THE BEST OF
Food & Wine

Swiss Chard Lasagna (p. 174)

Salad of Bitter Greens with Fallen Goat Cheese Soufflé (p. 45)

THE BEST OF
Food & Wine

Food & Wine
BOOKS

American Express Publishing Corporation
New York

Spicy Squid Salad (p. 67)

FOOD & WINE MAGAZINE

EDITOR IN CHIEF: Mary Simons
ART DIRECTOR: Dania Martinez Davey

FOOD & WINE BOOKS

EDITORIAL DIRECTOR: Judith Hill
EDITOR: Terri Mauro
DESIGNER: Nina Scerbo

MARKETING DIRECTOR: Mary V. Cooney
MARKETING/PROMOTION MANAGER: Roni Stein
OPERATIONS MANAGER: Ilene Polen-Lacombe
PRODUCTION MANAGER: Yvette Williams-Braxton

COVER PHOTO: SPRING VEGETABLE MEDLEY (P. 159)
BACK PHOTO: TOMATO AND CARAMELIZED ONION GALETTE (P. 205)

AMERICAN EXPRESS PUBLISHING CORPORATION
©1995 American Express Publishing Corporation

Published by American Express Publishing Corporation
1120 Avenue of the Americas, New York, New York 10036

ISBN 0-916103-24-2

Manufactured in the United States of America

CONTENTS

PAGE 9   Chapter 1 ▪ HORS D'OEUVRES & FIRST COURSES

25   Chapter 2 ▪ SOUPS

43   Chapter 3 ▪ SALADS

55   Chapter 4 ▪ FISH & SHELLFISH

81   Chapter 5 ▪ POULTRY

105   Chapter 6 ▪ MEAT

133   Chapter 7 ▪ PASTA & GRAINS

157   Chapter 8 ▪ VEGETABLES

183   Chapter 9 ▪ STUFFINGS & POTATOES

197   Chapter 10 ▪ PIZZAS, GALETTES & BREADS

221   Chapter 11 ▪ PRESERVES & CONDIMENTS

231   Chapter 12 ▪ DESSERTS

245   Chapter 13 ▪ CAKES & COOKIES

267   Chapter 14 ▪ PIES & TARTS

285   Chapter 15 ▪ FRUIT DESSERTS

Chocolate Zabaglione Cream Trifle (p. 233)

FOREWORD

THE 1995 EDITION OF **THE BEST OF FOOD & WINE** TAKES US ON A COOK'S TOUR OF THE world and lands us right back in the kitchen—our favorite place. We start the culinary trip with hors d'oeuvres and first courses that take their inspiration from Italy, Greece, Southeast Asia and right here in the United States. Inventive salads, many of them hearty enough to make a meal, also come from far and wide, as do flavorful soups and stews that span the seasons. Pastas and grains are now the cornerstone of a healthy diet, and we have a sizable sampling of them—from quick and easy Fettuccine with Radicchio and Sun-Dried Tomatoes to hearty Polenta with Butter and Cheese to Risotto with Zucchini Blossoms and Sage. Recipes for meat and fish, many from top restaurant chefs and our favorite cooking teachers, Julia Child, Jacques Pépin and Marcella Hazan, range from the exotic to the homey. Our desserts are all suitably scrumptious.

Not only will you relish the diversity reflected in this worldwide collection, but you'll welcome the ease with which you can make the dishes. We are fiercely proud of these recipes gathered from around the world. As always, they've been refined and perfected in the FOOD & WINE test kitchen.

May your meals be memorable and your parties great fun.

MARY SIMONS
Editor in Chief
FOOD & WINE Magazine

Chapter 1 ▪ HORS D'OEUVRES & FIRST COURSES

11   Pita Crisps

11   Black Bean Dip with Garlic

11   White Bean Puree with Mint

12   Green Olive and Anchovy Puree

12   Fiery Cream Cheese Dip

12   Goat Cheese and Thyme Spread

15   Goat Cheese, Walnut and Sun-Dried Tomato Spread

15   Spicy Peanut Dip

15   Caponata

16   Apple Haroset

16   Almond-Date Haroset

17   Salmon Mousse with Dill and Capers

17   Astier's Salmon Rillettes

18   Tuna Mousse with Lemon and Oregano

18   Pâté de Campagne with Pecans and Mushrooms

19   Chopped Liver

20   Hot Curried Nuts

20   Silky Peppers

21   Marinated Baby Artichokes in Oil

21   Oven-Roasted Tomatoes

23   Zucchini with Fresh Thyme

23   Green Dumplings with Shrimp and Peanuts

24   Low-Country Pickled Shrimp

Black Bean Dip with Garlic and White Bean Puree with Mint (top)
Green Olive and Anchovy Puree (p. 12) served in endive spears

PITA CRISPS

These are a perfect foil for any dip or spread, but they are also delicious by themselves. The seasonings can be varied—substitute poppy seeds, celery seeds or anise seeds for the sesame seeds; dried dill, basil or oregano for the thyme; and ground pepper with cumin or chili powder for plain pepper.

Makes About 96 Crisps

- **4 tablespoons unsalted butter, melted**
- **3 tablespoons olive oil**
- **6 6-inch white or whole wheat pita breads**
- **¼ cup sesame seeds (1½ ounces)**
- **1 tablespoon thyme**
- **1½ teaspoons freshly ground pepper**
- **½ cup freshly grated Parmesan cheese**

1. Preheat the oven to 350°. In a bowl, combine the butter and oil.

2. Trim the edges off the pita breads. Arrange the pitas on a baking sheet and bake for about 3 minutes, or until warm. Separate the top of each pita from the bottom and brush the inside of each half with the butter and oil.

3. Stack the pitas and cut them into eighths to form triangles. Arrange the triangles, buttered side up, on 2 baking sheets. In a small bowl, combine the sesame seeds, thyme and pepper and sprinkle the mixture on the pitas. Top with the Parmesan.

4. Bake the pita triangles for 8 minutes on the upper and lower racks of the oven. Switch the pans and bake for about 6 minutes longer, until toasted. Transfer the crisps to paper towels to cool. (The pita crisps can be kept for up to 1 week in an airtight container.)

—Bob Chambers

■

BLACK BEAN DIP WITH GARLIC

Tortilla chips are the natural partner for this hearty dip. For an attractive presentation, serve it side-by-side in the same bowl with the White Bean Puree with Mint, which follows.

Makes About 1½ Cups

- **1 19-ounce can black beans, drained and rinsed**
- **2 large garlic cloves, coarsely chopped**
- **2 tablespoons coarsely chopped onion**
- **2 tablespoons coarsely chopped fresh coriander (cilantro), plus additional sprigs for garnish**
- **1 tablespoon fresh lime juice**
- **½ teaspoon hot chili oil**
- **¼ teaspoon grated lime zest**
- **¼ teaspoon ground cumin**
- **¼ teaspoon thyme**
- **Salt and freshly ground pepper**

In a food processor, combine all the ingredients except the coriander sprigs. Add 1 tablespoon of water and process until smooth; add 1 more tablespoon of water for a thinner texture. Transfer the dip to a serving bowl and garnish with coriander sprigs.

—Marcia Kiesel

■

WHITE BEAN PUREE WITH MINT

This puree is delicious spread on water crackers or toast and topped with smoked mussels, clams or scallops. It can also be served with fennel or endive spears, red bell pepper strips or cucumber slices. ➤

Makes About 1½ Cups

½ **cup flat-leaf parsley leaves**
⅓ **cup fresh mint leaves plus additional sprigs, for garnish**
2 **garlic cloves, minced**
1 **small shallot, coarsely chopped**
1 **19-ounce can white kidney beans, drained and rinsed**
2½ **tablespoons fresh lemon juice**
¾ **teaspoon freshly ground black pepper**
½ **teaspoon salt**
½ **teaspoon ground cumin**
⅛ **teaspoon cayenne pepper**

In a food processor, pulse the parsley and mint leaves until finely chopped. Add the garlic and shallot and pulse until minced. Add the remaining ingredients and process until smooth. Transfer the puree to a serving bowl and garnish with mint sprigs.

—Bob Chambers

■

GREEN OLIVE AND ANCHOVY PUREE

This salty dip is nicely balanced by crisp vegetables, such as celery and fennel sticks.

Makes About 2½ Cups

1 **cup flat-leaf parsley plus additional sprigs, for garnish**
4 **2½-ounce jars or 2 cups pitted Spanish olives, drained and rinsed**
½ **cup bottled chopped pimientos, drained**
1 **2-ounce can flat anchovy fillets**
¼ **cup plain unsalted dry bread crumbs**
2 **tablespoons tomato paste**
1 **tablespoon capers, drained and rinsed**
1 **teaspoon finely grated lemon zest**
½ **teaspoon freshly ground pepper**
½ **pound cream cheese, at room temperature, cut into small pieces**

In a food processor, pulse the cup of parsley leaves until finely chopped. Add the olives, pimientos, anchovies with their oil, bread crumbs, tomato paste, capers, lemon zest and pepper and process until minced. Add the cream cheese and process until smooth. Transfer to a serving bowl and garnish with parsley sprigs

—Bob Chambers

■

FIERY CREAM CHEESE DIP

Serve this hot, garlicky dip with tortilla or potato chips, or whole-grain crackers.

Makes About 2 Cups

1 **pound cream cheese, at room temperature**
3 **large garlic cloves, minced**
3 to 4 **jalapeño peppers, minced**
2 **tablespoons minced fresh coriander (cilantro)**
Salt

In a food processor, process the cream cheese until smooth. Add the garlic and jalapeños and process until blended. Add the coriander and pulse just until combined. Season with salt and transfer to a serving bowl.

—Candy Voytershark

■

GOAT CHEESE AND THYME SPREAD

Serve this tangy dip with crostini, breadsticks or toast.

Makes 1 Cup

8 **ounces mild fresh goat cheese or robiola cheese** ➤

**Silky Peppers
(p. 20)**

**Goat Cheese
and Thyme
Spread**

Spicy Peanut Dip

2 teaspoons extra-virgin olive oil
2 teaspoons fresh thyme leaves

Combine all the ingredients in a food processor and blend until smooth and silky. Spoon the cheese into a ramekin and smooth the surface with a spatula or mound in a serving bowl. (The cheese spread can be refrigerated, covered, for up to 3 days. Let return to room temperature and stir well before serving.)

—Patricia Wells

■

GOAT CHEESE, WALNUT AND SUN-DRIED TOMATO SPREAD

Pair this tangy spread with breadsticks or fruit, such as red or white seedless grapes, slices of tart apple or Bosc pear, or wedges of kiwi.

Makes About 1½ Cups
4 ounces goat cheese, such as Montrachet, at room temperature
⅔ cup coarsely chopped walnuts (3 ounces)
4 oil-packed sun-dried tomato halves, drained and coarsely chopped
1 large garlic clove, coarsely chopped
1 teaspoon extra-virgin olive oil
¼ teaspoon thyme
Salt and coarsely ground pepper

In a food processor, combine all the ingredients and process until well blended but still slightly chunky. Transfer to a serving bowl. Alternatively, spoon the cheese into a small bowl lined with plastic wrap and refrigerate until firm, about 10 minutes. Unmold onto a plate and serve.

—Marcia Kiesel

■

SPICY PEANUT DIP

Serve this Indonesian-style dip with cooked shrimp, fresh vegetables or fried shrimp crackers.

Makes About 1 Cup
⅔ cup unsweetened coconut milk* or whole milk, at room temperature
½ cup chunky peanut butter, at room temperature
2 scallions, thinly sliced
2 garlic cloves, coarsely chopped
2 tablespoons fresh lime juice
1 tablespoon soy sauce
½ teaspoon hot chili oil*
¼ teaspoon dark sesame oil
¼ teaspoon grated lime zest

*Available at Asian markets

In a food processor, combine all the ingredients except half of the scallions. Process to a smooth paste. Transfer to a serving bowl and garnish with the reserved scallion slices.

—Marcia Kiesel

■

CAPONATA

Native to Sicily, caponata is a mixture of eggplant, red peppers, onions and celery punctuated with green olives, capers, vinegar and a touch of sugar. Each vegetable is cooked separately and then all are folded together toward the end.

Makes About 5 Cups
¾ cup plus 2 tablespoons extra-virgin olive oil
2 medium onions, halved crosswise and thinly sliced lengthwise
Sea salt   ➤

15

2 **red bell peppers, thinly sliced lengthwise and halved crosswise**
4 **garlic cloves, thinly sliced**
1 **16-ounce can crushed tomatoes in tomato sauce**
  Several parsley stems
  A few fresh thyme sprigs, plus 2 teaspoons fresh thyme leaves
6 **celery ribs from the heart with leaves, thinly sliced crosswise**
1 **medium eggplant (about 1 pound), cut into ½-inch cubes**
½ **cup red wine vinegar**
2 **tablespoons sugar**
¼ **cup drained capers, rinsed**
1 **cup Italian green olives (5 ounces), pitted**
  Freshly ground black pepper

1. In a large, deep, nonreactive skillet, combine ¼ cup of the olive oil with the onions and a pinch of salt. Cook over low heat, stirring occasionally, until soft and translucent, about 5 minutes. Add the peppers with another pinch of salt, cover and cook until softened, about 5 minutes. Add the garlic and cook just until fragrant, about 2 minutes. Add the tomatoes, parsley stems and thyme sprigs, cover and simmer gently, stirring from time to time, until the onions and peppers are tender, about 15 minutes.

2. Meanwhile, in another large skillet, heat 2 tablespoons of the oil. Add the celery ribs and leaves and cook over moderate heat, stirring occasionally, until beginning to soften, about 8 minutes. Transfer the celery to a bowl, season lightly with sea salt and stir in the thyme leaves.

3. In the same skillet, heat the remaining ½ cup olive oil. Add the eggplant and cook over moderate heat, tossing occasionally, until lightly browned, about 8 minutes. Transfer the eggplant and the celery to the skillet with the tomatoes, peppers and onions. Season with salt. Cover and simmer gently until all the vegetables are soft, about 20 minutes.

4. Meanwhile, in a small bowl, combine the vinegar and sugar; stir to dissolve.

5. Add the vinegar mixture, capers and olives to the vegetables and simmer over low heat to blend the flavors, 1 to 2 minutes. Season with salt and black pepper. Discard the parsley stems and thyme sprigs. Transfer the caponata to a large serving bowl to cool. Serve warm or at room temperature, but not chilled. (The caponata can be refrigerated for up to 2 days. Let return to room temperature before serving.)

—Patricia Wells

■

APPLE HAROSET

Haroset, a sweet fruit and nut mixture that is one of the symbolic foods of Passover, is eaten at the beginning of the meal.

Makes About 1½ Cups
2 **large Granny Smith apples, quartered and cored**
¾ **cup walnuts (about 3 ounces)**
¼ **cup kosher sweet red wine, such as Manischewitz**
2 **teaspoons honey**
1 **teaspoon cinnamon**

Place the apples and walnuts in a food processor. Pulse until fairly finely chopped. Transfer to a bowl and stir in the red wine, honey and cinnamon. (The haroset can be refrigerated, covered, for up to 6 hours.) Serve chilled or at room temperature.

—Susan Shapiro Jaslove

■

ALMOND-DATE HAROSET

For this version of haroset, dates are microwaved to plump them up.

Makes About 1 Cup
- ½ cup pitted dates (about 3 ounces)
- 1 cup whole blanched almonds (about 5 ounces)
- 3 tablespoons kosher sweet white wine, such as Manischewitz
- 1 tablespoon poppy seeds
- 1 teaspoon finely grated lemon zest
- ¼ teaspoon ground ginger

In a small microwaveable bowl, cover the dates with 1 cup of water. Microwave at full power for 1 minute. (Alternatively, cook the dates in 1 cup of boiling water until plumped, about 3 minutes.) Drain the dates, reserving ¼ cup of the cooking liquid. Transfer the dates and reserved liquid to a food processor with the almonds. Pulse until fairly finely chopped. Transfer to a bowl and stir in the white wine, poppy seeds, lemon zest and ground ginger. (The date haroset can be refrigerated, covered, for up to 2 days.) Serve chilled or at room temperature.

—Susan Shapiro Jaslove

■

SALMON MOUSSE WITH DILL AND CAPERS

This mousse is great served on pumpernickel toasts or piped onto cucumber rounds, fennel sticks or endive spears.

Makes About 2½ Cups
- 2 7½-ounce cans salmon, preferably red sockeye, drained and picked over
- 4 ounces smoked salmon, preferably Scottish
- 1 medium scallion, minced
- 1 small shallot, minced
- 2½ tablespoons fresh lemon juice
- ½ teaspoon thyme
- ¼ teaspoon freshly ground black pepper
- ¼ teaspoon cayenne pepper
- 4 tablespoons unsalted butter, softened
- 1 tablespoon coarsely chopped fresh dill plus small sprigs, for garnish
- 2 teaspoons capers, drained
- 1 ounce salmon roe for garnish (optional)

In a food processor, combine the canned salmon, smoked salmon, scallion, shallot, lemon juice, thyme and black and cayenne peppers. Pulse until blended. Add the butter, chopped dill and the capers and process until smooth. Transfer to a serving bowl and garnish with dill sprigs and salmon roe.

—Bob Chambers

■

ASTIER'S SALMON RILLETTES

Traditional rillettes are made by cooking seasoned pork or goose in its own fat until very tender and then pounding it to

Salmon Mousse with Dill and Capers

a coarse spread. The exalted version of this hors d'oeuvre served at Astier in Paris is made with fresh and smoked salmon. At the restaurant, it's served with slices of lemon along with cherry tomatoes and cucumbers drizzled with a simple vinaigrette.

6 to 8 Servings

- 1 **cup dry white wine**
- ½ **pound skinless fresh salmon fillet, coarsely chopped**
- 7 **tablespoons unsalted butter**
- ¼ **cup olive oil**
- 1 to 2 **teaspoons Cognac**
- 8 **ounces smoked salmon, finely chopped**
- 1 **tablespoon crème fraîche**
  Salt and freshly ground white pepper
  Toasted country bread, for serving

1. In a small nonreactive skillet, bring the white wine to a simmer over moderate heat. Add the fresh salmon and simmer until it turns opaque, about 2 minutes. Using a slotted spoon, transfer the salmon to a plate and drain off the liquid in the pan.

2. In the same skillet, melt the butter in the olive oil over low heat. Add the Cognac, smoked salmon and cooked fresh salmon. Simmer gently for 4 minutes, stirring with a wooden spoon to break up the fresh salmon. Remove the skillet from the heat. Stir in the crème fraîche until thoroughly incorporated. Season with salt and plenty of white pepper. Scrape the mixture into a small, deep terrine or ramekin. Cover and refrigerate for at least 24 hours and up to 5 days.

3. Let the salmon rillettes sit at room temperature for about an hour to soften slightly before serving. Serve the rillettes from the terrine and pass the warm toast separately.

—Alexander Lobrano

TUNA MOUSSE WITH LEMON AND OREGANO

This rich, vibrantly flavored dip is from the trattoria Cibrèo in Florence. Serve with breadsticks or crostini or with crisp vegetables, such as celery, fennel, bell pepper and cucumber.

Makes About 1 Cup

- 1 **6⅛-ounce can of Italian tuna packed in olive oil**
- 4 **tablespoons unsalted butter, softened**
- 1 **teaspoon finely grated lemon zest**
- 2 **tablespoons fresh lemon juice**
- 2 **tablespoons extra-virgin olive oil**
- ½ **teaspoon dried leaf oregano**
- 1 **garlic clove, minced**
  Salt and freshly ground pepper

Flake the tuna in the can with a fork and transfer, oil and all, to a food processor. Add the remaining ingredients and process until smooth and creamy. Season with salt and pepper. Transfer to a medium bowl and serve at room temperature.

—Patricia Wells

PATE DE CAMPAGNE WITH PECANS AND MUSHROOMS

Serve this pâté with cornichons, grainy mustard, such as moutarde de Meaux, and crusty French bread. Paired with a salad, it makes a perfect first course.

Makes 15 to 17 Slices

- 2 **pounds fatty pork chops on the bone**
- 1 **pound ground pork**

1 **egg**
1 **small onion, finely chopped (½ cup)**
½ **ounce dried cèpe or black chanterelle mushrooms (⅓ cup)**
¼ **cup dry white wine**
¼ **cup pecan pieces**
1 **tablespoon Cognac**
1 **tablespoon cornstarch**
1 **tablespoon salt**
1½ **teaspoons minced garlic**
¼ **teaspoon saltpeter (optional)**
1 **teaspoon black peppercorns**
½ **teaspoon allspice berries**
½ **teaspoon thyme leaves**
½ **teaspoon coriander seeds**
3 **bay leaves**
6 **ounces chicken livers, trimmed**

1. Bone the pork chops; reserve the bones for another use. Trim the chops to remove the outer layer of fat and any fatty portions of meat; set aside. Cut the lean meat into ¼-inch pieces and place in a bowl. Add the ground pork, egg, chopped onion, mushrooms, wine, pecan pieces, Cognac, cornstarch, salt, garlic and saltpeter, if using.

2. In a spice grinder, combine the black peppercorns, allspice berries, thyme leaves, coriander seeds and bay leaves. Grind to a fine powder and add to the pork mixture.

3. In a food processor, puree the reserved pork fat and fatty meat with the chicken livers until smooth. Add to the bowl and mix all the ingredients very well.

4. Pack the pâté mixture into a 10-by-3-by-3-inch enameled cast-iron pâté mold. (If you don't have one, use a rectangular glass loaf pan. The pâté will take a bit longer to cook in the wider mold.) Press a sheet of plastic wrap firmly against the surface of the meat, then cover with the pâté mold lid or foil. Refrigerate for at least 12 and up to 24 hours.

5. Preheat the oven to 325°. Uncover the mold and set in a roasting pan. Add enough lukewarm water to reach two-thirds of the way up the sides of the mold. Bake the pâté for 1 hour, and then reduce the heat to 300° and bake for 45 minutes longer, or until a meat thermometer inserted in the center registers 150° to 160°.

6. Remove the mold from the water bath. Let the pâté cool in the mold for 2 to 3 hours at room temperature, then refrigerate it for 1 day.

7. To unmold the pâté, dip the mold in a large pan of hot water; it may take as long as 1 minute to warm the mold sufficiently. Run a knife around the pâté to loosen it from the mold, then invert it on a large sheet of plastic wrap. Wrap the unmolded pâté in the plastic wrap and refrigerate it for at least 1 day and up to 1 week. Serve the pâté in ¾-inch slices.

—Jacques Pépin

■

CHOPPED LIVER

Serve the chopped liver with matzos. If you're using a food processor, quarter the eggs instead of chopping them.

8 Servings
Generous ¼ cup chicken fat (about 2 ounces), rendered (see Chicken Fat, at right)
1 **medium onion, coarsely chopped**
1 **pound chicken livers, halved and trimmed**
3 **large hard-cooked eggs, coarsely chopped**
1 **small onion, coarsely chopped**
Salt and freshly ground pepper

1. In a large heavy skillet, heat the chicken fat. Add the chopped onion and cook over moderate heat, stirring occasionally, until the onion is golden, about 10 minutes.

2. Add the chicken livers to the skillet and sauté over moderately high heat, breaking them up with a wooden spoon,

CHICKEN FAT

To render chicken fat, cook over moderate heat, turning occasionally, until melted, about 5 minutes. Discard the small, solid pieces that remain. The rendered fat can be refrigerated, covered, for up to 3 weeks or frozen for 6 months. Use the fat from uncooked chickens for rendering; one chicken will yield about ¼ cup of fat. Or ask your butcher for some.

—Susan Shapiro Jaslove

CURRY POWDER

Bright yellow with turmeric and fragrant with coriander, cumin, cinnamon, nutmeg, cloves, cardamom, fenugreek, peppercorns and chiles, this popular mix of ground spices grew out of the Anglo-Indian kitchens of the British raj. Spices are enhanced when cooked, so sauté curry powder with onions or garlic before adding it to a cooked dish.

—Nancie McDermott

until firm but slightly pink in the center, about 5 minutes. Remove from the heat and let cool slightly.

3. Using a meat grinder fitted with a medium blade, grind the liver mixture and the hard-cooked eggs into a medium bowl. Grind the small raw onion and stir it into the chopped liver. (Alternatively, pulse the small onion in a food processor until finely chopped. Quarter the hard-cooked eggs, add them to the processor and pulse 2 or 3 times to break them up. Add the cooked liver mixture and pulse until finely chopped but not smooth.)

4. Season the chopped liver with salt and pepper and transfer to a serving bowl. Cover and refrigerate until chilled, at least 1 hour or up to 2 days. Serve chilled or at room temperature.

—Susan Shapiro Jaslove

■

HOT CURRIED NUTS

Curry powder is not one spice, but a mixture of several. Brands vary, and freshness counts for a lot. For this recipe, use a blend with some heat. If you have a mild curry powder, perk it up with a pinch of cayenne.

Makes About 2½ Cups
1 tablespoon hot curry powder (see Note)
1 tablespoon mild vegetable oil, such as canola
11 ounces mixed unsalted roasted nuts, such as cashews, almonds, filberts and pecans (2½ cups)
½ teaspoon salt

In a heavy medium skillet, cook the curry powder in the oil, stirring occasionally with a wooden spoon, over moderate heat until very fragrant but not burned,

about 5 minutes. Stir in the mixed nuts and the salt and cook, stirring occasionally, until the nuts are nicely toasted, about 5 minutes longer. Let cool to room temperature. (The nuts will keep in an airtight container at room temperature for up to 5 days.)

NOTE: Try Kalustyan's Imperial Hot Curry Powder, which comes in 4-, 7- or 14-ounce bags. (Kalustyan, 123 Lexington Avenue, New York, NY 10016; 212-685-3451.)

—Diana Sturgis

■

SILKY PEPPERS

This tangy dish comes from the Al Forno restaurant in Providence, Rhode Island.

6 to 8 Servings
6 red and/or yellow bell peppers—quartered lengthwise, cored, seeded and deribbed
½ cup balsamic or red wine vinegar Sea salt
¼ cup extra-virgin olive oil

1. Place the peppers in a very large nonreactive skillet and toss with the vinegar and 1 teaspoon sea salt. Cover and cook the peppers over low heat, stirring occasionally, until soft and tender, about 30 minutes. (Most of the liquid will have evaporated by then.)

2. Transfer the peppers to a large platter. Beat the extra-virgin olive oil into the liquid in the skillet just until warmed through. Pour the liquid over the peppers and toss to coat. Season with sea salt. Let cool for at least 30 minutes before serving. (The peppers can be refrigerated for up to 3 days. Let return to room temperature before serving.)

—Johanne Killeen and George Germon

■

MARINATED BABY ARTICHOKES IN OIL

Baby artichokes are small yet fully mature artichokes that grow around the stems of large ones.

Makes About 1 Quart

2 cups Champagne vinegar
8 bay leaves, preferably fresh
2 teaspoons fine sea salt
2½ pounds baby artichokes (see Note), rinsed well
4 garlic cloves, halved
2 tablespoons minced fresh flat-leaf parsley
About 1½ cups extra-virgin olive oil

1. In a large nonreactive saucepan, combine 2 cups of water with the vinegar, 4 of the bay leaves and the salt.

2. Using a stainless steel knife, trim the stem of each artichoke to ½ inch. Peel the stem. Bend back the tough outer green leaves, one at a time, letting them snap off naturally at the base. Continue snapping off leaves until only a central cone of yellow leaves with pale green tips remains. Trim the tops of the leaves to just below the green tips. Depending on the size, halve or quarter the artichoke lengthwise and drop it immediately into the vinegar mixture to prevent browning. Repeat with the remaining artichokes.

3. Bring the artichokes and their liquid to a simmer over moderately high heat. Simmer until the artichokes are tender but still offer a bit of resistance when pierced, about 8 minutes. Drain the artichokes; discard the vinegar mixture and bay leaves.

4. While the artichokes are still warm, layer them in a sterilized 1-quart canning jar with the garlic, parsley and the remaining 4 bay leaves, ending with a layer of artichokes. Pour in enough of the oil to cover the artichokes completely and set aside until thoroughly cool. Cover tightly and refrigerate for at least 24 hours before serving. (The artichokes can be refrigerated for up to 2 months. Make sure that they are always completely covered with oil.)

NOTE: Baby artichokes are available by mail from Giant Artichoke, 11241 Merritt Street, Castroville, CA 95012; 408-633-2778.

—Patricia Wells

■

OVEN-ROASTED TOMATOES

Round or plum tomatoes work equally well in this recipe. Be sure to use a large well-seasoned pan to sear the tomatoes.

8 Servings

¼ cup extra-virgin olive oil
8 firm medium tomatoes (about 3½ pounds), cored and halved crosswise
Sea salt
2 teaspoons fresh thyme leaves

1. Preheat the oven to 400°. Heat the oil in a very large nonreactive skillet. Fit as many tomatoes as you can in the pan, cut sides down. Cook over high heat without moving the tomatoes until they are almost caramelized, 5 to 6 minutes. Using a spatula, carefully transfer the tomatoes, cooked sides up, to a 9-by-13-inch glass or ceramic baking dish. Repeat with the remaining tomatoes.

2. Pour the cooking juices over the tomatoes and season them lightly with sea salt; sprinkle with the thyme leaves. Bake the tomatoes in the middle of the oven until browned and sizzling, about 30 minutes. Serve hot, warm or at room temperature. (The tomatoes can be cooked up to 8 hours ahead and set aside at room temperature.)

—Patricia Wells

Green
Dumplings
with Shrimp
and Peanuts

ZUCCHINI WITH FRESH THYME

The zucchini can be broiled as directed below or grilled outdoors. Serve this simple dish warm or at room temperature on the day it is made.

4 to 6 Servings
- **5** small, firm zucchini (about 1¾ pounds), sliced lengthwise ¼ inch thick
- **3** tablespoons extra-virgin olive oil
  Sea salt
- **½** tablespoon fresh thyme leaves

1. Preheat the broiler. Cover a broiling pan with aluminum foil and place the zucchini slices side by side on the pan. Lightly brush with 1 tablespoon of the oil and season with salt. Broil about 5 inches from the heat for about 2 minutes, until golden brown. Remove the pan from the oven and turn each slice of zucchini with tongs; lightly brush with ½ tablespoon of the oil and season with the sea salt. Broil for about 2 minutes, until golden brown.

2. Transfer the zucchini to a shallow serving dish, overlapping the slices. Drizzle the remaining 1½ tablespoons oil on top and sprinkle with the thyme leaves. Serve warm or at room temperature. (The zucchini can be cooked up to 8 hours ahead and set aside at room temperature.)
—Patricia Wells

GREEN DUMPLINGS WITH SHRIMP AND PEANUTS

This is an adaptation of a favorite dumpling served at dim sum parlors in China.

Makes 20 Dumplings
Dough:
- **⅓** cup long-grain rice
- **1** cup (lightly packed) cornstarch, plus more for rolling
- **1** teaspoon salt

Filling:
- **1½** pounds bok choy, preferably baby bok choy, stem end trimmed
- **½** pound medium shrimp, shelled and deveined
- **2** large egg whites
- **1** large garlic clove, minced
- **2** teaspoons soy sauce
- **1** teaspoon minced fresh ginger
- **¼** teaspoon sesame oil
- **¼** teaspoon salt
  Large pinch of white pepper
- **3** tablespoons unsalted roasted peanuts
- **4** large scallions, finely chopped
  Soy sauce and chile bean paste, for serving

1. Make the dough: In a small saucepan, cover the rice with 1 cup of water and bring to a boil over high heat. Reduce the heat to low, cover and cook for 15 minutes. The rice will be soft and soggy. Scrape the rice into a food processor and set aside to cool slightly. Add the cornstarch and salt and process until the dough forms a firm, moist and slightly sticky ball, about 10 seconds. Scrape the dough out onto a work surface and knead briefly to smooth out. Roll the dough into a 15-inch log. Cover with plastic wrap and set aside.

2. Make the filling: In a large steamer, bring ½ inch of water to a boil over high heat. Pack the bok choy in the basket, cover and steam for 3 minutes. Transfer the basket to the sink; let the bok choy drain and cool slightly. Squeeze out as much excess liquid as possible. Finely chop and place in a large nonreactive bowl.

3. In a food processor, puree half of the shrimp with the egg whites for 20 seconds. Scrape into the bok choy and mix well. ➤

4. In a small bowl, combine the garlic, soy sauce, ginger, sesame oil, salt and white pepper. Pour the sauce, peanuts and scallions into the bok choy filling and mix thoroughly. Chop the remaining shrimp into ½-inch pieces and stir into the filling.

5. Unwrap the dough and cut the log into 4 even pieces. Rewrap all but 1 piece of dough. Cut the dough crosswise into 5 equal slices. Press each slice into a flat disk with your hands. Using a rolling pin, roll each disk into a 3½-inch round. Place a heaping tablespoon of the bok choy filling in the center of each round. Draw the dough up and pinch together at 3 places to surround the filling, leaving a small triangle of filling exposed on top (the dumpling should look like a 3-cornered hat with an exposed center of green).

6. Sprinkle cornstarch on a wide area of a work surface. Set the formed dumplings on top. Repeat with the remaining dough and filling. Drizzle some soy sauce and chile bean paste on a platter and set aside.

7. In a large steamer, bring ½ inch of water to a boil over high heat. Generously oil a metal steamer basket and arrange 4 to 5 dumplings without touching in the basket. Place the basket in the steamer, cover and steam for 3 minutes. Using a thin metal spatula, carefully transfer each dumpling to the prepared platter. Wipe the steamer basket clean and oil it again before steaming the remaining 3 or 4 batches of dumplings.

8. Eat the steamed dumplings hot, with your fingers, dipping them in the soy sauce and chile bean paste on the platter.

—Marcia Kiesel

■

LOW-COUNTRY PICKLED SHRIMP

Serve these pickled shrimp straight from the jar with long-handled forks or skewers or accompany the shellfish with a zippy parsley salad that's made from tender parsley leaves dressed with a lemon-shallot vinaigrette.

8 to 10 Servings

- **1 cup Champagne vinegar or tarragon vinegar**
- **4 nickel-size slices of fresh ginger**
- **¼ cup coriander seeds**
- **1 tablespoon mustard seeds**
- **1 tablespoon fennel seeds**
- **1 teaspoon whole allspice berries**
- **2 pounds medium shrimp**
- **1 medium Bermuda or other sweet onion, thinly sliced**
- **2 medium lemons, thinly sliced crosswise and seeded**
- **¾ cup drained small capers**
- **6 garlic cloves**
- **2 dried cayenne chiles, each broken into 2 or 3 pieces**
- **4 bay leaves, preferably fresh**
- **1 cup olive oil**
- **½ teaspoon salt**

1. In a medium nonreactive saucepan, combine the vinegar with ½ cup of water, the ginger slices, coriander seeds, mustard seeds, fennel seeds and allspice berries. Bring the liquid to a boil over moderately high heat. Lower the heat and simmer for 10 minutes. Let the pickling mixture cool completely.

2. Bring a large pot of water to a boil. Add the shrimp. Remove the pot from the heat and let stand until the shrimp have turned pink, about 3 minutes. Drain and let cool completely, then shell and devein the shrimp.

3. In a 6-cup glass jar or crock, tightly pack the shrimp with the onion and lemon slices, capers, garlic, chiles and bay leaves. Whisk the olive oil and salt into the pickling mixture and pour it into the jar. Cover tightly and refrigerate for at least 2 days or up to 1 week. Serve the shrimp slightly chilled.

—Ben Barker

Chapter 2 ▪ SOUPS

27 Chilled Tomato Soup with Garlic Oil, Basil and Mint

27 Corn Chowder

27 Spring Pea Soup with Scallops and Sorrel

28 Pea Soup with Coconut

30 Roasted Yellow Pepper Soup with Pico de Gallo

30 Smoky Potato Soup with Kale

31 Creamy Rutabaga Soup

32 Spinach Soup with Bean Thread Noodles

32 Corn and Crab Gazpacho

33 Curried Mussel Soup with Red Lentils and Yogurt

34 Miso Clam Soup With Julienned Vegetables and Shiitake Mushrooms

35 Brazilian-Style Shrimp and Coconut Soup

36 Chicken Broth with Fregula

39 Curried Mulligatawny Soup

40 Lobster and White Bean Soup

41 Soup of Broken Pasta and Beans with Fresh Basil

Chilled Tomato Soup with Garlic Oil, Basil and Mint

CHILLED TOMATO SOUP WITH GARLIC OIL, BASIL AND MINT

If you don't have a mortar, coarsely grind the peppercorns into a bowl, smash the garlic to a paste and mix it with the pepper.

4 Servings

- ½ teaspoon whole black peppercorns
- 1 large garlic clove
- 3 tablespoons extra-virgin olive oil
- 3 pounds beefsteak tomatoes, coarsely chopped
- 2 teaspoons balsamic vinegar
  Salt
- 2 tablespoons finely chopped fresh basil, preferably purple basil
- 2 tablespoons finely chopped fresh spearmint

1. In a mortar, pound the peppercorns to a coarse powder; add the garlic and pound to a paste. Stir 2 tablespoons of the oil into the paste. Set aside to macerate for 30 minutes. Strain and discard the solids.

2. Puree the tomatoes in a food processor. With the machine on, pour in the balsamic vinegar. Pour in the remaining 1 tablespoon olive oil and process until emulsified. Pass the soup through a coarse strainer set over a large nonreactive bowl. Season the soup with salt. Refrigerate until thoroughly chilled, about 1 hour.

3. To serve, stir the soup and pour into 4 chilled bowls. Drizzle the garlic oil over each serving and sprinkle the basil and spearmint on top.

—Marcia Kiesel

■

CORN CHOWDER

This low-fat chowder owes its taste and texture to pureed corn kernels and egg whites.

4 Servings

- 3 cups fresh corn kernels (from 5 ears) or 1 pound frozen corn, thawed
- 4 cups Chicken Stock (p. 36) or canned low-sodium broth
- ½ teaspoon finely grated fresh ginger
  Salt and freshly ground white pepper
- 3 large egg whites, lightly beaten
- 2 scallions, thinly sliced on the diagonal

1. In a blender or food processor, puree two-thirds of the corn kernels with ¾ cup of the Chicken Stock until almost smooth; some pieces of corn should remain.

2. In a medium saucepan, combine the remaining 3¼ cups Chicken Stock with the ginger, ¼ teaspoon salt and ⅛ teaspoon white pepper. Bring to a boil over high heat. Add the whole corn kernels and bring back to a boil. Cover and simmer over moderate heat for 5 minutes. Add the pureed corn and boil over high heat, stirring, until slightly thickened, about 2 minutes.

3. Stir the egg whites into the chowder and remove the pan from the heat. Stir until the whites form thin opaque strands. Season with salt and white pepper, ladle into bowls and sprinkle with the scallions.

—Eileen Yin-Fei Lo

■

SPRING PEA SOUP WITH SCALLOPS AND SORREL

A vegetable puree is the ideal base for low-fat soups. Flavorful, creamy pea soup is a delicious example.

❦ The sweet pea soup is best complemented by an oaky California Chardonnay, such as 1992 Liberty School or 1992 Stag's Leap Wine Cellars. ➤

27

4 Servings

1 teaspoon vegetable oil
4 medium shallots, finely chopped
1 fresh thyme sprig
¼ cup dry white wine
4 cups freshly shelled green peas
(about 4 pounds in the pod) or two
10-ounce packages frozen petite
peas, thawed
Salt and freshly ground pepper
4 sea scallops (3 ounces), sliced
horizontally in thirds
¼ cup coarsely torn fresh sorrel leaves
2 tablespoons coarsely chopped fresh
spearmint leaves

1. Heat the oil in a medium nonreactive saucepan. Add the chopped shallots and thyme sprig, cover and cook over low heat, stirring once, until the shallots are translucent, about 5 minutes. Add the wine and simmer for 2 minutes. Add the peas and 2½ cups of water and bring to a boil over high heat. Cover and cook over low heat until the peas are just tender, 5 to 8 minutes for fresh peas, 3 to 4 minutes for frozen.

2. Working in 2 batches, puree the soup in a food processor or blender. Pass through a coarse strainer into a bowl, pressing down on the solids.

3. Return the soup to the saucepan. Season with salt and pepper and bring to a simmer over moderately high heat. Add the sliced scallops and simmer, stirring, until just cooked through, about 2 minutes. Serve the soup garnished with the sorrel and spearmint.

—Marcia Kiesel

■

PEA SOUP
WITH COCONUT

The restaurant Arcadia in New York City, serves this delicate soup subtly flavored with coconut.

🍷 A crisp, fruity, not-quite-dry white would harmonize with the sweet peas and coconut yet have enough acidity to provide contrast. A German Riesling, such as 1991 Sichel Riesling or 1990 Lauerburg Bernkasteler Doctor Spätlese, is ideal.

4 Servings

2 tablespoons coriander seeds
3 tablespoons unsalted butter
1 large onion, finely chopped
⅓ cup shredded unsweetened
coconut* (about 1 ounce)
3½ cups Chicken Stock (p. 36) or
vegetable stock or canned
low-sodium chicken broth
1½ cups heavy cream
3 cups freshly shelled green peas
(about 3 pounds in the pod) or 1
pound frozen petite peas, thawed
1½ cups coarsely chopped fresh
spinach leaves
Salt and freshly ground pepper

*Available at health food stores

1. In a small skillet, toast the coriander seeds over high heat, shaking the pan, until the seeds are fragrant and lightly browned, about 2 minutes. Let cool slightly, then finely grind in a spice grinder or mortar.

2. Heat the butter in a large saucepan. Add the onion and cook over moderate heat, stirring, until translucent, about 10 minutes. Add the coconut, ground coriander and Chicken Stock and bring to a boil over moderately high heat. Lower the heat and simmer for 5 minutes. Add the cream and simmer for 3 minutes. Add the peas and cook just until tender, about 5 minutes for fresh, 2 minutes for frozen. Stir in the spinach.

3. Transfer the pea soup to a blender or food processor and puree until smooth. Pass the soup through a fine strainer set over a large bowl, pressing on the solids with a rubber spatula. Season with salt

Pea Soup with Coconut

and pepper. Cover and refrigerate until chilled, for at least 2 hours or up to 1 day. Spoon into chilled soup bowls and serve.

—Anne Rosenzweig

■

ROASTED YELLOW PEPPER SOUP WITH PICO DE GALLO

This creamy, deep yellow soup from the restaurant Star Canyon in Dallas, is topped with a spicy salsa and a spoonful of sour cream.

❦ The spiciness and heat imparted by the salsa point to a crisp white, such as 1991 Mouton Cadet Bordeaux Blanc Sec or 1992 Columbia Crest Sémillon from Washington State.

4 Servings
¼ teaspoon saffron threads
3 medium yellow bell peppers
1½ cups Chicken Stock (p. 36) or canned low-sodium broth
½ cup finely chopped onion
¼ cup finely chopped carrot
½ of a serrano or jalapeño chile, seeded and finely chopped
1 garlic clove, minced
½ cup cold heavy cream
½ cup cold milk
Salt
Pico de Gallo (recipe follows)
¼ cup sour cream

1. In a small bowl, soak the saffron in 1 tablespoon of warm water.
2. Roast the yellow peppers directly over a gas flame or under a broiler as close to the heat as possible, turning frequently, until charred all over. Transfer to a bowl, cover and let stand for at least 10 minutes. Peel the peppers and discard the cores, seeds and ribs. Coarsely chop the peppers.

3. In a medium nonreactive saucepan, combine the Chicken Stock, peppers, onion, carrot, serrano, garlic and the saffron with its soaking liquid. Bring to a boil over moderately high heat. Reduce the heat to low. Simmer until the vegetables just soften, about 5 minutes. Let cool slightly.
4. Transfer the yellow pepper mixture to a blender or food processor and puree until smooth. Pass the soup through a fine strainer set over a large bowl, pressing on the solids with a rubber spatula. Cover and refrigerate until the soup is chilled, at least 2 hours or for up to 1 day.
5. Stir the cream and milk into the soup. Season with salt. Ladle into chilled bowls. Garnish each serving with ¼ cup Pico de Gallo and 1 tablespoon sour cream.

Pico de Gallo
Makes About 1 Cup
½ pound ripe plum tomatoes
¼ cup minced red onion
1 small garlic clove, minced
1 small serrano chile, seeded and minced
½ tablespoon finely chopped fresh coriander (cilantro)
2 teaspoons fresh lime juice
Salt

Halve the tomatoes and discard the seeds and juice. Cut the tomato flesh into ¼-inch dice. In a small bowl, combine the tomatoes, red onion, garlic, chile, coriander and lime juice. Let stand for 30 minutes. Season with salt before serving.

—Stephan Pyles

■

SMOKY POTATO SOUP WITH KALE

Make this soup up to two days ahead. Cover and refrigerate; then rewarm over low heat.

❡ This satisfying soup, with its zesty flavor, is best paired with a tart, lemony wine that also has some fruitiness to balance the soup's saltiness. Dry Chenin Blanc—such as 1992 Preston or 1992 Chalone, both from California—would be ideal.

Makes 10 Cups
- 3 tablespoons unsalted butter
- 3 medium leeks—split, rinsed and thinly sliced crosswise
- 3 large garlic cloves, coarsely chopped plus 1 medium clove, minced
- 1 medium onion, coarsely chopped
- 1 bay leaf
- 1 cup dry white wine
- 8 cups Chicken Stock (p. 36) or canned low-sodium broth
- 2 smoked ham hocks
- 2 pounds red or all-purpose potatoes, peeled and cut into 2-inch pieces
- 1 dried chipotle chile*
- 1 tablespoon olive oil
- ½ pound kale, tough stems discarded, finely shredded
- 2 teaspoons fresh lemon juice
- 1 teaspoon finely grated lemon zest
  Salt and freshly ground black pepper

  *Available at Latin American markets or specialty food stores

1. In a large, heavy, nonreactive soup pot or casserole, melt the butter over moderately low heat. Add the leeks, coarsely chopped garlic, onion and bay leaf and cook, stirring often, until wilted, about 5 minutes. Increase the heat to high, pour in the wine and boil to reduce it by half. Add 8 cups of water, the Chicken Stock, ham hocks, potatoes and chipotle and bring to a boil. Reduce the heat to low and simmer until the potatoes are very tender, about 35 minutes. Remove the ham hocks and chile stem.

2. Working in batches, puree the soup in a food processor or blender and return it to the pot. Remove all the meat from the ham hocks, cut it into small pieces and add it to the soup.

3. In a large nonreactive skillet, warm the oil over moderate heat. Add the minced garlic and cook until fragrant, about 30 seconds. Add the kale and cook, stirring often, until bright green and wilted, about 5 minutes. Spoon the kale into the soup and simmer over moderately low heat until the kale is tender but still slightly crunchy, about 5 minutes. Season with the lemon juice, lemon zest, salt and black pepper and serve.

—Marcia Kiesel

■

CREAMY RUTABAGA SOUP

This soup has a wonderful taste, and you'd probably never guess it's made with turnips. You might also think it's a rich soup because it's so velvety smooth—the magical effect of pureed rice.

12 Servings
- 1½ tablespoons unsalted butter
- 2 medium celery ribs, sliced
- 1 large onion, sliced
- ⅓ cup white rice
- 3 pounds rutabagas, peeled and coarsely diced
- 4 cups Chicken Stock (p. 36) or canned broth
  Salt
- 2½ cups milk
  Freshly ground pepper
  Sour cream and chopped chives, for garnish

1. Melt the butter in a heavy 3-quart saucepan. Add the celery and onion and cook over moderately low heat, stirring frequently, until the onions are tender, about 8 minutes.

2. Stir in the rice, then add the rutaba-

gas, Chicken Stock and 3 cups of water. Bring to a simmer over high heat and stir. Season lightly with salt. Cover partially and simmer until the rutabagas are very tender, about 1 hour.

3. Puree the soup, adding a little milk if needed, in batches in a blender (not a food processor—the rice must be a very fine puree).

4. To serve, stir the remaining milk into the soup and bring to a simmer over moderate heat. Season to taste with salt and pepper. Ladle the soup into bowls and garnish with sour cream and chives.

—Julia Child

■

SPINACH SOUP WITH BEAN THREAD NOODLES

Chinese cooking, in spite of the oily food found in many take-out places, is naturally low in fat. The Chinese also include lots of vegetables in their meals to make them even more healthful. Here, spinach is mixed with thin noodles in a light broth, with a tiny amount of sesame oil added for flavor.

4 Servings

- 1 ounce bean thread noodles
- 6 cups Chicken Stock (p. 36) or canned low-sodium broth
- 1 tablespoon dry white wine
- 2 teaspoons minced fresh ginger
- 2 teaspoons minced garlic
  Salt
- 1 pound fresh spinach, stems trimmed and leaves torn in half
- 1 teaspoon Oriental sesame oil

1. In a small bowl, soak the noodles in warm water to cover until pliable, about 30 minutes. Drain and rinse, then cut the noodles into 4-inch lengths.

2. In a large nonreactive saucepan, combine the Chicken Stock, wine, ginger and garlic; season with salt. Cover and bring to a boil over high heat. Stir in the spinach and boil until the leaves are just tender, about 1 minute.

3. Stir in the noodles and bring back to a boil. Remove from the heat and stir in the sesame oil. Season with salt and serve in warmed soup plates.

—Eileen Yin-Fei Lo

■

CORN AND CRAB GAZPACHO

This dressed-up gazpacho is served at the famous Windsor Court Hotel in New Orleans. Substitute coarsely chopped boiled shrimp if you prefer it to crab.

6 Servings

- 3 pounds large ripe tomatoes— peeled, seeded and coarsely chopped
- 1 medium green bell pepper, coarsely chopped
- 1 small cucumber—peeled, seeded and coarsely chopped
- 1 small red onion, coarsely chopped
- 4 garlic cloves—2 coarsely chopped and 2 left whole and peeled
- ¼ cup extra-virgin olive oil
- 1 teaspoon rice wine vinegar or ½ teaspoon white wine vinegar Cayenne pepper
  Pinch of ground cumin
  Salt
  Freshly ground white pepper
- 1 cup fresh or frozen corn kernels
- 12 thin diagonal slices cut from a baguette
- ½ pound fresh lump crabmeat, picked over
- 1 tablespoon minced fresh basil

1. In a large bowl, combine the tomatoes, green pepper, cucumber, red onion, chopped garlic, 3 tablespoons of the olive oil, the rice vinegar, ¼ teaspoon cayenne and the cumin. Working in batches, process the mixture in a food processor or blender until blended but still chunky. Transfer to a large bowl and season with salt, white pepper and cayenne. Cover and refrigerate until chilled, at least 1 or up to 8 hours.

2. In a small saucepan, combine the corn with ¼ cup of water. Bring to a boil over moderately high heat and cook until just tender, 2 to 3 minutes. Drain and let cool.

3. Preheat the broiler. Arrange the baguette slices on a baking sheet and toast until golden. Rub the toasts with the whole garlic cloves and drizzle lightly with the remaining 1 tablespoon olive oil; keep warm.

4. To serve, stir the corn and crab into the gazpacho. Ladle the gazpacho into chilled soup plates and sprinkle with the basil. Serve with the warm garlic toasts.

—Kevin Graham

■

CURRIED MUSSEL SOUP WITH RED LENTILS AND YOGURT

In this soup, based on a traditional Indian recipe, lentils add body without masking the flavor of the mussels. Yogurt lightens the soup and gives it a delightful tang. You can use other kinds of lentils, and you can replace the mussels with clams.

4 First-Course Servings

2¼ **pounds small mussels, scrubbed and debearded**
1½ **cups dry white wine**
2 **tablespoons unsalted butter**
1 **medium onion, coarsely chopped**
2 **garlic cloves, finely chopped**
½ **teaspoon coarsely chopped fresh thyme**
1 **tablespoon Madras curry powder**
½ **cup red lentils, picked over and rinsed**
1¼ **cups plain yogurt**
2 **tablespoons finely chopped flat-leaf parsley**
Freshly ground black pepper
Cayenne pepper

1. Put the mussels in a heavy, medium, nonreactive saucepan. Add the wine, cover and cook over moderate heat until the mussels open, about 7 minutes. Remove the saucepan from the heat and let cool; discard any mussels that don't open.

2. Melt the butter in another medium nonreactive saucepan. Add the onion, garlic and thyme and cook over low heat, stirring occasionally, until the onion is translucent, about 10 minutes. Stir in the curry powder and cook until fragrant, about 1 minute. Add the lentils and 1½ cups of water. Cover and simmer over moderately low heat, stirring once or twice, until the lentils are tender, about 20 minutes. Remove from the heat and let cool for 10 minutes.

3. Shell the mussels and place them in a medium bowl. Slowly pour in the cooking liquid, leaving behind the grit at the bottom. Wipe out the saucepan.

4. Transfer half of the mussels and all the cooking liquid to a food processor or blender. Add the lentils and puree until the mixture is smooth. Using a ladle or a rubber spatula, work the puree through a coarse strainer into the clean saucepan. Stir in the remaining mussels, 1 cup of the yogurt and the chopped parsley and bring to a gentle simmer over low heat, stirring occasionally. If the soup is too thick, stir in a little water to thin it. Season with black pepper and cayenne. Ladle the soup into warmed bowls and garnish each serving with 1 tablespoon of yogurt.

—James Peterson

Miso Clam Soup with Julienned Vegetables and Shiitake Mushrooms

■

MISO CLAM SOUP WITH JULIENNED VEGETABLES AND SHIITAKE MUSHROOMS

Miso soup is so adaptable that once you've made the basic broth it's a snap to make variations by adding vegetables— cut into different shapes—and almost any kind of fish or shellfish. Serve this salty soup with rice crackers on the side.

4 First-Course Servings
Dashi (recipe follows)
1   large carrot, cut into 1½-inch-long matchsticks
1   medium leek, white and tender green, cut into 1½-inch-long matchsticks
4   medium shiitake mushrooms, stems discarded and caps thinly sliced
2   dozen littleneck clams, scrubbed
2   tablespoons medium (brown) miso*
1   tablespoon Japanese soy sauce
2   medium scallions, finely chopped
1   tablespoon finely chopped flat-leaf parsley

*Available at health food stores

1. In a medium saucepan, combine 3 cups of the Dashi with the carrot matchsticks, leek matchsticks and mushroom slices. Bring to a boil over moderately high heat. Reduce the heat to moderate, cover and simmer until the vegetables are just tender, about 5 minutes.

2. In another medium saucepan, combine the clams with the remaining 1 cup Dashi and bring to a simmer over moderately high heat. Reduce the heat to moderate, cover and simmer gently until the clams open, about 10 minutes. Transfer the clams to a bowl and let cool. Slowly pour the clam cooking liquid into the vegetables in the pan, leaving behind the grit at the bottom.

3. Shell half of the clams. Place 1 shelled clam in each unshelled clam, so that you have 12 clamshells with 2 clams inside each one.

4. In a small bowl, blend the miso with the soy sauce to form a smooth paste. Stir the paste into the soup. Add the scallions and parsley and simmer over moderate heat for 1 minute. Spoon the soup into warmed bowls. Arrange 3 of the double clams in each bowl just below the surface of the soup.

Dashi
Makes 1 Quart
1   18-inch piece of konbu, or giant seaweed (about 1 ounce)*
4   (unpacked) cups hana-katsuo, or shaved bonito (1 ounce)*

*Available at Japanese markets

1. Fold the seaweed in half and put in a medium saucepan. Add 6 cups cold water. Bring slowly to a simmer over low heat, about 15 minutes. Discard the konbu.

2. Bring the broth to a boil over moderately high heat. Add the hana-katsuo and remove the saucepan from the heat. Let stand for 1 minute. Pass the dashi through a fine strainer. Add water if necessary to make 1 quart. (The dashi can be prepared up to 1 day ahead. Cover and refrigerate.)

—James Peterson

■

BRAZILIAN-STYLE SHRIMP AND COCONUT SOUP

Based on a traditional Brazilian shrimp stew called *vatapá*, this rich soup benefits from the aromatic flavor combination of peanuts, coconut milk and lime juice.

8 First-Course or
6 Main-Course Servings

2 tablespoons unsalted butter
2 pounds medium shrimp, shelled
   and deveined, shells reserved
1 large onion, coarsely chopped
5 garlic cloves, finely chopped
2 small Thai, or bird, chiles,* or
   serrano chiles, finely chopped
2 tablespoons finely grated fresh
   ginger (from a 2-inch piece)
1 quart Chicken Stock (p. 36), canned
   low-sodium broth or water
8 medium plum tomatoes—peeled,
   seeded and coarsely chopped—
   or 2 cups canned Italian peeled
   tomatoes, drained and chopped
1 14-ounce can unsweetened coconut
   milk*
⅔ cup roasted unsalted peanuts or
   ½ cup creamy peanut butter
¼ cup fresh lime juice
¼ cup finely chopped fresh coriander
   (cilantro)

Salt and freshly ground pepper
Lime wedges, for garnish (optional)

*Available at Asian markets

1. Melt the butter in a medium, nonreactive saucepan. Add the shrimp shells, onion, garlic, chiles and ginger. Cook over low heat, stirring, until the onion is translucent, about 10 minutes. Add the Chicken Stock and simmer gently for 15 minutes.

2. Strain the shrimp broth and return it to the pan. Stir in the tomatoes and simmer for 10 minutes.

3. Meanwhile, in a food processor or blender, puree the coconut milk with the peanuts until smooth. Stir into the broth. Add the shrimp, lime juice and coriander. Simmer gently just until the shrimp curl and turn pink, about 3 minutes. Season with salt and pepper, ladle into warmed bowls and serve with lime wedges.

—James Peterson

Brazilian-Style
Shrimp and
Coconut
Soup

CHICKEN STOCK

This all-purpose recipe comes from the Food & Wine test kitchen.

Makes About 2 Quarts

7 pounds chicken backs or wings
2 medium onions, quartered
3 celery ribs, halved lengthwise

1. Combine the chicken parts, onions and celery in a stockpot and add 3 quarts of cold water. Bring to a boil over high heat. Reduce the heat to moderately low, cover partially and simmer for 2 hours.

2. Strain the stock through a colander set over a large bowl. Cover and refrigerate the stock for up to 3 days or freeze for up to 1 month. Skim off the fat before using.

■

CHICKEN BROTH WITH FREGULA

In Sardinia, chicken is most often used for making a clear broth (*brodo di pollo*). Ask your butcher for a boiling fowl, which has a great deal more flavor than a younger chicken and will stand up to longer boiling.

🍷 Look for Torbato Terre Bianche, Sardinia's finest dry white wine; it has a rich penetrating flavor that matches that of the island's best cooking.

6 Servings

1 4-pound boiling fowl, cut into 8 pieces, or 4 pounds bony chicken parts, such as backs, necks and wings, rinsed
1 medium tomato, fresh or canned, seeded and coarsely chopped
1 medium yellow onion, unpeeled and halved
1 medium carrot, halved
1 large celery rib, including leaves, halved
1 large fennel stalk, including feathery leaves
3 fresh flat-leaf parsley sprigs plus the stems from a bunch and ½ cup chopped leaves
1 bay leaf
¼ teaspoon black peppercorns
Salt
1 cup small Fregula (recipe follows) or pastina
½ cup freshly grated aged Pecorino cheese

1. In an 8-quart stockpot, combine the fowl, tomato, onion, carrot, celery, fennel, parsley sprigs and stems, bay leaf and peppercorns. Add enough cold water to cover the fowl by several inches. Cover the pot almost completely and bring to a boil. Lower the heat and simmer gently for 3 to 4 hours, occasionally skimming the foam from the surface; do not let the stock boil. Set aside to cool. Skim off as much fat as you can. Strain the broth through cheesecloth or a very fine sieve set over a clean stockpot. (The recipe can be made to this point up to 4 days ahead; refrigerate. Skim off any additional fat before proceeding.)

2. Bring the stock to a boil and reduce to 2½ quarts. If you like a stronger broth you can boil it down for about 10 minutes longer. Season with salt.

3. Add the Fregula. Simmer until al dente, about 5 minutes. Ladle the chicken broth and the pasta into warm bowls. Sprinkle with some of the chopped parsley and cheese.

Fregula
Makes About 2 Cups
¼ teaspoon (packed) saffron threads
¼ teaspoon salt
½ cup boiling water
About 2 cups fine semolina flour*

*Available at specialty food stores and Italian markets ➤

**Chicken Broth
with Fregula**

Curried Mulligatawny Soup

1. In a small bowl, steep the saffron and salt in the boiling water until dissolved, about 10 minutes.

2. Spread about ½ cup of the semolina flour in a wide shallow bowl. Using one hand, sprinkle some of the warm saffron water over the semolina. Rub the mixture to form crumbs. Using your dry hand, add more semolina. Keep sprinkling on more saffron water with your wet hand and adding more semolina flour with your dry hand until all the water and semolina have been added and firm but unevenly sized crumbs have formed. Add a little tap water if the crumbs are too dry and more semolina flour if the crumbs are too moist.

3. Spread the fregula on kitchen towels to dry for about 30 minutes. Using your hands, brush the crumbs into 1 pile of large and 1 pile of small crumbs. (The fregula can be refrigerated, covered, for up to 5 days.)

—Julia della Croce

■

CURRIED MULLIGATAWNY SOUP

Classic Indian Mulligatawny is often based on red lentils. This heartier version also includes chunks of potato and tart green apple.

6 Servings

- ¼ cup olive oil
- 1 large onion, finely chopped
- 2 medium carrots, finely diced
- 2 celery ribs, finely diced
- 4 large garlic cloves, minced
- 1½ tablespoons finely grated fresh ginger (from a 2-inch piece)
- 2 teaspoons Madras curry powder
- 1 teaspoon ground cumin
- ½ teaspoon ground coriander
- ½ teaspoon cayenne pepper
- ½ teaspoon freshly ground black pepper
- Rich Chicken Stock (recipe follows) and shredded chicken
- ½ pound red potatoes, peeled and cut into ½-inch dice
- 1 cup red lentils (4 ounces)
- ½ teaspoon thyme
- 2 medium Granny Smith apples
- 2 tablespoons fresh lemon juice
- ½ cup shredded unsweetened coconut* (about 1½ ounces)
- Salt
- Plain low-fat yogurt, for garnish

*Available at health food stores

1. Heat the olive oil in a large, heavy, nonreactive saucepan or enameled cast-iron casserole. Add the onion, cover and cook over moderately high heat, stirring occasionally, until translucent, about 3 minutes.

2. Add the carrots, celery, garlic and ginger to the saucepan. Cover and cook, stirring, for 3 minutes. Add the curry powder, cumin, coriander, cayenne and black pepper and stir until fragrant, about 1 minute.

3. Add the Rich Chicken Stock to the pan with the potatoes and lentils and bring to a boil over moderately high heat. Add the thyme, cover and simmer the soup over moderate heat, skimming, for 10 minutes.

4. Meanwhile, peel and core the apples, then cut them into ½-inch dice. Place in a medium bowl and toss with the lemon juice. Add the apples to the soup and bring to a boil over moderately high heat. Lower the heat and simmer, covered, until the potatoes and apples are tender, about 8 minutes.

5. Meanwhile, preheat the oven to 350°. Spread the shredded coconut on a small baking sheet and toast until golden, 6 to 8 minutes. ➤

6. Add the shredded chicken to the soup and cook until the chicken is heated through. Season with salt. Ladle the soup into bowls and garnish each serving with a spoonful of yogurt and a sprinkling of coconut.

Rich Chicken Stock
Makes 2 Quarts Stock Plus About
4 Cups Shredded Chicken

- 1   3½-pound chicken
- 1   pound unpeeled onions, trimmed and cut into eighths
- 2   celery ribs, halved lengthwise and coarsely chopped
- 1   large carrot, coarsely chopped
- 2   large garlic cloves, minced
- 1½ quarts Chicken Stock (p. 36) or canned low-sodium broth
- 2   cups dry white wine
     Bouquet garni: 5 flat-leaf parsley sprigs, 2 fresh thyme sprigs, 1 bay leaf and 5 black peppercorns tied in cheesecloth

1. Place the chicken in a large nonreactive stockpot. Add the onions, celery, carrot, garlic, stock, wine, bouquet garni and 1 quart of water and bring to a boil over moderately high heat. Lower the heat, cover partially and simmer, skimming occasionally, until the chicken is cooked through, about 1 hour.

2. Transfer the chicken to a large plate and let cool slightly. Discard the skin. Remove the meat from the bones and tear it into 2-inch shreds.

3. Strain the stock. If using immediately, skim off the fat and then blot the stock with paper towels. Alternatively, let the stock cool completely, then add the shredded chicken and refrigerate, covered, for up to 3 days or freeze for up to 1 month. Remove the fat from the cold stock. Rewarm the stock over moderate heat and strain, reserving the shredded chicken.

—Bob Chambers

■

LOBSTER AND WHITE BEAN SOUP

To give this soup body, half of the cooked beans are pureed. Italian cooks would be more likely to use shellfish such as shrimp, clams or mussels rather than lobster, but this is one of those soups you can play around with by adding vegetables (peas, fennel), various herbs (marjoram, thyme) and, of course, different shellfish. Serve the soup with Italian bread on the side. You can have your fishmonger cut up the live lobsters.

🍷 A fresh, fruity Chardonnay (one without excessive oak character) will accent the lobster flavor nicely here. Examples to look for include the 1992 Rothbury Estate from Australia and the 1991 Alexander Valley Vineyards from California.

6 First-Course or
4 Main-Course Servings

Beans:
- 1½ cups dried white beans, such as borlotti, white kidney or Great Northern, rinsed and picked over
- 1   medium onion, finely chopped
- 2   garlic cloves, finely chopped
     Bouquet garni: 3 fresh thyme sprigs, 10 flat-leaf parsley sprigs and 1 bay leaf
- 1   tablespoon sea salt

Soup:
- 2   tablespoons olive oil
- 1   medium onion, coarsely chopped
- 1   medium carrot, coarsely chopped
- 3   cups Chicken Stock (p. 36), canned low-sodium broth or water
- 6   medium plum tomatoes, coarsely chopped, or 1½ cups canned Italian peeled tomatoes, drained and coarsely chopped

1 cup dry white wine

3 1¼-pound live lobsters—heads halved lengthwise (sand sacks discarded), claws and tails removed but not cracked

4 tablespoons unsalted butter

4 1-inch slices of Italian bread, crusts removed, bread cut into ½-inch cubes

2 tablespoons finely chopped flat-leaf parsley

1 cup heavy cream

2 tablespoons balsamic vinegar
Table salt and freshly ground pepper

1. Prepare the beans: In a medium bowl, soak the beans in 3 cups of water for at least 3 hours or overnight. Drain and rinse the beans.

2. In a medium saucepan, combine the beans with 2 cups of water, the onion, garlic and bouquet garni. Bring to a boil over moderate heat. Cover and simmer over low heat for 30 minutes. Stir in the salt, cover and cook until the beans are tender, about 1 hour longer.

3. Meanwhile, prepare the soup: Heat the olive oil in a large enameled cast-iron casserole. Add the coarsely chopped onion and carrot, cover and cook over low heat, stirring occasionally, until the vegetables soften, about 10 minutes. Add the Chicken Stock, plum tomatoes, white wine and lobster pieces to the casserole. Cover and simmer, stirring, until the lobster pieces turn red, about 8 minutes. Remove from the heat. Transfer the lobster claws and tails to a bowl. Let cool for 5 minutes.

4. Remove the lobster tail meat from the shells in one piece and cut into ½-inch cubes. Place the meat in a medium bowl; reserve the shells.

5. Crack the lobster claws with a nutcracker or the back of a chef's knife. Remove the meat and cut into ½-inch cubes. Add it to the tail meat.

6. Break the lobster tail and claw shells into 1- to 2-inch pieces and return them to the casserole with any accumulated lobster juices. Bring to a boil, then simmer over moderate heat for 20 minutes. Pass the broth through a fine strainer and transfer to a medium casserole. (The recipe can be prepared to this point up to 1 day ahead. Cover and refrigerate the broth, lobster meat and cooked white beans separately. Reheat the broth before proceeding.)

7. Melt the butter in a medium skillet. Add the bread cubes and cook over moderate heat, stirring frequently, until golden brown, 4 to 5 minutes. Remove from the heat and stir in the parsley to coat the croutons.

8. In a blender or food processor, puree 2 cups of the cooked white beans with their liquid and 1 cup of the lobster broth until smooth. Stir the puree back into the remaining lobster broth. Add the remaining cooked beans, the lobster meat, the heavy cream and the balsamic vinegar and bring the soup to a simmer over moderate heat. Season with salt and pepper. Ladle the soup into warmed bowls or soup plates and garnish with the parslied croutons.

—James Peterson

■

SOUP OF BROKEN PASTA AND BEANS WITH FRESH BASIL

Lighter and more delicate than most bean and pasta dishes, this soup from the Modena area of Emilia-Romagna is traditionally made with maltagliati, haphazard cuts of pasta.

❦ Try Valpolicella Classico from the Veneto, one of the most charming of red wines, tender on the palate and packed

HOW TO MAKE MALTAGLIATI

To cut this irregularly shaped pasta, roll up a sheet of pasta like a jelly roll and then make angled cuts, first one way and then the other, to create triangles and trapezoids.

—Lynne Rossetto Kasper

with sensations of fruits. A Sangiovese di Romagna (from Emilia-Romagna), a young Dolcetto d'Alba (from Piedmont) or a light-bodied Zinfandel (from California) would also pair well.

4 to 6 Servings

- ½ **pound dried beans, such as cannellini (white kidney beans), toscanelli or borlotti (1 cup)**
- 3 **medium garlic cloves—1 crushed and 2 minced**
- 1 **large imported bay leaf**
  Generous pinch of ground cloves
- 6 **cups Chicken Stock (p. 36) or canned low-sodium broth**
- 3 **thin slices of lean pancetta, minced (about ¾ cup)**
- 2 **tablespoons extra-virgin olive oil**
- 1 **large onion, finely chopped**
- ⅓ **cup minced fresh flat-leaf parsley**
- 2 **cups peeled and chopped ripe fresh tomatoes (about 4 medium) or whole canned tomatoes, crushed**
  Salt and freshly ground pepper
- 1 **cup finely chopped fresh basil**
- ¼ **pound dried pappardelle or wide egg noodles, broken into bite-size pieces, or ⅓ pound fresh Egg Pasta (p. 142), cut into maltagliati (see How to Make Maltagliati, at left)**
- 1 **tablespoon cold unsalted butter**
- ½ **cup freshly grated Parmigiano-Reggiano cheese**

1. Place the beans in a large saucepan. Add cold water to cover by 2 inches and bring to a boil. Remove from the heat and let soak for 2 hours. Drain the beans and return them to the pan. Add the crushed garlic, bay leaf, cloves, 2 cups of the stock and enough water to cover by about 1½ inches. Simmer, partially covered, until the beans are soft and beginning to fall apart, 1 to 1½ hours; do not drain. (The beans can be refrigerated in their liquid for up to 1 day.)

2. Bring a medium saucepan of cold water to a boil for the pasta. Meanwhile, in a large nonreactive saucepan, cook the pancetta in the oil over moderate heat, stirring occasionally, until most of the fat has been rendered and the pancetta starts to brown, about 8 minutes. Add the onion and cook, stirring occasionally, until rich golden brown, about 8 minutes. Add the parsley and minced garlic and cook for 1 minute. Add 1 cup of stock and boil until reduced to a thin film on the bottom of the pan, about 5 minutes. Add the tomatoes and simmer for about 8 minutes.

3. Add the remaining 3 cups stock and the beans with their cooking liquid to the tomato mixture. Season with salt and pepper. Set aside 1 cup of the soup. Pass the rest through a food mill. Return the soup to the saucepan and stir in the reserved 1 cup. The soup should be the consistency of heavy cream; thin with water if necessary. Bring the soup to a simmer, add the basil and cook for 5 minutes.

4. Meanwhile, salt the boiling pasta water, stir in the pasta and cook until al dente, 3 to 4 minutes for fresh or 8 to 10 minutes for dried. Drain the pasta and add it to the soup.

5. Ladle the soup into warmed soup bowls. Shave small shards of the butter over each serving. Sprinkle generous spoonfuls of Parmigiano-Reggiano cheese around the melting butter and serve.

—Lynne Rossetto Kasper

Chapter 3 ▪ SALADS

45 Salad of Bitter Greens with Fallen Goat Cheese Soufflés

46 Spinach and Cherry Tomato Salad

46 Tomato and Arugula Salad

46 Black Bean Salad with Chipotle Vinaigrette

49 Mustard Slaw

49 Tomato, Cucumber and Red Onion Salad

50 Celery Salad with Anchovy Dressing

50 Chickpea and Celery Salad

51 Carrots with Cornichon Dressing

51 Carrot and Parsley Salad

51 Potato Salad with Green Beans, Bacon and Cremini Mushrooms

52 Sweet Potato Salad

53 Bulgur Salad with Watercress and Sunflower Seeds

54 Lemon, Cucumber and Pepper Salad

54 Pear and Watercress Salad

**Salad of Bitter
Greens with Fallen
Goat Cheese
Soufflé**

SALAD OF BITTER GREENS WITH FALLEN GOAT CHEESE SOUFFLES

Add a note of elegance to a dinner party menu with this special version of the winter-greens-and-goat-cheese theme.

8 Servings

Soufflés:
- ¼ cup plus 3 tablespoons freshly grated Parmesan cheese (about 2 ounces)
- 1 11-ounce log of mild fresh goat cheese, such as Montrachet
- ⅔ cup milk
- 2 tablespoons unsalted butter
- 3 tablespoons all-purpose flour
  Salt
- ¼ teaspoon freshly ground pepper
- 3 large egg yolks
- 2½ tablespoons chopped mixed fresh herbs, such as thyme, parsley and chives
- 6 large egg whites
  Boiling water

Salad:
- 4 Belgian endives
- 1 small head of frisée or chicory
- 1 small head of escarole
- 1 small head of radicchio
- ¼ cup minced shallots
- ¼ cup sherry vinegar
- 2 teaspoons dry mustard
- ¾ teaspoon freshly ground pepper
- ½ teaspoon salt
- ¾ cup olive oil
- ¼ cup vegetable oil

1. Make the soufflés: Preheat the oven to 350°. Generously butter eight ½-cup ramekins and sprinkle them with 3 tablespoons of the Parmesan cheese. Cut ⅓ of the log of goat cheese into 8 even slices. Crumble the remainder of the log.

2. Bring the milk to a boil in a small saucepan. Meanwhile, in a medium saucepan, melt the butter over moderately high heat. Add the flour and cook, stirring constantly, for 2 minutes. Gradually whisk in the milk and whisk vigorously until smooth. Remove from the heat and mix in the goat cheese, the remaining ¼ cup Parmesan, ½ teaspoon salt and the pepper. Let the soufflé base cool for 10 minutes.

3. Place the egg yolks in a medium bowl. Stir in a few tablespoons of the warm soufflé base until blended, then fold in the remaining soufflé base. Let cool to room temperature, then stir in the fresh herbs.

4. Beat the egg whites with a pinch of salt until stiff peaks form. Gently stir ⅓ of the beaten egg whites into the soufflé base to lighten it, then gently fold in the remaining whites until just incorporated.

5. Spoon 2 tablespoons of the soufflé mixture into each prepared ramekin and top with a reserved slice of goat cheese. Fill the ramekins with the rest of the soufflé mixture and place them in a large baking dish at least ½ inch apart. Set the baking dish in the middle of the oven. Pour enough boiling water into the pan to reach halfway up the ramekins.

6. Bake the soufflés for about 50 minutes, or until they are browned on top and beginning to shrink away from the sides of the ramekins. Remove the ramekins from the water bath and let cool on a rack for 15 to 20 minutes. (The soufflés can be made up to 4 hours ahead and set aside at room temperature. Reheat in a 325° oven for about 7 minutes, until warmed through.)

7. Prepare the salad: Tear all the greens into bite-size pieces. In a small bowl, steep the shallots in the vinegar for 1 hour. Stir in the mustard, pepper and salt. Slowly whisk in the olive oil and vegetable oil.

8. To serve, toss the greens with the dressing. Unmold each soufflé and place in the center of a plate. Surround with the salad and serve.

—Bob Chambers

FRESH CORIANDER

This delicate, leafy herb is also known as cilantro and Chinese parsley. It tastes a little like orange peel. Look for bunches with roots attached; they keep longer. In addition to using fresh coriander in Black Bean Salad with Chipotle Vinaigrette, at right, you can:

• Simmer a handful of sprigs (roots and all) in a stock.

• Chop the leaves and add to sauces, sautés and stir-fries just after removing from the heat.

• Add to potato salad or pasta salad.

• Sprinkle whole leaves on soups at serving time.

—Nancie McDermott

SPINACH AND CHERRY TOMATO SALAD

For this colorful salad, choose curly spinach rather than the more delicate flat-leaf variety. Store the trimmed greens in a covered bowl in the refrigerator to keep them crisp.

4 Servings

- 1 tablespoon balsamic vinegar
- 2 teaspoons Dijon mustard
- 1 teaspoon olive oil
- ½ pound cherry tomatoes, quartered
- ¼ teaspoon sugar
  Salt and freshly ground pepper
- ¾ pound curly spinach, stemmed and torn into 1-inch pieces
- 1 4-ounce bunch of watercress, large stems discarded

1. In a large bowl, whisk the vinegar with the mustard and olive oil. Add the tomatoes and sprinkle them with the sugar and ¼ teaspoon each of salt and pepper. Stir to coat and set aside for 30 minutes, stirring once or twice.

2. Add the spinach and watercress to the tomatoes and toss well. Season with salt and pepper and serve.

—Diana Sturgis

TOMATO AND ARUGULA SALAD

Garlic and herbs give plenty of flavor to this low-fat salad.

8 Servings

- 3 pounds tomatoes, cut into wedges
- 2 medium garlic cloves, minced
- 2 tablespoons balsamic vinegar
- ½ tablespoon olive oil
  Salt and freshly ground pepper
- ½ pound arugula, large stems discarded
- ¼ cup slivered fresh basil

In a large bowl, toss the tomato wedges with the minced garlic, balsamic vinegar and olive oil. Season with salt and pepper. (The tomato salad can be prepared up to 5 hours ahead. Cover and let stand at room temperature.) Arrange the arugula on a large serving platter and mound the tomatoes on top. Sprinkle the salad with the slivered basil and serve.

—Martha Rose Shulman

BLACK BEAN SALAD WITH CHIPOTLE VINAIGRETTE

Give bean salad a south-of-the-border twist with cumin, chipotle and cilantro.

12 Servings

- 2 teaspoons cumin seeds
- 1 tablespoon adobo sauce, from a can of chipotle chiles in adobo
- ¼ cup red wine vinegar
- ¾ cup extra-virgin olive oil
- 1 28-ounce can Italian peeled tomatoes, drained and cut into ¼-inch dice
- ¼ teaspoon sugar
- 8 cups cooked black beans or 5 15-ounce cans black beans, drained and rinsed
- ⅔ cup finely chopped red onion
- 2 tablespoons thinly sliced tender scallion greens
- ¼ cup finely chopped fresh coriander (cilantro)
- ¼ cup finely chopped flat-leaf parsley
  Coarse (kosher) salt
  Freshly ground pepper
- 4 ounces goat cheese, crumbled

1. In a small heavy skillet, toast the cumin seeds over moderate heat, shaking the pan constantly, until the seeds darken and become fragrant, 1 to 2 minutes. Let cool slightly. Using a mortar with a pestle, a spice mill or a coffee grinder reserved for spices, grind the seeds to a fine powder.

2. In a medium bowl, whisk the adobo sauce and cumin together. Add the vinegar and whisk in the olive oil. (The vinai-

grette can be prepared up to 8 hours before serving. Cover and let stand at room temperature.)

3. Two to 3 hours before serving, stir the tomatoes and the sugar together in a small bowl; let stand for 15 minutes. In a large serving bowl, combine the black beans, red onion, scallion greens, coriander and 3 tablespoons of the parsley. Fold in the tomatoes. Whisk the vinaigrette and add it to the salad, tossing gently but

Tomato and Arugula Salad

Black Bean Salad with
Chipotle Vinaigrette

thoroughly. Season with coarse salt and pepper and mix once again. Cover the salad and let stand in a cool place, stirring occasionally.

4. Just before serving, scatter the crumbled goat cheese over the salad and sprinkle with the remaining 1 tablespoon chopped parsley.

—Leslie Newman

■

MUSTARD SLAW

Two mustards and three peppers make this one super bowl of slaw.

12 Servings
2½ to 3 tablespoons Dijon mustard
  1 tablespoon superfine sugar
1½ teaspoons dry mustard
    Coarse (kosher) salt
  ½ teaspoon cayenne pepper
  ¼ teaspoon freshly ground white pepper
  ¼ teaspoon freshly ground black pepper
1⅔ cups mayonnaise
2½ pounds green cabbage—quartered, cored and shredded
  4 medium carrots, cut into 3-inch lengths and shredded

1. In a medium bowl, whisk the Dijon mustard, sugar, dry mustard, 1 teaspoon coarse salt, the cayenne and white and black peppers. Whisk in the mayonnaise. (The dressing can be refrigerated, covered, for up to 2 days.)

2. One to 2 hours before serving, toss the cabbage and carrots together in a large salad bowl. Add the dressing and mix thoroughly. Cover and refrigerate the slaw until ready to serve, stirring once or twice. Season with coarse salt and toss once again.

—Leslie Newman

Mustard Slaw

■

TOMATO, CUCUMBER AND RED ONION SALAD

A zesty Greek-style salad, this is especially easy to assemble.

4 Servings
  ½ medium red onion, thinly sliced
  2 tablespoons red wine vinegar
    Kosher salt
  1 large tomato, cut into ½-inch dice
  ½ European cucumber or 1 medium cucumber, thinly sliced
  2 teaspoons extra-virgin olive oil
  1 tablespoon coarsely chopped fresh basil plus additional sprigs, for garnish
    Freshly ground pepper
  2 6-inch pitas or about 4 ounces of flat Middle Eastern bread ➤

Carrots with Cornichon Dressing

¼ cup plus 2 tablespoons extra-virgin olive oil
2 1.7-ounce cans flat anchovy fillets in olive oil
3 garlic cloves, coarsely chopped
Freshly ground pepper

1. Prepare a large bowl of ice water. With a small, sharp knife make several 1½-inch-long cuts in each piece of celery. Place the celery in the ice water and refrigerate for at least 2 hours and up to 1 day. The cut pieces of celery will fan out into flowers.

2. In a food processor or blender, combine the olive oil, anchovies and their oil and the garlic; process or blend until smooth. Transfer to a small bowl.

3. Just before serving, drain and carefully dry the celery with a clean towel. Place in a large serving bowl. Toss with just enough of the dressing to lightly coat the celery. Serve immediately, passing the pepper mill.

—Patricia Wells

■

1. In a medium bowl, toss the red onion with the vinegar and ¼ teaspoon salt. Let stand for 10 minutes.

2. Drain the onion and return to the bowl. Add the tomato, cucumber, olive oil and chopped basil; toss gently. Season the salad with salt and pepper, garnish with the basil sprigs and serve. Accompany each portion with half a pita bread or one-quarter of the flat bread.

—Janet Hazen

■

CELERY SALAD WITH ANCHOVY DRESSING

This is an adaptation of a Roman salad traditionally made with puntarelle, local wild chicory. Here, celery is used instead.

6 to 8 Servings
1 bunch of celery (about 1½ pounds)—ribs separated, rinsed and trimmed into 2-inch lengths

CHICKPEA AND CELERY SALAD

Easy as can be, this salad can also be made up to five days before serving.

4 Servings
1 small onion, finely chopped
1 medium garlic clove, minced
1 anchovy fillet, mashed, plus 1 teaspoon of oil from the can
2½ tablespoons fresh lemon juice
2 tablespoons olive oil
1½ tablespoons chopped fresh flat-leaf parsley
2 teaspoons chopped capers
1 teaspoon chopped fresh thyme
½ teaspoon or more chopped fresh chile, such as serrano or jalapeño

2 cups drained cooked chickpeas
(from a 19-ounce can), rinsed
Salt and freshly ground black
pepper
2 large celery ribs, peeled and thinly
sliced crosswise

1. In a large bowl, mix together the
onion, garlic, anchovy fillet and anchovy
oil. Stir in the lemon juice, olive oil, parsley, capers, thyme and chile.
2. Fold in the chickpeas and season with
salt and pepper. Set aside at room temperature for a few hours to allow the flavors
to develop; stir from time to time. Just
before serving, stir in the celery.

—Marcia Kiesel

■

CARROTS
WITH
CORNICHON
DRESSING

The unusual combination of fresh tarragon and spearmint adds a special note to
this salad.

4 Servings
1 pound thin baby carrots
¼ cup finely chopped onion
⅓ cup diced cornichons or sour
gherkins
2 teaspoons chopped fresh tarragon
1 teaspoon chopped fresh spearmint
2 teaspoons fresh lemon juice
2 tablespoons olive oil
Salt and freshly ground
pepper

1. In a medium saucepan of boiling
water, cook the carrots until just tender,
about 5 minutes. Drain in a colander and
refresh with cold water.
2. In a large bowl, combine the onion,
cornichons, tarragon, spearmint, lemon
juice and olive oil. Add the carrots and

toss with the dressing. Season with salt
and pepper. Serve or cover and refrigerate
for up to 3 days.

—Marcia Kiesel

■

CARROT
AND PARSLEY
SALAD

This recipe has been adapted from *Fanny
at Chez Panisse* (HarperCollins).

4 Servings
1 small garlic clove, peeled
1 tablespoon plus 1 teaspoon red
wine vinegar
¼ cup light olive oil or vegetable oil
1 pound large carrots, finely grated
⅔ cup chopped fresh parsley
Salt

1. In a medium serving bowl, rub the
garlic back and forth against the tines of a
fork to make a juicy puree. Use the fork to
blend in the vinegar and oil.
2. Stir in the carrots and parsley, season
with salt and mix very well.

—Alice Waters

■

POTATO
SALAD WITH GREEN
BEANS, BACON
AND CREMINI
MUSHROOMS

A small quantity of lean bacon, preferably
from a German or Polish butcher, makes
this festive, quick-to-prepare salad hearty
enough for a main-dish meal.

2 Main-Course or 4 to 6 First-Course
Servings
1¼ pounds small boiling potatoes,
scrubbed under running water ➤

FLAVORED
VINEGARS

Place clean, dry
herbs in glass
bottles, fill with
vinegar and cork or
cap securely. The
flavor will permeate
the vinegar in a few
weeks. Use the tasty
vinegars to make
plain salads
interesting. The
vinegars will keep at
room temperature
for four to six
months.
• Use slender fresh
chives with their
blossoms attached
or bushy stems of
fresh rosemary, sage
or thyme in white
wine vinegar.
• Pair green or
purple basil with red
wine vinegar.
• Pack a bottle of
unseasoned rice
vinegar with
pounded stalks of
fresh lemon grass.
Store this vinegar in
the refrigerator.
• Make a colorful,
spicy mix with white
wine vinegar, dried
red chiles and a
combination of
black, red and green
peppercorns

1. In a large saucepan, cover the potatoes with cold water, add salt and bring to a boil over high heat. Reduce the heat and simmer until tender, about 20 minutes.

2. Meanwhile, in a salad bowl, combine ¼ cup of the olive oil with the vinegar, 1 teaspoon of salt and the white pepper.

3. Drain the potatoes. Peel them if you like, then quarter them and toss quickly with the dressing in the bowl.

4. In a medium nonstick skillet, heat 1 teaspoon of the olive oil over moderately high heat. Add the bacon and cook until crisp, about 5 minutes. Discard any fat from the pan. Add the bacon to the potatoes and toss.

5. Add the remaining 1 teaspoon olive oil to the skillet and cook the mushrooms over moderately high heat, shaking the pan, until lightly browned, about 2 minutes. Add the garlic and cook for 1 minute; shake the pan to avoid burning the garlic. Toss the mushrooms with the potatoes.

6. In a medium saucepan, bring 2 quarts of water to a boil over high heat. Add the beans and boil until just cooked through but still crisp, 3 to 4 minutes. Drain well. Toss the beans and basil with the potatoes. Season the salad with salt and black pepper and serve immediately.

—Lydie Marshall

■

SWEET POTATO SALAD

Pickled Pepper Relish makes a tangy counterpoint to the potato salad, but it can be omitted from the recipe.

8 to 10 Servings

2 pounds sweet potatoes, peeled and cut into ½-inch dice
  Salt
1 cup Pickled Pepper Relish (recipe follows)

**Sweet
Potato
Salad**

Salt
¼ cup plus 2 teaspoons olive oil
1 tablespoon red wine vinegar
⅛ teaspoon freshly ground white pepper
4 ounces sliced lean bacon, cut crosswise into ⅓-inch strips
6 ounces cremini mushrooms, stems trimmed or discarded, caps quartered
2 garlic cloves, thinly sliced
¾ pound haricots verts or thin green beans
¼ cup shredded fresh basil
  Freshly ground black pepper

2 tablespoons Dijon mustard
1 tablespoon honey
1 teaspoon minced garlic
1 teaspoon Worcestershire sauce
¾ cup olive oil
  Freshly ground pepper
¼ cup coarsely chopped fresh flat-leaf
  parsley

1. In a large heavy saucepan, cover the sweet potatoes with water. Add ½ teaspoon salt and bring to a boil over moderately high heat. Cook until just tender, about 10 minutes. Drain well, refresh briefly with cold water and drain again thoroughly.

2. In a large bowl, whisk the Pickled Pepper Relish with the mustard, honey, garlic and Worcestershire sauce. Gradually whisk in the olive oil. Fold in the sweet potatoes and season with salt and pepper. (The potato salad can be refrigerated, covered, for up to 2 days. Let return to room temperature before serving.) Stir the chopped parsley into the potato salad and serve warm or at room temperature.

Pickled Pepper Relish
Makes 3 Cups

2 dried chipotle chiles
1 large green bell pepper, cut into
  ¼-inch dice
1 medium red bell pepper, cut into
  ¼-inch dice
1 small yellow bell pepper, cut into
  ¼-inch dice
1 medium red onion, cut into ¼-inch
  dice
6 cups of boiling water
¾ cup cider vinegar
⅓ cup plus 1½ tablespoons sugar
1½ teaspoons salt
½ teaspoon celery seeds

1. In a small bowl, soak the chipotles in hot water to cover until softened, about 20 minutes. Drain the chiles, halve them and discard the seeds and stems.

2. In a medium nonreactive saucepan, cover the bell peppers and the red onion with the boiling water. Let stand for 10 minutes.

3. Drain the vegetables and return them to the saucepan. Stir in the chipotles, vinegar, sugar, salt and celery seeds and bring to a boil over moderately high heat. Lower the heat and simmer, stirring occasionally, until the peppers are just tender, about 15 minutes. Let cool completely. (The relish can be refrigerated, covered, for up to 1 week.) Discard the chipotles and serve.

—Ben Barker

■

BULGUR SALAD WITH WATERCRESS AND SUNFLOWER SEEDS

Generally you can keep grain salads, but this one is best on the day it is made.

4 Servings

¾ cup bulgur
1 small onion, chopped
1 bunch of watercress, tough stems
  discarded, the rest torn into sprigs
3 tablespoons roasted sunflower
  seeds
3 tablespoons fresh lemon juice
2 tablespoons olive oil
  Salt and freshly ground pepper

1. In a medium saucepan, cover the bulgur with 1½ cups water and bring to a boil over high heat. Reduce the heat to low, cover and cook for 15 minutes. Remove from the heat. Keep covered for 5 minutes.

2. Transfer the bulgur to a large bowl and stir occasionally until it has cooled to room temperature. Then stir in all the remaining ingredients. Serve immediately or cover and refrigerate until chilled.

—Marcia Kiesel

■

LEMON, CUCUMBER AND PEPPER SALAD

This cool, refreshing and easy-to-prepare salad is particularly welcome after a fish course.

4 to 6 Servings

2 small, firm, thick-skinned lemons, well washed
   Salt
1 red bell pepper
1 European seedless cucumber, sliced paper-thin
   Extra-virgin olive oil, for drizzling
   Freshly ground black pepper
1 tablespoon coarsely chopped flat-leaf parsley

1. Slice the lemons crosswise as thinly as possible—no thicker than ⅛ inch. With the tip of a paring knife, pick out the seeds, which secrete a bitter oil, from each lemon slice. Put the lemon slices in a small bowl and sprinkle them liberally with salt.

2. Cut the bell pepper lengthwise along its creases. Discard the core, seeds and ribs. Slice the pepper crosswise into very thin strips.

3. Line a serving platter or individual plates with concentric rings of cucumber slices. Drain the lemon slices and arrange them over the cucumber slices, allowing a border of cucumber slices to show. Arrange the red bell pepper strips over the lemon slices. Pour a thin stream of extra-virgin olive oil in a figure eight pattern over the salad. Sprinkle the salad with black pepper and the chopped flat-leaf parsley. Just before serving, sprinkle the salad with salt.

—Marcella Hazan

■

PEAR AND WATERCRESS SALAD

In this salad the sweet, delicate flavor of fresh pears complements the pepperiness of the watercress. Serve it with an assortment of blue cheeses, such as Roquefort, Fourme d'Ambert and Stilton.

4 Servings

1 tablespoon fresh lemon juice
2½ tablespoons extra-virgin olive oil
   Fine sea salt and freshly ground pepper
2 ripe Comice or Bartlett pears
1 medium bunch of watercress, large stems removed

1. Put the lemon juice in a large bowl. Whisk in the extra-virgin olive oil in a thin stream until incorporated. Season with sea salt and pepper.

2. Peel, halve and core the pears, then slice them lengthwise ⅓ inch thick. Fold the pears into the dressing and set aside for 30 minutes.

3. Add the watercress to the pears, toss well and serve.

—Patricia Wells

Chapter 4 ▪ FISH & SHELLFISH

57   Lobster Salad with Fennel and Orange

57   Grilled Scallop Skewers with Grilled Tomato Sauce

58   Shrimp Salad with Celery, Olives and Tomatoes

59   Poached Shrimp with Coriander and Rice

60   Malay Prawn Curry

60   Skewered Shrimp with Fennel and Orange

62   Lump Crab Chiles Rellenos with Chimayo Cream Sauce

63   Soft-Shell Crabs with Ginger-Lime Sauce

65   Grilled Squid Salad with Tomato and Mint Bruschetta

67   Spicy Squid Salad

67   Baked Whole Fish Stuffed with Shellfish

68   Fish in a Foil Packet

69   Grilled Brook Trout with Pancetta

70   Broccoli Rabe and Potato Hash with Smoked Trout

70   Seared Pompano with Grapefruit Essence and Spinach

72   Cod Steaks with Red Pepper Sauce

72   Poached Cod with Tomatoes and Fennel

75   Salt Cod Ragout on Steamed Spinach

76   Grilled Swordfish Sicilian Style

77   Grilled Swordfish with Salsa Verde

77   Grilled Salmon with Potato-Herb Dressing

78   Steamed Salmon

78   Grilled Whole Bluefish Rubbed with Garlic and Rosemary

79   Spicy Tuna and Green Bean Salad with Tomatoes

**Lobster Salad with
Fennel and Orange**

LOBSTER SALAD WITH FENNEL AND ORANGE

This salad can be made through step four up to one day ahead. Cover and refrigerate the lobster, orange and dressing separately.

8 Servings

- 6 1½-pound cooked lobsters
- 5 navel oranges
- 1 tablespoon fennel seeds
- 2 tablespoons fresh lemon juice
- 1½ tablespoons chopped fresh tarragon
- 1 tablespoon plus 1 teaspoon Dijon mustard
- 2 teaspoons finely grated orange zest
- 1 teaspoon freshly ground pepper
- ½ teaspoon salt
- ½ cup extra-virgin olive oil
- 2 tablespoons vegetable oil
- 2 pounds fennel bulbs with feathery fronds—bulbs trimmed, cored and sliced paper thin plus 1 tablespoon chopped fronds
- 1 pound jicama, peeled and cut into very thin 3-inch matchsticks
  Fresh tarragon sprigs or fennel fronds, for garnish

1. Crack the lobsters and remove all the meat from the shells, keeping the pieces as intact as possible. Set aside the 8 prettiest claws for garnish. Halve the tails lengthwise; pull out and discard the veins. Cut the tails and the 4 remaining claws into ½-inch pieces and place them in the bowl.

2. Juice one of the oranges into a small bowl. Peel the remaining 4 oranges with a sharp knife, removing all of the bitter white pith. Cut in between the membranes to release the sections into another bowl. Squeeze the remaining membranes over the bowl of juice. Strain the orange juice.

3. In a small skillet, toast the fennel seeds over moderately high heat until fragrant and lightly colored, 2 to 3 minutes. Let cool. Grind in a spice grinder or mortar.

4. Add the fennel seeds to the orange juice along with the lemon juice, tarragon, mustard, orange zest, pepper and salt. Whisk in the olive and vegetable oils.

5. One hour before serving, stir the 1 tablespoon chopped fennel fronds into the dressing. Toss the lobster meat with ⅔ cup of the dressing. Toss the 8 claws with ⅓ cup of the dressing. In separate bowls, toss the fennel and jicama with the remaining dressing.

6. To serve, arrange the fennel in the center of each plate. Arrange the jicama around the fennel. Mound ½ cup of the lobster in the center and garnish with the reserved claws, orange segments and tarragon sprigs.

—Bob Chambers

■

GRILLED SCALLOP SKEWERS WITH GRILLED TOMATO SAUCE

The deep, haunting flavor of bay leaves is quite pronounced in these skewers. Soak the leaves before grilling so that they won't burn. To keep the delicate scallops from sticking, make sure that the grill is very hot and is well oiled before cooking.

4 Servings

- 20 bay leaves (see Bay Leaves, p. 58)
  Boiling water
- 1½ pounds medium sea scallops, muscles discarded
- 3 garlic cloves, minced
- ¼ teaspoon ground cloves
- ½ cup olive oil
- 1 medium yellow bell pepper, cut into 1-inch dice
- 1 medium red bell pepper, cut into 1-inch dice
- 1 medium orange bell pepper, cut into 1-inch dice
  Fine sea salt ➤

BAY
LEAVES

If you can find
them, use fresh bay
leaves for the
Grilled Scallop
Skewers with
Grilled Tomato
Sauce. Fresh or
dried, the leaves
should be soaked
in cold or warm
water for about 20
minutes to prevent
burning.

—Erica De Mane

Freshly ground pepper
Grilled Tomato Sauce (recipe
follows)

1. Put the bay leaves in a medium bowl.
Add boiling water to cover and soak the
bay leaves until softened, about 30 minutes. Drain and transfer the bay leaves to
a large bowl.

2. Add the scallops, garlic and cloves to
the bowl. Stir in the olive oil, cover and let
marinate at room temperature for at least
1 or up to 3 hours.

3. Light a grill. Thread the scallops, alternating colors of yellow, red and orange
bell pepper and the bay leaves on 4 long
metal skewers. Brush any remaining marinade over the skewers and season with sea
salt and pepper.

4. Cook the skewers on an oiled grill for
about 2½ minutes per side, just until grill
marks appear and the scallops feel firm.
Spoon the Grilled Tomato Sauce into the
center of 4 large plates. Place a scallop
skewer on the pool of tomato sauce on
each plate and serve immediately.

Grilled Tomato Sauce
Makes About 2½ Cups

5 ripe medium tomatoes, halved and
   seeded
¼ cup extra-virgin olive oil plus more,
   for brushing
1 garlic clove
1 teaspoon light brown sugar
   Fine sea salt
   Freshly ground pepper
2 tablespoons balsamic vinegar

1. Light a grill. Brush the tomatoes
lightly with olive oil and grill for about 5
minutes, turning once, until they are softened and browned; don't let the skins
blacken and burn.

2. Transfer the tomatoes to a food processor or blender. Add the ¼ cup of oil,
the garlic, brown sugar and ¼ teaspoon
each sea salt and pepper. Process until

smooth. (The sauce can be prepared up to
3 hours ahead; cover and let stand at
room temperature. Rewarm before proceeding with the next step.)

3. Stir the balsamic vinegar into the
tomato sauce and season with sea salt and
pepper. Serve warm.

—Erica De Mane

■

SHRIMP SALAD
WITH CELERY,
OLIVES AND
TOMATOES

Skinny strips of celery make this one of
the freshest-tasting shrimp salads around.
Season the salad with salt just before serving; otherwise the salt will draw too much
juice from the tomatoes and make the
salad watery.

4 to 6 Servings

   Salt
3 tablespoons wine vinegar
2 dozen medium shrimp in their
   shells
4 large celery ribs, peeled and cut
   into 1½-by-¼-inch strips
4 ripe plum tomatoes (⅔ pound)—
   peeled, seeded and cut into
   1½-by-¼-inch strips
8 black Greek olives, pitted and sliced
   lengthwise into ¼-inch strips
2 tablespoons finely chopped flat-leaf
   parsley
   Freshly ground pepper
⅓ cup extra-virgin olive oil

1. Bring 3 quarts of water to a boil in a
large saucepan. Add 1 tablespoon salt and
1 tablespoon of the vinegar. Put the
shrimp in the pan. One minute after the
water returns to a boil, drain the shrimp.
As soon as the shrimp are cool enough to
handle, shell and devein them and transfer
to a serving bowl.

2. Add the celery strips, plum tomatoes, Greek olives and chopped flat-leaf parsley to the shrimp. Season liberally with pepper, add the olive oil and the remaining 2 tablespoons vinegar and toss thoroughly. (The salad can be prepared several hours ahead and refrigerated. Let return to room temperature and season with salt just before serving.)

—Marcella Hazan

■

POACHED SHRIMP WITH CORIANDER AND RICE

Low-in-fat shrimp are flavored with the liquid they're poached in—a stock made with cilantro, ginger and scallions.

4 Servings

Poached Shrimp:
- 1½ pounds medium shrimp
- 1 tightly packed cup fresh coriander (cilantro) leaves plus additional sprigs, for garnish
- 4 scallions, each cut into 3 pieces
- 1 3-inch piece of fresh ginger, crushed
- ¼ cup dry white wine
- 1 teaspoon distilled white vinegar
- 2 teaspoons sugar
- 1 teaspoon salt
- ¼ teaspoon whole white peppercorns
- 5 cups cooked white rice, for serving

Dipping Sauce:
- 2 tablespoons dry white wine
- 2 teaspoons light soy sauce
- 1 teaspoon distilled white vinegar
- 3 tablespoons Chicken Stock (p. 36) or canned low-sodium broth
- ½ teaspoon finely grated ginger
- 1 large scallion, thinly sliced on the diagonal

1. Shell the shrimp, leaving the tail shells on; reserve the shells. Devein the shrimp, cover and refrigerate.

2. In a medium nonreactive saucepan, combine the shrimp shells, coriander, scallions, ginger, wine, vinegar, sugar, salt and white peppercorns. Add 5 cups of water, cover and bring to a boil over high heat. Lower the heat and simmer for 30 minutes.

3. Prepare the dipping sauce: in a small bowl, combine all the ingredients. Set aside at room temperature.

4. Strain the poaching liquid and return it and the crushed ginger to the pan. Bring to a boil over high heat. Add the shrimp and cook, stirring frequently, until they curl and turn pink, about 2 minutes.

5. Transfer the shrimp to plates. Garnish with the coriander sprigs and serve with the rice and dipping sauce.

—Eileen Yin-Fei Lo

MARCELLA HAZAN'S FAVORITE FAMILY MEAL

❦ For the shrimp salad and the pasta, look for a light and fragrant Pinot Grigio, preferably from a good producer in the Collio district of Friuli, such as Puiatti. For the stuffed fish, you'll want a full-bodied white with depth and length of taste, such as a Chardonnay from central Italy. Fine examples are Caparzo's Le Grance, Antinori's Cervaro della Sala and Ama's Vigna al Poggio.

Shrimp Salad with Celery, Olives and Tomatoes
(page 58)

■

Spaghetti with Fresh Tuna and Roasted Red Peppers
(page 144)

■

Baked Whole Fish Stuffed with Shellfish
(page 67)

■

Lemon, Cucumber and Pepper Salad
(page 54)

■

Ricotta Fritters
(page 244)

VEGETABLE GHEE

A solid vegetable shortening made from various oils, vegetable ghee is frequently used in India as a less expensive alternative to butter-based ghee (a kind of clarified butter). The shortening is available at Indian markets.

—Jennifer Brennan

■

MALAY PRAWN CURRY

This prawn (shrimp) curry, as served in the sultanate of Brunei, is exceedingly spicy-hot. The original recipe from the Malay Archipelago includes four times the amount of crushed red pepper called for here.

4 Servings

2 tablespoons vegetable ghee or canola oil (see Vegetable Ghee, at left)
1 large yellow onion, thinly sliced
6 garlic cloves, finely chopped
1 fresh lemon grass stalk*—white bulb and 2 inches of green tops—minced
5 fresh or dried curry leaves*
6 green tomatoes (or unripened red ones), coarsely chopped, and their liquid
3 cups unsweetened coconut milk*
2 tablespoons minced fresh ginger
1 tablespoon crushed red pepper
1 tablespoon dried shrimp powder* or ground dried shrimp
1 teaspoon shrimp paste*
1 teaspoon turmeric
1 teaspoon tamarind concentrate* dissolved in 2 tablespoons hot water or ½ tablespoon molasses dissolved in 2 tablespoons fresh lemon juice
1 pound large shrimp, shelled and deveined
Salt

*Available at Asian markets

1. In a wok, heat the ghee until shimmering. Add the onion, garlic, lemon grass and curry leaves and stir-fry over moderately high heat until the onions are translucent, about 5 minutes.

2. Immediately add the tomatoes and their liquid. Stir in the coconut milk, ginger, crushed red pepper, shrimp powder, shrimp paste, turmeric and tamarind mixture. Simmer over moderate heat until the tomatoes soften and the gravy thickens, about 10 minutes. (The recipe can be prepared to this point up to 2 days ahead; refrigerate. Bring to a simmer over moderate heat before proceeding.)

3. Stir in the shrimp and simmer until just cooked through, about 5 minutes. Season with salt and serve.

—Jennifer Brennan

■

SKEWERED SHRIMP WITH FENNEL AND ORANGE

Grilled shrimp is popular in towns along the southern Italian coast, and Sicilian cooking often features this combination of fennel and orange. Serve the shrimp with rice.

6 Servings

½ cup olive oil
2 tablespoons fennel seeds, ground
Grated zest of 2 oranges
Grated zest of 1 lemon
¼ teaspoon crushed red pepper
1½ pounds large shrimp, shelled and deveined
2 medium fennel bulbs—halved, cored and cut into 1-inch chunks, thick layers separated
2 medium red onions, cut into 1-inch chunks
3 medium oranges, halved lengthwise and sliced crosswise ⅓ inch thick
Salt

1. In a small bowl, combine the olive oil, fennel seeds, grated orange and lemon zests and the crushed pepper. ➤

Malay Prawn Curry

2. Thread the shrimp, fennel, onions and oranges onto 6 metal skewers. Arrange the skewers in a shallow baking dish and brush them with the marinade. Cover and refrigerate for 3 to 4 hours, turning occasionally.

3. Light a grill. Cook the shrimp skewers on an oiled grill for about 2 minutes per side, brushing occasionally with any remaining marinade, until the shrimp turn pink. Sprinkle lightly with salt and serve.

—Erica De Mane

■

LUMP CRAB CHILES RELLENOS WITH CHIMAYO CREAM SAUCE

For this tasty first course, served at Mike's on the Avenue in New Orleans, use Anaheim chiles that are about seven inches long so that the ends peek out of the phyllo dough. Instead of being just fried, these untraditional stuffed chiles, which can also be eaten as a main course, are quickly fried and then rolled in the phyllo and baked.

❡ To set off the flavors and heat of the spicy *rellenos,* try a rich, fruit-scented Chardonnay, such as 1991 Sonoma-Cutrer Russian River Ranches.

10 Servings

Chiles Rellenos:
- 3 cups vegetable oil, for frying
- 10 large Anaheim chile peppers
- 1 pound lump crabmeat, picked over
- ½ cup fresh bread crumbs
- ¼ cup minced red onion
- 2 tablespoons mayonnaise
- 2 tablespoons fresh lime juice
- 1 tablespoon minced fresno chile or jalapeño pepper
- 1 tablespoon finely chopped fresh coriander (cilantro)
- ½ tablespoon Dijon mustard
- 1 teaspoon coarse (kosher) salt
- 1 large egg, lightly beaten
- 10 strips of Monterey Jack cheese, 3 inches long and ¼-inch thick (2 ounces)
- 5 sheets of phyllo dough
- ¼ cup unsalted butter, melted
  Chimayo Cream Sauce (recipe follows)

Jicama Salad:
- 4 8-inch corn tortillas, quartered and cut into ⅛-inch-thick strips
- 2 fresh ears of corn
- ½ medium red bell pepper, cut into 2-by-⅛-inch sticks
- ½ pound jicama, peeled and cut into 2-by-⅛-inch sticks
- 2 teaspoons minced jalapeño pepper
- 1½ tablespoons fresh lime juice
  Pinch of cayenne pepper
  Table salt

1. Prepare the *chiles rellenos:* In a large saucepan, heat the oil to 375°. Add 2 of the whole chile peppers and fry over moderately high heat until blistered all over, 1 to 2 minutes. Plunge the chile peppers in a bowl of ice water and drain on paper towels. Repeat with the remaining chile peppers. Strain the oil and reserve for frying the tortillas.

2. Peel the skin from the blistered chile peppers and make a slit from the stem to the tip of each one. Using a pair of scissors, cut out the cores and seeds. Rinse each chile pepper and pat it dry with paper towels.

3. In a medium bowl, gently break up the crabmeat. Fold in the bread crumbs, red onion, mayonnaise, lime juice, fresno chile, fresh coriander, mustard and coarse salt. Stir in the egg. Stuff the chiles with the crab mixture and carefully insert a

slice of cheese in each one. Close the chiles by folding one edge over the other and set aside.

4. Make the jicama salad: Light a grill or preheat the oven to 500°. In a large skillet, heat the reserved frying oil to 375°. Working in 2 or 3 batches, add the tortilla strips and fry over moderately high heat, stirring, until golden brown and crisp, about 3 minutes. Drain on paper towels.

5. Husk the corn, leaving the innermost layer and silk on. Rinse the corn to saturate it. Grill or roast the corn, turning occasionally, for about 15 minutes, or until charred and crisp-tender. Let cool, then peel off the outer layer and remove the silk. Slice the kernels from each ear of corn. Transfer to a medium bowl and toss with the red bell pepper, jicama and jalapeño. (The recipe can be prepared to this point up to 1 day ahead. Refrigerate the *chiles rellenos* and jicama salad separately; store the tortilla strips in an airtight container.)

6. Preheat the oven to 375°. Cut the phyllo sheets in half lengthwise to form ten 6-by-17-inch rectangles. Lay one rectangle on a work surface with the short end toward you. Keep the remaining phyllo rectangles covered with a damp towel. Lightly brush the rectangle with some of the melted butter. Place one *chile relleno* at the rectangle end near you, positioning it in the center so that the stem and tip of the chile stick out. Roll up the chile in the phyllo rectangle to form a neat cylinder and set it, seam side down, on a large baking sheet. Repeat with the remaining phyllo rectangles, melted butter and chiles. Bake the *chiles rellenos* for about 25 minutes, until the phyllo is golden brown.

7. Toss the jicama salad with the lime juice and season with cayenne and table salt. Spoon about ¼ cup of the Chimayo Cream Sauce on each of 10 plates and set a *chile relleno* on top. Spoon the jicama

salad alongside and garnish with a mound of fried tortilla strips. Serve, passing any remaining sauce separately.

Chimayo Cream Sauce
Makes About 3 Cups
1 stick (8 tablespoons) unsalted butter
2 tablespoons minced red onion
1 garlic clove, minced
2½ tablespoons tomato paste
2 tablespoons minced chimayo chile or other mild chile, such as Anaheim or poblano
3 cups heavy cream
Coarse (kosher) salt

Melt the butter in a large skillet. Add the onion and garlic and cook over moderate heat until translucent, about 3 minutes. Add the tomato paste and chile and stir in the cream. Simmer over moderate heat, stirring, until thickened, about 10 minutes. Season with coarse salt. (The chimayo sauce can be refrigerated, covered, for up to 1 day. Reheat gently just before serving.)

—Mike Fennelly

■

SOFT-SHELL CRABS WITH GINGER-LIME SAUCE

At the restaurant Gautreau's in New Orleans, this main-course dish is topped with fried shoestring potatoes. It's accompanied by a black-bean salad made from cooked dried beans flavored with scallions, fresh coriander, minced jalapeño, ground cumin and a little of the Lemon Vinaigrette.

♆ To balance the fried crabs and complement the tangy ginger-lime sauce, try either a fresh, fruity, spicy German

Gewürztraminer, such as 1990 Dürkheimer Feuerberg Dry Spätlese from the Rhine Valley, or a crisp, flavorful California Sauvignon Blanc, such as 1990 Kalin Cellars Reserve from Potter Valley.

4 Servings

Seasoned Flour:

2 cups all-purpose flour, sifted
¾ teaspoon salt
¼ teaspoon cayenne pepper
¼ teaspoon ground coriander
¼ teaspoon ground cumin
¼ teaspoon paprika
¼ teaspoon freshly ground white pepper

Ginger-Lime Sauce:

1 cup dry white wine
½ cup fresh lime juice
½ small red onion, thinly sliced
1 medium jalapeño pepper, thinly sliced crosswise
1 garlic clove, minced
1½ teaspoons minced fresh ginger
1 teaspoon ground ginger
1 teaspoon ground coriander
1 teaspoon paprika
½ teaspoon finely grated lime zest
6 fresh coriander sprigs (cilantro)
2 tablespoons heavy cream
2 sticks (½ pound) cold unsalted butter, cut into tablespoons
Salt and freshly ground white pepper

6 cups bite-size pieces of frisée
⅓ cup plus 1 tablespoon minced red onion
1½ tablespoons finely chopped fresh coriander (cilantro)
Lemon Vinaigrette (recipe follows)
Salt and freshly ground pepper
½ cup olive oil
8 cleaned medium soft-shell crabs
½ cup thinly sliced scallion greens
⅓ cup finely diced seeded fresh tomatoes

1. To make the seasoned flour, combine all of the ingredients in a medium bowl and set aside.

2. Prepare the ginger-lime sauce: In a medium nonreactive saucepan, combine the wine, lime juice, onion, jalapeño, garlic, fresh and ground ginger, ground coriander, paprika, lime zest and fresh coriander sprigs. Bring to a boil over moderately high heat and cook until reduced to ½ cup, 10 to 12 minutes. Let cool, then strain into a small nonreactive saucepan.

3. Reheat the ginger-lime mixture. Add the heavy cream and bring to a simmer over moderate heat. Remove the saucepan from the heat and whisk in the butter, 2 or 3 pieces at a time, adding another batch when the previous one has been incorporated. Reheat the sauce briefly from time to time to keep it very warm; do not let the sauce boil or it will separate. Season the sauce with salt and white pepper and set aside.

4. In a large bowl, toss the frisée with 1 tablespoon of the minced red onion, ½ tablespoon of the chopped fresh coriander and ¼ cup of the Lemon Vinaigrette. Season with salt and pepper.

5. Heat ¼ cup of the olive oil in each of 2 large skillets until almost smoking. Spread the seasoned flour on a large plate. Dredge the soft-shell crabs in the seasoned flour, shaking off the excess. Add 4 of the crabs to each skillet, top side down, and fry over high heat, turning once, until the crabs are crisp and reddish-orange, about 2 minutes per side. Transfer the crabs to a large plate and keep warm in a low oven.

6. Gently reheat the ginger-lime sauce over moderate heat, whisking, until very warm; do not boil.

7. To serve, mound the frisée salad in the center of each of 4 large warmed plates and sprinkle the scallion greens, the diced tomatoes and the remaining ⅓ cup minced red onion around. Top each

serving with 2 soft-shell crabs. Spoon 3 to 4 tablespoons of the ginger-lime sauce on the crabs and around each plate. Sprinkle the crabs with the remaining 1 tablespoon of chopped fresh coriander and serve immediately.

Lemon Vinaigrette
Makes About ¾ Cup

- ½ teaspoon Dijon mustard
- ¾ teaspoon coarse (kosher) salt
- ¼ teaspoon freshly ground white pepper
- ¼ cup fresh lemon juice
- ½ cup vegetable oil
- 2 tablespoons extra-virgin olive oil

In a small bowl, combine the Dijon mustard, the coarse salt and the white pepper. Whisk in the lemon juice, then slowly whisk in the vegetable oil and then the extra-virgin olive oil. (The vinaigrette can be refrigerated, covered, for up to 2 days. Let it return to room temperature before serving.)

—Larkin Selman

■

GRILLED SQUID SALAD WITH TOMATO AND MINT BRUSCHETTA

Grilling is one of the best ways to prepare squid; the quick cooking keeps it very tender. If baby squid is not available, use the same amount of cleaned large squid, cook until opaque and slice it into rings after grilling.

❢ Savory flavors predominate in this squid salad, which narrows the choice to an equally tart, aromatic white, such as 1991 Ceretto Arneis "Blangé" from Italy or a 1991 Dry Creek Fumé Blanc from California.

6 First-Course Servings

- ⅓ cup fresh lemon juice
- ¼ cup plus 2 tablespoons extra-virgin olive oil
- 1 tablespoon drained small capers
- 1 tablespoon finely chopped fresh dill
- Coarse salt
- Freshly ground pepper
- 1½ pounds cleaned baby squid, with tentacles reserved
- 5 medium scallions, trimmed
- 2 small tender celery ribs with their leaves—ribs very thinly sliced and leaves left whole
- 5 sprigs fresh flat-leaf parsley, stems discarded
- Tomato and Mint Bruschetta (recipe follows)

1. Light a grill. In a large bowl, mix the lemon juice with ¼ cup of the oil, the capers and dill. Season with coarse salt and pepper and set aside at room temperature.

2. Brush the squid bodies, the tentacles and the scallions with the remaining 2 tablespoons oil. Cook on an oiled grill for about 1¼ minutes per side, just until grill marks appear and the squid turns opaque; don't overcook or the squid will be tough.

3. Transfer the squid to the bowl of caper dressing. Slice the scallions ¼ inch thick, add to the bowl and toss to combine. Season with coarse salt and pepper. Let stand at room temperature for 30 minutes.

4. Add the celery slices and leaves and the parsley to the squid and toss. Spoon the salad onto the warm Tomato and Mint Bruschetta and serve.

Tomato and Mint Bruschetta
6 First-Course Servings

- 1 pound ripe medium tomatoes, seeded and finely chopped
- ¼ cup extra-virgin olive oil, plus more for brushing
- ¼ cup (tightly packed) minced fresh basil leaves   ➤

Spicy Squid Salad

1½ tablespoons minced fresh mint
   leaves
 2 garlic cloves—1 minced and 1
   halved
   Salt and freshly ground pepper
12 ½-inch-thick slices of crusty Italian
   bread

1. In a medium bowl, toss the tomatoes with ¼ cup of the olive oil, the basil, minced fresh mint leaves and minced garlic. Season with salt and pepper and let stand for 3 hours.

2. Light a grill. Toast the bread on the grill on both sides. Rub the toasts with the halved garlic clove and brush lightly with olive oil.

3. Place a heaping tablespoon of the tomato mixture on each toast and serve immediately.

—Erica De Mane

■

SPICY SQUID SALAD

Variations of this refreshing seafood salad can be found on antipasto tables throughout Italy. The textures of this version are particularly appealing: pleasantly chewy squid, crisp celery and soft green olives.

6 Servings
⅔ cup extra-virgin olive oil
⅓ cup fresh lemon juice
 4 garlic cloves, minced
¾ teaspoon crushed red pepper, or
   more to taste
 4 tender celery ribs from the heart
   with leaves, minced
20 drained pimiento-stuffed green
   olives, sliced crosswise
   Sea salt
   Freshly ground black pepper
 2 pounds very fresh, small whole
   squid

1. In a medium serving bowl, stir together the oil, lemon juice, garlic and crushed red pepper. Add the celery and olives and toss to coat. Season with sea salt and black pepper.

2. Clean the squid (see How to Clean Squid, at right). In a large saucepan, bring 3 quarts of water to a rolling boil. Add 2 teaspoons sea salt. Add the squid and cook just until opaque and tender, less than 1 minute. (Begin testing the squid after about 30 seconds.) Drain thoroughly but do not rinse.

3. Transfer the hot squid to the bowl of olives and dressing and toss well. Cover and refrigerate for at least 3 hours or overnight. Season with additional sea salt and black pepper before serving.

—Patricia Wells

■

BAKED WHOLE FISH STUFFED WITH SHELLFISH

A whole fish is stuffed with clams, mussels and shrimp, then tightly sealed in parchment paper or foil and baked in the oven, where it braises in its own juices. Once cooked, the fish is extraordinarily moist and infused with a medley of sea fragrances. The most agreeable way to serve the fish is whole, with the head and tail intact, but completely boned. If you have an obliging fish dealer, have him do it for you. If he is not so obliging, have him fillet the fish, leaving the skin on. Then sandwich the two fish fillets around the stuffing.

6 Servings
 1 dozen littleneck clams, scrubbed
 1 dozen small mussels, scrubbed and
   debearded
 6 medium shrimp, shelled and
   deveined   ➤

HOW TO CLEAN SQUID

• Rinse and drain thoroughly.
• Slice off the tentacles just above the eyes.
• Squeeze out and discard the hard little beak just inside the tentacles at the point where they joined the head.
• Using your fingers, pull out the innards and the quill from the body and discard. Do not worry about removing the grayish-pink skin.
• Slice the bodies crosswise into ½-inch rings.
• Cut the tentacles in half lengthwise.
• Rinse the squid thoroughly and drain.

—Patricia Wells

1 small onion, very thinly sliced
2 garlic cloves, lightly smashed
½ cup extra-virgin olive oil
⅓ cup fine dry bread crumbs
3 tablespoons fresh lemon juice
2 tablespoons finely chopped flat-leaf parsley
½ teaspoon salt
¼ teaspoon freshly ground pepper
1 4-pound whole sea bass, red snapper or salmon, boned but with head and tail intact

1. Arrange the clams and mussels in a heavy skillet or flameproof casserole large enough that they don't need to be piled more than 3 deep. Cover and turn the heat to high. Cook, checking and turning the mussels and clams frequently, until they just begin to open, about 6 minutes. Remove them from the pan promptly as they open.

2. Working over a bowl, shell the mussels and clams, allowing the meat and any juices to fall into the bowl. Add any cooking juices from the pan, leaving behind the sand and grit. Set aside for 20 to 30 minutes to allow the shellfish to release any sand.

3. Using a slotted spoon, transfer the mussels and clams to a clean medium bowl. Line a strainer with paper towels and strain the shellfish juices into the bowl. (The shellfish can be prepared 2 to 3 hours ahead.)

4. Wash the shrimp in cold water and pat thoroughly dry. Add them to the bowl. Add the onion and garlic to the bowl, then add the olive oil, bread crumbs, lemon juice, parsley, salt and pepper and toss thoroughly.

5. Preheat the oven to 475°. Wash the fish in cold water inside and out, then pat thoroughly dry with paper towels. Lay a double thickness of parchment paper or heavy-duty foil on a long, shallow baking dish or rimmed baking sheet, bearing in mind that there must be enough paper to

close over the whole fish. Pour some of the liquid in the mixing bowl over the parchment, tipping the baking dish to spread it evenly.

6. Place the fish in the center of the parchment paper and stuff it with the contents of the bowl, reserving some of the liquid. If you are using fillets, sandwich the stuffing between them. Use the reserved liquid to moisten the fish. Fold the parchment over the fish, crimping the edges to seal tightly all around; tuck the ends under the fish.

7. Bake the fish in the upper third of the oven for 35 minutes or until just cooked through. Remove the fish from the oven and let rest for 10 minutes before unwrapping. (If the baking dish is not presentable, transfer the wrapped fish to a platter.) With scissors, cut open the parchment, trimming down to the edge of the dish. Don't attempt to lift the fish out of the paper because it will break apart. Bring the fish to the table to present it whole. Slice the fish across as you might a roast and serve it directly from the parchment, spooning some of the cooking juices over each portion.

—Marcella Hazan

■

FISH IN A FOIL PACKET

This fresh-tasting, low-fat dish doesn't require a great deal of effort. Red snapper fillets are grilled or baked in foil with bell pepper strips and white wine. The juices become the sauce.

4 Servings
1 large red bell pepper, cut into 2-by-⅜-inch strips
1 large yellow bell pepper, cut into 2-by-⅜-inch strips
2 large garlic cloves, very thinly sliced

2 **teaspoons chopped fresh thyme**
2 **teaspoons chopped fresh rosemary**
¼ **teaspoon crushed red pepper**
   Kosher salt
4 **6-ounce skinless red snapper or sea**
   bass fillets, about ½ inch thick
1 **teaspoon extra-virgin olive oil**
   Freshly ground black pepper
2 **tablespoons dry white wine**
2 **teaspoons finely chopped fresh**
   flat-leaf parsley
4 **cups steamed white rice, for**
   serving

1. Light a grill or preheat the oven to 400°. In a medium bowl, toss the red and yellow bell pepper strips with the sliced garlic, chopped thyme and rosemary, crushed red pepper and ½ teaspoon of the salt. Rub the snapper fillets with the extra-virgin olive oil and season with salt and pepper.

2. Set a stack of four 18-by-12-inch rectangles of heavy-duty aluminum foil on a work surface, short ends toward you. Spoon one-quarter of the red and yellow bell pepper strips onto the lower half of the rectangle. Lay 1 snapper fillet on top and drizzle with 1½ teaspoons of the wine. Fold over the top half of the rectangle to loosely cover the fish and crimp the edges together securely. Repeat with the remaining bell pepper strips, fish fillets and wine.

3. To grill, place the foil packets on the rack and cover with a lid. Cook for 6 minutes. Rotate the packets to ensure even cooking and cook for about 6 more minutes, or until the fish is cooked through. Alternatively, arrange the packets on a large baking sheet and bake for about 15 minutes.

4. Cut open the packets. Transfer the fish fillets to large plates and spoon the bell peppers and sauce on top. Sprinkle with the chopped parsley and serve with the steamed rice.

—Janet Hazen

■

GRILLED BROOK TROUT WITH PANCETTA

A hinged wire basket makes the job of grilling the pancetta-wrapped trout much simpler.

❢ The sweetness of the fish and the bitter notes of sage suggest a fruity-spicy white wine, such as the 1991 Antinori Galestro from Italy or the 1991 Mark West Gewürztraminer from California.

4 Servings
Lemon-Sage Mayonnaise:
1½ **cups mayonnaise**
3 **tablespoons fresh lemon juice**
2 **teaspoons finely grated lemon**
   zest
1½ **teaspoons finely chopped fresh**
   sage
1 **teaspoon Dijon mustard**
   Salt
2 **pinches of cayenne pepper**

4 **¾-pound brook trout, cleaned,**
   with heads and tails intact
   Freshly ground pepper
8 **fresh sage sprigs plus additional**
   sprigs for garnish
½ **pound pancetta, thinly sliced**
   (about ¹⁄₁₆ inch)
⅓ **cup fresh lemon juice**
¼ **cup olive oil**
   Lemon wedges, for serving

1. Make the lemon-sage mayonnaise: In a small bowl, mix the mayonnaise with the lemon juice, zest, sage, Dijon mustard, ⅛ teaspoon salt and the cayenne. Cover and refrigerate for up to 3 hours.

2. Light a grill. Season each of the trout inside and out with salt and pepper. Place 2 sage sprigs in the cavity of each fish. Wrap the pancetta around the trout. Tie

the fish with a piece of cotton string to hold the pancetta in place. Rub the fish first with the lemon juice and then with the olive oil.

3. Grill the trout on an oiled grill for about 5 minutes, until nicely browned. Turn the trout and grill for about 7 minutes longer, or until the fish is cooked through and the pancetta is nicely browned.

4. Discard the string. Transfer the trout to a serving platter or individual plates. Garnish with the sage sprigs and lemon wedges and serve.

—Erica De Mane

■

BROCCOLI RABE AND POTATO HASH WITH SMOKED TROUT

An unusual flavor combination and a thick, crisp crust make this hash special.

4 to 6 Servings
2 **pounds broccoli rabe, woody stems discarded**
1½ **pounds Yukon Gold or Yellow Finn potatoes (about 2 inches in diameter), unpeeled**
3 **tablespoons vegetable oil**
1 **medium onion, cut into ½-inch dice**
½ **of a red bell pepper, cut into ½-inch dice**
4 **ounces smoked trout fillet, broken into ½-inch pieces**
  Salt and freshly ground black pepper
2 **tablespoons unsalted butter**
  Hot pepper sauce, for serving

1. In a large steamer, bring 1 inch of water to a boil over high heat. Pack the broccoli rabe in the steamer basket, cover and steam for 3 minutes. Transfer the steamer basket to the sink and let the broccoli rabe drain and cool slightly. Lightly squeeze out any excess liquid and coarsely chop.

2. Put the potatoes in a large pan, add enough water to cover and cook over moderately high heat until tender, about 20 minutes. Drain and let cool slightly, then peel and cut into 1-inch pieces.

3. In a large nonreactive skillet, warm 1 tablespoon of the oil over moderately high heat. Add the onion and bell pepper and cook, stirring, until softened, about 4 minutes. Transfer to a large bowl.

4. Add the steamed broccoli rabe, the potatoes and the smoked trout to the red bell pepper and onion. Season with salt and black pepper.

5. Wipe the skillet clean. Add 1 tablespoon each of the butter and the remaining oil and turn the heat to moderately high. When the fat is very hot, add half of the hash mixture, pressing down slightly to form an even layer in the pan. Lower the heat to moderate and cook undisturbed until a thick crust forms on the bottom, about 5 minutes.

6. Using a sturdy metal spatula and a firm, quick motion, flip as much of the hash as possible in 1 piece; turn over the remaining pieces of hash. Cook the hash on the other side until heated through, about 2 minutes. Scrape the hash out onto a large platter. Lightly wipe out the skillet and repeat with the remaining butter, oil and hash. Serve hot with the hot pepper sauce passed separately.

—Marcia Kiesel

■

SEARED POMPANO WITH GRAPEFRUIT ESSENCE AND SPINACH

This dish, from The Four Seasons Ocean Grand in Palm Beach, Florida, is an exciting mix of Gulf Coast ingredients:

white-fleshed fish, citrus fruit and rock lobster tails. If pompano is unavailable, substitute Dover sole or flounder.

♀ The fish, with Grapefruit Essence and other citrus flavors, calls for a light- to medium-bodied white wine with a spicy and floral bouquet. A good choice is 1991 Firestone Gewürztraminer from Santa Barbara.

4 Servings

- 1 large Ruby Red or other pink grapefruit
- 4 strips of lean bacon (about 2 ounces), sliced crosswise ¼ inch thick
- 3 garlic cloves—2 thinly sliced, 1 minced
- 4 3-inch-long strips of orange zest, thinly sliced lengthwise
- 4 3-inch-long strips of lemon zest, thinly sliced lengthwise
- ¼ cup canola oil
- 8 4- to 5-ounce skinless pompano fillets
  Salt and freshly ground pepper
- 1 tablespoon finely chopped fresh lemon thyme or regular thyme
- 2 tablespoons extra-virgin olive oil
- 1 small shallot, minced
- 4 4-ounce frozen rock lobster tails (optional)—thawed, removed from the shell and cut into 1-inch pieces
- 6 medium plum tomatoes—peeled, seeded and cut into ¼-inch dice
- 1 pound fresh spinach—stems discarded, small leaves left whole and large leaves torn into 2-inch pieces
- 2 tablespoons snipped fresh chives (1-inch pieces)
- 2 tablespoons slivered fresh basil leaves
  Grapefruit Essence (recipe follows)

1. Using a small sharp knife, peel the grapefruit, removing all the bitter white pith. Cut in between the membranes to release the sections; set aside.

2. In a small skillet, cook the bacon over moderate heat until crisp. Transfer to paper towels to drain. Pour off all but 1 tablespoon of the bacon fat from the pan. Add the sliced garlic, turn the heat to low and cook until golden, about 1 minute. Add the orange and lemon zests and cook for 30 seconds. Remove from the heat and stir in the bacon.

3. Preheat the oven to 200°. In a large skillet, heat half of the canola oil until smoking. Season the pompano fillets with salt, pepper and the thyme. Add 4 fillets to the skillet and cook over moderately high heat, turning once, until well browned, 2 to 3 minutes per side. Transfer the fish to a large baking sheet with sides and keep warm in a low oven. Repeat with the remaining canola oil and pompano.

4. Wipe out the skillet and add the extra-virgin olive oil. Add the minced garlic and the shallot and cook over moderately low heat until softened, about 30 seconds. Add the lobster meat, if using, and cook, stirring, until the lobster is white throughout, 4 to 5 minutes. Stir in ½ cup of the tomatoes and cook until just heated through.

5. Put the spinach in a large bowl. Pour the hot tomato mixture on top of the spinach and toss well. Season with salt and pepper. Add the remaining tomato to the citrus zest and bacon mixture and reheat gently over low heat. Stir in the chives and basil.

6. Arrange the spinach on 4 large dinner plates. Arrange 3 grapefruit sections on the side of each plate. Place 2 pompano fillets over the spinach. Add any accumulated juices from the pompano to the Grapefruit Essence and drizzle 2 to 3 tablespoons around each plate. Top the pompano with the bacon mixture and serve at once. ➤

71

Grapefruit Essence
Makes About ⅔ Cup

1½ cups freshly squeezed Ruby Red
    or other pink grapefruit juice
1½ cups Zinfandel
6   large garlic cloves, minced
1   large shallot, minced
10 whole black peppercorns
1   large bay leaf
⅓   cup heavy cream
3   tablespoons unsalted butter
    Salt
    Freshly ground pepper

1. In a medium nonreactive saucepan, boil the grapefruit juice, wine, garlic, shallot, peppercorns and bay leaf over high heat until the mixture is reduced to 1¼ cups, about 15 minutes. Add the cream, lower the heat to moderate and simmer until thickened, about 5 minutes. Strain into a small saucepan and set aside at room temperature for up to 4 hours.

2. Just before serving, reheat the sauce gently over low heat, whisking constantly; do not boil. Remove the sauce from the heat and whisk in the butter, 1 tablespoon at a time, briefly reheating the sauce to keep it very warm. Season with salt and pepper.

—Hubert Des Marais

■

COD STEAKS WITH RED PEPPER SAUCE

Steamed thin green beans and baby red potatoes in their jackets would make ideal partners for this dish.

❢ The red pepper sauce contributes sharp, savory and herbaceous flavors to the dish, making crisp Sauvignon Blanc the first choice for this dish. Look for 1991 Cloudy Bay Vineyards from New Zealand and 1991 Handley Cellars from California.

4 Servings

1   large red bell pepper—halved,
    cored, seeded and deribbed
1   tablespoon olive oil
½   teaspoon white wine vinegar
½   teaspoon minced garlic
    Salt
4   6- to 8-ounce cod steaks, cut
    1 inch thick
2   teaspoons chopped fresh
    parsley

1. Put the red pepper halves, cut sides down, in a steamer basket and place over boiling water in a large saucepan. Cover and steam over moderate heat for 15 minutes. Transfer the red pepper to a plate to cool for 10 minutes, then peel with a small knife.

2. Transfer the steamed red pepper to a food processor and puree. Add the olive oil, vinegar, garlic and ¼ teaspoon of salt and pulse to blend. Transfer the sauce to a small nonreactive saucepan and warm over low heat.

3. Arrange the cod steaks in the steamer basket in a single layer. Sprinkle with salt and place the basket over boiling water in the saucepan. Cover and steam over moderate heat until the cod steaks are just cooked through, about 10 minutes. Remove the steaks from the steamer and let them drain on paper towels for a minute. Peel off the skin with a fork if desired. Transfer the cod steaks to a serving platter or individual plates and spoon the warm sauce over the top. Sprinkle with the parsley and serve at once.

—Stephanie Lyness

■

POACHED COD WITH TOMATOES AND FENNEL

Fennel, leek, garlic, basil and orange zest give this low-fat dish plenty of flavor. ➤

**Cod Steaks with
Red Pepper Sauce**

Salt Cod Ragout on Steamed Spinach

♈ The tomatoes and fennel add both an acid bite and an herbal note to this fish dish—characteristics that will go well with a crisp 1991 Dry Creek Fumé Blanc from California or a 1992 Henri Bourgeois Sancerre "Bonne Bouches" from France.

4 Servings

½ teaspoon fennel seeds
2 teaspoons olive oil

1 large fresh fennel bulb— halved, cored and finely chopped
1 large leek, white and tender green portion, finely chopped
2 garlic cloves, minced
1 28-ounce can Italian peeled tomatoes, coarsely chopped, with their liquid
½ teaspoon finely grated orange zest

1 **bay leaf**
 Salt
 Freshly ground pepper
4 **6-ounce cod fillets, about ¾ inch
 thick**
2 **tablespoons finely chopped fresh
 basil**

1. Grind the fennel seeds in a spice grinder (or in a coffee grinder reserved for spices) or in a mortar with a pestle. Alternatively, finely chop the fennel seeds with a large knife.

2. Heat the olive oil in a large nonreactive skillet. Add the chopped fresh fennel, the chopped leek and the minced garlic cloves, cover the skillet and cook over moderately low heat, stirring occasionally, until the vegetables are translucent, about 5 minutes. Add the chopped Italian tomatoes with their liquid, the ground fennel seeds, the grated orange zest, the bay leaf and a pinch each of salt and freshly ground pepper.

3. Bring the tomato sauce to a boil over moderately high heat. Lower the heat, cover and simmer, stirring occasionally, until the sauce is slightly thickened, about 20 minutes.

4. Season the cod fillets with salt and pepper and nestle them in the tomato sauce. Spoon a little of the sauce over the fish, cover and simmer gently until the fillets are just cooked through, 8 to 10 minutes.

5. Transfer the fish fillets to a serving platter, cover loosely with foil and keep warm. Discard the bay leaf from the tomato sauce and bring the sauce to a boil over moderately high heat. Cook until the tomato sauce is thickened, about 3 minutes. Add any accumulated juices from the fish fillets and season the tomato sauce with salt and freshly ground pepper. Stir in the chopped fresh basil, spoon the tomato sauce over the cod fillets and serve at once.

—Georgia Chan Downard

SALT COD RAGOUT ON STEAMED SPINACH

This ragout was inspired by Jacques Pépin's "Bacalao Gloria." Allow two days to soak the salt cod.

❦ The salty, meaty fish and the sharp accents of bell peppers and sun-dried tomatoes require a fruity white. A ripe, round California Sauvignon Blanc, such as 1991 Estancia or 1992 Lakespring, fits the bill perfectly.

6 First-Course Servings
12 **ounces thick, center-cut skinless
 and boneless salt cod**
3 **tablespoons olive oil**
4 **large garlic cloves, thinly sliced
 lengthwise**
2 **medium onions, thinly sliced
 lengthwise**
1 **red bell pepper, thinly sliced
 lengthwise**
1½ **cups Chicken Stock (p. 36) or
 canned low-sodium broth**
¼ **cup oil-packed sun-dried tomato
 halves, drained and thinly sliced**
6 **Calamata olives, pitted and thinly
 sliced**
4 **pounds spinach, preferably the
 crinkly variety, large stems
 discarded
 Salt and freshly ground black
 pepper**

1. In a large bowl, combine the salt cod and enough cold water to cover by 1 inch. Refrigerate the cod for 2 days, changing the water 2 or 3 times a day. Transfer the salt cod to a medium saucepan, add enough fresh cold water to cover by 1 inch and bring to a simmer over moderate heat. Drain the cod in a

TIPS ON COOKING SWORDFISH

Slow, prolonged cooking dries out swordfish. To keep the fish moist, cook it very briefly at very high heat. For this kind of cooking, a ½-inch-thick steak is ideal, 1 inch is too much. If you have steaks that are 1 inch thick or thicker, remove the skin and, using a broad, sharp knife, divide the slices into 2 thinner ones.

—Marcella Hazan

colander. Separate the cod into large, naturally formed flakes, discarding any bones, membranes or skin.

2. In a large nonreactive skillet, warm the olive oil over moderately high heat. Stir in the garlic, onions and red bell pepper, cover and cook over low heat, stirring occasionally, until tender, about 10 minutes. Add the Chicken Stock, sun-dried tomatoes and olives and bring to a simmer over moderate heat. Stir in the salt cod and simmer until the cod is warmed through, 1 to 2 minutes. Cover and set aside while you steam the spinach. (The ragout can be made up to 1 day ahead and refrigerated.)

3. In a large steamer, bring 1½ inches of water to a boil over high heat. Pack half of the spinach into the steamer basket, cover tightly and steam until tender, about 4 minutes. Transfer the spinach to a colander to drain. Repeat with the remaining spinach. Very lightly press on the cooked spinach to remove excess water without mashing the leaves.

4. Arrange the spinach around the rim of a large platter. Season the salt cod ragout with salt and black pepper and reheat until warmed through if necessary. Spoon the ragout into the center of the platter and serve.

—Marcia Kiesel

■

GRILLED SWORDFISH SICILIAN STYLE

In the entire canon of fish cookery, nothing can surpass the juiciness, spicy fragrance and uncloaked simplicity of *pesce spada al salmoriglio*, grilled swordfish Sicilian style, simply brushed with olive oil, lemon juice and oregano. Swordfish *salmoriglio* is one of the fastest and most delicious things one can cook on an

outdoor grill, but it tastes just about as good when cooked indoors under a very hot broiler.

❡ This dish calls for a brisk, fragrant, refreshing white. Among Sicilian wines, an excellent choice would be Corvo's Colomba Platino. Another good match would be a Gavi, cool and flinty with the flavor of ripe citrus, particularly fine when produced by a top maker like La Giustiniana.

4 to 6 Servings
Salt
2 tablespoons fresh lemon juice
2 teaspoons chopped fresh oregano or 1 teaspoon dried
¼ cup extra-virgin olive oil
Freshly ground pepper
2 pounds ½-inch-thick swordfish steaks

1. If using a charcoal grill, light it in time for white ash to form before cooking. If using an outdoor gas grill or the broiler, preheat for at least 15 minutes.

2. Put a liberal amount of salt, about 2 teaspoons, in a small bowl. Add the lemon juice and beat with a fork until the salt has dissolved. Mix in the oregano. Trickle in the olive oil, drop by drop, beating it in with the fork to blend it with the lemon juice. Stir in several grindings of pepper.

3. When the grill or broiler is ready, place the swordfish steaks close to the heat source and grill for about 2 minutes, then turn and grill the other side for less than 2 minutes.

4. Transfer the swordfish steaks to a warmed serving platter or individual plates. Prick each of the steaks in several places with a fork to allow the sauce to penetrate deeply.

5. Use a spoon to beat and, at the same time, to pour the *salmoriglio* mixture over the swordfish steaks, spreading it evenly. Serve at once.

—Marcella Hazan

■

GRILLED SWORDFISH WITH SALSA VERDE

Grilling is a particularly good method for cooking meaty swordfish. Grilled vegetables, such as eggplant, yellow squash and bell peppers, make a wonderful accompaniment. Plain olive oil can be substituted for the spicy Olio Santo used to brush the swordfish steaks.

🍷 These meaty swordfish steaks need a full-flavored white wine to stand up to their savory flavor. A tart, penetrating Italian wine, such as 1992 Poggio alle Gazze, or a crisp California white wine, such as 1992 Gavilan Pinot Blanc, would be an ideal choice.

6 Servings
Salsa Verde:
- ½ cup (tightly packed) fresh flat-leaf parsley leaves
- 2 tablespoons drained capers
- 1 tablespoon Dijon mustard
- 1 large garlic clove
- ¼ cup extra-virgin olive oil
- 1½ tablespoons fresh lemon juice Salt
- ¼ teaspoon freshly ground pepper

- 6 8-ounce swordfish steaks, cut ½ inch thick
- ½ cup Olio Santo (recipe follows) or extra-virgin olive oil

1. Make the salsa verde: Combine the parsley leaves, capers, Dijon mustard, garlic clove, olive oil, lemon juice, ¼ teaspoon salt and the pepper in a food processor or blender. Process until the parsley, capers and garlic are very finely minced, but the mixture is not completely smooth. (The sauce can be prepared up to 3 hours ahead; cover and let stand at room temperature.)

2. Light a grill. Brush the swordfish steaks on both sides with Olio Santo. Grill the swordfish steaks on an oiled grill for 2 minutes, basting occasionally with Olio Santo. Turn the steaks, sprinkle them lightly with salt and grill them for about 2 minutes longer, until the steaks are just cooked through. Transfer the steaks to a large platter and serve with the salsa verde.

Olio Santo
Makes 2 Cups
- 2 cups olive oil
- 6 large fresh basil leaves
- 2 or 3 dried red chiles

In a glass jar, combine the oil with the basil and dried chiles. Cover and refrigerate for at least 10 days or up to 1 month.
—Erica De Mane

■

GRILLED SALMON WITH POTATO-HERB DRESSING

This light main course is served with mixed lettuces and a roasted-potato-thickened salad dressing flavored with basil and dill.

🍷 The applelike fruitiness of a dry Riesling with good acidity will round out the flavor of the sweet grilled shallots and salmon in this dish. Two good choices from Alsace are 1989 Marc Kreydenweiss and 1988 Cuvée Frédéric Emile Trimbach.

6 Servings
- 1½ pounds skinless center-cut salmon fillet, cut into 12 even pieces
- 20 medium shallots—18 peeled and 2 minced
- 3 tablespoons sugar
- 1 teaspoon coarse (kosher) salt ➤

¾ **cup plus 2 tablespoons extra-virgin olive oil**

1 **medium Idaho potato (about 6 ounces)**

¼ **cup plus 1 tablespoon fresh lemon juice**

½ **cup finely chopped fresh dill**

½ **cup finely chopped fresh basil
Table salt and freshly ground pepper**

9 **small new red potatoes (about 14 ounces)**

4 **cups mixed lettuces, such as mâche, frisée and radicchio**

1. Place the salmon fillet and the 18 shallots in a large shallow glass or ceramic dish. In a small bowl, combine the sugar, coarse salt, minced shallots and 2 tablespoons of the olive oil and spoon over the salmon and shallots. Turn the salmon pieces and whole shallots to coat evenly, then cover and refrigerate for 2 hours.

2. Preheat the oven to 400°. Prick the Idaho potato all over and bake for about 45 minutes, or until tender. Let cool slightly. Halve the potato. Scoop the flesh into a medium bowl. Mash well with a potato masher or fork. Stir in the lemon juice and remaining ¾ cup oil, then the dill, basil, 1 teaspoon salt and ¾ teaspoon pepper. Cover and let stand at room temperature.

3. Light a grill or preheat the oven to 500°. If grilling, thread the marinated whole shallots on 2 skewers. If roasting, spread the shallots on a baking sheet. Grill or roast the shallots for 15 to 20 minutes, turning once, until tender and crusty brown. Transfer the shallots to a plate.

4. In a medium saucepan, cover the red potatoes with 1 inch of water. Bring to a boil over high heat and cook until tender, about 12 minutes. Drain and let cool slightly.

5. Meanwhile, if using the oven, preheat the broiler. Grill or broil the salmon on 1 side only until crusty brown on the outside and medium rare in the center, about 2 minutes.

6. Spoon the potato dressing onto 6 plates and set 2 pieces of salmon on each. Mound the lettuces in the center and season with table salt and pepper. Cut the red potatoes into ½-inch slices and arrange them on the plates. Scatter the grilled shallots on top.

—Jim Galileo

■

STEAMED SALMON

All this simple dish calls for is a perfect piece of fish. Ask the fishmonger for fillets cut from the middle, not the tail end.

4 Servings

4 **6-ounce salmon fillets with skin, about 1 inch thick
Salt**

Put the salmon fillets in a steamer basket in a single layer. Season with salt and place over boiling water in a large saucepan. Cover and steam over moderate heat until just cooked through, about 8 minutes.

—Stephanie Lyness

■

GRILLED WHOLE BLUEFISH RUBBED WITH GARLIC AND ROSEMARY

Bluefish is not native to Italian waters, but is inexpensive and plentiful in the United States in the summer. Its flavor stands up to bold seasoning, such as this classic Italian combination of rosemary and garlic.

❦ The oiliness of bluefish, accented by rosemary and garlic, requires an assertive dry white, such as 1992 Corvo Bianco from Italy or 1992 CVNE Monopole from Spain.

4 to 6 Servings

¼ cup plus 2 tablespoons olive oil
5 large garlic cloves, peeled
2 heaping tablespoons fresh rosemary leaves
1 tablespoon coarse salt
1 tablespoon freshly ground pepper
1 4-pound bluefish, cleaned, with head and tail intact
   Lemon wedges, for serving

1. Light a grill. In a food processor or blender, combine ¼ cup of the olive oil with the garlic, rosemary, salt and pepper. Process to a smooth paste.

2. Cut 2 shallow slashes in each side of the bluefish. Rub three-quarters of the garlic-rosemary paste inside and outside the fish. Stir the remaining 2 tablespoons olive oil into the remaining garlic-rosemary paste and set aside.

3. Grill the fish on an oiled grill for 15 to 20 minutes, brushing occasionally with the reserved garlic-rosemary paste, until the skin is nicely browned and no longer sticks to the grill. Turn the fish and grill for about 10 minutes longer, brushing occasionally, until opaque throughout. Transfer the bluefish to a large platter, garnish with lemon wedges and serve.

—Erica De Mane

Steamed Salmon

Simi, or a Sicilian white, such as 1990 Corvo Bianco.

■

SPICY TUNA AND GREEN BEAN SALAD WITH TOMATOES

If you want to serve this up-to-date tuna salad as a main dish rather than a first course, double the ingredients.

🍷 Hot chile pepper adds bite to this tuna salad, making a simple, straightforward wine the best choice. Choose a crisp white that can stand up to the acidic flavors—a California Sauvignon Blanc, such as 1991

4 Servings

½ pound green beans or yellow wax beans, cut into 1-inch lengths
3 tablespoons extra-virgin olive oil
2 tablespoons finely chopped Calamata olives
2 medium garlic cloves, minced
2 anchovy fillets, mashed with 1 teaspoon of their oil
1 tablespoon fresh lemon juice
½ to 1 teaspoon minced fresh chile, such as jalapeño or serrano
1 3½-ounce can olive oil-packed tuna, drained and lightly flaked
4 medium red tomatoes, cut into thin wedges ➤

Spicy Tuna and Green Bean Salad with Tomatoes

Salt and freshly ground black pepper

2 tablespoons chopped fresh basil

1. In a medium saucepan of boiling water, cook the green beans until just tender and brightly colored, 3 to 4 minutes. Drain in a colander and refresh with cold water.

2. In a nonreactive bowl, using a wooden spoon, mix the olive oil, chopped olives, minced garlic, mashed anchovies, lemon juice and minced chile. Fold in the tuna and beans.

3. On a large serving platter, arrange the tomato wedges in a circle leaving a small open space in the center. Season lightly with salt and black pepper. Spoon the tuna and bean salad into the center of the platter. Sprinkle the chopped fresh basil over the tuna and tomatoes and serve.

—Marcia Kiesel

Chapter 5 ▪ POULTRY

83   Roast Chicken with Herbs

83   Steamed Chicken with Chinese Mushrooms

84   Garlicky Chicken

85   Chicken in Green Sauce

86   Stewed Chicken with Pastis

88   Thai Chicken and Eggplant Curry

89   Curried Chicken with Spinach and Carrots

90   Curried Chicken Moghlai

92   Normandy-Style Rock Cornish Hens

93   Roast Capon

94   Turkey Cutlets with Grainy Mustard and Sage

95   Turkey Tonnato

96   Turkey and Pinto Bean Chili

97   Turkey Burgers

98   Steamed Duck Breast

98   Roast Duck with Balsamic Vinegar, Summer Greens and Duck Liver Crostini

100   Crisp Peppered Quail with Country Ham and Spicy Crayfish Hominy

101   Grilled Quail with Cumin

103   Pan-Roasted Quail

103   Squab on Mushroom Toasts with Mixed Greens and Blackberry Dressing

Roast Chicken with Herbs

ROAST CHICKEN WITH HERBS

This recipe has been adapted from *Fanny at Chez Panisse* (HarperCollins).

❦ If you like to serve white wine with chicken, try a 1991 Qupé Santa Barbara Chardonnay. If you prefer red wine, look for a 1990 Château de Montmirail Gigondas or a 1990 Château de Montmirail Vacqueyras.

4 Servings
- 1 **4-pound chicken**
- 1 **garlic clove, peeled**
- 1 **teaspoon chopped fresh rosemary**
- 1 **teaspoon chopped fresh thyme**
- 1 **teaspoon chopped fresh oregano or marjoram**
- ¼ **teaspoon freshly ground pepper**
- ½ **teaspoon salt**
- 1 **tablespoon olive oil**

1. Preheat the oven to 375°. Rinse the chicken inside and out with cold water. Remove the pockets of fat just inside the chest cavity, then pat dry.

2. Hold the tines of a fork against a plate and rub the garlic clove against them to make a juicy puree. Blend in all the remaining ingredients.

3. Rub the herb paste all over the outside of the chicken. Set the chicken on a rack in a roasting pan, breast side up; roast for 20 minutes. Turn the chicken over and roast breast side down for another 20 minutes. Then turn it over again and roast breast side up for 35 minutes longer.

4. Remove the chicken from the oven, cover loosely with foil and let rest for 15 to 20 minutes before carving. (This resting time is very important for all roasted meats, for it makes them tender and juicy.) Before serving, collect the juices from the roasting pan and skim off the clear fat. Moisten the slices of meat with the tasty juices.

—Alice Waters

■

STEAMED CHICKEN WITH CHINESE MUSHROOMS

This recipe highlights two of the most popular and healthful techniques of Chinese cooking, marinating and steaming. Marinating enhances taste while adding only a touch of oil, and steaming brings out flavor with no oil at all. Here, the chicken is marinated in a ginger-soy sauce mixture and then steamed with shiitake mushrooms so that it stays juicy and absorbs the meaty mushroom flavor.

❦ A glass of off-dry, fruity white, such as a California Chenin Blanc, balances the savory spiciness of the flavors here. Look for 1992 Pine Ridge or 1991 Robert Mondavi.

4 Servings
- 7 **large dried shiitake or Chinese black mushrooms**
- 3 **tablespoons Chicken Stock (p. 36) or canned low-sodium broth**
- 1 **tablespoon oyster sauce**
- 1 **tablespoon dry white wine**
- 2 **teaspoons peanut oil**
- 1½ **teaspoons light soy sauce**
- 1½ **teaspoons sugar**
- 1 **teaspoon ginger juice (see How to Make Ginger Juice, at right)**
- 1 **teaspoon distilled white vinegar**
- 1 **teaspoon Oriental sesame oil**
- 2 **teaspoons cornstarch**
- ½ **teaspoon salt**
  Pinch of freshly ground white pepper
- 1 **pound skinless, boneless chicken breast halves, trimmed of fat and cut into 1-inch cubes** ➤

HOW TO MAKE GINGER JUICE

To make 1 teaspoon of ginger juice, peel a ½-inch piece of fresh ginger. Grate it and then transfer the grated ginger to a fine strainer and press with the back of a spoon to squeeze out the juice.

—Eileen Yin-Fei Lo

4 scallions—white portions cut into
1-inch pieces plus 3 tablespoons
thinly sliced scallion greens
½ small red bell pepper, cut into
⅛-inch strips

1. In a medium bowl, soak the mushrooms in warm water to cover until softened, about 30 minutes. Rinse the mushrooms. Discard the stems and slice the mushroom caps ¼ inch thick.

2. In a 9-inch glass or ceramic pie plate, combine the Chicken Stock, oyster sauce, wine, peanut oil, soy sauce, sugar, ginger juice, vinegar and sesame oil. Stir in the cornstarch and season with the salt and white pepper. Add the chicken, mushrooms and scallion whites and stir to coat. Cover and refrigerate for 1 hour.

3. Fill a wok or steamer fitted with a rack with water to 1 inch below the rack. Cover and bring to a boil. Place the pie plate on the rack, cover and steam over moderate heat, turning once, until the chicken is cooked through, about 20 minutes.

4. Transfer the chicken and vegetables to warmed plates. Garnish with the pepper strips and scallion greens. Serve at once.

—Eileen Yin-Fei Lo

BUYING CHICKEN

You can, of course, start with a whole chicken, cut it up yourself and make stock out of the remains (neck, back, gizzard and any bones or meaty scraps). That's the most economical, old-fashioned way to buy chicken for stew and other dishes requiring parts. Or choose any one or a combination of chicken parts, including the most expensive—the boneless and skinless breast. I vote for the bone-in thigh myself. It has juicier meat with a nicer texture and definitely more flavor (meat cooked on the bone always has more flavor). Thighs are far cheaper, too, than breasts. The least expensive of the cuts is the leg-thigh combination; the thighs alone are a few cents more per pound. The drumstick is the most expensive of leg cuts, although it contains considerably less meat per bone than the others.

—Julia Child

■

GARLICKY CHICKEN

Bourride is a lively, intensely garlicky fish stew from Provence. Its unique flavor comes from a final enrichment with aioli, the famous Mediterranean garlic mayonnaise. Marvelous with fish, this stew is equally delicious when made with chicken, and it's time to give those birds something new to think about. To make bourride, you start out with the familiar robust base of onions, leeks, garlic and tomatoes cooked in olive oil. Then the chicken is put in, followed by wine, stock, herbs and seasoning. The final touch is blending in the aioli.

🍷 A strong dry white wine, like a Chardonnay or Côtes du Rhône, or a not-too-fruity red, like a Beaujolais, would go well with the stew.

6 Servings

Stew:
¾ cup sliced onions
¾ cup sliced leeks, white and tender green only
2 tablespoons olive oil
3 medium garlic cloves, pureed
3 cups chopped, peeled and seeded plum tomatoes—half fresh and half canned
3 to 4 pounds bone-in chicken parts
Salt and freshly ground pepper
3 cups Chicken Stock (p. 36) or canned broth
2½ cups dry white wine
2 imported bay leaves
½ teaspoon thyme
½ teaspoon fennel seeds, crushed
3 pinches of saffron threads
1 3-inch strip dried orange peel
¼ teaspoon hot pepper sauce
Boiled potatoes
¼ cup chopped fresh parsley

Aioli:

- **6 large garlic cloves**
- **Salt**
- **½ cup (lightly packed) fresh bread crumbs**
- **½ teaspoon white wine vinegar**
- **6 egg yolks**
- **½ to 1 cup fruity olive oil**

1. In a large, heavy, flameproof casserole, cook the onions and leeks in the olive oil over moderate heat until soft but not brown, 4 to 5 minutes. Stir in the garlic and tomatoes. Cover and cook until the tomatoes begin to exude their juices, about 5 minutes. Uncover and boil over moderately high heat, stirring frequently, until the mixture is almost dry, 4 to 5 minutes.

2. Season the chicken with salt and pepper and arrange the pieces in the casserole, spreading the vegetables over and around them. Cover and cook for 5 minutes, then turn the chicken and cook for 5 minutes longer. Pour in the Chicken Stock and wine, adding just enough liquid to barely cover the chicken. Add the bay leaves, thyme, fennel seeds, saffron, orange peel and hot pepper sauce. Season lightly with salt and pepper. Cover and simmer for 15 to 25 minutes, depending on the cuts you've selected. The chicken is done when the meat feels just springy at the fleshiest part and the juices run clear yellow if the meat is pierced.

3. Transfer the chicken to a plate. Remove the skin. Tip the casserole and skim the fat from the cooking juices. Return the chicken to the casserole. (The stew can be made to this point up to 1 day ahead. Refrigerate it uncovered, then cover when chilled.)

4. Make the aioli: Puree the garlic cloves in a mortar. Add ½ teaspoon salt and pound to a fine paste. Pound in the bread crumbs and a few drops of the vinegar. Add the egg yolks and pound to a thick and sticky mass. Whisk in the oil by droplets to make a thick sauce. If the aioli becomes very stiff, whisk in drops of vinegar. Season with salt. If not serving shortly, cover with plastic wrap and refrigerate.

5. Bring the stew just to a simmer. Gradually and by dribbles, whisk 1 cup of the hot cooking liquid into the aioli. Pour the aioli into the casserole and swirl slowly over moderate heat for several minutes until the sauce thickens to the consistency of light cream. Be very careful not to let the sauce come near a simmer (the yolks will scramble), but you must let it heat to the point of thickening; it will register over 160°, enough to kill off any harmful bacteria! Discard the bay leaves.

6. Ladle the stew into warm soup plates. Add a serving of potatoes and garnish with the parsley. Serve immediately, with a fork, knife and spoon.

—Julia Child

∎

CHICKEN IN GREEN SAUCE

There are many variations on this Central American classic. Serve with rice, black beans and warm tortillas.

6 Servings

- **6 whole chicken legs—thighs and drumsticks separated**
- **1 medium onion, quartered**
- **5 medium garlic cloves**
- **1 imported bay leaf**
- **Salt**
- **⅓ cup sesame seeds (1½ ounces)**
- **¼ cup raw shelled pumpkin seeds (1 ounce)**
- **½ pound tomatillos, husks discarded, rinsed**
- **3 large scallions, thinly sliced**
- **4 large romaine lettuce leaves, coarsely chopped (2 cups)**
- **2 to 3 jalapeño chiles, seeded and coarsely chopped** ➤

½ cup coarsely chopped fresh flat-leaf parsley
½ cup coarsely chopped fresh coriander (cilantro) leaves and tender stems
1½ tablespoons fresh lime juice
1 tablespoon sugar
   Freshly ground black pepper

1. In a large enameled cast-iron casserole, combine the chicken, onion, 3 of the garlic cloves and the bay leaf. Cover with 2 quarts of cold water. Stir in 1 tablespoon of salt and bring to a simmer over moderate heat. Simmer for 20 minutes.

2. Strain the chicken parts in a colander set over a bowl; reserve the broth. Discard the onion, garlic cloves and bay leaf. Set the casserole aside.

3. In a medium skillet, lightly toast the sesame seeds over moderate heat, stirring, until golden. Set aside to cool. Repeat with the pumpkin seeds. In a spice mill or mortar, grind the seeds together until coarsely ground.

4. In a food processor, puree the remaining 2 garlic cloves with the tomatillos, scallions, romaine, jalapeños, parsley, coriander and ground sesame and pumpkin seeds.

5. Skim the fat from the surface of the reserved chicken broth. Add 1½ cups of the broth to the food processor and process until smooth.

6. Pour the sauce into the reserved casserole. Stir in 1½ cups of the chicken broth and bring to a simmer over moderately low heat. (Reserve any remaining chicken broth for another use.) Nestle the chicken into the sauce and simmer until very tender and the sauce is thickened, about 30 minutes.

7. Transfer the chicken to a serving platter. Stir the lime juice and sugar into the sauce. Season with salt and black pepper. Spoon the sauce over the chicken and serve at once.

—Ilana Sharlin Stone

■

STEWED CHICKEN WITH PASTIS

To intensify the garlic flavor, top each serving with a tablespoon of Garlic Butter (recipe follows).

8 Servings

1 cup pastis or other anise liqueur
¼ cup olive oil
¼ teaspoon crumbled saffron threads
   Salt and freshly ground pepper
4 large whole chicken breasts on the bone (about 5 pounds), split and skinned
1 pound onions, thinly sliced
7 medium garlic cloves, 6 minced and 1 peeled
3 pounds tomatoes—peeled, seeded and coarsely chopped
2 cups Chicken Stock (p. 36) or canned low-sodium broth
¾ cup coarsely chopped fresh flat-leaf parsley
1 teaspoon fennel seeds, lightly crushed
2 pounds waxy potatoes, such as Yukon Gold, peeled and cut into ¾-inch dice
   Eight ¾-inch-thick slices of Italian bread

1. In a large bowl, whisk together the pastis, 2 tablespoons of the olive oil, the crumbled saffron threads, 1 teaspoon salt and ½ teaspoon pepper. Add the skinned chicken breasts and turn to coat in the marinade. Cover and refrigerate, for at least 4 hours or overnight, turning the breasts occasionally.

2. Heat the remaining 2 tablespoons oil in a large, enameled, cast-iron casserole. Add the onions, cover and cook over moderately low heat, stirring occasionally, until the onions are softened, about 8

minutes. Stir in the minced garlic and cook for 2 minutes. Add the tomatoes and 1 teaspoon salt and cook, stirring occasionally, until the tomatoes are softened and most of the liquid has evaporated, about 15 minutes.

3. Add the chicken breasts with their marinade, the Chicken Stock, 2 cups of water, ½ cup of the parsley and the crushed fennel seeds to the casserole. Bring to a boil over moderate heat and simmer, turning the breasts occasionally, until the chicken is just cooked through, about 30 minutes. Transfer the chicken to a plate and let cool slightly, then remove the breast meat in 1 piece from the bones.

4. Boil the cooking liquid over moderately high heat until slightly thickened, about 10 minutes. Add the diced potatoes and simmer until the potatoes are tender, 10 to 12 minutes. Add the breast meat to the casserole and season with salt and pepper. (The recipe can be prepared to this point up to 1 day ahead; cover and refrigerate.)

5. Preheat the broiler. Toast the bread slices until golden. Let cool slightly, then rub them on both sides with the peeled garlic clove.

6. To serve, warm the chicken in the broth over moderate heat. Place 1 chicken breast in each of 8 shallow bowls and ladle the potatoes and broth on top. Sprinkle with the remaining ¼ cup parsley and accompany each serving with a garlic toast.

Garlic Butter
Makes ½ Cup

2 large heads of garlic, separated into cloves and peeled
1 bay leaf
Salt
Cayenne pepper

1. In a medium saucepan, cover the peeled garlic cloves with 1 quart of water. Bring the water to a boil over high heat,

Stewed Chicken with Pastis

then drain. Return the garlic to the pan, add 1 quart of water and bring to a boil. Boil for 5 minutes. Drain, return the garlic to the pan and add a third quart of water, the bay leaf and 1 teaspoon salt. Bring to a boil, then lower the heat to moderate and simmer until the garlic is softened, about 35 minutes. Drain, reserving ¼ cup of the cooking liquid; discard the bay leaf.

2. In a food processor, puree the cooked garlic with ⅛ teaspoon cayenne pepper, adding 1 to 2 tablespoons of the cooking liquid to make a smooth, slightly thick puree.

3. Season the garlic puree with salt and additional cayenne pepper. (The puree can be made up to 2 days ahead; cover and refrigerate.) Serve the garlic puree at room temperature or warm.

—Martha Rose Shulman

THAI CHICKEN AND EGGPLANT CURRY

Thai Chicken and Eggplant Curry

Buy fresh coriander (cilantro) with roots still attached. The roots are used to make a paste, which is the base of this Thai curry. Serve with sliced cucumbers sprinkled with chopped peanuts and coriander leaves.

6 Servings

6 small dried red chiles—stemmed, seeded and finely chopped
6 medium shallots, coarsely chopped
6 medium garlic cloves, coarsely chopped
6 fresh coriander (cilantro) roots, cleaned and coarsely chopped
1 fresh lemon grass stalk*—white bulb and 2 inches of green tops— finely chopped

1 teaspoon shrimp paste*
1 teaspoon Laos powder (dried galangal or ka)*
1 teaspoon freshly ground black pepper
½ teaspoon salt
½ teaspoon cinnamon
¼ cup plus 1 tablespoon safflower or canola oil
2½- to 3-pound frying chicken, cut into 6 pieces (legs, thighs and breast halves), skinned if desired
2 medium Japanese eggplants, cut into 1-inch chunks
1 teaspoon tamarind concentrate* dissolved in 2 tablespoons hot water or ½ tablespoon molasses dissolved in 2 tablespoons fresh lemon juice
2 tablespoons fish sauce (nam pla)*
  Coarsely chopped fresh coriander (cilantro) leaves, for garnish

*Available at Asian markets

1. In a mortar or a food processor, mash or chop the chiles, shallots, garlic, coriander roots, lemon grass, shrimp paste, Laos powder, black pepper, salt and cinnamon to a coarse paste.

2. In a wok, heat the oil until shimmering. Add the spice paste and stir-fry over moderate heat until the mixture turns light brown and the aroma mellows, about 3 minutes.

3. Add the chicken and stir-fry until the meat is coated with the spice paste, 3 to 4 minutes. Add 1 cup of water to the wok. Arrange the chicken pieces so that they are partially submerged in the liquid; simmer over low heat, turning occasionally, until the chicken is tender and just cooked through, about 15 minutes. (The recipe can be prepared to this point up to 2 days ahead; refrigerate. Bring to a simmer over moderate heat before proceeding with the next step.)

4. Add the eggplant chunks, tucking them in between the chicken pieces. Cover and simmer over low heat until tender, about 5 minutes.

5. Uncover and stir in the tamarind mixture and fish sauce. Sprinkle the coriander leaves on top and serve.

—Jennifer Brennan

■

CURRIED CHICKEN WITH SPINACH AND CARROTS

Remove the curried chicken breasts from the heat immediately after adding the buttermilk so that the milk doesn't curdle. For a spicier curry, add more crushed red pepper.

🍷 The mild spiciness of the chicken and raita would be nicely supported by a simple, soft, fruity California white or blush wine, such as 1991 Girard Chenin Blanc or 1993 Monteviña White Zinfandel.

4 Servings
1 teaspoon arrowroot
1¼ cups nonfat buttermilk
1½ teaspoons curry powder
1 teaspoon ground cumin
  Salt
1 pound boneless skinless chicken breasts, cut into 1-inch cubes
½ pound carrots, cut into ⅜-by-2-inch matchsticks
1 teaspoon canola oil
1 medium shallot, finely chopped
2 medium garlic cloves, finely chopped
  1-inch piece of fresh ginger, peeled and finely chopped
¼ teaspoon crushed red pepper
1½ pounds fresh spinach, rinsed and stems trimmed
4 cups boiled white rice, for serving ➤

FISH SAUCE

This intensely fishy, salty brown liquid made from fresh anchovies—called *nam pla* in Thailand, *nuoc mam* in Vietnam, *tuk trey* in Cambodia, *ngan pya ye* in Burma and *patis* in the Philippines, is the heart and soul of Southeast Asian food. Rich in protein and vitamin B, it's a pungent foil at meals centered on lots of unseasoned rice. Use in stir-fries, sautés and soups as a background flavoring or in dressings and dipping sauces.

—Nancie McDermott

1. In a small bowl, dissolve the arrow-root in 1½ tablespoons of water. In a large bowl, combine ½ cup of the buttermilk with the arrowroot mixture, ½ teaspoon of the curry, the cumin and ½ teaspoon salt. Add the chicken cubes to the marinade and stir to coat. Cover and refrigerate to allow the chicken to marinate for at least 1 or up to 3 hours.

2. Put the carrots in a small saucepan. Add water to cover. Bring to a boil over moderately high heat. As soon as the water comes to a boil, drain the carrots, rinse with cold water and drain again thoroughly.

3. Heat the canola oil in a large nonstick skillet. Add the blanched carrot sticks, shallot, garlic, ginger, remaining 1 teaspoon curry powder and the crushed red pepper. Cook over moderately low heat, stirring frequently, until fragrant and the shallots are softened, about 5 minutes.

4. Drain the chicken and add it to the skillet. Raise the heat to moderately high and sauté, stirring occasionally, until the chicken pieces are well browned and cooked through, about 8 minutes. Using a slotted spoon, transfer the chicken to a plate, cover with foil and keep warm.

5. Add the spinach with the water that clings to it to the carrots in the skillet and stir until just limp, 1 to 2 minutes. Return the chicken to the skillet. Stir in the remaining ¾ cup buttermilk and immediately remove the skillet from the heat. Season with salt. Divide the rice among 4 large plates, spoon the curried chicken on top and serve at once.

—Andrea Chesman

■

CURRIED CHICKEN MOGHLAI

An ideal candidate for freezing, this dish not only retains its flavor, but the taste of the sauce is actually enhanced after a few weeks in the freezer.

❦ The spicy, mild heat of this dish calls for a slightly dry fruity white that's acidic enough to contrast with the sour cream's richness. Look for Rieslings, especially German ones, such as 1991 Deinhard Riesling Dry or 1991 Dr. Fischer Ockfener Bockstein Kabinett.

6 to 8 Servings

12 skinless, boneless chicken breast halves (about 4 pounds)
   Salt and freshly ground black pepper
About ¼ cup all-purpose flour
 1 stick (8 tablespoons) unsalted butter
 5 medium onions, finely chopped
 6 garlic cloves, minced
 1 tablespoon finely grated fresh ginger
 ½ teaspoon ground cumin
 ½ teaspoon cumin seeds
 ½ teaspoon turmeric
 ½ teaspoon caraway seeds
   Cayenne pepper
 1 35-ounce can Italian peeled tomatoes, coarsely crushed, with their liquid
 2 cups Chicken Stock (p. 36) or canned low-sodium broth
 3 cups sour cream
 ½ cup (packed) light brown sugar
 1 tablespoon tomato paste
 1 teaspoon crushed red pepper
 1 teaspoon saffron threads
 ½ teaspoon ground cardamom
 ¼ teaspoon ground cloves
 ¼ teaspoon freshly grated nutmeg
   Cooked basmati rice, for serving
   Fresh coriander (cilantro) sprigs, for garnish

1. Season the chicken breasts on both sides with salt and black pepper and coat lightly with the flour, shaking off the excess. Melt 4 tablespoons of the butter in a large nonreactive skillet. Add 6 breasts and cook over moderately high heat, turning once, until golden, about 4 minutes per side. Transfer to a large plate and cook the remaining 6 breasts. ➤

Curried Chicken Moghlai

2. Melt the remaining 4 tablespoons butter in the skillet. Add the onions and cook over moderate heat, stirring, until softened, about 10 minutes. Stir in the garlic and ginger. Cook until softened, about 3 minutes. Add the ground cumin, cumin seeds, turmeric, caraway seeds and ¼ teaspoon cayenne and cook for 1 minute. Stir in the crushed tomatoes with their liquid and the Chicken Stock. Transfer to a heavy pot.

3. Add the chicken to the casserole. Bring to a simmer over moderately low heat; simmer for 10 minutes. Stir in the sour cream, brown sugar, tomato paste, crushed red pepper, saffron, cardamom, cloves and nutmeg. Cover and cook over low heat for 30 minutes. Uncover and cook, stirring occasionally, until the chicken is tender and the sauce thickened, about 45 minutes longer; the sauce will not be completely smooth. Season with salt and cayenne. Serve with basmati rice and garnish with fresh coriander sprigs.

—Ann Chantal Altman

FREEZING TIPS

• Check the temperature of your freezer. It should register 0°.
• Undercook food when planning to freeze. It will finish cooking when reheated.
• Freeze food in small portions. It will freeze more quickly, attract less water during freezing and be easier to defrost and reheat.
• Wrap food tightly. If using freezer bags, squeeze out all the air before sealing. If using heavy-duty plastic wrap, place it directly on the food's surface to protect it from the dry freezer air. Or double wrap food with two layers of regular plastic or one of plastic and one of foil. Since foil conforms to the food's shape better, it is more likely to prevent freezer burn, which occurs when dry air draws the moisture out of food, discoloring and eventually spoiling it.
• Remember that water expands as it freezes. Food with a high liquid content expands by about 10 percent when frozen. When storing soups, stews or stocks, leave at least an inch of room at the top. Place plastic wrap directly on the food's surface and cover with a lid. This allows for expansion but protects the surface from exposure.
• Defrost food carefully. Thaw frozen food in the refrigerator or microwave. Thawing at room temperature encourages spoilage.

NORMANDY-STYLE ROCK CORNISH HENS

Apples are at the center of Norman cuisine; here apples, cider, Calvados and cider vinegar flavor the hens. Serve with a crisp potato pancake.

❦ A sweet, creamy sauce and the apples add a richness to these birds that a smooth white with a crisp contrast would embellish. Ideal choices would be 1991 Antinori Orvieto "Campogrande" from Italy and 1990 Trimbach Pinot Blanc or 1991 Labouré-Roi Bourgogne Chardonnay.

4 Servings

1 **pound small white boiling onions, unpeeled**
4 **Rock Cornish hens (about 1½ pounds each)**
 Salt
 Freshly ground white pepper
2 **Gala, Rome Beauty or McIntosh apples—peeled, halved and cored**
3 **tablespoons unsalted butter**
6 **medium shallots, minced**
1 **quart Chicken Stock (p. 36) or canned low-sodium broth**
1½ **cups unpasteurized apple cider**
1 **cup heavy cream**
1 **tablespoon Calvados**
1 **tablespoon cider vinegar**
 Chopped fresh parsley, for garnish

1. In a medium saucepan of boiling water, blanch the onions for 1 minute. Drain and transfer to a bowl of ice water to cool; then peel.

2. Season the Rock Cornish hens inside and out with salt and white pepper. Place an apple half in the cavity of each hen. Truss the hens with kitchen twine, tying the legs closed and tucking the wings underneath the body.

3. In a large enameled cast-iron casserole, melt the butter over moderately high heat. Add the hens, breast side down, and cook, turning, until the hens are nicely browned all over, about 10 minutes. Transfer to a platter. Add the onions and shallots to the casserole, lower the heat to moderate and cook, stirring frequently, until golden, about 6 minutes. Using a wooden spoon, stir in the Chicken Stock and apple cider, scraping the bottom of the casserole to loosen any browned bits; bring to a boil.

4. Return the hens to the casserole, breast side up, and baste with the liquid. Cover and simmer over moderate heat for 45 minutes, basting occasionally, and turning the hens over halfway through. (The recipe can be made to this point up to 1 day ahead. Let the liquid and the hens cool separately, then return the hens to the casserole, cover and refrigerate overnight. Skim the fat from the sauce; cover and rewarm over moderate heat for about 20 minutes.) Transfer the hens to a broiling pan.

5. Preheat the broiler. Skim the fat from the sauce. Stir in the cream and boil over moderately high heat until reduced to 2½ cups, about 20 minutes. Stir in the Calvados and cider vinegar and simmer for 2 minutes. Season with salt and white pepper and remove from the heat.

6. Broil the hens until nicely browned. Transfer the hens to serving plates and discard the twine. Spoon the onions and sauce over the hens and garnish with chopped parsley.

—Ilana Sharlin Stone

■

ROAST CAPON

In addition to capon, you can use this recipe for a roasting chicken of about seven pounds.

12 Servings

Normandy-Style Rock Cornish Hens

1   **7- to 7½-pound capon**
    Salt
    Freshly ground pepper
1½ **tablespoons softened unsalted**
    butter
1   **large carrot, chopped**
1   **onion, chopped**

1. Preheat the oven to 450°. Season the cavity of the capon with salt and pepper and truss the capon with kitchen string. Rub the butter all over the capon and set it breast up on a rack in a roasting pan. Roast on the middle rack of the oven for 10 minutes. ➤

2. Turn the capon on its side and roast for 10 minutes. Baste with the fat accumulated in the pan. Turn it on its other side and roast for 10 minutes longer. Baste again and lower the temperature to 350°.

3. Roast the bird for another 20 minutes, basting twice. Season lightly with salt, turn to its other side and add the carrot and onion to the pan. Roast another 20 minutes, basting twice. Turn breast up and sprinkle with salt. Roast, basting occasionally, 45 to 55 minutes longer, until the juices run clear when the inner thigh is pierced. When the bird is lifted up, the last juices to run from the vent should be clear yellow.

4. Transfer the capon to a carving board and let rest for at least 20 minutes. Spoon the fat from the roasting pan.

—Julia Child

JULIA CHILD'S CHRISTMAS

Oysters on the half shell
Smoked salmon on buttered pumpernickel
Crudités
🍷 Piper-Sonoma Brut

■

Creamy Rutabaga Soup (p. 31)
🍷 Hugel Riesling

■

Roast Capon (p. 93)

**Roast Double Loin of Pork
with Port Wine Sauce** (p. 118)

Classic Mashed Potatoes (p. 190)

Broccoli-Sauced Cauliflower (p. 168)

Winter Squash with Crouton Stuffing (p. 179)
🍷 Sanford Pinot Noir

■

Bûche de Noël (p. 253)
🍷 Sparkling Vouvray

■

Coffee and liqueurs

■

TURKEY CUTLETS WITH GRAINY MUSTARD AND SAGE

Lean turkey cutlets are a natural for low-fat cooking, and when cooked with just a little oil in a nonstick skillet, they make a quick and tasty sauté.

🍷 A fruity Pinot Noir is just the right light red wine to balance the mustard sauce and roasted vegetables. Look for exemplary bottlings, such as 1991 Labouré-Roi Pinot Noir Bourgogne from France or 1991 Napa Ridge Pinot Noir from California.

4 Servings

½ teaspoon vegetable oil
1 pound turkey cutlets, pounded ¼ inch thick
Freshly ground pepper
¼ cup plus ½ tablespoon dry white wine
2 cups Chicken Stock (p. 36) or canned low-sodium broth
1 tablespoon grainy mustard
8 fresh sage leaves
1 teaspoon arrowroot or potato starch
Salt

1. Heat the oil in a large nonstick skillet. Sprinkle the turkey cutlets with ¼ teaspoon pepper. Add half the cutlets to the skillet and cook over high heat, turning once, until nicely browned outside but still slightly pink inside, 1 to 2 minutes per side. Transfer to a platter and keep warm in a low oven. Repeat with the remaining turkey cutlets.

2. Add ¼ cup of the wine to the skillet. Cook over moderately high heat until reduced by half, scraping up any browned

bits. Add the Chicken Stock and mustard and boil for 4 minutes. Add the sage and cook until the liquid is reduced by half, about 4 minutes.

3. In a small bowl, dissolve the arrowroot in the remaining ½ tablespoon white wine and stir into the sauce. Bring the sauce back to a boil until thickened and season with salt and pepper. Add the turkey and turn to coat with the sauce. Transfer the turkey to the platter and spoon the sauce on top.

—Katherine Alford

■

TURKEY TONNATO

Once the turkey is cooked, you'll have a lovely broth to strain and use for making soup or stew. If you don't want to make your own mayonnaise for the sauce, one and one-third cups prepared mayonnaise can be used in place of the egg yolks and oil in step three.

Serves 12
1 **6-pound bone-in turkey breast**
2 **cups dry white wine or French vermouth**
2 **cups Chicken Stock (p. 36) or canned broth**
1 **cup chopped onions**
1 **cup chopped celery**
1 **cup chopped carrots**
 Bouquet garni: 2 fresh thyme sprigs, 2 fresh parsley sprigs and 2 bay leaves, tied together with white string
 Salt
1 **7-ounce can oil-packed tuna, drained**
1 **2-ounce can flat anchovy fillets, drained**
¼ **cup drained capers**
½ **teaspoon finely grated lemon zest**

2 to 3 **tablespoons Dijon mustard**
1 **large garlic clove, minced**
4 **egg yolks**
1 **cup virgin olive oil**
1 **teaspoon fresh lemon juice**
 Freshly ground white pepper
 For garnish: drained capers, chopped fresh parsley and lemon wedges

1. Put the turkey breast in a large pot or casserole, skin side up. Add the wine, Chicken Stock, chopped onions, celery, carrots and bouquet garni. Pour in enough water to cover the turkey breast by 1 inch. Bring to a simmer and season lightly with salt. Skim off the scum that rises to the surface.

2. Loosely cover the pot and gently simmer the turkey breast for about 1½ hours, until an instant-read thermometer inserted deep into the meat but not touching the bone measures 165°. Let the

Turkey Tonnato

turkey cool in its broth for at least 1 hour. Transfer the turkey breast to a large platter to cool completely, then refrigerate for up to 3 days. (You can also refrigerate the turkey overnight in its broth, but be sure to peel off the skin before the meat has cooled completely.)

3. In a food processor, puree the tuna with the anchovy fillets, capers, grated lemon zest, Dijon mustard and garlic. Add the egg yolks and process until the mixture thickens. With the machine on, gradually add the olive oil in a very thin stream; the sauce will become thick and creamy. Season with the lemon juice and salt and pepper.

4. Cut each turkey breast half from the carcass in one piece. Slice the meat at an angle across the grain ¹⁄₁₆ to ¹⁄₈ inch thick. Spoon a thin layer of sauce on a serving platter or individual plates. Arrange the turkey on top, spreading each slice with some of the sauce. Garnish with the capers, chopped fresh parsley and lemon wedges and serve.

—Julia Child

■

TURKEY AND PINTO BEAN CHILI

Corn bread is the ideal accompaniment to this newfangled chili.

❦ This dish needs a young, not-so-subtle Cabernet Sauvignon, such as 1991 Los Vascos or 1990 Cousiño-Macul, both from Chile, or serve a crisp lager, such as Beck's, Grolsch or Heineken.

6 to 8 Servings
- 1 **cup dried pinto beans (about 5 ounces), picked over and rinsed**
- 2 **large ancho chiles**
- 1 **large guajillo chile**
- ¼ **cup plus 2 tablespoons olive oil**
- 2½ **pounds skinless, boneless turkey leg meat, cut into ¾-inch cubes (from three 2-pound whole legs)**
  Salt and freshly ground black pepper
- 1 **medium onion, finely chopped**
- 4 **garlic cloves, minced**
- 1 **tablespoon ground cumin**
- 2 **teaspoons Madras curry powder**
- 2 **teaspoons coarsely chopped fresh thyme or 1 teaspoon dried**
- ½ **teaspoon cinnamon**
  Pinch of ground nutmeg
- 1 **quart Chicken Stock (p. 36) or canned low-sodium broth**
- 1 **large tomato—peeled, seeded and coarsely chopped—or 1 cup drained and coarsely chopped canned tomatoes**
- 1 **6-ounce can tomato paste**
- 1 **tablespoon sugar**
- 2 **bay leaves**
- 1 **large green bell pepper, cut into ¾-inch dice**
- 1 **large yellow or red bell pepper, cut into ¾-inch dice**
- ½ **cup finely chopped fresh coriander leaves (cilantro)**
- 1 **small red onion, finely chopped**

1. Place the pinto beans in a medium saucepan and add 6 cups of water. Bring to a boil over moderately high heat and boil for 3 minutes. Remove from the heat and let stand for 1 hour.

2. In a medium bowl, soak the ancho and guajillo chiles in 3 cups of hot water until softened, about 20 minutes. Pour off the soaking liquid, reserving 1½ cups. Stem and seed the chiles and transfer them to a food processor or blender with the reserved soaking liquid. Puree until smooth. Pass the puree through a fine strainer into a small bowl.

3. Heat 3 tablespoons of the oil in a large enameled cast-iron casserole. Season the turkey with salt and pepper. Add some of the meat to the casserole in a single layer and cook over moderately high heat until well browned all over, about 4 minutes. Transfer the cooked turkey to a large plate and brown the remaining meat in batches.

4. Heat 1 more tablespoon of the olive oil in the casserole. Add the onion and garlic and cook over moderate heat, stirring occasionally, until translucent, about 3 minutes. Add the cumin, curry, thyme, cinnamon and nutmeg and cook, stirring, until fragrant, 1 to 2 minutes. Add the Chicken Stock and bring to a boil over moderately high heat. Boil until reduced by ¼, about 6 minutes.

5. Return the turkey to the casserole and add the pureed chiles, chopped tomato, tomato paste, sugar and bay leaves. Bring to a boil over moderately high heat. Lower the heat and simmer until the turkey is tender, about 1 hour. Discard the bay leaves.

6. Meanwhile, drain the pinto beans and return them to the pan. Add 6 more cups of water and bring to a boil over moderately high heat. Lower the heat, cover partially and simmer until tender, about 1 hour. Drain the beans and add them to the chili.

7. Heat the remaining 2 tablespoons olive oil in a large skillet until almost smoking. Add the green and yellow bell peppers and cook over moderately high heat, stirring, until browned, about 3 minutes. Transfer to paper towels to drain, then stir them into the chili. (The chili can be prepared up to 3 days ahead; cover and refrigerate. Rewarm slowly over moderate heat.)

8. Stir half of the coriander into the chili and season with salt. Spoon the chili into bowls. Garnish with the chopped red onion and the remaining coriander.

—Grace Parisi

TURKEY BURGER TRIMMINGS

Garlic–Red Pepper Marinade
Makes 1¼ Cups

¾ cup safflower oil
¼ cup Dijon mustard
¼ cup minced garlic (about 10 large cloves)
3 tablespoons red wine vinegar
1½ teaspoons crushed red pepper
½ teaspoon salt

Combine all the ingredients in a nonreactive bowl. Use or cover tightly and refrigerate for up to 1 week.

Fresh Plum Sauce with Basil
Makes 2 Cups

1½ pounds ripe purple plums, pitted and cut into 1-inch chunks
⅓ cup balsamic vinegar
½ cup shredded fresh basil
½ teaspoon freshly ground pepper
¼ teaspoon salt

1. In a medium nonreactive saucepan, bring the plums and vinegar to a boil over high heat. Cover and reduce the heat to moderately low. Cook the plums, stirring often, until tender, about 10 minutes.

2. Puree the plums in a food processor. Strain the puree into a nonreactive bowl. Stir in the basil, pepper and salt and let cool. Use or cover tightly and refrigerate for up to 1 week.

—Bob Chambers

TURKEY BURGERS

Serve these burgers as you would any other—on a bun with sliced onions and tomatoes, pickles, ketchup or mustard and fried potatoes. If you like, use the Garlic–Red Pepper Marinade and Fresh Plum Sauce with Basil, above. Brush the formed ground-turkey patties with the marinade and serve the cooked burgers with the sauce. ➤

Makes 4 Burgers

- **1 pound ground turkey**
- **½ cup fresh bread crumbs**
- **⅓ cup finely chopped flat-leaf parsley**
- **1 egg, lightly beaten**
- **¾ teaspoon salt**
- **½ teaspoon freshly ground pepper**
- **1 tablespoon safflower oil**
- **1 small onion, finely chopped**
- **1 small garlic clove, minced**
- **4 grilled or toasted hamburger buns**

1. In a medium bowl, mix the turkey with the bread crumbs, parsley, egg, salt and pepper. Cover and refrigerate.

2. Light the grill. Heat the oil in a small skillet. Add the onion and cook over high heat until beginning to brown, 3 to 4 minutes. Stir in the garlic and remove from the heat. Let cool to room temperature, then stir into the turkey mixture.

3. Form the turkey into 4 patties. Cook on an oiled grill for about 6 minutes per side, or until an internal temperature of 145° is reached. Serve on the buns.

—Bob Chambers

■

STEAMED DUCK BREASTS

Steamed duck breasts are extremely moist and tender. These are finished off under the broiler to crisp the skin. They can then be served whole or sliced crosswise. If you prefer your duck breasts completely lean, steam them a minute or so longer than directed and remove the skin before serving.

4 Servings

- **4 6-ounce boneless duck breasts, skin on**
- **Salt and freshly ground pepper**

1. Preheat the broiler. Season the duck breasts on both sides with salt and pepper. Put them in a steamer basket, skin side down, and place over boiling water in a large saucepan. Cover and steam over moderate heat for about 5 minutes for medium rare.

2. Transfer the breasts to a small baking sheet, skin side up. Broil for 3 minutes or until the skin is crisp. Let the duck breasts rest for about 4 minutes before serving.

—Stephanie Lyness

■

ROAST DUCK WITH BALSAMIC VINEGAR, SUMMER GREENS AND DUCK LIVER CROSTINI

In a restaurant the ducks would usually be cooked ahead of time and then recrisped in the oven. If you prefer, you can carve and serve the birds as soon as they come out of the oven.

❦ This dish needs a fruity red wine with enough acidity and tannin and hints of sweet earthiness to stand up to the fattiness of the duck. For an exceptional choice, try 1985 Barbaresco Gallina di Neive from Bruno Giacosa.

4 Servings

Roasted Ducks:
- **1 cup balsamic vinegar**
- **½ cup soy sauce**
- **⅓ cup Dijon mustard**
- **1 tablespoon yellow mustard seeds**
- **1 tablespoon dried rosemary**
- **1 tablespoon cracked black peppercorns**
- **½ large onion, coarsely chopped**
- **1 tablespoon coarsely chopped garlic**
- **2 5-pound ducks, rinsed and dried, necks and livers reserved**

Sauce and Greens:
- **3 tablespoons extra-virgin olive oil**
- **2 large shallots, coarsely chopped**

1 medium carrot, coarsely chopped
1 medium celery rib, peeled and coarsely chopped
2 cups dry red wine
2 bay leaves
¼ teaspoon dried thyme
¼ teaspoon dried rosemary
1 quart Chicken Stock (p. 36) or canned low-sodium broth
20 large Sicilian green olives—halved, pitted and rinsed
1 tablespoon balsamic vinegar
Salt and freshly ground pepper
2 large garlic cloves, thinly sliced
1 pound assorted summer greens, such as watercress, spinach and mustard greens, stems trimmed

Duck Liver Crostini (recipe follows)

1. Prepare the roasted ducks: Preheat the oven to 350°. In a very large bowl, combine all the ingredients except the ducks. Remove the wing tips from the ducks and reserve for the sauce. Trim the skin around the neck, leaving just enough to cover the meat. Prick the ducks all over with a fork and add them to the marinade, turning to coat inside and out.

2. Set the ducks on a rack in a roasting pan. Pour the marinade on top. Roast for about 3 hours, or until the ducks are dark brown and almost all the fat is rendered.

3. Meanwhile, prepare the sauce: Chop the reserved duck necks and wing tips. Heat 1 tablespoon of the olive oil in a large nonreactive skillet. Add the neck and wing pieces and brown over moderate heat, turning occasionally, about 5 minutes.

4. Discard the fat from the pan. Add the shallots, carrot and celery and cook until browned, 2 to 3 minutes. Add the wine, bay leaves, thyme and rosemary and cook over high heat until reduced to a thick glaze, about 10 minutes. Lower the heat, add the Chicken Stock and simmer until the sauce lightly coats the back of a spoon, 15 to 20 minutes. Strain into a small non-

Steamed Duck Breasts

reactive saucepan and boil over moderately high heat until reduced to ½ cup, 2 to 3 minutes. Stir in the olives and vinegar and season with salt and pepper. (The recipe can be prepared to this point up to 4 hours ahead. Cover and set the ducks and sauce aside separately at room temperature.)

5. Preheat the oven to 450°. Heat the remaining 2 tablespoons oil in another large nonreactive skillet. Add the garlic and cook over low heat, stirring, until fragrant, about 2 minutes. Add the greens and cook over high heat, stirring, until wilted but still slightly crunchy, 1 to 2 minutes.

6. Partially bone the ducks, keeping the breasts attached to the legs: For each duck, cut along both sides of the breastbone. Using the bone as your guide, slide the knife under the meat to free a breast half and then continue carving with your knife to free the leg at the hip joint where it meets the carcass. Season the ducks on both sides with salt and pepper and set

them skin side down on a baking sheet with sides. Roast until heated through and the skin is crisp, about 10 minutes.

7. To serve, transfer each duck half to a large warmed plate and mound the greens alongside. Spoon the sauce and olives around the duck halves and accompany each serving with one of the Duck Liver Crostini.

Duck Liver Crostini
4 Servings

 4 ½-inch-thick slices of Italian bread
1½ tablespoons extra-virgin olive oil
 2 whole duck livers, trimmed and halved
   Salt and freshly ground pepper
 1 small red onion, thinly sliced

1. Preheat the oven to 350°. Lightly brush the bread on both sides with ½ tablespoon olive oil. Set the slices on a baking sheet and toast until golden, about 10 minutes.

2. Meanwhile, heat the remaining 1 tablespoon oil in a small skillet. Season the livers with salt and pepper, add them to the skillet and cook over moderately high heat, turning once, until browned on the outside and medium-rare, 2 to 3 minutes. Transfer the livers to a plate. Reduce the heat to low, add the onion and cook, stirring, until softened, 3 to 4 minutes. Top each toast with a piece of liver and some onion and serve warm.

—Jody Adams

■

CRISP PEPPERED QUAIL WITH COUNTRY HAM AND SPICY CRAYFISH HOMINY

If you can't find live crayfish for this first course served at Magnolia Grill in Durham, North Carolina, use medium shrimp.

♟ The pepperiness of a fruity young California Zinfandel will complement the spiciness of the dish. Try a 1990 or 1991 Mazzocco or Ridge Paso Robles Zinfandel.

6 First-Course Servings

 6 partially boned quail (about 4 ounces each), halved
 2 tablespoons bourbon
 1 tablespoon molasses
 2 teaspoons coarsely ground black pepper
 3 tablespoons fresh thyme plus additional sprigs, for garnish
 ½ cup peanut oil
1½ pounds live crayfish, cleaned
 3 ounces thinly sliced country ham, such as Smithfield or prosciutto, cut into ⅛-inch strips
 1 small onion, finely diced
 1 medium celery rib, peeled and finely diced
 ⅓ cup finely diced red bell pepper
 ⅓ cup finely diced green bell pepper
 1 tablespoon minced garlic
   Freshly ground black pepper
 ½ teaspoon fennel seeds, ground
 ½ teaspoon paprika
 ¼ teaspoon cayenne pepper
   Tomato-Crayfish Stock (recipe follows) or 2 cups Chicken Stock (p. 36) or canned low-sodium broth
 1 16-ounce can cooked hominy, drained and rinsed
   Salt
 1 medium tomato—peeled, seeded and cut into ¼-inch dice
 2 scallions, thinly sliced on the diagonal

1. Make an incision through the skin at the base of each quail breast and tuck in the leg. In a large shallow dish, combine the bourbon, molasses, coarsely ground pepper, 1 tablespoon of the thyme and ¼ cup of the peanut oil. Add the quail and stir to coat. Cover and marinate in the refrigerator for at least 4 hours.

2. Cook the crayfish in a large pot of boiling water until bright red, about 8 minutes. Drain and rinse briefly under cold water. Peel and devein the crayfish, reserving 6 whole ones for garnish. Reserve the crayfish shells for the stock.

3. Heat the remaining ¼ cup peanut oil in a large skillet. Add the ham and cook over high heat, stirring, until crisp, about 2 minutes. Transfer to paper towels to drain. Add the onion, celery and red and green bell peppers to the skillet and cook over moderately low heat until softened, about 5 minutes. Add the garlic, 2 teaspoons black pepper, ground fennel seeds, paprika and cayenne and cook for 1 more minute.

4. Add the Tomato-Crayfish Stock to the skillet and bring to a boil over high heat. Lower the heat and simmer until reduced by a third, about 10 minutes. Add the hominy and cook until heated through; season with salt and pepper. (The recipe can be prepared to this point up to 1 day ahead. Cover and refrigerate the quail, crayfish, ham and hominy separately.)

5. Light a grill or preheat the broiler. Reheat the hominy if necessary. Stir in the crayfish tails, the ham, the diced tomato and the remaining 2 tablespoons thyme. Cook over moderate heat until just warmed through.

6. Grill or broil the quail, skin side away from the heat, for 2 minutes. Turn and continue grilling until the skin is crisp and the meat is pink, 2 to 3 minutes longer. Season with salt.

7. To serve, spoon the hominy onto 6 plates and set 2 quail halves on top of each serving. Sprinkle on the sliced scallions and garnish each plate with a whole crayfish and thyme sprigs.

Tomato-Crayfish Stock
Makes 2 Cups
1 **pound large plum tomatoes, coarsely chopped**
  Reserved crayfish shells
1 **cup dry white wine**

2 **cups Chicken Stock (p. 36) or canned low-sodium broth**
2 **bay leaves**

Combine all the ingredients in a medium nonreactive saucepan and bring to a boil over high heat. Boil until the liquid is reduced to 2 cups, about 20 minutes. Strain and let cool.

—Ben Barker

■

GRILLED QUAIL WITH CUMIN

The flavors in this dish are reinforced with little piles of coarse salt, lemon zest, fresh coriander and more cumin on your plate for dipping the quail into as you eat it.

4 Servings
2 **tablespoons cumin seeds**
4 **large quail (about 6 ounces each)**
3 **tablespoons extra-virgin olive oil**
  Fine sea salt
¼ **cup coarsely chopped fresh coriander (cilantro)**
1½ **teaspoons finely grated lemon zest, preferably from organic lemons**
  Coarse sea salt

1. In a small dry skillet, toast the cumin seeds over moderate heat, stirring, until fragrant, about 3 minutes. Transfer to a mortar, spice mill or coffee grinder and pulverize.

2. Place 1 quail, breast side down, on a work surface. Using poultry shears, cut along 1 side of the backbone. Turn the quail over and press down on the breast with the heel of your hand to flatten the bird. Using a small sharp knife, make a tiny slit in the bottom of one of the thighs. Insert the tip of the opposite drumstick into the slit and pull it through. Repeat with the remaining quail.

3. In a small bowl, combine 1 tablespoon

of the ground cumin with the oil and stir to make a paste. Using a pastry brush, evenly spread the cumin paste all over the quail. Set aside for 30 minutes.

4. Light a grill or preheat the broiler. Season the quail well with fine sea salt. Place the birds skin side down on the grill or skin side up on a baking sheet under the broiler and cook for 5 minutes, until the skin is nicely browned. Turn the birds over with tongs and cook for 5 more minutes. Turn a second time and cook until the juices run clear when a thigh is pierced with a knife, about 5 minutes longer.

Clockwise from top left: **Roast Duck with Balsamic Vinegar, Summer Greens and Duck Liver Crostini (p. 98); Crisp Peppered Quail with Country Ham and Spicy Crayfish Hominy (p. 100); Pan-Roasted Quail; and Squab on Mushroom Toasts with Mixed Greens and Blackberry Dressing**

Sprinkle the quail lightly with fine sea salt, transfer to a plate or board and let rest for 5 minutes. To serve, place each quail on a warm dinner plate and surround it with small piles of the chopped fresh coriander, grated lemon zest, coarse salt and the remaining ground cumin.

—Patricia Wells

■

PAN-ROASTED QUAIL

What sets domestic and game birds apart from all other meats is the succulence, the saturated tenderness of their flesh; when carefully cooked through and through, the meat falls off the bone and releases pearls of juice at the slightest pressure. The most dependable way of achieving this result is this old-fashioned, but so reliable Italian pan-roasting method.

6 Servings
12 quail, preferably fresh
12 thin slices pancetta
12 fresh or dried sage leaves
2 tablespoons unsalted butter
1 tablespoon vegetable oil
 Salt and freshly ground pepper
½ cup dry white wine
 Polenta or mashed potatoes, for serving

1. Wash the quail thoroughly inside and out under cold running water, then place in a large colander to drain for at least 20 minutes. Pat the quail dry with kitchen towels. Stuff the cavity of each bird with 1 slice of pancetta and 1 sage leaf.

2. Put the butter and oil in a large, heavy, nonreactive skillet and turn the heat to high. When the fat is hot, add all the quail in a single layer and cook until browned on one side. Gradually turn them and continue cooking until they are evenly browned all over. Sprinkle the quail with salt and pepper, then add the white wine and turn the birds once.

3. Let the wine bubble for about 1 minute, then lower the heat to moderate and partially cover the pan, setting the lid slightly askew. Cook the quail until the meat feels very tender when poked with a fork and comes easily away from the bone, 45 minutes to 1 hour. Check from time to time to see that there is sufficient juice in the pan to keep the birds from sticking; if not, add 1 or 2 tablespoons of water. When the quail are done, transfer them to a warmed serving platter.

4. Add ¼ cup of water to the skillet. Boil over high heat, scraping the bottom of the pan with a wooden spoon to loosen any cooking residues, until the water boils away and only a few drops of dark pan juices for each bird remain. Pour the juices over the quail and serve with polenta or mashed potatoes.

—Marcella Hazan

■

SQUAB ON MUSHROOM TOASTS WITH MIXED GREENS AND BLACKBERRY DRESSING

Have your butcher remove the breasts from the squab; use the rest of the bird to make a flavorful stock.

❦ This salad pairs well with a fruity red Burgundy or Pinot Noir because the dressing is not overly acidic. Try a fragrant 1990 or 1991 Pinot Noir from the Williams Selyem Winery in Sonoma.

6 Servings
Mushroom Toasts:
6 ¾-inch-thick slices Italian bread, crusts removed
¼ cup plus 1 tablespoon olive oil ➤

3 garlic cloves—1 peeled and 2
minced
1 pound mixed fresh mushrooms,
such as shiitakes, portobellos,
chanterelles and oyster mushrooms
1 tablespoon fresh thyme leaves
Salt and freshly ground pepper

¼ cup shelled unsalted pistachios
(1 ounce)
2 tablespoons olive oil
6 whole boneless squab breasts, split
Salt and freshly ground pepper
Blackberry Dressing (recipe follows)
1 small head of radicchio, finely
shredded
6 cups mixed lettuces, such as red
oak leaf, frisée, mâche, radicchio
and arugula
30 blackberries, for garnish

1. Prepare the mushroom toasts: Preheat the oven to 425°. Lightly brush the bread on both sides with 2 tablespoons of the oil and transfer to a baking sheet with sides. Toast for about 5 minutes, or until golden brown. Let the bread cool slightly, then rub each slice on both sides with the peeled garlic clove.

2. Scatter the mushrooms on the baking sheet and sprinkle with the remaining 3 tablespoons olive oil, the minced garlic and the thyme. Season with salt and pepper. Roast in the oven for about 15 minutes, until the mushrooms are browned and fragrant. Coarsely chop the mushrooms.

3. Wipe off the baking sheet and spread the pistachios on it. Toast for about 5 minutes, until fragrant; finely chop. (The recipe can be prepared to this point up to 6 hours ahead. Set the toasts, mushrooms and nuts aside separately, covered, at room temperature.)

4. Heat the olive oil in a large heavy skillet until almost smoking. Season the squab breasts with salt and pepper and place in the pan, skin side down. Cook over moderately high heat until the skin is browned and crisp, about 3 minutes. Turn the breasts over and cook until browned on the outside and medium-rare, about 3 minutes longer. Transfer to a large plate and let stand for 5 minutes.

5. Spread the mushrooms on the garlic toasts and warm them in a low oven. Cut each squab breast crosswise into 2 or 3 slices. Cut each warm mushroom toast diagonally in half and top each half with a sliced breast.

6. To serve, spoon 1 tablespoon of the Blackberry Dressing around the perimeter of 6 large plates. Sprinkle the plates with the pistachios and radicchio. In a large bowl, toss the mixed lettuces with 3 tablespoons of the dressing. Set 2 squab toasts on each plate and mound the mixed lettuces between the toasts. Scatter the blackberries on the plates and serve the remaining Blackberry Dressing alongside.

Blackberry Dressing
Makes About 1 Cup
1 cup blackberries
1 medium shallot, minced
¼ cup blackberry vinegar, raspberry
vinegar or white wine vinegar
½ cup canola oil
½ teaspoon salt
½ teaspoon freshly ground pepper

Puree the blackberries in a food processor or blender and strain into a small bowl. Stir in the shallot and vinegar. Whisk in the oil, salt and pepper.
—Nancy Oakes

Chapter 6 ▪ MEAT

107   Spinach-Stuffed Veal Rolls in Tarragon Tomato Sauce

107   Veal Shanks with White Beans

108   Le Grand Colbert's Calf's Liver with Sherry Vinegar and Pearl Onions

109   Wine-Merchant Steak

110   Mom's Brisket with Dried Fruits

113   Estouffade of Beef with Apricots, Almonds and Raisins

114   New York Bowl of Red

115   Smoky Beef and Red Bean Chili

117   Middle Eastern Meatballs with Swiss Chard

118   Roast Double Loin of Pork with Port Wine Sauce

119   Hickory-Smoked Pork Tenderloins

120   North Carolina Chopped Barbecue

122   Malaccan Devil's Curry

123   Pork and Black Bean Chili Verde

124   Choucroute Garnie

126   Roast Leg of Lamb with Garlic

127   Poppy Seed-Coated Lamb Loins with Curried Couscous and Tamarind Chipotle Sauce

129   Pot-Roasted Lamb with Juniper Berries

129   Lamb, Spinach and Potato Curry with Banana Raita

131   Lamb and White Bean Chili

Spinach-Stuffed Veal
Rolls in Tarragon
Tomato Sauce

SPINACH-STUFFED VEAL ROLLS IN TARRAGON TOMATO SAUCE

Veal roulades in a flavorful sauce make a great freeze-ahead meal.

6 to 8 Servings

- 2 pounds fresh spinach, stemmed and leaves washed
- 6 tablespoons unsalted butter
- 2 medium shallots, finely chopped
- 2 medium garlic cloves, minced
- 10 ounces mushrooms, finely chopped
  Salt and freshly ground pepper
- ½ pound ground pork
- 1 cup fresh bread crumbs
- 1 large egg
- 1 large egg yolk
- 2 tablespoons freshly grated Parmesan cheese
- ⅛ teaspoon ground nutmeg
- 12 veal scaloppine (2¼ pounds)
- 1 medium onion, finely chopped
- 1 35-ounce can Italian peeled tomatoes, coarsely chopped, with their liquid
- ¾ cup dry white wine
- 1½ tablespoons fresh tarragon, coarsely chopped, or ½ teaspoon dried plus additional sprigs, for garnish (optional)
- 1 teaspoon finely grated orange zest

1. In a large saucepan, place the spinach with the water that clings to it. Cook over moderately high heat just until wilted, 4 to 5 minutes. Drain well. Coarsely chop the spinach and transfer to a medium bowl.

2. Heat 2 tablespoons of the butter in a medium nonstick skillet. Add the shallots and half the garlic and cook over moderate heat until fragrant, 1 to 2 minutes. Add the mushrooms and cook, stirring occasionally, until they begin to brown, about 10 minutes. Season with salt and pepper and let cool.

3. Add the mushroom mixture to the spinach along with the pork, bread crumbs, egg, egg yolk, Parmesan cheese and nutmeg. Mix well.

4. Spread 6 of the scaloppine on a work surface and season with salt and pepper. Divide half the stuffing evenly among the scaloppine; spread the stuffing on the narrower end of the veal. Starting at the narrow end, roll up the scaloppine in an even cylinder and tie the rolls at both ends with kitchen string. Repeat with the remaining scaloppine and stuffing. Season the rolls with salt and pepper.

5. Heat the remaining 4 tablespoons butter in an enameled cast-iron casserole. Add 6 veal rolls and cook over moderately high heat until browned, about 10 minutes. Transfer to a plate and repeat with the remaining rolls.

6. Add the onion and remaining garlic to the casserole. Cook over moderate heat, stirring, until softened, about 5 minutes. Add the tomatoes, white wine, dried tarragon, if using, and orange zest. Bring to a boil over moderately high heat and cook until slightly thickened, about 10 minutes. Season with salt and pepper. Return the veal rolls to the casserole, cover and simmer over low heat until tender, about 25 minutes.

7. Cut off and discard the strings from the veal rolls. Stir the fresh chopped tarragon into the sauce and garnish with sprigs of fresh tarragon.

—Ann Chantal Altman

■

VEAL SHANKS WITH WHITE BEANS

This veal and bean stew was inspired by the classic Italian preparation osso buco. The veal shanks should fit snugly in the casserole; it's okay if they touch each other slightly. ➤

❦ This is clearly a red wine dish, and an Italian Barolo would cut across the succulent flavors. Look for medium-bodied examples, such as 1988 Ceretto "Zonchera" or 1988 Prunotto.

6 Servings

½ cup dried porcini mushrooms
1 28-ounce can whole Italian peeled tomatoes and their liquid
¼ cup plus 1 tablespoon extra-virgin olive oil
6 2-inch-thick meaty pieces of veal shank
   Salt and coarsely ground pepper
½ cup all-purpose flour, for dredging
1 large onion, finely chopped
1 medium carrot, finely chopped
2 medium celery ribs, finely chopped
7 garlic cloves, minced
½ cup dry white wine
1½ tablespoons finely chopped fresh thyme
1 tablespoon minced fresh sage
2 15½-ounce cans of cannellini beans, drained and rinsed, or 4 cups cooked white beans
   Chopped fresh flat-leaf parsley

1. In a medium bowl, steep the mushrooms in 1½ cups of hot water until softened, about 20 minutes. Remove the mushrooms and squeeze out any excess water over the bowl. If the liquid is gritty, strain through a sieve lined with a coffee filter; set aside. Coarsely chop the mushrooms and set aside.

2. In a food processor or food mill, puree the tomatoes and their liquid.

3. In a large Dutch oven or heavy, nonreactive, flameproof casserole, heat 2 tablespoons of the olive oil over high heat until shimmering. Meanwhile, season the veal with salt and coarse pepper and dredge the meaty sides of the shanks in flour; shake off the excess. Place the veal shanks, cut side down, in the casserole and cook until browned on both sides.

Transfer the shanks to a plate. Turn off the heat for 1 minute to allow the pan to cool slightly.

4. Add the onion, carrot and celery and cook over moderate heat, stirring frequently, until the onion is translucent, about 8 minutes. Add the reserved porcini mushrooms and half of the garlic and cook for 2 minutes. Add the wine and cook for 1 minute, scraping the bottom of the pan to loosen any browned bits. Add the pureed tomatoes, reserved mushroom liquid and thyme and bring to a boil.

5. Reduce the heat to moderately low. Return the shanks to the pan and simmer until very tender, turning occasionally and spooning the sauce over them, about 1¾ to 2 hours.

6. In a medium skillet, heat the remaining 3 tablespoons olive oil over moderately low heat. Add the remaining minced garlic and the sage and cook, stirring, until fragrant, 3 to 5 minutes. Add the cannellini beans and cook just to warm through, about 7 minutes. If necessary, add a little water to moisten the beans but not enough to make them soupy. Season with salt and coarsely ground pepper.

7. To serve, transfer the shanks to individual serving bowls. If the sauce is too thin, boil to reduce it slightly. Season with salt and pepper. Place a generous spoonful of the beans in each bowl. Spoon the sauce over the meat and beans. Garnish with chopped parsley and serve.

—Ilana Sharlin Stone

■

LE GRAND COLBERT'S CALF'S LIVER WITH SHERRY VINEGAR AND PEARL ONIONS

This version of a brasserie classic—sautéed calf's liver with pearl onions—comes from Le Grand Colbert in Paris.

🍷 The richness of this dish, with a sherry vinegar reduction, points to an assertive but straightforward red—a country wine such as a California Zinfandel. Look for 1991 Rodney Strong "Old Vines" or 1991 Rosenblum Cellars.

4 Servings

- 16 pearl onions, peeled and trimmed
- 3½ tablespoons cold unsalted butter
- 1 teaspoon sugar
- 1 tablespoon sherry vinegar
- 1 cup Chicken Stock (p. 36) or canned low-sodium broth
- 2 tablespoons vegetable oil
- 4 ½-inch-thick slices of calf's liver (about 6 ounces each)
  Salt and freshly ground pepper

1. In a medium nonreactive saucepan, combine the onions with 2 tablespoons of the butter, the sugar and 2 tablespoons of water. Cook over moderately low heat, stirring once or twice, until the onions are dark brown, about 8 minutes. Stir in the sherry vinegar, scraping the bottom of the pan with a wooden spoon to loosen any browned bits. Stir in the Chicken Stock and cook over moderate heat until the onions are tender, about 10 minutes.

2. In a large skillet, melt ½ tablespoon of the butter in the vegetable oil over high heat. Season the calf's liver slices with salt and pepper, add them to the skillet and cook, turning once, until well browned, about 4 minutes per side. Transfer the liver to plates.

3. Bring the onions to a simmer over high heat. Cut the remaining 1 tablespoon butter into 3 pieces. Remove the onions from the heat and swirl in the butter. Season with salt and pepper. Spoon some of the onions and sauce over each serving of calf's liver.

—Alexander Lobrano

Wine-Merchant Steak

WINE-MERCHANT STEAK

Entrecôte marchand de vin, a traditional French bistro dish, consists of a nicely seared steak topped with a red-wine butter sauce. In keeping with the trend toward lighter fare, the fat in this classic has been reduced. The recipe is from *Today's Gourmet* (KQED, Inc.).

4 Servings

- 4 boneless New York strip, shell or sirloin-tip steaks, cut ¾ inches thick (9 ounces each)
  Salt and freshly ground pepper
- 2 tablespoons extra-virgin olive oil
- ¼ cup finely chopped shallots
- 4 large mushrooms (about 4 ounces), stems discarded, caps cut into julienne strips ➤

STEWING TIPS

● If possible, buy your meat from a butcher instead of a supermarket so that you can have control over how the meat is cut. What supermarkets package as stew meat is usually too small and irregularly shaped; when cooked the pieces may shrivel into odd-size bits.

● Tossing a handful of pantry ingredients into the pot is the right idea, but go easy on the seasonings—the flavors will develop as the dish cooks. Make sure your spices are fresh and your aromatics—celery, carrot and onion—crisp.

● Use homemade stock if you can; if not, low-sodium canned broth is a fine substitute. Choose good-quality wine or beer, since its flavor will be integrated into the dish. The amount of liquid used depends on the type of meat and the duration of cooking. The less cooking time required, the less liquid needed. Shanks, brisket and pot roast, which are usually cooked whole or in large pieces, require the most time and liquid. Poultry and cubed stew meat require less time and liquid. Whatever you are making, the meat must be, at the very least, covered with liquid.

—Ilana Sharlin Stone

1½ teaspoons finely chopped garlic
1 cup red Beaujolais
1 cup Chicken Stock (p. 36) or canned low-sodium broth
2 tablespoons Worcestershire sauce
1 tablespoon Dijon mustard
½ teaspoon potato starch dissolved in 2 teaspoons water
1 tablespoon finely chopped chives

1. Trim the steaks, removing all visible fat and sinews. Season with ½ teaspoon each of salt and pepper.

2. Heat the oil in a very large heavy skillet over high heat. When it is hot, add the steaks and sauté until well browned, 2½ to 3 minutes on each side for medium-rare. Transfer the steaks to a platter and keep warm.

3. Add the chopped shallots to the drippings in the skillet and sauté over moderately high heat for 10 seconds. Add the mushroom strips and chopped garlic and sauté for 1 minute. Stir in the Beaujolais and boil it down until 2 tablespoons remain, about 6 minutes. Add the Chicken Stock and boil to reduce the mixture to ½ cup, 4 to 5 minutes.

4. Add the Worcestershire sauce and mustard and mix well. Stir in the dissolved potato starch and bring the sauce to a boil. Season with salt.

5. Arrange the steaks on warmed dinner plates. Stir any meat juices on the platter into the sauce. Spoon the sauce over the steaks. Garnish with the chives and serve.

—Jacques Pépin

■

MOM'S BRISKET WITH DRIED FRUITS

Cook the meat a day ahead. Not only does it taste better the next day but it's also easier to skim the fat from the sauce when it's chilled. Serve the meat and its sweet sauce with potato pancakes or boiled new potatoes tossed with butter and parsley.

10 to 12 Servings

3 tablespoons unsalted butter
3 large onions, coarsely chopped
2 12-ounce bottles of beer
1 bay leaf
5 pounds beef brisket, trimmed of nearly all surface fat (4½ pounds trimmed)
   Salt and freshly ground pepper
½ packed cup pitted prunes (4 ounces)
½ packed cup dried apricot halves (3¼ ounces)
½ packed cup dried sour cherries (3 ounces)
¼ cup light brown sugar
3 tablespoons fresh lemon juice
2 tablespoons brandy
2 teaspoons finely grated lemon zest
¼ teaspoon ground ginger
1 cinnamon stick   ➤

Mom's Brisket
with Dried Fruits

Estouffade of Beef with Apricots, Almonds and Raisins

1. Preheat the oven to 350°. In a large Dutch oven or heavy, nonreactive, flameproof casserole, melt the butter over moderate heat. Add the onions and cook, stirring often, until golden, about 10 minutes. Stir in the beer and bay leaf and scrape the pan to loosen any browned bits.

2. Season the meat generously on both sides with salt and pepper. Add to the pan. Spoon the liquid over the top. Bring to a simmer. Cover and braise in the oven 3 to 3½ hours, basting often and turning over halfway through, until fork-tender.

3. Using tongs and a large spatula, move the brisket to a plate and let cool. When the cooking liquid is cool, return the meat to the pan, cover and refrigerate overnight.

4. Discard the solid fat on top of the cooking liquid. Cook the brisket over moderate heat until warmed through, about 30 minutes. Transfer to a cutting board, let cool slightly and slice across the grain ¼ inch thick. Arrange the slices on a heatproof platter, cover snugly with foil and keep warm in a 200° oven.

5. Meanwhile, pour the cooking liquid into a medium saucepan along with the prunes, apricots, cherries, brown sugar, lemon juice, brandy, lemon zest, ginger and cinnamon stick. Bring to a simmer over moderately low heat and cook until the sauce has thickened and the fruit has plumped, about 15 minutes. Discard the cinnamon stick. Season well with salt and pepper. Spoon the warm compote over the brisket and serve.

—Ilana Sharlin Stone

■

ESTOUFFADE OF BEEF WITH APRICOTS, ALMONDS AND RAISINS

Be sure to use meaty shanks for this dish. Estouffade is a good choice to make ahead or even freeze.

♟ Beef goes with many red wines, but the sweetness of the pureed fruit calls for a red with its own distinctive fruitiness to match the meat. A young California Zinfandel, such as 1991 Preston or 1991 Caymus, would be ideal.

8 Servings

- ½ **pound dried apricots**
- 1½ **cups boiling water**
- 4½ **pounds boneless beef shanks or boneless tip roast, cut into 1½-inch cubes**
  Salt and freshly ground pepper
- ¾ **teaspoon cinnamon**
- ½ **cup olive oil**
- 2 **large onions, finely chopped**
- 6 **garlic cloves, minced**
- 2 **teaspoons ground cumin**
- 1 **teaspoon ground coriander**
- ¼ **teaspoon ground cloves**
- ½ **cup dry white wine**
- 2 **cups canned crushed tomatoes with their liquid**
- 3½ **cups beef stock or broth**
- 2 **bay leaves**
- ½ **cup raisins**
- ½ **cup slivered blanched almonds, for garnish**
- 2 **tablespoons finely chopped flat-leaf parsley, for garnish**
  Cooked egg noodles, for serving

1. In a medium bowl, soak the dried apricots in the boiling water until plumped, about 30 minutes. Drain.

2. In a large bowl, toss the beef cubes with 1 teaspoon salt, 1 teaspoon pepper and the cinnamon. In a large heavy skillet, heat 4 tablespoons of the olive oil until almost smoking. Add half the beef cubes to the pan and cook over high heat, turning, until well browned on all sides, 8 to 10 minutes. Transfer the beef to a large plate. Add 1 more tablespoon of the oil and brown the remaining beef. ➤

3. Add the remaining 3 tablespoons oil to the pan. Add the onions and cook over moderate heat until softened, about 10 minutes, scraping up any browned bits from the bottom of the pan. Add the garlic, cumin, coriander and cloves and cook, stirring, until the spices are aromatic, about 3 minutes. Add the white wine and cook until almost all the liquid is evaporated, about 2 minutes. Stir in the crushed tomatoes with their liquid and the beef stock. Add the apricots to the pan, reserving 8 for garnish. Simmer the sauce for 2 minutes.

4. Working in batches, puree the sauce in a food processor until smooth, about 20 seconds. Transfer the puree to an enameled cast-iron casserole. Add the beef and bay leaves and bring to a simmer over moderate heat. Cover and cook over low heat, stirring occasionally, for 1¾ hours. Uncover and simmer for 15 minutes. Add the raisins and simmer until the meat is very tender and the sauce is thick, about 15 minutes longer. Discard the bay leaves and season with salt and pepper.

5. To freeze the estouffade, let cool completely, then refrigerate until cold. Transfer to plastic containers, covering the beef cubes with sauce. Press plastic wrap against the surface of the sauce, then seal the containers and freeze for up to 1 month.

6. To reheat the beef, let thaw in the refrigerator for 24 hours. Remove the plastic wrap, transfer the meat to an enameled cast-iron casserole and rewarm over low heat, stirring occasionally. Alternatively, reheat the beef in a microwave oven according to the manufacturer's instructions.

7. Preheat the oven to 350°. Toast the slivered almonds on a baking sheet for about 7 minutes, until golden. Slice the reserved apricots. Garnish the estouffade with the apricots, almonds and parsley. Serve with egg noodles.

—Ann Chantal Altman

NEW YORK BOWL OF RED

Jonathan Levine, director of the New York State Chili Cook-Off and a member of the International Chili Society Advisory Board, has won awards in New York and Maryland for his version of the classic bowl of red. This is a variation of his recipe. He uses a mild, dark New Mexico red-chile powder for color and flavor. Blended chili powder is spicier.

6 to 8 Servings

1½ teaspoons cumin seeds
5 pounds trimmed beef brisket, cut into ¾-inch cubes
Salt and freshly ground pepper
6 garlic cloves, minced
4 medium jalapeños, finely chopped
2 medium onions, finely chopped
½ cup commercial chili powder (see Note)
3 tablespoons pure red mild chile powder,* such as dark New Mexico
1½ teaspoons ground coriander
4 cups beef stock or broth or water
1 35-ounce can Italian peeled tomatoes, coarsely chopped, with their liquid
1½ teaspoons oregano, crumbled
½ pound coarsely ground beef chuck
2 scallions, white and tender green portions, thinly sliced (optional)

*Available at specialty food stores and Latin American markets

1. In a small dry skillet, toast the cumin seeds over moderate heat, stirring constantly, until fragrant, about 2 minutes. Grind the cumin in a spice mill or mortar.

2. Heat a large enameled cast-iron casserole. Season the brisket with salt and pepper. Working in batches, add the meat

to the casserole and cook over moderately high heat until well browned all over, about 8 minutes. Transfer each batch to a large plate.

3. Add the garlic, jalapeños and onions to the casserole and cook over moderate heat, stirring occasionally, until softened, about 4 minutes. Add the commercial chili powder and pure red chile powder, coriander and half of the ground cumin and cook, stirring, for 2 minutes.

4. Return the cooked brisket to the casserole and add the beef stock, tomatoes and their liquid, and the oregano. Bring to a boil over moderately high heat, then lower the heat and simmer gently, stirring occasionally, for 3 hours. Stir in the ground chuck, season with salt and cook until the brisket is very tender and the sauce is thickened, about 1 hour longer. Stir in the remaining cumin and simmer for 15 minutes. Garnish with the scallions, if desired, and serve.

NOTE: Rather than commercial chili powder, Jonathan Levine recommends using Reno Red Chili Mix, available by mail order from Stewart's Chili Company, P.O. Box 574, San Carlos, CA 94070.

—Grace Parisi

■

SMOKY BEEF AND RED BEAN CHILI

Corn and toasted pumpkin seeds add new flavors and textures to this old favorite.

8 Servings

2 cups dried red or pink beans (1 pound), picked over and rinsed

7 garlic cloves—1 left whole and 6 minced

4 ancho chiles

2 chipotle chiles

1½ cups raw pumpkin seeds (about 6 ounces)

3 tablespoons vegetable oil

2 pounds lean stewing beef, cut into 1-inch cubes
Salt and freshly ground black pepper

1 large yellow onion, finely chopped

1 28-ounce can crushed tomatoes

1 6-ounce can tomato paste

3 tablespoons ground cumin

1 tablespoon sugar

3 cups fresh corn kernels or 1 pound thawed frozen corn

5 medium scallions, thinly sliced

1 red onion, minced
White rice and sour cream, for serving

1. Place the red beans and whole garlic clove in a medium saucepan. Add 6 cups of water. Bring to a boil over moderately high heat and boil for 3 minutes. Remove from the heat and let stand for 1 hour.

2. Soak the chiles in 4 cups of hot water until softened, about 20 minutes. Pour off the soaking liquid, reserving 1½ cups. Stem and seed the chiles and transfer them to a food processor or blender with ½ cup of the reserved soaking liquid. Puree until smooth. Pass the puree through a fine strainer into a small bowl.

3. Preheat the oven to 350°. Spread the pumpkin seeds on a baking sheet and toast until fragrant, about 7 minutes. Set aside ⅓ of the pumpkin seeds for garnish. Transfer the remaining seeds to a food processor and pulse until finely ground.

4. Heat the oil in a large enameled cast-iron casserole. Season the beef cubes with salt and black pepper. Add some of the meat to the casserole in a single layer and cook over high heat until well browned all over, about 6 minutes. Transfer the meat to a large plate and brown the remaining beef cubes in batches.

5. Add the yellow onion and minced garlic to the casserole and cook over moderate heat, stirring occasionally, until translucent, about 3 minutes. ➤

Middle Eastern Meatballs with Swiss Chard

6. Return the meat to the casserole and add the pureed chiles, crushed tomatoes, tomato paste, the remaining 1 cup reserved chile liquid and 2 cups of water. Stir in the ground pumpkin seeds, the cumin, the sugar and 1 tablespoon salt. Bring to a boil over moderately high heat. Lower the heat, cover partially and simmer gently until the beef is very tender, about 2 hours.

7. Meanwhile, drain the beans and garlic clove. Return them to the pan, add 6 more cups of water and bring to a boil over moderately high heat. Lower the heat, cover partially and simmer until the beans are tender, about 1¼ hours. Drain the beans, discarding the garlic. Stir the beans into the chili with the corn and scallions. (The chili can be prepared up to 3 days ahead; cover and refrigerate. Rewarm slowly over moderate heat.)

8. Season the chili with salt and sprinkle the red onion and reserved toasted pumpkin seeds on top. Serve with rice and sour cream on the side.

—Grace Parisi

MIDDLE EASTERN MEATBALLS WITH SWISS CHARD

Serve these beef and lamb meatballs with couscous, rice or pita.

♟ A hearty red is the best accompaniment to this dish. A flavorful young Côtes du Rhône, such as 1991 Domaine de la Guichard or 1990 Guigal, would work particularly well.

6 to 8 Servings
3 tablespoons unsalted butter
¾ cup pine nuts (about 4½ ounces)
2 medium leeks, white part only, coarsely chopped
1 pound ground beef chuck
1 pound ground lamb
2 eggs, lightly beaten
⅓ cup unseasoned dry bread crumbs
1½ teaspoons ground cumin
1 teaspoon ground allspice
Salt and freshly ground pepper
2 28-ounce cans Italian peeled tomatoes and their liquid
½ cup all-purpose flour, for dredging
3 tablespoons fresh lemon juice
2 bunches of Swiss chard (about 3 pounds), large stems discarded, leaves and small stems chopped

1. In a small skillet, melt 1 tablespoon of the butter over moderate heat. Add the pine nuts and cook, shaking the pan, until toasted, 2 to 3 minutes. Transfer to a plate to cool.

2. In a saucepan of boiling water, blanch the leeks for 1 minute; drain in a colander. Rinse with cold water to cool; drain. Finely chop the leeks in a food processor. Add the ground chuck and lamb and process to blend.

3. Transfer the meat mixture to a large bowl. Add ½ cup of the toasted pine nuts, the beaten eggs, bread crumbs, cumin, allspice and 1½ teaspoons each of salt and pepper. Mix well. Form the mixture into 1-inch meatballs and place on a baking sheet. Cover and refrigerate to firm up slightly, about 30 minutes.

4. In a food processor, puree the tomatoes and their liquid.

5. In a large enameled cast-iron casserole, melt 1 tablespoon of the remaining butter over moderately high heat. Place the flour in a medium bowl. Dredge the meatballs in the flour, shaking off any excess. Add half of the meatballs to the casserole and cook, turning, until nicely browned all over, about 5 minutes. Using a slotted spoon, transfer the meatballs to a plate. Fry the remaining meatballs in the remaining 1 tablespoon butter. Return the first batch of meatballs to the casserole. ➤

6. Stir in 1½ cups of water, the pureed tomatoes and the lemon juice and bring to a boil. Simmer over moderately low heat for 20 minutes, stirring frequently. Stir in the Swiss chard and cook until tender, about 10 minutes. Season with salt and pepper. Before serving, sprinkle the remaining toasted pine nuts on top.

—Ilana Sharlin Stone

■

ROAST DOUBLE LOIN OF PORK WITH PORT WINE SAUCE

Ask the butcher to chop up the bones removed from the pork loins so that you can use them for making the sauce.

16 Servings

Spice mixture:
- 2 dried sage leaves
- 1 teaspoon black peppercorns
- 1 small bay leaf
- ¼ teaspoon whole allspice berries
- ¼ teaspoon thyme
- 1½ tablespoons salt

Meat:
- 2 2- to 2½-pound centercut boneless pork loins
- 1 onion, coarsely chopped
- 1 carrot, coarsely chopped
- 2 garlic cloves, smashed

Sauce:
- 3 tablespoons vegetable oil
  Reserved pork bones
- 2 carrots, cut into 1-inch pieces
- 1 large onion, chopped
- 3 tablespoons all-purpose flour
- 4 cups hot Chicken Stock (p. 36) or canned broth
- ½ cup dry white wine or French vermouth
- 2 tomatoes, chopped
- 2 celery ribs, chopped
- 3 large garlic cloves, smashed
  Pinch of rosemary leaves
- ½ cup loosely packed parsley stems
  Salt and freshly ground pepper
- 2 to 3 tablespoons dry port

1. Make the spice mixture: In a spice grinder or a blender, grind all the dried herbs and spices to a fine powder. Empty the spices into a bowl and stir in the salt.

2. Rub the spice mixture all over the pork loins. Align the loins with the fat sides out and with the tapered end of one against the widest end of the other. Tie the roast at 1-inch intervals with kitchen string and refrigerate for 24 to 48 hours.

3. Meanwhile, make the sauce base: Heat the oil in a large stainless steel or enameled cast-iron casserole. Add the reserved pork bones and brown them in the oil over high heat, stirring and tossing frequently, 3 to 5 minutes. Add the carrots and onion and continue stirring until the vegetables are lightly colored.

4. Stir in the flour. Toss and cook over moderate heat to brown the flour, about 2 minutes. Remove from the heat and let cool for several minutes.

5. Gradually stir in the hot Chicken Stock to blend with the flour. Add the white wine, tomatoes, celery and garlic and bring to a simmer over moderately high heat, skimming as necessary. Add the rosemary leaves and parsley stems, cover loosely and simmer for about 2 hours.

6. Strain the sauce base, pressing hard on the solids to release the flavorful juices. Season with salt and pepper. Let cool, then cover and refrigerate until you're ready to make the sauce.

7. Preheat the oven to 350°. Arrange the pork in a roasting pan, fattiest side up. Roast in the middle of the oven for 1½ hours, basting the meat every 30 minutes with the fat that has accumulated in the pan. Add the onion, carrot and garlic to the pan and continue roasting the pork,

basting occasionally, for 30 to 45 minutes longer, until the internal temperature reaches 160°. Transfer the roast to a carving board and cover loosely with foil.

8. Spoon the fat (not the roasting juices) out of the roasting pan. Skim the solidified fat from the surface of the chilled sauce base. Add the sauce base to the pan and bring to a simmer over moderate heat, scraping up the browned bits from the bottom and mashing the roasting vegetables. Strain the sauce into a small pan, pressing hard to extract all the juices. Season with salt and pepper, add the port and bring to a simmer, skimming any fat from the surface.

9. To serve, untie the roast. Using a sharp knife, carve the pork straight down into slices less than ¼ inch thick; the slices will separate as you serve them. Pass the sauce separately.

—Julia Child

■

HICKORY-SMOKED PORK TENDERLOINS

Smoking is best suited to a smoker or a charcoal grill, although many gas grills can now hold wood chips; check the manufacturer's instructions to be sure. Allow time for the meat to marinate overnight.

8 Servings
¼ cup bourbon
2 tablespoons molasses
4 garlic cloves, crushed
10 fresh thyme sprigs, coarsely chopped
6 fresh sage sprigs, coarsely chopped
2 bay leaves, preferably fresh, coarsely chopped or crumbled
1 tablespoon crushed red pepper
¼ cup olive oil
2 pork tenderloins, (about 2½ pounds total), trimmed

1½ cups dry hickory chips
Salt
Abundance Plum Chutney (recipe follows)

1. In a small bowl, whisk the bourbon with the molasses. Add the garlic, thyme, sage, bay leaves and crushed red pepper. Stir in the olive oil. Place the pork in a large glass baking dish. Pour the marinade over the meat and turn to coat. Cover and refrigerate overnight, turning occasionally.

2. Light a smoker or a charcoal or gas grill. Let the pork tenderloins return to room temperature. In a large bowl, cover the hickory chips with water and let soak for 30 minutes.

3. Drain the hickory chips and put them on the hot coals in the smoker or charcoal grill or add them to the gas grill according to the manufacturer's instructions. Place a rack about 5 inches from the heat. Season the tenderloins with salt and set them on the rack. Cover and smoke for 25 minutes. Turn the tenderloins, cover and smoke for about 25 minutes longer, until an instant-read thermometer reaches 150°. Transfer to a cutting board and let cool for at least 15 minutes.

4. Wipe the excess marinade from the pork. Slice the tenderloins about ¼ inch thick and serve warm or at room temperature with Abundance Plum Chutney.

Abundance Plum Chutney
Makes 7 Cups
2 tablespoons peanut oil
2 large onions, finely chopped
1 teaspoon Madras curry powder
1 cup cider vinegar
½ cup granulated sugar
½ cup light brown sugar
½ teaspoon ground allspice
3 whole cloves
1 3-inch cinnamon stick
1 teaspoon freshly ground white pepper ➤

3 pounds firm abundance or other tart plums, pitted and cut into ¾-inch pieces

½ cup dried cranberries,* dried sour cherries* or dried currants

*Available at specialty food stores

1. Heat the oil in a large nonreactive saucepan. Add the onions and cook over moderate heat, stirring occasionally, until softened, about 12 minutes. Stir in the curry powder and cook for 2 minutes. Add the vinegar, granulated and brown sugars, the allspice, cloves, cinnamon and white pepper and bring to a boil over moderately high heat. Lower the heat and simmer, stirring occasionally, for 20 minutes.

2. Stir in the plums and the dried cranberries. Simmer over low heat, stirring occasionally, until the plums are tender but still hold their shape, about 12 minutes. Discard the cloves and cinnamon stick and let cool completely. (The chutney can be refrigerated, covered, for up to 1 week. Let return to room temperature before serving.)

—Ben Barker

■

NORTH CAROLINA CHOPPED BARBECUE

Nothing could be finer. And this tangy, cayenne-peppered pork barbecue, which can be prepared up to a month in advance, is simple to make. Just let the meat simmer for two and a half hours, then roast it for two hours, and finally— when it's already falling apart anyway— chop it and mix it with the sauce. But you must allow enough time to simmer, roast, chop and sauce in one continuous process; if the meat gets cold or dries out between steps, it will not absorb the sauces properly. If you're freezing the barbecue, it may need extra perking up with additional barbecue sauce and hot pepper sauce before serving.

❦ The rich, sharp and savory tastes here call for beer. Alternatively, try a dry-style white Zinfandel, such as 1992 Buehler or 1992 De Loach.

12 to 15 Servings

2 bone-in picnic shoulder pork roasts (about 6 pounds each), skin removed

12 medium garlic cloves

3 cups cider vinegar

Mopping and Mixing Sauces:
Coarse (kosher) salt

3½ cups cider vinegar

1 tablespoon cayenne pepper

¾ teaspoon sugar
Freshly ground black pepper

¾ cup bottled barbecue sauce, plus more for serving (see Note)
Hot pepper sauce, for serving

1. In a very deep nonreactive stockpot or casserole, place the pork, garlic and vinegar; if necessary, divide them evenly between 2 smaller pots. Add water to cover by 2 inches. Bring to a boil over high heat, skimming occasionally. Reduce the heat to moderately low, cover partially and simmer for 2½ hours, adding boiling water as needed to keep the meat covered.

2. Transfer the roasts to a lightly oiled rack set in a large roasting pan; reserve the garlic and ½ cup of the simmering liquid.

3. Prepare the Mopping Sauce: Preheat the oven to 350°. In a large bowl, mash the garlic to a paste with 1 teaspoon coarse salt. Add the vinegar, ¼ cup of the reserved simmering liquid, the cayenne, sugar and ¼ teaspoon black pepper and mix well. Set aside 1½ cups of this Mopping Sauce for making the Mixing Sauce.

4. Using a wide pastry brush, sop the pork roasts all over with the remaining Mopping Sauce and place them in the

oven. Immediately lower the temperature to 300°. Roast for about 2 hours, basting every 15 minutes and turning once, until the meat is slightly crusty outside, very tender and moist inside and just about falling from the bone.

5. Set the roasts on a large chopping board and cover to keep warm and moist. Proceed to making the Mixing Sauce. Discard any fat from the roasting pan. Place the pan over very low heat and add ½ cup of the reserved Mopping Sauce. Scrape the pan to loosen the caramelized juices and browned bits, stirring quickly and constantly so that none of the flavorful liquid evaporates. Remove from the heat and pour every last drop of this "essence of barbecue" back into the remaining Mopping Sauce. Add the remaining ¼ cup pork simmering liquid. Stir in the ¾ cup barbecue sauce and season with coarse salt. This is the Mixing Sauce, a potent potion that will mellow considerably as the barbecue "ripens." ➤

SUPER BOWL SUPPER

This menu plays by all the Super Bowl rules: 1. Give them food that's easy to recognize; 2. Give them food that's easy to love; 3. Give them food that's easy to eat; and 4. Give them food that's easy to clean up after.

North Carolina Chopped Barbecue
(at left)

**Roasted Potato Wedges
with Salsa de Cilantro à la Presilla**
(page 193)

Mustard Slaw
(page 49)

Black Bean Salad with Chipotle Vinaigrette
(page 46)

■

Arline Rodman's Minnesota Cheesecake
(page 243)

North Carolina Chopped Barbecue

Malaccan Devil's Curry

6. Using your fingers, discard the bones and fat from the pork roasts. Pull the pork into shreds. With a large heavy knife, finely chop the lean pork. Transfer the meat to a large bowl.

7. Add half of the Mixing Sauce to the chopped pork and mix well. Gradually blend in the remaining Mixing Sauce. Let cool to room temperature, then cover tightly and refrigerate for at least 12 hours to let the flavor develop. (The chopped barbecue can be refrigerated for up to 2 days or frozen for up to 1 month.)

8. Let the barbecue return to room temperature. Reheat the barbecue in a 300° oven or in a microwave oven until warmed through. Season with coarse salt and black pepper and put a bottle of hot pepper sauce and a bowl of barbecue sauce on the table to serve with the barbecue.

NOTE: Real North Carolina barbecue is, of course, cooked over an open pit of hickory coals, but this is difficult to manage in your living room. Bottled smoky-flavored barbecue sauce, used sparingly and only as a seasoning, gives the Mixing Sauce an authentic Tarheel tang. Look for one that's got a good balance of heat and smoke and that isn't too sweet.

—Leslie Newman

■

MALACCAN DEVIL'S CURRY

To concentrate the flavor of this Singaporean curry, marinate the pork overnight. You can cut back the heat by using fewer dried red chiles. Serve the dish with steamed green beans mixed with chopped red bell peppers and roasted cashews.

6 Servings

3 tablespoons white wine vinegar

2 tablespoons dark soy sauce

1½ pounds boned and trimmed pork shoulder, cut into ¾-inch cubes

2 tablespoons safflower or canola oil

1 large red or Spanish onion (10
ounces), coarsely chopped
3 medium garlic cloves, minced
8 small dried red chiles, minced
2-inch piece of fresh ginger, peeled and
finely chopped
1½ teaspoons black mustard seeds,
crushed
1½ teaspoons fenugreek powder
1 teaspoon Laos powder (dried
galangal or ka)*
1 teaspoon shrimp paste*
1 teaspoon turmeric
1 fresh lemon grass stalk*—white bulb
and 2 inches of green tops—minced
6 candlenuts (kemiri nuts)* or
macadamia nuts, ground in a food
processor
1¾ cups beef stock or an even mixture
of canned broth and water
½ teaspoon salt
¼ teaspoon freshly ground black
pepper

*Available at Asian markets

1. In a nonreactive bowl, sprinkle the vinegar and soy sauce over the pork. Mix well and set aside to marinate for at least 30 minutes.

2. In a wok, heat the oil until shimmering. Add the onion and garlic and stir-fry over moderately high heat for 2 minutes. Add the chiles, ginger, mustard seeds, fenugreek, Laos powder, shrimp paste and turmeric and stir-fry for 2 minutes. Add the lemon grass and candlenuts.

3. Increase the heat to high and transfer the pork cubes to the wok, reserving the marinade. Stir-fry the meat until thoroughly coated with the spice paste, about 2 minutes.

4. Add the beef stock and reserved pork marinade; season with the salt and black pepper. Cover and simmer until the meat is tender, about 20 minutes. (The recipe can be prepared to this point up to 2 days ahead; refrigerate. Bring to a boil over

moderately high heat before proceeding.) Uncover and simmer, stirring, until the sauce thickens, about 15 minutes.

—Jennifer Brennan

■

PORK AND BLACK BEAN CHILI VERDE

This dish uses the potent habañero chile, whose heat dissipates only slightly with cooking. You can substitute one Scotch bonnet or three serranos for the habañero. Or omit it altogether and use a mild chile.

6 to 8 Servings
1½ cups dried black beans (about 10
ounces), picked over and rinsed
4 medium poblano chiles
4 medium cubanelle chiles (Italian
frying peppers)
3 medium green bell peppers
1 medium habañero chile
1 pound fresh spinach, stemmed
10 medium tomatillos—husked,
rinsed and quartered
5 scallions, coarsely chopped
1 meaty smoked ham hock (about
1 pound)
2 bay leaves
3 tablespoons vegetable oil
2 pounds trimmed boneless pork
shoulder or butt, cut into 1-inch cubes
Salt and freshly ground black pepper
1 medium onion, finely chopped
6 garlic cloves, minced
1 tablespoon sugar
1 tablespoon ground cumin
1 cup finely chopped fresh
coriander leaves (cilantro)
Tortilla chips or corn bread and
sour cream, for serving

1. Place the black beans in a medium saucepan and add 6 cups of water. Bring to a boil over moderately high heat and

boil for 3 minutes. Remove from the heat and let stand for 1 hour.

2. Meanwhile, roast the poblanos, cubanelles, bell peppers and habañero under the broiler as close to the heat as possible or over a gas flame, turning frequently, until blackened all over. Transfer them to a paper bag and let steam for 10 minutes. Peel the chiles and peppers under running water and remove the cores, seeds and ribs. Drain and pat dry. Place them all in a food processor or blender with the spinach, tomatillos and scallions and puree until smooth.

3. Drain the black beans and return them to the saucepan. Add the ham hock, bay leaves and 6 more cups of water. Bring to a boil over moderately high heat. Cover and simmer over low heat until the beans are tender, about 1½ hours. Drain the beans, reserving 1 cup of the liquid; discard the bay leaves. Remove the meat from the ham hock, cut it into ¾-inch pieces and set aside.

4. Heat 2 tablespoons of the oil in a large enameled cast-iron casserole. Season the pork cubes with salt and black pepper. Add some of the meat to the casserole in a single layer and cook over high heat until well browned all over, about 5 minutes. Transfer the cooked pork to a plate and brown the remaining meat in batches.

5. Heat the remaining 1 tablespoon oil in the casserole. Add the onion and garlic and cook over moderate heat, stirring occasionally, until translucent, about 3 minutes.

6. Return the browned pork to the casserole with the chile and spinach puree, sugar, cumin and 1 teaspoon salt. Bring to a boil over moderately high heat. Lower the heat and simmer gently until the meat is very tender, about 2 hours. Stir in the black beans and cubed ham with the reserved cooking liquid. (The chili can be prepared up to 3 days ahead; cover and refrigerate. Rewarm slowly over moderate heat.)

7. Season the chili with the coriander and salt. Spoon the chili into bowls and serve with tortilla chips and sour cream.

—Grace Parisi

■

CHOUCROUTE GARNIE

Choucroute garnie—wine-simmered sauerkraut "garnished" with pork—has a marvelous earthiness.

8 Servings
½ **pound sliced lean smoked bacon, cut crosswise into ½-inch strips**
3 **pounds yellow onions**
8 **large garlic cloves**
8 **cups Chicken Stock (p. 36) or six 10½-ounce cans low-sodium broth**
1 **bottle (750 ml) dry Alsace Gewürztraminer**
2 **teaspoons freshly ground pepper**
1 **teaspoon salt**
8 **pounds sauerkraut, drained and lightly rinsed**
1 **tablespoon vegetable oil (optional)**
1½ **pounds garlic sausage, skinned and sliced ½ inch thick**
1¼ **pounds kielbasa or other smoked sausage, cut into 2-inch pieces**
8 **1-inch-thick smoked pork chops**
8 **good-quality hot dogs Boiled potatoes and Dijon mustard, for serving**

1. Preheat the oven to 300°. In a large, heavy, nonreactive casserole, cook the bacon over moderately high heat until crisp, 5 to 6 minutes. Transfer to paper towels to drain. Pour all but 3 tablespoons of the fat into a bowl and reserve for another use.

2. Add the onions to the casserole, cover and cook over moderately high heat, stirring often, until translucent, 5 to 6 minutes. Uncover and increase the heat to

Choucroute
Garnie

NEW YEAR'S EVE DINNER

Foie gras mousse

Mandarin Beluga caviar

Toast points

🍷 Veuve Clicquot Brut

■

Lobster Salad with Fennel and Orange
(page 57)

■

Choucroute Garnie
(page 124)

Boiled potatoes

🍷 1991 Leon Beyer Alsace Gewürztraminer

■

Salad of Bitter Greens with Fallen Goat Cheese Soufflés
(page 45)

■

Green Apple Sorbet with Calvados
(page 287)

Pistachio Crumbles
(page 262)

■

Espresso

Chocolate truffles

Cognac

sausage and cook over moderately high heat until well browned on both sides, about 5 minutes. Remove and set aside. Repeat with the kielbasa.

5. Raise the oven temperature to 325°. Reheat the sauerkraut over moderately high heat until warmed through. Drain the sauerkraut, reserving the liquid.

6. Divide the sauerkraut between two 9-by-13-by-2-inch glass or ceramic baking dishes. Arrange the garlic sausage, kielbasa and pork chops on top. Pour ⅔ cup of the reserved sauerkraut liquid over the meats in each dish. Cover tightly with foil and bake for 1 hour.

7. Shortly before serving, in a medium nonreactive saucepan, bring the remaining sauerkraut liquid to a simmer over high heat. Add the hot dogs; simmer until warmed through. Arrange the hot dogs on the choucroute and serve with boiled potatoes and plenty of mustard.

—Bob Chambers

■

ROAST LEG OF LAMB WITH GARLIC

Garlicky leg of lamb goes well with a great range of side dishes—pasta or potatoes, peperonata or ratatouille, green or dried beans, to suggest a few.

8 to 10 Servings

1 **7- to 8-pound leg of lamb, well trimmed, at room temperature**
9 **medium garlic cloves—3 thinly sliced and 6 unpeeled and smashed**
1 **large onion, coarsely chopped**
1 **large carrot, cut into ¾-inch dice**
3 **fresh thyme sprigs plus 2 tablespoons fresh thyme leaves**
2 **teaspoons finely grated lemon zest Salt and freshly ground pepper**
2 **tablespoons olive oil**
1 **cup Chicken Stock (p. 36) or canned low-sodium broth**

high. Cook, stirring, until the onions have begun to brown, 7 to 9 minutes longer.

3. Add the garlic and cook for 1 minute. Stir in the Chicken Stock, wine, pepper and salt. Add the sauerkraut and the reserved bacon. Cover and bring to a boil over high heat, stirring occasionally. Cover tightly and bake the sauerkraut in the oven for 2 hours. (The sauerkraut can be prepared ahead to this point and refrigerated for up to 4 days or frozen for up to 2 weeks.)

4. Heat the vegetable oil, if desired, or 1 tablespoon of the reserved bacon fat in a large skillet. Add the slices of garlic

1. Preheat the oven to 350°. Using the tip of a sharp knife, make 1½-inch-deep slits all over the lamb. Press the garlic slices into the slits.

2. Spread the onion, carrot, smashed garlic and thyme sprigs in a large roasting pan. In a small bowl, combine the thyme leaves, lemon zest and 1 teaspoon each of salt and pepper. Stir in the oil. Rub the mixture evenly over the lamb, then place the lamb on top of the vegetables in the roasting pan.

3. Roast the lamb for about 2 hours, or until an instant-read thermometer inserted in the thickest part of the leg registers 150° for medium meat. Transfer the lamb to a carving board, cover with foil and let stand for 15 minutes.

4. Discard the fat from the pan. Set the pan over 2 burners, add the Chicken Stock and bring to a boil over moderately high heat, scraping up any browned bits. Strain the juices into a small saucepan and boil over moderately high heat, skimming occasionally, until reduced by half, about 5 minutes. Season with salt and pepper.

5. Carve the lamb and arrange the slices on a warmed serving platter. Stir any accumulated meat juices into the pan gravy, pour into a sauceboat and serve with the lamb.

—Susan Shapiro Jaslove

■

POPPY SEED-COATED LAMB LOINS WITH CURRIED COUSCOUS AND TAMARIND CHIPOTLE SAUCE

For this recipe—a specialty of Carlos' in Highland Park, Illinois—have your butcher bone the loins from two 5½-pound whole saddles of lamb and then cut them in half crosswise. Ask for the meat scraps and the bones, cut into three-inch lengths, to use for the Lamb Stock.

♟ A full-flavored red wine will nicely balance the lamb and the sweet, smoky, spicy flavors in this dish. A rich, lush 1990 Sterling Merlot from the Napa Valley is a good choice.

6 Servings
Tamarind Sauce:
1 tablespoon vegetable oil
1 medium carrot, finely chopped
1 medium onion, finely chopped
1 medium celery rib, finely chopped
8 large garlic cloves, coarsely chopped
2 cups dry red wine
1 teaspoon cracked black pepper
1 teaspoon fresh thyme
1 bay leaf
1 quart Lamb Stock (recipe follows)
⅓ cup tamarind pulp*
⅔ cup plus ½ cup boiling water
1 dried chipotle chile*
1 tablespoon honey
Salt and freshly ground black pepper

Couscous:
2 tablespoons olive oil
4 large garlic cloves, minced
2 large shallots, minced
1 tablespoon curry powder
½ cup dry white wine
1 cup Lamb Stock (recipe follows)
¾ cup couscous
Salt and freshly ground black pepper

1 stick (8 tablespoons) unsalted butter
4 12-ounce boneless lamb loins (see headnote)
Salt and freshly ground black pepper
½ cup poppy seeds
1 tablespoon finely chopped fresh flat-leaf parsley

*Available at specialty food stores ➤

127

1. Make the tamarind sauce: In a large nonreactive saucepan, heat the vegetable oil. Add the carrot, onion, celery and garlic and cook over moderately high heat, stirring often, until lightly browned, about 8 minutes. Add the red wine and cook over high heat until reduced to 1 tablespoon, about 10 minutes. Stir in the cracked black pepper, thyme and bay leaf. Pour in the Lamb Stock and boil until reduced to 1½ cups, about 25 minutes. Strain into a small saucepan and set aside.

2. Meanwhile, in a medium bowl, cover the tamarind pulp with ⅔ cup of the boiling water and set aside to dissolve for about 10 minutes. Press through a coarse strainer into the saucepan with the lamb sauce. In another bowl, cover the chipotle with the remaining ½ cup boiling water and set aside to soften for about 10 minutes. Remove the stem and seeds and finely dice the chipotle; add to the sauce.

3. Bring the tamarind sauce to a simmer, whisking, over moderately high heat. Whisk in the honey and season with salt and pepper. Remove from the heat. (The recipe can be prepared to this point up to 2 days ahead; cover and refrigerate.)

4. Make the couscous: Preheat the oven to 350°. Heat the olive oil in a small skillet. Add the garlic and shallots and cook over moderately low heat until translucent, about 4 minutes. Add the curry powder and cook, stirring, for 1 minute. Add the wine, increase the heat to high and boil until reduced completely, about 4 minutes. Stir in the Lamb Stock and bring to a boil.

5. Place the couscous in a heatproof bowl and pour the stock on top. Cover and let stand until the stock is absorbed and the couscous is tender, about 8 minutes. Uncover, fluff with a fork and season with salt and pepper. Pack the couscous into six ½-cup ramekins and keep hot in the oven.

6. In a small saucepan, melt the butter over low heat. Remove from the heat and, using a small ladle, skim the foam off the surface. Pour the clear butter into a large skillet, stopping when you reach the milk solids at the bottom; discard the milk solids.

7. Season the lamb loins with salt and pepper. Spread the poppy seeds on a large plate and press the meat onto the seeds to coat thinly.

8. Heat the clarified butter in the skillet until smoking. Add 2 of the loins and cook over high heat, turning once, until browned on the outside and medium-rare, 3 to 4 minutes per side. Transfer to a warm platter and cover loosely with foil. Repeat with the remaining lamb. Let the lamb rest for about 5 minutes, then cut each loin into 9 slices.

9. To serve, rewarm the tamarind sauce over low heat. Spoon the sauce onto 6 warmed plates. Sharply tap each ramekin and unmold the couscous onto each plate. Arrange 6 slices of lamb on the sauce. Sprinkle the parsley over the couscous and serve.

Lamb Stock
Makes About 6 Cups

- 2½ **pounds lamb bones, cut into 3-inch pieces**
- 2 **pounds lamb meat scraps**
- 1 **large carrot, cut into 1-inch pieces**
- 1 **medium onion, coarsely chopped**
- 1 **medium celery rib, cut into 1-inch pieces**
- 8 **garlic cloves, peeled**
- 2 **tablespoons whole black peppercorns**
- 1 **fresh thyme sprig**
- 1 **bay leaf**

1. Preheat the oven to 500°. In a roasting pan, brown the lamb bones and scraps in the oven for about 30 minutes. Add the carrot, onion, celery and garlic and roast for about 10 minutes, until the vegetables brown. Transfer the browned bones and vegetables to a stockpot. Set the roasting pan over 2 burners on high heat. When

sizzling, add 1 cup of water and scrape the bottom of the pan with a wooden spoon to loosen the browned bits.

2. Add the contents of the roasting pan to the stockpot with the peppercorns, thyme sprig and bay leaf. Cover with 13 cups of water and bring to a boil, then simmer over low heat, skimming occasionally, for about 5 hours. Strain and let cool, then refrigerate. Skim the fat before using. (The stock can be refrigerated for up to 3 days or frozen for up to 1 month.)

—Don Yamauchi

■

POT-ROASTED LAMB WITH JUNIPER BERRIES

Of all Italian lamb recipes, this best suits the lamb sold in American markets. It is made from older, grass-fed animals whose firm meat responds better to this kind of cooking than the delicate flesh of the very young, milk-fed lambs Italian butchers usually handle. This recipe is from *Essentials of Classic Italian Cooking* (Knopf).

4 Servings

2½ to 3 pounds lamb shoulder with some bone, cut into 3-inch pieces
1 cup dry white wine
1 tablespoon chopped carrot
2 tablespoons chopped onion
1 tablespoon chopped celery
2 garlic cloves, smashed
1 fresh rosemary sprig
1½ teaspoons lightly crushed juniper berries
Salt and freshly ground pepper

1. Put all the ingredients in a medium enameled cast-iron casserole. Cover and cook over moderately low heat for 2 hours, turning the meat every 30 minutes.
2. Set the lid slightly ajar and increase the heat to moderate. Cook for 1½ hours longer, turning the lamb occasionally. The meat should feel very tender when prodded with a fork. If there is still quite a bit of liquid in the casserole, uncover, raise the heat and reduce it to a less runny consistency. Season the meat with salt.

3. Tip the casserole and spoon off the fat. Transfer the meat and all its juices to a warmed serving platter or individual plates and serve at once.

—Marcella Hazan

■

LAMB, SPINACH AND POTATO CURRY WITH BANANA RAITA

The banana raita given here is a simple, cooling condiment. Serve this Indian dish with basmati rice.

6 Servings

Banana raita:
2 large ripe but firm bananas, sliced ¼ inch thick
1 cup good-quality whole milk yogurt
Generous pinch of ground cardamom

Curry:
3 pounds boneless trimmed lamb shoulder, cut into 1-inch cubes
Salt and freshly ground black pepper
¼ cup vegetable oil
2 large onions, finely chopped
4 medium garlic cloves, minced
4 serrano chiles, seeded and minced
1½ tablespoons minced fresh ginger
1½ tablespoons garam masala*
1 tablespoon ground coriander
1½ teaspoons turmeric
1 teaspoon ground cumin
¼ teaspoon ground cloves
3 large tomatoes—peeled, seeded and chopped
2 cups Chicken Stock (p. 36) or canned broth ➤

LAMB TIPS

• The best cut of lamb to use for pot roasting is the shoulder, which you must have the butcher cut into cubes. Do not use the leg or the chops; these cuts tend to dry out when cooked this way.
• If some of the pieces from the shoulder have a bone, don't worry. When the meat is done, it is so tender that it comes away from the bone easily.
• Before serving, tip the pot and spoon off any liquefied fat.
• If you are making Pot-Roasted Lamb with Juniper Berries, at left, a day ahead, reduce the amount of juniper so that its aroma won't become too strong.

—Marcella Hazan

Lamb, Spinach and Potato Curry with Banana Raita

3 medium baking potatoes, peeled, cut into 1-inch cubes and reserved in cold water
1 tablespoon brown sugar
1½ pounds spinach, stems discarded, leaves coarsely chopped

*Available at Indian markets and some supermarkets

1. Make the banana raita: Combine all the ingredients in a medium bowl. Refrigerate while you make the curry.

2. Make the curry: Season the lamb with salt and black pepper. In a large Dutch oven or nonreactive flameproof casserole, heat the oil over moderately high heat. Working in batches, add a single layer of lamb cubes without crowding and brown on all sides, about 10 minutes. Transfer to a plate. Repeat with the remaining lamb cubes.

3. Add the onions to the casserole and cook over moderately high heat until golden brown, about 5 minutes. Add the garlic, serrano chiles and ginger and cook until fragrant, about 2 minutes. Add the *garam masala*, coriander, turmeric, cumin and cloves and cook, stirring constantly, for 1 minute.

4. Return the lamb to the casserole and stir, coating the meat with the spice mixture and scraping the bottom of the pan to loosen any browned bits. Add the tomatoes, Chicken Stock and 3½ cups of water and bring to a boil over high heat. Lower the heat to moderate, cover partially and simmer for 1 hour.

5. Drain the potatoes, pat dry and add to the casserole. Cook until the sauce is thickened slightly, about 10 minutes. Stir in the brown sugar and spinach and cook until the spinach is wilted and the potatoes are tender, about 3 minutes longer. Season with salt and black pepper. Serve the lamb curry hot; pass the banana raita separately.

—Ilana Sharlin Stone

CHILE PEPPERS

The following chiles can be found in supermarkets, specialty food shops and Latin American markets. Dried chiles are also available by mail through such sources as Los Chileros de Nuevo Mexico (505-471-6967) and Mo Hotta-Mo Betta (800-462-3220).

Dried chiles
- **CHIPOTLE:** Fiery hot. These are dried, smoked jalapeños with a smoky, earthy flavor.
- **GUAJILLO:** Moderately hot. Smooth, brownish red skin and tangy, citrus, apricot taste.
- **ANCHO:** Mild to moderately hot. These are dried poblanos with wrinkled, dark brownish red skin and a deep, earthy flavor.
- **PASILLA (or NEGRO):** Mild to moderately hot. Off-black skin with a smoky scent and a taste like unsweetened fruit leather.
- **NEW MEXICO RED:** Mild to moderately hot. Smooth, brick-red skin and a taste of tea and dried apricots.

Fresh chiles
- **HABANERO:** Explosively hot. Green when young, orange and red when ripe, with a fresh floral flavor.
- **JALAPENO:** Moderate to very hot. Green or sometimes red with a fruity, fresh taste; widely available.
- **POBLANO:** Mild to moderately hot. A rich, earthy flavor and slightly bitter aftertaste.
- **CUBANELLE (Italian Frying Pepper):** Sweet. Yellowish green, sometimes orange skin. More flavorful than bell peppers.
- **BELL PEPPERS:** Sweet. Green, red, yellow, orange, purple or even brown. All are sweet, though the green have a tangy edge.

■

LAMB AND WHITE BEAN CHILI

Dried New Mexico chiles lend a sweet and subtle flavor to this meaty chili. Use one chipotle chile for mild to moderate spiciness, two if you like it hot.

❡ The meaty, smoky flavors here call for a hearty red. A California Zinfandel, such as 1990 De Loach or 1991 Ridge "Sonoma," would be a satisfying choice, as would a flavorsome ale, such as Bass or Samuel Smith. ➤

6 Servings

- 1 **cup dried white beans (about ½ pound), such as Great Northern or navy, picked over and rinsed**
- 4 **ounces smoked slab bacon**
- 4 **large dried New Mexico red chiles**
- 1 **large chipotle chile**
- 3 **tablespoons olive oil**
- 1½ **pounds trimmed boneless lamb shoulder, cut into 1-inch cubes Salt and freshly ground black pepper**
- 1 **medium onion, finely chopped**
- 3 **garlic cloves, minced**
- 1½ **tablespoons ground cumin**
- 2 **teaspoons coarsely chopped fresh thyme or 1 teaspoon dried**
- 1 **teaspoon coarsely chopped fresh oregano or ½ teaspoon dried**
- 1 **28-ounce can crushed tomatoes**
- 1 **6-ounce can tomato paste**
- 2 **tablespoons sugar**
- 3 **bay leaves Steamed white rice, for serving**

1. Place the white beans and smoked bacon in a medium saucepan and add 6 cups of water. Bring to a boil over moderately high heat and boil for 3 minutes. Remove the saucepan from the heat and let stand for 1 hour.

2. In a medium bowl, soak the New Mexico and chipotle chiles in 3 cups of hot water until softened, about 20 minutes. Pour off the soaking liquid, reserving 1 cup. Stem and seed the chiles and transfer them to a food processor or blender with the reserved soaking liquid. Puree until smooth. Pass the puree through a fine strainer into a small bowl.

3. Heat the olive oil in a large enameled cast-iron casserole. Season the lamb cubes with salt and black pepper. Add some of the meat to the casserole in a single layer and cook over high heat until the lamb is well browned all over, about 5 minutes. Transfer the cooked lamb cubes to a large

plate and brown the remaining meat in batches.

4. Add the onion and garlic to the casserole and cook over moderate heat, stirring occasionally, until translucent, about 3 minutes. Add the cumin, thyme and oregano and cook, stirring, until fragrant, about 2 minutes.

5. Return the lamb to the casserole. Add the pureed chiles, crushed tomatoes, tomato paste, sugar, bay leaves and ¾ cup of water. Bring to a boil over moderately high heat. Lower the heat, cover partially and simmer gently until the meat is very tender, about 1½ hours. Discard the bay leaves.

6. Meanwhile, drain the beans and bacon. Return them to the pan, add 6 more cups of water and bring to a boil over moderately high heat. Lower the heat, cover partially and simmer until the beans are tender, about 1 hour; drain. Coarsely chop the bacon and add it to the chili with the beans. (The chili can be prepared up to 3 days ahead; cover and refrigerate. Rewarm slowly over moderate heat.)

7. Season the chili with salt. Spoon into bowls and serve with white rice.

—Grace Parisi

Chapter 7 ▪ PASTA & GRAINS

135   Capellini with Fresh Tomatoes, Basil and Garlic Croutons

135   Fettuccine with Radicchio and Sun-Dried Tomatoes

136   Wild Mushroom Linguine

137   Perciatelli with Zucchini and Lemon

138   Penne with Cauliflower, Onions and Olive Oil

139   Spaghetti with Fava Beans

139   Pasta Puttanesca

141   Pasta and Potatoes

142   Tuscan Ricotta and Spinach Ravioli with Sage

144   Spaghetti with Fresh Tuna and Roasted Red Peppers

145   Seafood Cannelloni

146   Veal and Linguine alla Pizzaiola

147   Penne with Ragù of Ground Pork and Beef

147   Fettuccine with Sausage and Green Olives

149   Farfalle with Spicy Sausage and Smoked Mozzarella

150   Orecchiette with Porcini and Pancetta

151   Pappardelle with Pork, Porcini and Herbs

153   "Guitar" Maccheroni with Lamb Ragù

154   Fried Rice with Peas and Sun-Dried Tomatoes

154   Risotto with Zucchini Blossoms and Sage

155   Cheese Grits Soufflé over Turnip Greens

156   Creamy Polenta with Butter and Cheese

Capellini with Fresh Tomatoes, Basil and Garlic Croutons

CAPELLINI WITH FRESH TOMATOES, BASIL AND GARLIC CROUTONS

Spaghettini or spaghetti can take the place of the thinner capellini used here.

4 Servings

- 4 tablespoons unsalted butter, melted
- 3 large garlic cloves, minced
- 4 cups cubed Italian bread (½-inch pieces)
  Coarse (kosher) salt
- 4 large tomatoes, coarsely chopped
- ½ serrano or jalapeño pepper, minced (optional)
- 1 pound capellini
- ¼ cup extra-virgin olive oil
  Freshly ground black pepper
- 2 cups coarsely chopped fresh basil

1. Preheat the oven to 400°. In a large covered pot, bring 4 quarts of water to a boil over high heat.

2. Meanwhile, in a small bowl, combine the butter and two-thirds of the garlic. Place the bread cubes on a large rimmed baking sheet and toss them with the garlic butter. Bake for about 10 minutes or until the croutons are golden. Season with salt.

3. In a large serving bowl, toss the chopped tomatoes with the serrano pepper and the remaining garlic.

4. Add 2 tablespoons salt to the boiling pasta water. When it returns to a boil, add the capellini and cook, stirring occasionally, until al dente, about 3 minutes. Drain, allowing enough water to remain to keep the pasta moist.

5. Add the pasta to the tomatoes, drizzle with the olive oil and toss well. Season with salt and pepper. Sprinkle the basil and half of the croutons over the pasta and serve, passing the remaining croutons at the table.

—Marcia Kiesel

■

FETTUCCINE WITH RADICCHIO AND SUN-DRIED TOMATOES

Cream mellows the bitter radicchio and sharp sun-dried tomatoes into a harmonious sauce.

4 to 6 Servings

- 2 cups heavy cream
- 6 large garlic cloves, finely chopped
  Coarse (kosher) salt
- ½ teaspoon freshly ground pepper
- 2 large heads of radicchio (1 pound), thinly sliced crosswise
- 1 pound fettuccine
- 5 ounces oil-packed, sun-dried tomatoes, drained and coarsely chopped (⅔ cup)
- 1 cup freshly grated Parmesan cheese (about 4 ounces)

1. In a large covered pot, bring 4 quarts of water to a boil over high heat.

2. Meanwhile, in a large skillet, bring the cream and chopped garlic cloves to a simmer over moderate heat. Season with salt and the pepper, reduce the heat to moderately low and simmer for 2 minutes. Add all but a small handful of radicchio to the garlic cream and cook, stirring occasionally, until the radicchio is wilted and the cream is slightly thickened, 8 to 10 minutes.

3. Add 2 tablespoons salt to the boiling pasta water. When it returns to a boil, add the fettuccine and cook, stirring occasionally, until al dente, about 7 minutes. Drain well and return the pasta to the pot. ➤

135

4. Add the radicchio mixture and toss. Add the sun-dried tomatoes and Parmesan and toss again. Transfer the pasta to a large warmed bowl and sprinkle with the reserved radicchio.

—Diana Sturgis

∎

WILD MUSHROOM LINGUINE

Fresh oyster and shiitake mushrooms, browned in a nonstick skillet, and reconstituted dried porcini are tossed with linguine to produce a dish with an earthy mushroom flavor. Blanched carrot sticks are added for color and sweetness, and yogurt cheese (made by draining plain nonfat yogurt) is stirred in at the end to infuse the pasta with a creamy tang. Because there's so little fat in this dish, you can top the pasta with a generous sprinkling of Parmesan. Start this recipe one day ahead to allow the yogurt plenty of time to drain.

4 Servings

- 1 **cup plain nonfat yogurt**
- ½ **cup dried porcini mushrooms (½ ounce)**
- 1 **tablespoon olive oil**
- 1 **pound oyster mushrooms, stems trimmed and tops quartered**
  Salt and freshly ground pepper
- 1 **pound fresh shiitake mushrooms, stems discarded and caps quartered**
- 1 **large carrot, cut into 2-by-¼-inch matchsticks**
- ¾ **pound dried linguine**
- 5 **medium shallots, thinly sliced**
- 3 **large garlic cloves, minced**
- ½ **cup dry white wine**
- 1½ **teaspoons finely chopped fresh thyme**
- ¼ **cup finely chopped fresh flat-leaf parsley or chervil**
- ¼ **cup freshly grated Parmesan cheese**

1. Spoon the yogurt into a stainless steel strainer set over a medium bowl. Cover and let the yogurt drain overnight in the refrigerator.

2. Discard the accumulated liquid from the yogurt and wipe out the bowl. Transfer the yogurt cheese to the bowl, stir until smooth and allow to come to room temperature.

3. In a small bowl, cover the dried porcinis with 1 cup of hot water. Let stand until softened, about 20 minutes.

4. Bring a large pot of salted water to a boil. In a large nonreactive skillet, heat 1 teaspoon of the oil until it begins to smoke. Add the oyster mushrooms in a single layer, cover and cook over moderately high heat for 2 minutes. Stir, cover and continue cooking until the mushrooms are browned, about 2 minutes longer. Season

Wild Mushroom Linguine

with salt and pepper and transfer to a plate. Repeat with 1 more teaspoon of the oil and the shiitake mushrooms; add them to the oyster mushrooms.

5. Remove the porcinis from the soaking liquid. Rinse, coarsely chop and add them to the browned mushrooms; reserve the soaking liquid.

6. Put the carrot sticks in a strainer. Place the strainer in the pot of boiling water and cook until the carrots are just tender, about 3 minutes. Transfer the carrots to paper towels to drain.

7. Cook the linguine in the boiling water, stirring occasionally, until al dente, about 8 minutes. Drain the linguine, allowing enough water to remain to keep the pasta moist. Return it to the pot.

8. While the pasta cooks, heat the remaining 1 teaspoon oil in the skillet. Add the shallots, cover and cook over low heat, stirring occasionally, until translucent, about 3 minutes. Add the garlic and cook, stirring, for 1 minute. Raise the heat to high, add the wine and boil for 2 minutes. Pour in the reserved mushroom soaking liquid, stopping when you reach the grit at the bottom. Add the carrot sticks and thyme and cook until the carrots are heated through, 1 to 2 minutes.

9. Add the carrot mixture to the linguine along with the mushrooms and toss to combine. Stir in the yogurt cheese and parsley and season with salt and pepper. Divide the pasta among 4 plates and sprinkle each serving with 1 tablespoon of Parmesan.

—Marcia Kiesel

■

PERCIATELLI WITH ZUCCHINI AND LEMON

You can substitute any maccheroni-type pasta for the long, tubular perciatelli called for here.

TIPS FOR QUICK PASTAS

The following suggestions will help you get pasta on the table faster. Remember, organization is key.

• Before you start cooking, select ingredients that do not require much preparation, such as canned tomatoes and anchovies, prosciutto and ground beef. To get a good head start, buy freshly grated Parmesan cheese.

• Put the pasta water on to boil before you begin making the sauce, and cover the pot so the water boils more quickly. Then assemble and prepare your ingredients.

• Cook ingredients that need to be blanched (tough vegetables like broccoli and carrots) in the boiling pasta water. Remove them with a slotted spoon before you add the pasta. This method is efficient and adds flavor and nutrients to the water.

• To peel garlic quickly, smash the cloves with the flat side of a heavy knife, then slip off the skins. If you have a sturdy garlic press, push the cloves through without peeling them first. Cut shallots and onions in half lengthwise, then trim the ends and peel off the skins.

• Use a mini food processor to chop fresh herbs and chiles.

4 to 6 Servings

½ cup dry white wine
¼ teaspoon saffron threads
2 tablespoons olive oil
4 medium zucchini, cut into 2-by-½-inch sticks
   Coarse (kosher) salt and freshly ground pepper
1 tablespoon unsalted butter
4 large shallots, thinly sliced
2 garlic cloves, minced
1 cup Chicken Stock (p. 36) or canned low-sodium broth
1 pound perciatelli
½ cup heavy cream
2 teaspoons finely grated lemon zest
¼ cup freshly grated Parmesan cheese

1. In a large covered pot, bring 4 quarts of water to a boil over high heat.

2. Meanwhile, in a small nonreactive saucepan, warm the wine over moderate heat. Remove from the heat, crumble in the saffron and set aside. ➤

Penne with Cauliflower, Onions and Olive Oil

3. In a large skillet, heat the olive oil until smoking. Add half of the zucchini sticks in a single layer and cook over high heat until browned on the bottom, about 2 minutes. Transfer the zucchini to a plate. Repeat with the remaining zucchini, then season the sticks with salt and pepper. Cover with foil and keep warm.

4. Melt the butter in the skillet. Add the shallots, cover and cook over moderately low heat, stirring once, until softened and lightly browned, about 4 minutes. Add the garlic and cook, stirring, until fragrant, about 1 minute. Raise the heat to high, add the Chicken Stock and the saffron-infused wine and boil until reduced by half, about 4 minutes.

5. Add 2 tablespoons salt to the boiling pasta water. When the water returns to a boil, add the perciatelli and cook, stirring occasionally, until the pasta is al dente, about 8 minutes.

6. Add the cream to the sauce and boil over high heat until reduced to 1 cup, about 5 minutes. Season with salt and pepper and stir in the lemon zest.

7. Drain the pasta well and return it to the pot. Add the cream sauce and the Parmesan cheese and toss well. Transfer the pasta to a large warmed platter. Gently tuck in half of the fried zucchini and scatter the rest on top.

—Marcia Kiesel

PENNE WITH CAULIFLOWER, ONIONS AND OLIVE OIL

If you serve this dish as a first course, follow it with a light main course and possibly fruit and cheese to end the meal.

🍷 Try Salice Salentino, a blend of two native red Apulian grapes: Negro-amaro, which gives it firmness, and Malvasia Nera, which endows it with charm and aroma.

6 Servings
1 **large head of cauliflower (2½ to 3 pounds), trimmed and cut into 1-inch florets**
  Salt
½ **cup olive oil**
2 **medium onions, sliced lengthwise ⅓ inch thick**
1 **pound penne rigate or other ridged tubular pasta**
1 **tablespoon chopped fresh parsley**
  Pinch of crushed red pepper
  Freshly ground black pepper

1. In a large covered pot, bring 6 quarts of cold water to a boil. Add the cauliflower and 2 tablespoons of salt and boil until almost tender, 4 to 5 minutes. Using a slotted spoon, transfer the cauliflower to a bowl. Do not discard the water.

2. In a heavy, medium, nonreactive saucepan, warm the oil over moderately low heat. Add the onions and cook, stirring occasionally, until golden brown, 20 to 30 minutes.

3. When the onions are almost done, return the cauliflower water to a boil. Add the penne and cook until almost al dente, about 7 minutes. Add the cauliflower and cook until the penne is al dente and the cauliflower is heated through,

about 1 minute longer. Set aside 1 cup of the pasta cooking water, then drain. Transfer the cauliflower, pasta and reserved pasta water to a warmed bowl.

4. Quickly reheat the oil and onions and add them to the penne. Season with the parsley, crushed red pepper, salt and black pepper. Serve at once.

—Anna Amendolara Nurse

■

SPAGHETTI WITH FAVA BEANS

Calabria, where this dish hails from, is still a poor region of Italy. The people use vegetables that are inexpensive there, such as fava beans, onions, bell peppers, tomatoes and wild mushrooms. The taste and texture of fresh fava beans are worth the effort of peeling them. If you can't find them, substitute frozen lima beans.

❦ Try this dish with a Savuto from Calabria, an appealing, brightly colored red wine with a spicy fragrance, or substitute the youngest available Chianti.

4 Servings
3 pounds fresh fava beans, shelled, or one 10-ounce package of frozen large lima beans, thawed
1 large ripe tomato, coarsely chopped
1 small onion, finely chopped
½ cup extra-virgin olive oil
Salt
1 pound spaghetti

1. In a large saucepan of boiling salted water, blanch the shelled fava beans for 2 minutes. Drain and let cool slightly. Peel off the tough skins.

2. In a large covered pot, bring 4 quarts of cold water to a boil for the pasta. Meanwhile, in a nonreactive skillet large enough to hold the cooked pasta, spread

the fava beans in a single layer. Add the tomato, onion and ¼ cup of the oil; season with salt. Cover and cook over low heat until the vegetables are tender, about 10 minutes. (If using frozen lima beans, add them to the skillet after the tomato and onion have cooked for 5 minutes.)

3. Meanwhile, salt the boiling pasta water, add the spaghetti and cook until almost al dente, about 8 minutes. Drain and add to the skillet with the vegetables; toss well. Cook over moderate heat until the spaghetti is nicely al dente, about 2 minutes. Transfer the pasta to a deep serving dish, stir in the remaining ¼ cup oil and serve at once.

—Lorenza de' Medici

■

PASTA PUTTANESCA

The fame of *puttanesca* (the prostitute's pasta sauce) is widespread. A quick, down-to-earth, hearty sauce that originated in Naples, it is one of the few completely authentic southern Italian dishes to have become well known in Rome and indeed all over Italy.

❦ If, when in Rome, you eat as the Romans do, the soft, peachy, easygoing quality of Frascati is a congenial white wine for dishes like this one.

6 to 8 Servings
½ cup olive oil
3 garlic cloves, finely chopped
½ teaspoon crushed red pepper
1½ pounds ripe fresh tomatoes— peeled, seeded and chopped
¾ cup black Gaeta olives (about 5 ounces), pitted
¼ cup drained capers, rinsed
3 salt-packed anchovies, rinsed and patted dry, or 6 oil-packed anchovy fillets, drained ➤

Pasta and Potatoes

¼ cup finely chopped fresh
   flat-leaf parsley, plus more for
   garnish
1 teaspoon dried leaf oregano,
   crushed
   Salt
1⅓ pounds vermicelli or spaghetti
   Freshly ground black pepper

1. In a large covered pot, bring 6 quarts of cold water to a boil for the pasta. Meanwhile, in a nonreactive skillet large enough to hold the cooked pasta, warm the oil over moderate heat. Add the garlic and cook until it is browned, about 5 minutes. Stir in the crushed red pepper, then add the tomatoes, olives and capers and cook over moderately high heat for 10 minutes.

2. Finely chop the anchovies and add them to the skillet. Stir in the parsley and oregano and cook for 2 minutes. Season with salt.

3. Salt the boiling pasta water, add the vermicelli and cook until al dente. Drain and toss with the sauce. Garnish with chopped parsley if desired. Serve at once and pass the pepper mill.

—Jo Bettoja

■

PASTA
AND
POTATOES

Pasta e patate is enjoyed in Naples, as well as in other parts of Campania and throughout southern Italy.

❡ The local wines in Campania by Mastroberardino are good choices. Greco di Tufo, produced in the Avellino district and one of Italy's tastiest, most mouth-filling white wines, will stand up to this hearty dish. Two light reds—Avellanio and Lacryma Christi del Vesuvio—will also pair well.

6 Servings

2 ounces pancetta, finely chopped
2 tablespoons olive oil
1 medium onion, finely chopped
1 medium carrot, finely chopped
1 tender celery rib, finely chopped
¼ cup chopped fresh flat-leaf parsley
1 pound all-purpose potatoes,
   peeled and cut into small dice
1 garlic clove, finely chopped
2 cups Chicken Stock (p. 36)
2 cups canned Italian peeled
   tomatoes, coarsely chopped,
   and their liquid
   Salt and freshly ground pepper
1 pound tubetti or ditalini
½ cup freshly grated Pecorino Romano
   or Parmigiano-Reggiano cheese

1. In a large, heavy, nonreactive saucepan, cook the pancetta in the olive oil over moderate heat until lightly browned, about 8 minutes. Add the onion, carrot, celery and parsley and cook, stirring often, until the vegetables are lightly browned, about 8 minutes.

2. In a large covered pot, bring 4 quarts of cold water to a boil for the pasta. Meanwhile, add the potatoes and garlic to the saucepan and cook over moderate heat, stirring, for 2 minutes. Add the Chicken Stock, lower the heat and simmer for 15 minutes.

3. Add the tomatoes and their liquid to the saucepan. Season with salt and pepper and cook until the potatoes are very tender, about 15 minutes.

4. Meanwhile, salt the boiling pasta water. Add the *tubetti* and cook until al dente, about 7 minutes. Set aside 1 cup of the pasta cooking water, then drain the pasta and stir it into the sauce. If the pasta seems dry, add the pasta water as needed. Cook, stirring, until the pasta is coated with sauce, about 2 minutes. Transfer the pasta to a warm bowl and stir in the cheese.

—Michele Scicolone

TUSCAN RICOTTA AND SPINACH RAVIOLI WITH SAGE

This homemade ravioli dough produces gossamer wrappers for the rich filling. Ricotta cheese is popular in Tuscany, and spinach is a native vegetable. The mixture, along with sage, frequently used in Tuscan cooking, makes for a striking combination.

⊻ The Tuscan town of San Gimignano produces Vernaccia di San Gimignano, a rich and sometimes spicy white that is a match for this herbaceous dish.

6 Servings

- 2¼ **pounds fresh spinach, stems discarded**
- ¾ **cup fresh ricotta cheese**
- 2 **large eggs**
- ½ **cup freshly grated Parmesan cheese (about 2 ounces)**
- ⅛ **teaspoon cinnamon**
- ⅛ **teaspoon freshly grated nutmeg**
- ⅛ **teaspoon ground white pepper**
  Salt
  Egg Pasta (recipe follows)
- 1 **stick (8 tablespoons) unsalted butter**
- 20 **large fresh sage leaves**
  Freshly ground black pepper
  Freshly grated Parmesan cheese

1. Wash the spinach leaves and transfer them to a large saucepan with some water still clinging. Cover and cook over moderate heat, stirring once, until wilted, about 3 minutes. Let cool slightly. Using your hands, squeeze as much water from the spinach as possible and finely chop. Transfer to a large bowl. Stir in the ricotta, eggs, Parmesan, cinnamon, nutmeg, white pepper and a pinch of salt. Set the filling aside.

2. Turn the Egg Pasta dough out onto a lightly floured surface and knead until smooth and slightly elastic, about 5 minutes. Cover with a towel and let rest for 5 minutes. Cut the dough in half. Keep 1 piece covered while you work with the other. Using a pasta machine, roll the dough through successively narrower settings until you reach the thinnest setting. (If the pasta sheet is too long to handle comfortably, cut it in half and roll the 2 pieces of dough separately.) Lay the sheet of dough flat on a work surface and cover with a towel. Repeat the process with the remaining piece(s) of dough.

3. In a large covered pot, bring 4 quarts of cold water to a boil for the pasta. Meanwhile, place 1 of the pasta sheets on a lightly floured surface. Spoon or pipe 1-teaspoon mounds of filling in 2 rows on the pasta sheet, spacing the mounds about 1¼ inches from the edges and each other. Drape the second pasta sheet on top. With your fingers, press down around the mounds to seal the 2 sheets, and to create little square shapes. Using a pizza wheel or a sharp knife, cut the ravioli into squares.

4. Add 2 tablespoons of salt to the boiling pasta water. Working in 4 or 5 batches, carefully slide the ravioli off a spatula or a large spoon into the water. Cook until the ravioli float to the surface and are al dente, about 2 minutes. Using a slotted spoon, transfer the ravioli to a colander to drain.

5. While the ravioli cook, melt the butter in a large skillet over low heat. Add the sage leaves and cook for 2 minutes. Carefully add the cooked ravioli to the skillet. Toss gently. Season with salt and black pepper. Transfer to a warmed platter, sprinkle with Parmesan and serve at once.

Egg Pasta
Makes 1¼ Pounds

- **About 3 cups all-purpose flour**
- ½ **teaspoon salt**
- 4 **large eggs** ➤

Tuscan Ricotta and Spinach Ravioli with Sage

By hand: Mound the flour on a work surface and make a well in the center of the mound. Sprinkle the salt over the flour. Crack the eggs into the well. Beat the eggs with a fork or with your fingers; then begin incorporating the flour until the dough can be formed into a ball (you may not need all of the flour). Using your hands, knead the dough for at least 15 minutes, sprinkling it with a little more flour when it feels sticky. Form the dough into a ball, cover with a bowl and let rest for 15 minutes.

In a food processor: Mix the eggs for a few seconds. Gradually add the flour, stopping as soon as a ball forms on the blades (you may not need all of the flour). Transfer the dough to a work surface and knead for 5 minutes. Form the dough into a ball, cover with a bowl and let rest for 15 minutes.

—Pino Luongo

**Seafood
Cannelloni**

SPAGHETTI WITH FRESH TUNA AND ROASTED RED PEPPERS

This recipe has been adapted from *The Classic Pasta Cookbook,* by Giuliano Hazan (Dorling Kindersley).

4 to 6 Servings

 2 **red bell peppers**
 1 **small yellow onion, thinly sliced**
 ⅓ **cup extra-virgin olive oil**
    Salt
 1 **pound spaghetti**
 1 **teaspoon minced garlic**
 ½ **pound fresh tuna, cut into ½-inch chunks**
 ¼ **cup dry white wine**
 1 **tablespoon finely chopped flat-leaf parsley**
 2 **tablespoons drained capers**
    Freshly ground black pepper

1. Roast the red peppers over a gas flame or under the broiler, turning until the skins are charred all over. Place the peppers in a bowl, cover tightly with plastic wrap and set aside for 20 minutes. Halve the peppers and remove the cores. Scrape off the skins and the seeds. Cut the peppers into 1½-by-¼-inch strips.

2. Bring 4 quarts of water to a boil in a large pot. Meanwhile, in a large nonreactive skillet, cook the onion in the olive oil over moderately low heat until soft and golden, about 3 minutes.

3. Add 1 tablespoon salt to the boiling water. Drop in the spaghetti and stir until all the strands are submerged. Bring the water back to a boil and cook the spaghetti until al dente.

4. While the spaghetti cooks, add the garlic to the onion in the skillet and cook over moderately high heat for 1 minute. Add the tuna and cook, stirring often,

until it just loses its raw color, 1 to 2 minutes. Add the roasted peppers and stir for 30 seconds. Add the wine and simmer for about 1 minute, then stir in the parsley and capers. Season with salt and pepper and remove from the heat.

5. As soon as the spaghetti is cooked, drain it well and return it to the pot. Stir in the tuna mixture. Transfer to a bowl or platter and serve at once.

—Marcella Hazan

■

SEAFOOD CANNELLONI

You can make this creamy pasta dish ahead of time and freeze it. If you're serving it right away, skip steps nine and ten. Sprinkle the parsley over the pasta and bake in a 350° oven for about 20 minutes, until hot and bubbling and golden on top.

8 Servings

Filling:
- ½ ounce dried porcini mushrooms
- 1 cup boiling water
- 1 tablespoon tomato paste
- 4 tablespoons unsalted butter
- 3 medium shallots, finely chopped
- ½ pound fresh white mushrooms, stems discarded and caps finely chopped
- ⅓ cup dry vermouth
- 1 pound sea scallops, cut into ¼-inch dice
- ½ pound lump crabmeat, picked over
- ½ pound small shrimp—shelled, deveined and cut into ¼-inch dice
- 1¼ cups freshly grated Parmesan cheese
- 2 large egg yolks, lightly beaten
- ¼ cup finely chopped flat-leaf parsley
- 2 tablespoons finely chopped fresh basil
- 1 tablespoon fresh lemon juice
  Salt and freshly ground pepper

Béchamel sauce:
- 1 quart milk
- 1 cup heavy cream
- 1 bay leaf
- 2 fresh thyme sprigs or ¼ teaspoon dried
- 4 tablespoons unsalted butter
- ¼ cup plus 2 tablespoons all-purpose flour
- 1 tablespoon fresh lemon juice
- ½ teaspoon hot pepper sauce
  Pinch of freshly grated nutmeg

- 16 wide lasagna noodles (see Note)

1. Prepare the filling: In a small bowl, soak the dried porcini in the boiling water until softened, about 15 minutes.

2. Using a slotted spoon, remove the mushrooms from the soaking liquid. Rinse and coarsely chop them. Pour the soaking liquid into a bowl, stopping when you reach the grit at the bottom. Stir in the tomato paste until dissolved.

3. Melt 4 tablespoons of the butter in a large nonreactive skillet. Add the shallots. Cook over moderately high heat, stirring, until softened, about 4 minutes. Add the porcini and fresh mushrooms and cook, stirring, until the fresh mushrooms soften, about 10 minutes. Add the vermouth and cook until evaporated, 3 to 4 minutes.

4. Add the scallops, crabmeat and shrimp to the pan and cook, stirring, until just cooked through, about 5 minutes. Remove from the heat and stir in 1 cup of the Parmesan, the egg yolks, 2 tablespoons of the parsley, the basil and lemon juice. Season with salt and pepper.

5. Prepare the béchamel sauce: In a medium saucepan, bring the milk, cream, bay leaf and thyme just to a boil. In another medium saucepan, melt the butter. Whisk in the flour over moderate heat until the mixture lightens, about 3 minutes. Remove from the heat and whisk in the hot milk. ➤

6. Bring the mixture to a simmer over moderately low heat, whisking constantly. Add the tomato-mushroom liquid. Simmer, whisking occasionally, until the sauce thickens, about 10 minutes. Discard the bay leaf and thyme. Stir in the lemon juice and hot pepper sauce. Season well with salt, pepper and the nutmeg. Stir ½ cup of the béchamel sauce into the seafood.

7. In a large pot of boiling salted water, cook the noodles until soft and pliable, about 3 minutes for instant and 30 seconds for fresh. Drain and transfer to damp tea towels.

8. Pour 1 cup of béchamel sauce into the bottom of each of two 8-inch square baking dishes. Lay a lasagna noodle on a work surface with the longer end toward you. Spread 3 heaping tablespoons of the seafood filling evenly along the long side of the noodle. Roll up the filling in the lasagna noodle to form a neat cylinder and set it seam side down in one of the baking dishes. Repeat with the remaining noodles and filling. Spoon the remaining béchamel sauce over the cannelloni and sprinkle the remaining ¼ cup Parmesan on top.

9. To freeze the cannelloni, let cool completely, then refrigerate until cold. Double wrap each dish tightly in plastic wrap. Place each dish in a large freezer bag. Seal and freeze for up to 1 month.

10. To reheat the cannelloni, let thaw in the refrigerator for 24 hours. Preheat the oven to 375°. Remove the plastic wrap and sprinkle the cannelloni with the remaining 2 tablespoons parsley. Cover with foil and bake for 1 hour. Uncover and bake until heated through and the top is browned, about 15 minutes. Alternatively, reheat the cannelloni in a microwave oven according to the manufacturer's instructions and brown the top in a 450° oven.

NOTE: Use either Delverde Instant Lasagne Ondine or 1½ pounds fresh lasagna noodles. Curly dried lasagna noodles are too thick for this dish.

—Ann Chantal Altman

■

VEAL AND LINGUINE ALLA PIZZAIOLA

The classic southern Italian Vitello alla Pizzaiola (Veal Pizza-Maker's Style) satisfies our modern appetite for hearty, low-fat fare. Lean veal scallops are first browned, then simmered with crushed tomatoes, garlic, white wine and dried oregano (more pungent than the fresh herb) to infuse the meat with flavor.

❦ A medium-bodied red—especially an Italian Barbera—is the right choice here. Try the 1991 Giacomo Conterno or 1990 Azelia. They have the tart, bright flavors to match this tomato-and-garlic accented dish and enough body to stand up to the taste of the veal.

4 Servings

1½ tablespoons extra-virgin olive oil
¾ pound veal scaloppine, pounded ⅛ inch thick
   Salt and freshly ground pepper
2 large garlic cloves, minced
½ cup dry white wine
2 cups canned crushed tomatoes with their liquid
2 tablespoons coarsely chopped flat-leaf parsley
½ teaspoon oregano, crumbled
¾ pound linguine

1. Bring a large pot of salted water to a boil.

2. Heat the oil in a large nonstick skillet. Season the veal on both sides with salt and pepper and add to the pan in a single layer. Cook over moderately high heat until browned, about 2 minutes. Turn the veal, scatter the garlic in the pan and cook until the scaloppine is browned, about 2 minutes longer. Transfer the veal to a plate.

3. Add the wine to the skillet and boil over moderately high heat until reduced to 2 tablespoons, about 3 minutes. Stir in the tomatoes, ½ cup of water, the parsley and oregano and season with salt and pepper. Bring to a simmer over moderately low heat. Return the veal to the pan and cook, stirring occasionally, until the sauce is thickened and the veal is tender, about 15 minutes.

4. Meanwhile, add the linguine to the boiling water. Cook, stirring occasionally, until al dente, about 6 minutes. Drain the pasta and transfer to a large warmed bowl. Spoon the tomato sauce over the pasta and toss well. Transfer to warmed plates and serve the veal alongside.

—Michele Scicolone

■

PENNE WITH RAGU OF GROUND PORK AND BEEF

Cavatelli or fusilli would also be good with this chunky pork and beef *ragù*.

❦ The hearty, meaty sauce points to an equally hearty, but not heavy, red. A simple French country wine, such as 1991 Réserve St Martin Syrah or 1990 La Vieille Ferme Côtes du Rhône Réserve, would be excellent.

4 to 6 Servings

- ¼ **cup olive oil**
- ½ **pound lean ground pork**
- ½ **pound lean ground sirloin**
  Coarse (kosher) salt
- ½ **teaspoon freshly ground black pepper**
- 2 **medium onions, very thinly sliced**
- 2 **garlic cloves, minced**
- 1½ **pounds plum tomatoes, coarsely chopped**
- ⅔ **cup Chicken Stock (p. 36) or canned low-sodium broth**
- 1 **tablespoon tomato paste**
- 2 **teaspoons oregano**
- ½ **teaspoon crushed red pepper**
- 2 **tablespoons unsalted butter**
- 1 **pound penne**
- ¼ **cup coarsely chopped fresh flat-leaf parsley**
  Freshly grated Parmesan cheese, for serving

1. In a large covered pot, bring 4 quarts of water to a boil over high heat.

2. Meanwhile, heat 1 tablespoon of the oil in a large, heavy, nonreactive skillet. Crumble in the pork and beef. Season with salt and the pepper and cook over moderately high heat, stirring, until browned, about 8 minutes. Transfer the meat to a plate.

3. Heat the remaining 3 tablespoons oil in the skillet. Add the onions and garlic and cook over moderately high heat, stirring occasionally, until softened, about 8 minutes. Stir in the tomatoes, Chicken Stock, tomato paste, oregano, crushed red pepper and the browned meat with its juices and simmer for 8 minutes. Stir in the butter.

4. Add 2 tablespoons salt to the boiling pasta water. When it returns to a boil, add the penne and cook, stirring occasionally, until the pasta is al dente, about 8 minutes. Drain the pasta and return it to the pot. Add the meat sauce and the parsley and toss. Transfer to a large warmed bowl and serve at once. Pass the Parmesan separately.

—Tracey Seaman

■

FETTUCCINE WITH SAUSAGE AND GREEN OLIVES

This dish hails from Ascoli Piceno in the Marches in Italy, where fresh pasta is still made in most homes nearly every day. ➤

**Fettuccine
with Sausage
and Green
Olives**

♟ Verdicchio dei Castelli di Jesi, a brac-
ing and savory white wine from the
Marches in Italy, has a light citrus quality that echoes the freshly grated lemon
zest in the sauce.

4 Servings

¾ ounce dried porcini mushrooms
Boiling water
1 tablespoon mild olive oil

½ pound coarse-grained Italian pork
sausage, thinly sliced
4 tablespoons unsalted butter
4 ounces white mushrooms, thinly
sliced
2 tablespoons chopped fresh
parsley
1 teaspoon freshly grated lemon
zest
1 medium garlic clove, minced

    Salt and freshly ground pepper
12 to 18 large, sweet, green olives,
      such as Baresi Dolce, pitted and
      cut into thin strips
  1 pound fresh fettuccine or
      ¾ pound dried egg fettuccine or
      tagliatelle
  2 tablespoons extra-virgin olive oil

1. Cover the dried porcini mushrooms with boiling water and set aside to soak for at least 30 minutes. Drain, rinse under cold water and pat dry. Chop the mushrooms coarsely.

2. In a large covered pot, bring 4 quarts of cold water to a boil for cooking the pasta. Meanwhile, in a skillet, warm the mild olive oil over moderately high heat. Add the Italian pork sausage and cook, stirring, until the sausage is browned, about 10 minutes.

3. Melt the butter in a nonreactive skillet large enough to hold the pasta. Add the sliced white mushrooms and the chopped porcini mushrooms and cook over moderately high heat until the mushrooms begin to give off some liquid, about 5 minutes. Add the chopped parsley, grated lemon zest, minced garlic and salt and pepper and cook, stirring, for 2 minutes. Add the sausage, lower the heat to moderate and cook, stirring, for 5 minutes. Add the olives and cook until heated, about 1 minute.

4. Salt the boiling pasta water, add the fettuccine and cook until the pasta is al dente, 3 to 4 minutes for fresh fettucine, 8 to 10 minutes for dried. Set aside 1 cup of the pasta cooking water, then drain the pasta and transfer it to the skillet. Add the extra-virgin olive oil and a couple of tablespoons of the reserved pasta water. Cook for 1 minute while tossing constantly to coat the strands of pasta. If the fettucine seems dry, add more of the pasta water. Serve immediately right from the skillet.

—Anna Del Conte

■

FARFALLE WITH SPICY SAUSAGE AND SMOKED MOZZARELLA

Orecchiette or conchiglie make a fine alternative to the butterfly-shaped pasta used in this recipe.

❦ The hot sausage here calls for a spicy, full-flavored red wine like a California Zinfandel. Look for such bottlings as 1990 Beringer or 1989 Louis M. Martini.

4 to 6 Servings
  1 pound hot Italian sausage
  2 tablespoons unsalted butter
  2 tablespoons olive oil ➤

**Farfalle
with Spicy
Sausage
and Smoked
Mozzarella**

1 cup fresh sage leaves
1 medium onion, thinly sliced
2 large garlic cloves, minced
2 cups Chicken Stock (p. 36) or
 canned low-sodium broth
 Coarse (kosher) salt
1 pound farfalle
1 pound smoked mozzarella, cut
 into ½-inch cubes
 Freshly ground pepper

1. In a large covered pot, bring 4 quarts of water to a boil over high heat. Meanwhile, in a medium saucepan, cover the hot Italian sausage with cold water and bring the water to a boil over moderately high heat. Lower the heat to moderate and simmer until the sausage is cooked through, about 7 minutes. Drain and let cool slightly, then cut the sausage into ¼-inch slices.

2. In a large skillet, melt 1 tablespoon of the butter in the oil. Add the sage leaves and cook over moderately high heat, stirring once or twice, until crisp, about 2 minutes. Transfer the sage leaves to a plate.

3. Melt the remaining 1 tablespoon butter in the skillet. Add the onion and garlic and cook over moderately low heat, stirring, until softened, about 4 minutes. Raise the heat to high, add the Chicken Stock and boil until reduced to 1 cup, about 8 minutes.

4. Add 2 tablespoons salt to the boiling pasta water. When it returns to a boil, add the farfalle and cook, stirring occasionally, until the pasta is al dente, about 8 minutes. Drain the pasta well and return it to the pot.

5. Stir the reduced stock mixture and the sausage into the pasta and fold in the smoked mozzarella. Season with salt and pepper. Transfer to a large warmed serving platter and scatter the crisp sage leaves over the top. Serve the farfalle immediately.

—Marcia Kiesel

■

ORECCHIETTE WITH PORCINI AND PANCETTA

Fusilli or maccheroni campagnoli can replace the orecchiette called for here.

4 to 6 Servings

1 ounce dried porcini mushrooms
¼ pound pancetta, finely chopped
2 medium onions, finely chopped
 Coarse (kosher) salt
1 pound orecchiette
1 cup heavy cream
½ cup finely shredded fresh basil
 Freshly ground pepper
 Freshly grated Parmesan cheese

1. In a large covered pot, bring 5 quarts of water to a boil over high heat. In a bowl, soak the porcini in 3 cups of hot water until softened, about 15 minutes.

2. Meanwhile, heat a large, heavy skillet. Add the chopped pancetta and cook over moderate heat, stirring occasionally, until lightly browned, about 5 minutes. Add the onions and cook, stirring, until slightly softened, about 3 minutes.

3. Add 2 tablespoons salt to the boiling pasta water. When the water returns to a boil, add the orecchiette and cook, stirring occasionally, until al dente, about 15 minutes.

4. Drain the porcini, reserving the soaking liquid. Rinse and chop the mushrooms, then add them to the skillet. Pour in the mushroom liquid, stopping when you reach the grit. Add the cream and basil and season with salt and pepper. Boil over moderate heat until reduced by half, about 5 minutes. Correct seasonings.

5. Drain the pasta and return it to the pot. Add the sauce and toss. Transfer to a large warmed bowl and serve, passing the Parmesan separately.

—Tracey Seaman

PAPPARDELLE WITH PORK, PORCINI AND HERBS

Pappardelle are wide strips of pasta that are traditionally teamed with hare or wild-boar sauce. Here they are combined with some classic Umbrian ingredients: pork, fennel, sage, leeks and porcini.

🍷 Serve the tightly knit, wiry Torre di Giano Il Pino of Umbria—one of Italy's most elegant white wines, with a cool, flowery scent—which nimbly trims the richness of this dish.

Orecchiette with Porcini and Pancetta

6 Servings

⅞ ounce dried porcini mushrooms (about ⅔ cup)
1 cup hot water
¼ cup plus 2 tablespoons olive oil
¼ pound fennel bulb, thinly sliced (about 1 cup)
1 large leek, white part only, thinly sliced crosswise ➤

1 large garlic clove, minced
¼ cup minced fresh sage leaves plus more for garnish
¼ cup minced fresh fennel fronds plus more for garnish
Fine sea salt
Coarsely ground pepper
6 ounces cremini, shiitake or button mushrooms, stems discarded, caps thinly sliced
2 pounds lean boneless pork loin, cut into 1-inch pieces
½ cup dry white wine
½ cup Chicken Stock (p. 36) or canned broth
½ teaspoon red wine vinegar or fresh lemon juice
1 pound Fresh Pappardelle (recipe below)

FRESH PAPPARDELLE
Makes 1 Pound

2 cups unbleached all-purpose flour
⅛ teaspoon salt
3 large eggs
1 teaspoon extra-virgin olive oil

1. Mound the flour on a work surface and sprinkle the salt over it. Make a well in the center and add the eggs and oil. Using a fork, mix the liquid ingredients until smooth, then begin incorporating the flour until the dough can be formed into a ball.

2. Using your hands, gradually work in the flour until a smooth dough forms (you may not need all the flour; push any excess aside). Knead the dough for 5 minutes, then cover with a bowl and let rest for 10 minutes.

3. Cut the dough in half. Keep 1 piece covered on a lightly floured surface while you work with the other. Flatten the dough slightly with a rolling pin. Using a manual pasta machine, roll the dough through successively narrower settings until you reach the thinnest setting. Spread the sheet of pasta flat on a lightly floured surface.

4. Halve the sheet of pasta crosswise, then cut each half crosswise into 1½-inch-wide strips. Place the noodles on clean kitchen towels while you roll out and cut the remaining dough. (The pappardelle will keep in a cool place covered with kitchen towels for up to 5 days.)

—Mary Ann Esposito

1. In a small bowl, cover the dried porcini mushrooms with the hot water. Let soak until the mushrooms are softened, about 30 minutes.

2. Meanwhile, in a large, heavy, nonreactive skillet, heat ¼ cup of the oil. Add the fennel and leek and cook over moderate heat until slightly softened, about 4 minutes. Stir in the garlic and cook for 3 minutes longer. Add 2 tablespoons each minced sage and fennel fronds, season with sea salt and pepper and cook, stirring occasionally, for 3 minutes. Transfer the vegetables to a dish.

3. Add 1 more tablespoon of oil and the fresh mushrooms to the skillet and cook over high heat until the mushrooms begin to soften and give off some of their liquid, about 3 minutes. Season with sea salt and pepper. Add the mushrooms and their liquid to the other vegetables.

4. Add the remaining 1 tablespoon oil to the skillet. Pat the pork dry with paper towels and season with sea salt and pepper. Add one-third of the pork to the skillet and brown the pieces evenly over high heat. Remove the cooked pork pieces with a slotted spoon and set aside. Repeat with the remaining pork in 2 batches. Return all the meat to the pan, pour in the white wine and cook for 3 minutes. Stir in the Chicken Stock and all the cooked vegetables and lower the heat to maintain a simmer.

5. Drain the porcini mushrooms, reserving the liquid. Cut the porcini into small pieces and add them to the skillet. Strain the porcini soaking liquid into the skillet through cheesecloth or a sieve lined with paper towels. Cover the skillet and gently simmer on low heat until the pork is fork-tender, about 1 hour. Stir in the red wine vinegar.

6. Shortly before the meat is done, in a large covered pot, bring 4 quarts of cold water to a boil for the pasta. Salt the water, add the Fresh Pappardelle and cook until the pasta is al dente, 2 to 4

minutes. Drain the pasta and transfer it to a large serving platter. Pour the meat sauce over the pasta and toss gently. Garnish with the remaining 2 tablespoons each minced sage and fennel leaves and serve at once.

—Mary Ann Esposito

■

"GUITAR" MACCHERONI WITH LAMB RAGU

If one mentions food from Abruzzo, the first thing that comes to mind is *la chitarra*, "the guitar," a culinary instrument consisting of a wood frame strung with evenly spaced wires. A sheet of pasta is placed on the wires, and a rolling pin is pressed over it, cutting the dough into noodles. Today most cooks, even those in Abruzzo, rely on a pasta machine, which is much less time-consuming.

❦ Montepulciano d'Abruzzo, made in Abruzzo from a local grape of the same name, is a warm and supple, yet very lively red wine that is compatible with many dishes, including the lamb *ragù* here.

6 Servings

- 2 red bell peppers
- 1 green bell pepper
- ¼ cup extra-virgin olive oil
- 2 medium garlic cloves, smashed
- 2 imported bay leaves
- ¾ pound lean ground lamb
- ¼ cup dry white wine
- 1 35-ounce can pureed tomatoes
- 2 to 3 fresh basil leaves, coarsely chopped, or ½ teaspoon dried
  Coarse (kosher) salt
  Freshly ground black pepper
  Egg Pasta (p. 142)
  Freshly grated Pecorino Romano cheese

1. Make the lamb *ragù:* Roast the red and green peppers directly over a gas flame or under the broiler as close to the heat as possible, turning often, until charred. Transfer the peppers to a paper bag and set them aside to steam for 10 minutes. Using a small sharp knife, scrape off the blackened skin and remove the cores, seeds and ribs. Cut lengthwise into thin strips.

2. In a large, heavy, nonreactive saucepan, heat the oil. Add the garlic and the bay leaves. Cook over moderately high heat for 3 minutes. Add the lamb and cook, stirring, until browned, about 8 minutes. Add the wine and simmer until almost evaporated. Add the tomatoes. Fill the can with 1½ cups of water and add to the pan. Season with the basil, coarse salt and black pepper. Reduce the heat to moderately low, cover and simmer the sauce for 45 minutes to 1 hour, stirring often. Add the roasted pepper strips during the last 10 minutes.

3. Cut the Egg Pasta dough into 4 equal pieces. Work with 1 piece of dough at a time, keeping the other pieces covered with a bowl. Flatten the dough with your hands. Using a pasta machine, start rolling the dough through the largest setting. Sprinkle the dough with flour, fold into thirds lengthwise and roll again. Do this 2 more times until smooth and not sticky.

4. Move the rollers to the next setting and roll the dough through without folding. Continue rolling the dough through successively narrower settings until the dough is the desired thickness. Spread the pasta sheets on a kitchen towel to dry for 10 minutes (not longer or the dough will become difficult to cut).

5. Feed the pasta sheets through the thin cutters of the pasta machine. Spread the noodles on kitchen towels. Repeat with the remaining 3 pieces of dough. (The noodles will keep in a cool place covered with kitchen towels for up to 5 days.)

6. In a large covered pot, bring 6 quarts

of cold water to a boil for the pasta. Stir in 3 tablespoons of coarse salt. When the water returns to a boil, stir in the Egg Pasta. Cover the pan so that the water quickly returns to a boil. Uncover and cook the pasta until al dente, 2 to 4 minutes. Drain immediately and toss with the hot *ragù*. Serve immediately with the grated Pecorino cheese passed separately.

—Anna Teresa Callen

■

FRIED RICE WITH PEAS AND SUN-DRIED TOMATOES

Although stir-frying is often thought to be a high-fat cooking method, it uses very little fat when done properly. Sun-dried tomatoes add a distinctive taste.

4 Servings

- 1½ cups extra-long-grain rice
- 1 tablespoon plus 1 teaspoon peanut oil
- 3 large eggs
- Pinch of salt
- Freshly ground white pepper
- 1½ tablespoons oyster sauce
- 1 tablespoon Chicken Stock (p. 36) or canned low-sodium broth
- 2 teaspoons light soy sauce
- 1 teaspoon dry white wine
- ¾ teaspoon sugar
- ½ teaspoon Oriental sesame oil
- 1½ teaspoons minced fresh ginger
- 1¼ cups shelled fresh or thawed frozen green peas
- 4 oil-packed sun-dried tomato halves—rinsed, patted dry and cut into ½-inch dice
- 4 scallions, thinly sliced
- 3 tablespoons minced fresh coriander

1. In a large saucepan, cover the rice with cold water. Rub the rice between your hands. Drain well and repeat the rinsing process 2 more times. Return the rice to the pan, add 1½ cups of cold water and let soak for 2 hours.

2. Heat 1 teaspoon of the peanut oil in a medium skillet. Lightly beat the eggs with the salt and a pinch of white pepper. Pour the eggs into the skillet and cook, stirring with a fork, until scrambled, 2 to 3 minutes. Transfer to a plate and cut into ½-inch pieces.

3. Bring the rice in the saucepan to a boil over high heat. Boil, stirring with a chopstick, until most of the water evaporates, about 4 minutes; the rice will still be hard. Cover and cook over very low heat, stirring occasionally, until tender, about 10 minutes. Stir the rice to loosen it and let cool.

4. In a bowl, combine the oyster sauce, Chicken Stock, soy sauce, wine, sugar, sesame oil and a pinch of white pepper.

5. Set a wok over high heat for 30 seconds. Add the remaining 1 tablespoon peanut oil and swirl to coat until a wisp of white smoke appears. Add the ginger and stir-fry for 10 seconds. Add the peas and stir-fry for 20 seconds. Add the cooked rice. Stir-fry until very hot, 2 to 3 minutes.

6. Add the oyster sauce mixture to the wok. Stir until the rice is thoroughly coated. Stir in the eggs, tomatoes, scallions and coriander. Mix well and serve.

—Eileen Yin-Fei Lo

■

RISOTTO WITH ZUCCHINI BLOSSOMS AND SAGE

This succulent dish from the restaurant Drago in Santa Monica can be served either as a main course or as a prelude to fish or meat. At the restaurant, the risotto is garnished with thin slices of steamed baby zucchini, julienned Parmesan cheese and finely diced tomato.

❦ A delicate Italian spumante or a non-sparkling light white without an over-abundance of fruit will best complement the subtle flavor of the zucchini blossoms and the aroma of the sage. Two candidates are Berlucchi Brut Rosé metodo champenois, from the Franciacorta region of Lombardy, and 1990 Livon Pinot Grigio, from Collio in the Friuli-Venezia Giulia region.

4 Servings
- 4 baby yellow or green zucchini, preferably with blossoms attached
- 3 tablespoons olive oil
- 8 large fresh sage leaves
- ¾ pound zucchini blossoms (about 60)
- 7 cups Chicken Stock (p. 36) or canned low-sodium broth
- 1 small onion, minced
- 2 cups arborio rice (12 ounces)
- ½ cup dry white wine
- ¼ cup plus 1 tablespoon freshly grated Parmesan cheese
- 2 tablespoons unsalted butter
  Salt and freshly ground white pepper

1. Thinly slice the baby zucchini lengthwise, keeping the slices attached at the blossom end. Press each of the zucchini gently to fan out the slices. Carefully transfer the fanned zucchini to a steamer basket set over ½ inch of boiling water. Cover and steam until crisp-tender, about 3 minutes.

2. Heat 2 tablespoons of the olive oil in a large skillet. Add the sage leaves and cook over high heat until crisp, about 1 minute. Using a slotted spoon, transfer the sage to paper towels to drain. Add the zucchini blossoms to the skillet and cook, stirring, until the zucchini is slightly wilted, about 3 minutes.

3. Heat the Chicken Stock in a medium saucepan and simmer gently over low heat. Heat the remaining 1 tablespoon oil in a large nonreactive saucepan. Add the onion and cook over moderate heat until translucent, about 4 minutes. Raise the heat to moderately high, add the rice and stir for 2 minutes, until each of the grains is coated with oil.

4. Add the wine and boil until reduced to 2 tablespoons, about 1 minute. Add 1 cup of the simmering Chicken Stock and cook, stirring constantly, just until absorbed. Add another cup of the simmering stock and stir continuously until absorbed. Repeat the process until the rice is tender but still firm to the bite and bound with creamy liquid, about 15 minutes total.

5. Remove the pan from the heat and stir in the sautéed sage leaves and zucchini blossoms. Stir in the Parmesan cheese and the butter and season with salt and white pepper. Spoon the risotto into bowls and garnish each serving with a zucchini fan.

—Celestino Drago

∎

CHEESE GRITS SOUFFLE OVER TURNIP GREENS

Southern flavors predominate in this slimmed-down soufflé. Egg whites alone, rather than whole eggs, work just fine.

6 Servings
- 1 cup quick grits
- 2½ pounds turnip greens, large stems discarded
- 2 tablespoons unsalted butter
- 1 tablespoon canola oil
- 2 medium garlic cloves, minced
- 1 medium onion, finely chopped
- ½ teaspoon crushed red pepper ➤

OYSTER SAUCE

Made from a salty extract of dried oysters, this thick, shiny, coffee-colored sauce (sold in bottles) is strong, delicious and essential in the Cantonese pantry. Add to stir-fries and sauces during cooking. Drizzle over blanched or steamed broccoli, baby bok choy or spinach shortly before serving.

—Nancie McDermott

Salt and freshly ground black pepper
1 **cup coarsely grated Monterey Jack cheese (4 ounces)**
½ **cup coarsely grated sharp Cheddar cheese (2 ounces)**
4 **large egg whites**

1. Preheat the oven to 375°. Butter a 9-by-13-inch enameled cast-iron baking dish or heavy gratin dish.

2. In a medium saucepan, bring 4 cups of water to a simmer over moderately high heat. Whisk in the grits and reduce the heat to low. Cover and cook, stirring occasionally, until creamy, about 7 minutes. Pour the grits into a large bowl and let cool, stirring often to prevent a skin from forming.

3. In a large nonreactive saucepan of boiling water, cook the turnip greens until they are tender, about 5 minutes. Drain the greens in a colander and lightly squeeze out excess water. Chop the greens coarsely.

4. In a large nonreactive skillet, melt the butter in the oil over low heat. Add the garlic and the onion and cook until softened, about 5 minutes. Increase the heat to high and add the greens, stirring to heat through. Season with the crushed red pepper, salt and black pepper. Spread the greens evenly in the prepared baking dish.

5. Using a rubber spatula, fold the grated Monterey Jack cheese and Cheddar cheese into the bowl of cooled grits along with ½ teaspoon each of the salt and the black pepper.

6. In a large stainless steel bowl, whisk the egg whites with a pinch of salt until firm but not overly stiff peaks form. Mix ⅓ of the egg whites into the grits with a rubber spatula to lighten slightly. Then fold in the remaining whites lightly but thoroughly (some streaks of egg white can remain). Spread the mixture over the greens, smoothing the surface.

7. Bake the soufflé in the upper third of the oven for 30 minutes, until it is well risen and lightly browned on top. Serve immediately.

—Marcia Kiesel

■

CREAMY POLENTA WITH BUTTER AND CHEESE

This recipe has been adapted from *Fanny at Chez Panisse* (HarperCollins).

4 Servings
1 **teaspoon salt**
1 **cup polenta (not instant)**
Unsalted butter and freshly grated Parmesan cheese, for serving

1. In a heavy medium saucepan, bring 4 cups of water to a boil. Reduce the heat to low and add the salt. Slowly pour the polenta into the water, stirring constantly. Keep stirring for about 5 minutes, until the polenta is evenly thickened and soupy. Adjust the heat to the lowest setting so that the polenta barely bubbles. Cook for 30 to 45 minutes, stirring every few minutes to keep it from sticking to the pan. If it gets too thick, just add water in small amounts until it is the consistency you want.

2. When it is done, eat it right away with butter and Parmesan cheese.

—Alice Waters

Chapter 8 ▪ VEGETABLES

159   Spring Vegetable Medley

159   Artichoke Hearts with Tomatoes and Balsamic Vinegar

160   Gratinéed Asparagus with Parmesan and Fried Eggs

161   Green Beans with Tomato and Fresh Coriander

161   Blue Lake Beans with Red Wine–Sweet Onion Pickle

162   Fresh Fava Beans with Escarole and Tomato

164   Baby Artichoke, Spinach and Fava Bean Ragout

166   New Year's Peas and Greens

167   Carefree Boston Baked Beans

167   Skillet-Steamed Broccoli with Lemon

167   Grilled Broccoli-Stuffed Onions

168   Broccoli-Sauced Cauliflower

169   Stir-Fried Cabbage with Green and Red Peppers

169   Marinated Fennel, Pearl Onions and Celery

170   Spinach and Red Pepper Gratin

172   Mixed Greens

173   Stir-Fried Collards with Apple and Balsamic Vinegar

174   Swiss Chard Lasagna

175   Oven-Roasted Parsnips with Onions and Chestnuts

176   Roasted Red Peppers with Vinaigrette

176   Peperonata

177   Roasted Vegetable and Hominy Chili

177   Garden Squash and Pea Medley

178   Zucchini and Carrots Parmesan

179   Zucchini Parmesan

179   Corn, Squash and Green Chile Stew

179   Winter Squash with Crouton Stuffing

180   Fried Green Tomatoes

181   Vegetarian Kofta Curry

Spring Vegetable Medley

SPRING VEGETABLE MEDLEY

Make long, thin, garlic-rubbed toasted croutons from country sourdough bread to accompany this medley. You can create your own vegetable combination. Just remember to cook the vegetables in order of mildest-tasting to strongest-tasting.

❣ The tarragon undertone would find an attractive flavor echo in a simple, not-too-oaky West Coast Chardonnay, such as 1992 Columbia Crest from Washington State or 1991 St. Clement from California.

4 Servings

- 1 dozen baby carrots (about 3 ounces), peeled, or 1 medium carrot, peeled and cut into 2-by-½-inch sticks
- ½ cup snow peas
- 4 small radishes with ½ inch of the tops, halved lengthwise
- 18 thin asparagus stalks, tips trimmed to 2 inches, stems discarded
- 6 thin scallions, trimmed to 4-inch lengths of both white and green parts
  Stems of 2 broccoli stalks (about 5 ounces), peeled and sliced diagonally ¼ inch thick
- 4 small white turnips (6 ounces total), peeled and cut lengthwise into sixths
- 4 tablespoons unsalted butter
- 4 fresh thyme sprigs
- 1 tablespoon fresh lemon juice
  Salt and freshly ground pepper
- 10 arugula or sorrel leaves, thinly sliced lengthwise
- 5 fresh flat-leaf parsley sprigs, minced
- 1 tablespoon snipped fresh chives
- 1 teaspoon finely chopped fresh tarragon or scant ½ teaspoon dried

1. In a large nonreactive saucepan, bring 6 cups of salted water to a boil. Fill a large bowl with cold water. Add the vegetables individually to the boiling water in the following order and cook until crisp-tender as follows: about 5 minutes for the carrots, 1 minute for the snow peas, 2 minutes for the radishes, 2 minutes for the asparagus tips, 2 minutes for the scallions, 2 minutes for the broccoli stems and 3 minutes for the turnips. Using a slotted spoon, transfer each vegetable as it's cooked to the cold water to cool, then drain well. Reserve 1 cup of the vegetable cooking water.

2. In a large skillet, combine the butter, thyme sprigs and the reserved cooking liquid over moderate heat until the butter is melted. Add all the cooked vegetables and warm them over moderately low heat. Season with the lemon juice and salt and pepper and shake the skillet back and forth to blend the sauce. Stir in the arugula leaves, parsley, chives and tarragon and cook for 1 minute to thoroughly blend the flavors. Discard the thyme sprigs and serve at once.

—Deborah Madison

■

ARTICHOKE HEARTS WITH TOMATOES AND BALSAMIC VINEGAR

This vegetable dish would be a good accompaniment to any simply cooked poultry, fish or meat.

4 Servings

- 1 lemon, halved
- 4 artichokes
- 1 pound ripe tomatoes
- 1 tablespoon olive oil
- ¼ cup chopped red onion
- 1 large clove garlic, minced ➤

ASPARAGUS
TIPS

• Buy asparagus only when the spears are firm and the buds at the tip are tightly closed. Green asparagus should have a bright, dewy hue with no hint of yellow.

• To prepare asparagus for cooking, first trim off the ends. Holding a stalk with the tip facing you and using a small, sharp knife, begin at the base and strip off the thin fibrous skin all around. Soak the asparagus in cold water for 10 minutes, then rinse in two changes of water.

• To cook, choose a pan that's large enough to accommodate the asparagus lying flat. Fill it with water and bring to a boil. Add 1 tablespoon salt for every pound of asparagus. When the water returns to a rolling boil, add the asparagus and cover. When the water boils again, uncover and cook the asparagus until tender when pierced at the thickest part with a fork. Drain immediately.

—Marcella Hazan

½ teaspoon chopped fresh thyme
1 tablespoon balsamic vinegar
2 teaspoons chopped fresh parsley
¼ teaspoon salt
⅛ teaspoon freshly ground pepper

1. Fill a medium bowl with water. Squeeze the juice from the lemon halves into the bowl and then add the lemon halves to the bowl.

2. Prepare the artichokes one at a time. Pull off all the outer leaves, bending them down so that they break naturally, until you reach the yellowish cone of softer leaves. Lay the artichoke on its side and, using a stainless steel knife, cut off the cone of leaves flush with the heart. Cut out the purplish leaves, down to the fuzzy choke; rub all the cut sides with one of the lemon halves. Cut off the stem and all the dark green outer parts and leaves so that the entire heart is yellowish white. Scoop out the fuzzy choke with a spoon. Rub the artichoke heart all over with the lemon half and drop it in the bowl of water to prevent it from discoloring.

3. Cut out the stem ends of the tomatoes. Put the tomatoes in a steamer basket and place the basket over boiling water in a large nonreactive saucepan or deep skillet. Cover and steam over moderate heat for 30 seconds. Refresh the tomatoes in cold water, pat dry and peel. Cut the tomatoes in half and scoop out the seeds with your fingers. Dice the tomatoes and set aside.

4. Place the artichoke hearts, stem sides up, in the steamer basket and place the basket over boiling water. Cover and steam over moderate heat until tender, 20 to 25 minutes.

5. Meanwhile, heat the oil in a medium nonreactive skillet. Add the onion, garlic and thyme and cook over moderate heat, stirring, until the onion is translucent, about 3 minutes. Stir in the tomatoes, vinegar, parsley, salt and pepper and remove from the heat.

6. When the artichokes are done, cut them into eighths and add them to the tomato mixture. Toss gently over moderate heat until warmed through. Serve hot or at room temperature.

—Stephanie Lyness

■

GRATINEED ASPARAGUS WITH PARMESAN AND FRIED EGGS

The coming of asparagus is an event that Italian cooks celebrate by giving the vegetable a starring role. One of the most winning presentations is achieved by gratinéing cooked asparagus under a blanket of freshly grated Parmesan and topping them with a fried egg. In a menu it takes the place of a meat dish.

4 Servings
2 pounds fresh asparagus, trimmed and cooked
Salt
⅔ cup freshly grated Parmigiano-Reggiano cheese
Unsalted butter
4 large eggs
Freshly ground pepper

1. Preheat the oven to 450°. Butter an oval or rectangular baking dish.

2. Align the cooked asparagus in the dish in partly overlapping rows, sprinkling each row with salt and Parmigiano-Reggiano cheese and dotting with butter. Bake on the top shelf of the oven for about 15 minutes, until a light golden crust forms on top. Arrange the gratinéed asparagus on 4 warm dinner plates.

3. In a large skillet, melt 2 tablespoons of butter over moderately high heat until the foam begins to subside. Break the eggs into the pan, sprinkle with salt and fry. Slide a fried egg over each portion of

asparagus. Spoon the juices from the baking pan over the eggs. Sprinkle with pepper and serve.

—Marcella Hazan

■

GREEN BEANS WITH TOMATO AND FRESH CORIANDER

Green beans done in this manner—boiled until crisp-tender, then plunged into ice water to halt the cooking—taste wonderful with any vibrant, full-flavored dressing. Since beans vary in size and tenderness, taste as you cook. Remove them from the heat as soon as they go from raw to cooked.

4 Servings
- 2 teaspoons sherry vinegar
  Fine sea salt
- 2 tablespoons extra-virgin olive oil
- 1½ tablespoons minced shallot
- 1 ripe medium tomato—peeled, seeded and cut into ¼-inch dice
  Coarse sea salt
  Ice water
- 1 pound thin French green beans (haricots verts)
- 2 tablespoons chopped fresh coriander (cilantro)

1. In a small bowl, whisk together the vinegar and a pinch of fine sea salt. In a second bowl, stir together the oil and shallot. Set aside for 1 hour.

2. Place the diced tomato in a fine sieve, sprinkle with 1 teaspoon of coarse sea salt and let drain while you proceed.

3. Fill a large bowl with ice water. In a large saucepan, bring 3 quarts of water to a boil over high heat with 1 teaspoon of coarse salt. Add the green beans, return to a boil over moderately high heat and cook until crisp-tender, about 5 minutes. Drain

the beans and immediately plunge them into the ice water to cool for 1 to 2 minutes. Drain thoroughly in a colander and pat dry. (The beans can be prepared up to 4 hours ahead and refrigerated.)

4. Transfer the beans to a large bowl. Whisk together the vinegar and shallot oil; add to the green beans along with the tomato and coriander. Toss well and serve.

—Patricia Wells

■

BLUE LAKE BEANS WITH RED WINE–SWEET ONION PICKLE

You can use Blue Lake, Kentucky Wonder or any variety of green beans that are available for this salad. The yellow wax beans make it more colorful.

8 Servings
Onion Pickle:
- ⅔ cup red wine vinegar
- ⅔ cup dry red wine, preferably Cabernet Sauvignon
- ⅓ cup sugar
- 2 bay leaves, preferably fresh
- 10 black peppercorns, crushed
  Salt
- 1½ pounds Bermuda or other sweet onions, thinly sliced

Beans:
- 1 pound green string beans, stemmed, with tender tips left on
- 1 pound yellow wax beans, stemmed, with tender tips left on
- 1 large European cucumber—halved, seeded and thinly sliced on the diagonal
- ¼ cup peanut oil

1. Prepare the onion pickle: In a small nonreactive saucepan, combine the vinegar, wine, sugar, bay leaves, peppercorns

Blue Lake Beans with Red Wine–Sweet Onion Pickle

again. Add the yellow beans and cucumber to the bowl. (The beans and cucumber can be refrigerated, covered, for up to 6 hours. Let return to room temperature before serving.)

4. Discard the bay leaves from the onion pickle. Toss the onion pickle with the beans. Add the peanut oil and toss again. Season with salt and serve.

—Ben Barker

■

FRESH FAVA BEANS WITH ESCAROLE AND TOMATO

In this hearty side dish, the vegetables are steamed separately first and then cooked together briefly. When buying fava beans, choose slender, bright green, fresh-looking pods; the beans will be small and sweet. Larger beans tend to be starchy.

4 Servings
- 1 ripe medium tomato
- 3 pounds fresh fava beans, shelled
- 3 packed cups escarole cut into 1-inch-wide strips (from a 1-pound head)
- 1½ tablespoons olive oil
- 1 medium onion, thinly sliced
- 2 medium garlic cloves, smashed
- ½ teaspoon chopped fresh thyme
  Salt
- 1 tablespoon chopped fresh parsley
- 1 tablespoon red wine vinegar
  Freshly ground pepper

and 1 teaspoon salt and bring to a boil over moderately high heat. Pour the hot liquid into a medium bowl and add the onions. Let cool, then cover and refrigerate for at least 2 hours or overnight.

2. Prepare the beans: Bring a large saucepan of salted water to a boil. Add the green beans and cook over moderately high heat until crisp-tender, about 5 minutes. Using a slotted spoon, transfer the beans to a colander, refresh with cold water and drain thoroughly. Transfer to a large bowl.

3. Add the yellow beans to the boiling water and cook over moderately high heat until crisp-tender, about 6 minutes. Drain, refresh with cold water and drain

1. Cut out the stem end of the tomato. Put the tomato in a steamer basket and place the basket over boiling water in a large nonreactive saucepan. Cover and steam over moderate heat for 30 seconds. Refresh the tomato in cold water and pat dry. Peel with a small knife. Cut the tomato in half crosswise and scoop out the seeds with your fingers. Cut the flesh into ¼-inch strips. ➤

Fresh Fava Beans with Escarole and Tomato

STEAMING KNOW-HOW

The steamer basket or rack must sit more than one inch from the floor of the pot to allow sufficient room for the steaming liquid. The basket or rack can be raised off the floor of the pot with small, empty tin cans or crumpled pieces of aluminum foil. The water must be at least one inch deep and should not touch the bottom of the steamer basket or rack; less than one inch of water will slow the steaming time.

• Bring water to a boil in the steamer pot over high heat.

• Add the food to the steamer in a basket or insert, or on a rack.

• The steamer should be covered, but a tight-fitting lid is not critical. You can use a piece of aluminum foil. Simply cover the pan with the foil, then press the foil tightly around the edges.

• Adjust the heat so that the water simmers hard enough for steam to puff energetically from under the lid. Moderate heat should suffice.

• Begin timing when steam is visible.

• The rate of evaporation of the steaming liquid depends on the size of the pan (the larger the area, the faster the evaporation), the fit of the lid and the amount of liquid given off by the food being cooked. Keep a pot of boiling water on the stove to replenish the steaming liquid as needed.

• If you open the lid of the steamer briefly to check the cooking progress, add about one minute to the total steaming time.

—Stephanie Lyness

2. Put the fava beans in the steamer basket and place over boiling water in the saucepan. Cover and steam over moderate heat until tender, 8 to 10 minutes. Transfer the fava beans to a plate to cool slightly.

3. Add the escarole to the steamer and steam for 3 minutes. Remove and set aside. Drain off the water.

4. In the same saucepan, combine the olive oil, onion, garlic, thyme and ¼ teaspoon of salt. Cover and cook over low heat for 5 minutes, stirring once or twice. Add the parsley and ½ cup of water and bring to a boil. Cover partially and simmer until the liquid has reduced to 2 tablespoons, about 5 minutes.

5. Peel the fava beans: split the tough skins with your fingers and pop out the tender beans. Add the beans, escarole and the vinegar to the onion mixture in the saucepan. Toss gently and cook over low heat for 2 minutes to marry the flavors and warm through. Season with salt and pepper. Remove from the heat and stir in the tomato. Serve warm or at room temperature.

—Stephanie Lyness

■

BABY ARTICHOKE, SPINACH AND FAVA BEAN RAGOUT

This ragout is particularly good served with soft polenta. If you can't find fava beans, try fresh lima beans.

4 Servings

½ cup fresh whole wheat or white bread crumbs
¼ cup finely grated Parmesan cheese
¼ cup chopped fresh flat-leaf parsley
2 pounds young fava beans, shelled
1 large lemon
16 fresh baby artichokes
¼ cup extra-virgin olive oil
4 small shallots, finely chopped
3 small garlic cloves, minced
1 tablespoon finely chopped fresh thyme or 1 teaspoon dried
Salt and freshly ground pepper
12 ounces tender young spinach
2 tablespoons finely chopped fresh tarragon or 2 teaspoons dried

1. In a small dry skillet, toast the bread crumbs over moderate heat, stirring often, until golden, 2 to 3 minutes. Transfer to a bowl and toss with the cheese and half of the parsley.

2. Bring a medium saucepan of water to a boil. Add the fava beans and boil for 1 minute. Drain and rinse with cold water; then, using your thumbnail, pinch off the tough outer skins.

3. Squeeze the juice from the lemon into a bowl filled with 6 cups of water. Break off and discard all the outer leaves of the artichokes until you reach the tender inner yellow leaves. Using a small sharp knife, cut 1 inch off the tops of the artichokes and trim the bottoms. Quarter the artichokes and place them in the lemon water.

4. In a large nonreactive skillet, warm the oil over moderately high heat. Drain the artichokes in a fine strainer, reserving 1½ cups of the lemon water. Pat the artichokes dry. Add them to the hot oil and cook, stirring, until nicely browned on the edges, about 5 minutes.

5. Stir in the shallots and garlic and cook for 2 minutes. Stir in the fava beans, thyme, 1 teaspoon of salt, ½ teaspoon of pepper and the reserved lemon water. Cover and cook, stirring occasionally, until the artichokes are tender, about 15 minutes.

6. Stir in the spinach until wilted, then stir in the tarragon and the remaining 2 tablespoons parsley. Season with salt and pepper, sprinkle the vegetables with the seasoned bread crumbs and serve.

—Deborah Madison

Baby Artichoke, Spinach and Fava Bean Ragout

New Year's Peas and Greens

■

NEW YEAR'S PEAS AND GREENS

Eating hoppin' John—a southern dish of black-eyed peas and rice—on New Year's Day is supposed to bring good luck. This new dish follows that tradition.

Makes 6 to 8 Side-Dish Servings

- 1 **cup dried black-eyed peas, picked over**
- 3 **ounces smoked bacon* (about 4 slices)**
- 3 **garlic cloves, finely chopped**
- 1 **large onion, coarsely chopped**
- 1 **tablespoon plus 1 teaspoon minced fresh ginger**
- 2 **medium carrots, sliced crosswise ½ inch thick**
- 1 **small dried red chile**
- 1 **pound mustard greens, tough stems and large ribs discarded**
- 1 **tablespoon vegetable oil**
- ½ **of a jalapeño chile, minced**
- 2 **tablespoons tomato paste**

Salt and freshly ground black pepper
Red wine vinegar or apple cider vinegar, for serving

*Available at butchers and specialty food stores

1. Put the peas in a medium bowl and add enough cold water to cover by 1 inch. Let soak overnight.

2. The following day, in a large nonreactive saucepan, cook the bacon over moderate heat until slightly crisp. Coarsely chop the bacon and set aside. Pour off all but 1½ tablespoons of the fat from the saucepan. Add the garlic, onion and 1 tablespoon of the ginger and cook, stirring often, until fragrant, about 4 minutes.

3. Drain the peas and add them to the saucepan along with the carrots and dried red chile. Cover with 6 cups of cold water and bring to a boil. Reduce the heat to low and simmer, stirring occasionally, until the peas are tender, about 45 minutes.

4. In a large steamer, bring 1 inch of water to a boil over high heat. Pack the mustard greens in the steamer basket, cover and steam for 5 minutes. Transfer the steamer basket to the sink and let the greens drain and cool slightly, then coarsely chop.

5. In a large nonreactive skillet, warm the oil over moderately high heat. Add the remaining 1 teaspoon ginger, the reserved bacon and the jalapeño and cook until fragrant, about 30 seconds. Add the tomato paste and cook until shiny and beginning to brown, about 2 minutes. Add the mustard greens and stir until thoroughly coated, about 1 minute.

6. Scrape the greens into the black-eyed peas, stir well and simmer over low heat for 5 to 10 minutes. Remove the dried red chile. Season the greens and peas with salt and black pepper. Serve in bowls and pass the vinegar separately.

—Marcia Kiesel

CAREFREE BOSTON BAKED BEANS

Boston baked beans are cooked long and slowly, so that they literally caramelize in their juices. There's no soaking, no fussing—you just dump everything into the pot at night, and the next morning they are done.

Makes About 2 Quarts

- 1 2-inch square of salt pork, cut into matchsticks
- 2 cups small white beans, rinsed and picked over
- 1½ teaspoons salt
- 2 large garlic cloves, minced
- 2 tablespoons dark unsulfured molasses
- 2 tablespoons Dijon mustard
- ½ teaspoon thyme
- 2 imported bay leaves
- ½ tablespoon grated fresh ginger
- 6 grinds pepper

Put all the ingredients plus 5 cups of water in an electric slow-cooker, cover and cook on low for 12 to 14 hours, regulating the heat to maintain an almost simmer. (Or cook in a tightly covered casserole in a 225° oven. Add a little boiling water if the beans begin to look dry.) They are done when they turn a dark reddish caramel brown. Correct the seasoning before serving.

—Julia Child

SKILLET-STEAMED BROCCOLI WITH LEMON

Grated lemon zest, lemon juice and shallots add extra flavor to simple, low-fat steamed broccolli.

4 Servings

- 1 teaspoon olive oil
- 2 large shallots, minced
- 1 large bunch of broccoli (1½ pounds), cut into 1-inch florets
- ½ teaspoon finely grated lemon zest
  About 2 tablespoons fresh lemon juice
  Salt and freshly ground pepper

Heat the olive oil in a medium nonstick skillet. Add the shallots and cook over moderately high heat, stirring occasionally, until softened, about 1 minute. Add the broccoli, ¼ cup of water and the lemon zest, cover and simmer, shaking the pan occasionally, until the broccoli is crisp-tender, 3 to 4 minutes. Stir in the lemon juice. Season the broccoli with salt and pepper and serve.

—Georgia Chan Downard

GRILLED BROCCOLI-STUFFED ONIONS

Don't throw away your broccoli stems. Peel off the skin with a paring knife, then slice and steam the stems. You'll be surprised at how delicious they are.

4 Servings

- 2 large Spanish onions
- ¼ cup pine nuts
- 1½ tablespoons olive oil, plus a little more for brushing
- 4 cups very small broccoli florets, finely chopped (from 1 bunch)
- 1 medium garlic clove, minced
- 2 tablespoons freshly grated Parmesan cheese
  Salt and freshly ground pepper

1. Preheat the oven to 400°. Bring a large saucepan of water to a boil. With a knife, make a lengthwise cut just to the

---

BEAN FACTS

- About 2½ cups of water are needed to cook each cup of beans.
- One cup of uncooked beans makes 3 cups of cooked beans.
- Beans may be cooked 2 to 3 days ahead and refrigerated.

center of each onion. Drop the onions into the saucepan and boil until the outer layers are just tender and translucent, about 5 minutes. Drain and refresh with cold water. Separate the onion layers; you will need twelve good-sized ones for stuffing.

2. Toast the pine nuts in a small baking pan in the oven for about 4 minutes, until golden brown. Remove from the pan and let cool completely.

3. Heat the olive oil in a large skillet. Add the chopped broccoli and cook over moderately high heat, stirring, until bright green and barely cooked, about 2 minutes. Stir in the garlic and cook for another minute. Stir in the Parmesan cheese and season with salt and pepper. Transfer the broccoli to a bowl to cool to room temperature. (The broccoli filling can be prepared up to 1 day ahead and refrigerated.)

4. Just before filling the onions, stir the toasted pine nuts into the broccoli. Place a few tablespoons of the broccoli mixture at one edge of each layer of onion and tightly roll up.

5. Light a medium-hot grill. Press two 10-inch bamboo skewers crosswise through a stuffed onion roll to secure it. Skewer 2 more stuffed onion rolls on the same pair of skewers, one at a time. Repeat with the remaining stuffed onions; you should have 4 pairs of skewers with 3 rolls on each.

6. Lightly brush the onions with olive oil and season with salt and pepper. Grill the onions for 5 to 6 minutes per side, until lightly charred and heated through.

—Marcia Kiesel

■

BROCCOLI-SAUCED CAULIFLOWER

This wintry vegetable dish is composed of simple steamed cauliflower florets dressed with tiny broccoli buds in lemon butter sauce. Although most of the elements can be prepared ahead, it does need to be finished at the last minute.

12 Servings
- **2 large heads of broccoli**
- **¼ cup Chicken Stock (p. 36) or canned broth**
- **¼ cup fresh lemon juice**
  Finely grated zest of 1 lemon
- **½ teaspoon salt**
- **½ cup clarified unsalted butter plus 1 stick (8 tablespoons) cold unsalted butter, cut into ½-inch slices**
  Freshly ground pepper
- **2 large, firm heads of cauliflower, trimmed into 2-inch florets**

1. Cut the broccoli florets into tiny buds with tiny bits of stem. (Save the rest of the broccoli for soup.) Cover and refrigerate.

2. Make the base for the sauce: In a nonreactive saucepan, boil the Chicken Stock, lemon juice and zest, salt and 2 tablespoons of the cold butter over high heat until reduced to a syrupy ¼ cup, about 2 minutes. Season with pepper and set aside.

3. Shortly before serving, steam the cauliflower: Pour 1½ inches of water into a large saucepan with a steamer basket. Add the cauliflower, cover tightly and bring to a vigorous boil over high heat. Lower the heat to moderate and steam the cauliflower until just tender but with a gentle crunch, 5 to 8 minutes.

4. Meanwhile, heat the clarified butter in a skillet over moderate heat. Add the broccoli buds and cook, stirring occasionally, until just tender, 3 to 4 minutes.

5. Set the sauce base over moderately high heat and bring to a boil. Whisk in the remaining 6 tablespoons cold butter, a few pieces at a time, until creamy and thoroughly incorporated. Remove from the heat and fold in the broccoli buds.

6. Arrange the cauliflower on a warmed platter. Spoon the broccoli sauce over all.

—Julia Child

■

STIR-FRIED CABBAGE WITH GREEN AND RED PEPPERS

Stir-fried strips of green cabbage and bright bell peppers perk up a plate with plenty of color and crunch and don't require a lot of oil.

4 Servings

½ teaspoon peanut oil
½ teaspoon sesame oil
½ tablespoon finely grated fresh ginger
   Salt
1 pound green cabbage, cored and cut into 3-by-¼-inch strips
1 tablespoon dry white wine
½ medium green bell pepper, cut into ⅛-inch strips
½ medium red bell pepper, cut into ⅛-inch strips
   About 3 tablespoons Chicken Stock (p. 36) or canned low-sodium broth

1. Set a wok over high heat for 30 seconds. Add the peanut oil and the sesame oil and spread to coat the wok. Heat until a wisp of white smoke appears, then add the grated ginger and ½ teaspoon salt and stir-fry for 10 seconds. Add the strips of cabbage and stir-fry for 30 seconds. Drizzle the white wine down the side of the wok and stir to combine. Add the green and red bell peppers and stir-fry for 1 minute.

2. Add 3 tablespoons of the Chicken Stock to the wok. Cook, stirring frequently, until the cabbage and bell pepper strips are just tender, about 7 minutes. Add more stock as necessary during cooking if the vegetables look dry. Season with salt.

—Eileen Yin-Fei Lo

TIPS ON STIR-FRYING

• Stir-frying is terrific for health-conscious eaters because the intense heat cooks food without the need for much added fat. And just a little peanut or sesame oil—perhaps redolent with chiles or ginger for an extra kick—will have a definite impact on the flavor.
• Adding a small amount of chicken stock, white wine or water to the wok will slightly steam the foods being stir-fried, helping them to cook through.
• Another advantage of stir-frying is that it allows the partnering of foods with very different textures. Some successful pairings: tender cabbage and crisp bell peppers (as in Stir-Fried Cabbage with Green and Red Peppers, at left), carrots and cucumbers, broccoli stems and baby corn.

—Eileen Yin-Fei Lo

■

MARINATED FENNEL, PEARL ONIONS AND CELERY

This vegetable medley can be served as a first course or as an accompaniment to simply cooked seafood, poultry or meat. The red pearl onions called for below are pretty, but they taste just the same as the white ones.

4 Servings

1½ pounds medium fennel bulbs
12 red pearl onions
1   cup dry white wine
    Juice of 1 lemon
3   tablespoons olive oil
4   fresh thyme sprigs
1   small bay leaf
1   tablespoon chopped fresh parsley
½   teaspoon salt
½   teaspoon coriander seeds
½   teaspoon whole black peppercorns
4   tender inner celery ribs, peeled and cut into 2½-inch lengths
⅓   cup golden raisins
    Boiling water   ➤

1. Trim the fennel bulbs and remove any tough outer layers. Quarter each bulb through the root end.

2. Put the pearl onions in a steamer basket and place over boiling water in a large nonreactive saucepan or deep skillet. Cover and steam over moderate heat for 2 minutes. Remove the steamer basket from the pan and pour out the water. Peel the onions and trim the root ends.

3. In the same saucepan, combine the wine, lemon juice, olive oil, thyme sprigs, bay leaf, parsley and 2 cups of water. Cover and bring to a boil. Arrange the fennel in a single layer in the steamer basket and place over the boiling liquid. Sprinkle with the salt, coriander seeds and peppercorns. Cover and steam over moderate heat for 5 minutes.

4. Arrange the celery around and on top of the fennel. Add the pearl onions and raisins. Cover and steam until tender, about 15 minutes longer. (Add boiling water to the pan if necessary.)

5. Transfer the contents of the steamer basket to a serving dish or bowl. Discard the bay leaf. Boil the steaming liquid over high heat until reduced to ⅔ cup, 4 to 5 minutes. Pour over the vegetables and let cool to room temperature before serving.

—Stephanie Lyness

∎

SPINACH AND RED PEPPER GRATIN

This bright, pepper-studded spinach gratin requires a minimum of oil. It can be assembled hours ahead of time and baked at the last minute.

8 Servings

1   large red bell pepper
6   pounds fresh spinach
2   teaspoons extra-virgin olive oil
2   large eggs
⅔   cup skim milk

5   medium garlic cloves, minced
2   teaspoons coarsely chopped fresh thyme or 1 teaspoon dried, crumbled
1½ teaspoons salt
¾   teaspoon freshly ground black pepper
3   tablespoons fresh or dry bread crumbs
2   tablespoons freshly grated Parmesan cheese

1. Preheat the oven to 400°. In a small roasting pan, roast the pepper, turning occasionally, for about 45 minutes, or until browned and softened. Transfer the roasted pepper to a bowl, cover tightly and let steam for 20 minutes. Leave the oven on.

2. Working over a strainer set over a large bowl to catch the juices, peel off the roasted pepper skin and remove the core, ribs and seeds. Cut the pepper lengthwise into ¼-inch strips and set aside.

3. Bring a large pot of salted water to a boil. Working in batches, blanch the spinach in the boiling water until wilted. Transfer the cooked leaves to a bowl of cold water and repeat with the remaining spinach. Drain and squeeze the cooked spinach to remove as much liquid as possible, then coarsely chop the leaves.

4. Lightly coat a 10-inch round glass or ceramic baking dish with ½ teaspoon of the olive oil. Beat the eggs and skim milk into the red pepper liquid. Stir in the chopped spinach, garlic, thyme, salt and black pepper. Spoon the mixture into the prepared dish and sprinkle the bread crumbs and Parmesan cheese on top. Arrange the bell pepper strips on top in a starburst pattern and drizzle with the remaining 1½ teaspoons olive oil. (The gratin can be prepared to this point up to 5 hours ahead; cover and refrigerate.)

5. Bake the gratin for about 30 minutes, until it is cooked through and lightly browned. Let cool slightly, then cut into 8 wedges and serve warm.

—Martha Rose Shulman

Spinach and Red Pepper Gratin

MIXED GREENS

Wilted greens—escarole, arugula, napa cabbage and radicchio—make for a colorful combination.

4 Servings

½ cup Chicken Stock (p. 36), canned low-sodium broth or water
1½ teaspoons minced garlic
½ pound napa cabbage, torn into 2-inch pieces
½ pound arugula, stemmed, leaves torn in half
½ pound radicchio, torn into 2-inch pieces
½ pound escarole, torn into 2-inch pieces
Salt and freshly ground pepper
1 teaspoon walnut oil

Place the Chicken Stock and garlic in an enameled cast-iron casserole. Cover and cook over moderately high heat until the garlic is softened, about 1 minute. Add the greens and season with salt and pepper. Cover and cook, stirring, until just wilted, about 2 minutes. Transfer the greens to a serving dish, drizzle the walnut oil on top and season with salt and pepper.

—Katherine Alford

Swiss Chard

Bok Choy

Kale

Broccoli Rabe

Turnip Greens

Mustard Greens

■

STIR-FRIED COLLARDS WITH APPLE AND BALSAMIC VINEGAR

For a simpler variation of this dish, replace the onion and apple with one large minced clove of garlic.

4 Side-Dish Servings

½ **pound collard greens, stems and thick center ribs discarded**
1½ **tablespoons canola oil or unsalted butter**
1 **small onion, thinly sliced**
1 **small tart apple, such as Winesap or greening—peeled, halved, cored and thinly sliced lengthwise**
1 **tablespoon balsamic vinegar**
Salt and freshly ground pepper

1. In a large nonreactive saucepan of boiling water, cook the collards over high heat for 5 minutes. Drain and let cool slightly, then cut into 1-inch pieces.

2. In a large nonreactive skillet, heat the oil. Add the onion and cook over moderately high heat, stirring, until wilted and lightly caramelized, about 2 minutes. Add the apple slices and cook until tender, 2 minutes longer. Stir in the collards until thoroughly combined. Increase the heat to

GREENS: QUICK-FIX COOKING SUGGESTIONS

Spinach

Collards

• **Swiss chard:** Boil the stems until softened. Add the leaves and cook until just tender. Drain, return to the pot and cook until excess moisture has evaporated. Flavor with olive oil, butter, vinegar or lemon juice and salt and pepper.

• **Bok choy:** Cook shredded pieces in a clear soup. Or stir-fry in hot peanut oil flavored with ginger and garlic for 2 minutes in a wok or wide skillet. Add a bit of water or broth, cover and cook until the leaves are tender. Season with soy sauce and sesame oil.

• **Kale:** Slice the leaves into wide strips and add to stews and soups, such as hearty vegetable or lentil, for the last 10 minutes of cooking.

• **Spinach:** Sauté in olive oil or olive oil and butter until wilted and excess liquid has evaporated, then season with vinegar or lemon juice, and salt and pepper. For quick creamed spinach, wilt the leaves with the water clinging to them in a hot skillet. Remove from the heat, lightly squeeze and drain off any excess liquid. Stir in room-temperature sour cream, lots of chopped scallions, salt and freshly ground black pepper. Try it on top of a baked potato.

• **Broccoli rabe:** Heat olive oil in a wide skillet. Stir in chopped garlic and broccoli rabe and turn to coat well. Add enough stock or water to coat the bottom of the pan, cover and cook over low heat, stirring occasionally, until tender. Uncover and cook to evaporate any liquid; season to taste. Use as a topping for pasta or as a bed for fish or poultry.

• **Turnip greens:** Cook the leaves until tender in just enough boiling water or stock to keep them from sticking to the pan. In the southern manner, serve with as much butter as you dare.

• **Mustard greens:** Blanch the leaves, drain, refresh and gently squeeze out excess moisture. Chop and reheat in a skillet with olive oil or butter or in a bit of chicken broth and seasonings. Use as a side dish or as a stuffing for poultry or calzones.

• **Collards:** For a traditional southern preparation, boil the leaves in ham broth. Or heat olive oil in a wide skillet, gradually add sliced collard leaves and, if desired, an equal amount of thinly sliced green cabbage, stirring until wilted. Add a bit of stock or water, cover and braise, stirring occasionally, until the greens are tender. Uncover and cook to evaporate any excess liquid; season to taste.

Swiss Chard Lasagna

3 tablespoons unsalted butter
1 small onion, finely chopped
2 tablespoons all-purpose flour
2 cups milk
1 bay leaf
   Salt and freshly ground pepper
1 pound shiitake mushrooms, stems discarded, caps sliced ¼ inch thick
2 medium shallots, minced
2 cups ricotta cheese (8 ounces)
2 cups grated mozzarella cheese (8 ounces)
2 large garlic cloves, minced
1 large egg yolk
½ cup grated Parmesan cheese (about 2 ounces)

high, add the balsamic vinegar and cook, stirring, until the greens are evenly coated, about 1 minute. Remove from the heat, season with salt and pepper and serve.

—Marcia Kiesel

■

SWISS CHARD LASAGNA

In this lasagna, layers of Swiss chard leaves take the place of noodles.

♟ This dish is complemented by a medium-bodied, smooth red, such as Rioja. A 1988 Marqués de Murrieta Reserva or 1988 Marqués de Riscal is an excellent choice.

8 Servings

2 pounds red Swiss chard, stems removed up to an inch from the leaves

1. In a large steamer, bring ½ inch of water to a boil over high heat. Pack half of the Swiss chard in the steamer basket, cover and steam until tender but not too soft, 3 to 4 minutes. Transfer to a colander and repeat with the remaining chard. Let drain until cool, then separate the leaves and spread them out in a single layer on paper towels, pressing them lightly to remove excess moisture. Gently roll up the towels to keep the leaves from drying out.

2. In a medium nonreactive saucepan, melt 1 tablespoon of the butter over moderate heat. Add the onion and cook until slightly softened, about 3 minutes. Using a wooden spoon, stir in the flour and increase the heat to high. Whisk in the milk and bring to a boil, whisking until smooth, about 4 minutes. Add the bay leaf and simmer over low heat, whisking often, until the sauce is shiny and the floury taste is gone, about 10 minutes. Pass the sauce through a coarse strainer set over a bowl, pressing the onion with a rubber spatula and scraping the bottom of the strainer. Season with salt and pepper. Put plastic wrap directly on the surface of the sauce to prevent a skin from forming.

3. In a large skillet, melt the remaining 2 tablespoons butter over high heat. Stir in the mushrooms and shallots. Cover and

cook, stirring once, until the mushrooms are well browned, about 5 minutes. Season with salt and pepper and transfer to a plate.

4. In a medium bowl, mix the ricotta, mozzarella and garlic and season with salt and pepper. Stir in the egg yolk.

5. Preheat the oven to 375°. Remove the plastic wrap from the white sauce and squeeze any sauce clinging to it back into the bowl. Spread ¼ cup of the sauce on the bottom of a 9-by-13-inch glass or enameled baking dish or oval gratin dish. Unfold the chard leaves and divide into 4 equal parts. Arrange ¼ of the leaves in an even layer over the sauce. Using a rubber spatula, lightly spread ½ of the ricotta mixture on top of the leaves. Continue to layer in the following manner: ¼ of the chard, all of the mushrooms, ¾ cup of the white sauce, 3 tablespoons of the Parmesan, another ¼ of chard, the remaining ricotta mixture, 2 more tablespoons of Parmesan, the remaining chard and the remaining white sauce. Sprinkle the remaining 3 tablespoons Parmesan on top.

6. Bake in the upper third of the oven for 35 to 40 minutes, until bubbling and lightly browned on top. Let the lasagna rest for 10 to 15 minutes before serving

—Marcia Kiesel

■

OVEN-ROASTED PARSNIPS WITH ONIONS AND CHESTNUTS

Roasted parsnips and onions, combined with chestnuts (an exceptionally low-fat nut) make a health-conscious accompaniment for turkey or chicken.

4 Servings
¾ **pound fresh chestnuts**
½ **pound pearl onions**
½ **tablespoon unsalted butter**
½ **tablespoon vegetable oil**
1¼ **pounds parsnips, peeled and cut into ½-inch cubes**
   Salt
   Freshly ground pepper
1½ **cups Chicken Stock (p. 36) or canned low-sodium broth**
1 **teaspoon minced fresh thyme leaves**
1 **tablespoon coarsely chopped flat-leaf parsley**

1. Make an incision across each chestnut. In a medium saucepan, cover the chestnuts with water and bring to a boil over moderate heat. Boil for 4 minutes. Remove from the heat.

2. Remove 2 or 3 chestnuts at a time from the water and peel off the shells and skins. If the skins stick, reheat the chestnuts in the hot water. Break the peeled nuts into ½-inch pieces.

3. Bring a medium saucepan of water to a boil. Add the pearl onions and cook for 4 minutes. Drain, rinse and drain again. Trim the root end from each onion and slip off the skin.

4. Preheat the oven to 450°. Place the butter and the vegetable oil in a large rimmed baking sheet and heat in the oven for 3 minutes. Coat the baking sheet with the melted butter and oil. Spread the pearl onions and the parsnip cubes on top; season with salt and pepper. Roast the vegetables for about 25 minutes, stirring occasionally, until they are tender and browned.

5. Meanwhile, in a small saucepan, combine the chestnuts with the Chicken Stock and thyme. Season with salt and pepper. Bring to a boil over high heat and cook until the liquid has reduced by two-thirds, about 5 minutes.

6. Transfer the roasted onions and parsnips to a bowl and add the chestnuts with their liquid. Sprinkle with the chopped parsley and serve.

—Katherine Alford

ROASTED RED PEPPERS WITH VINAIGRETTE

This recipe has been adapted from *Fanny at Chez Panisse* (HarperCollins).

4 Servings

6 firm red bell peppers, halved
   lengthwise, cored and seeded
   Pure olive oil, for rubbing
1 shallot
   Salt
2 tablespoons red wine vinegar
5 to 6 tablespoons extra-virgin olive oil

1. Preheat the oven to 375°. Rub the bell pepper skins with pure olive oil and put them on a baking sheet, cut sides down. Bake for 30 to 40 minutes, until the peppers are tender and the skins are blistered and browned. Remove from the oven and let cool.

2. While the peppers cook, slice the shallot very thin and put it in a medium bowl. Add a pinch of salt and the vinegar. Let soak for 15 to 20 minutes, then stir in the extra-virgin olive oil.

3. Pull the skins off the peppers. Slice the peppers lengthwise and toss them with the vinaigrette. Taste to see if the balance of vinegar and oil is right; you might need to add more of one or the other.

—Alice Waters

PEPERONATA

Poblano or jalapeño peppers give an untraditional twist to this Italian dish.

Makes About 2 Quarts

3 tablespoons olive oil
5 medium red bell peppers
5 medium yellow bell peppers
2 large green poblano peppers or 1
   green bell pepper and 2 jalapeño
   peppers
1 large Spanish onion, halved
   lengthwise and cut into 1-inch
   wedges
10 unpeeled garlic cloves
6 fresh thyme sprigs
   Salt and freshly ground black pepper
½ cup finely chopped fresh basil

1. Preheat the oven to 400°. Coat the bottom of a large roasting pan with 1 tablespoon of the olive oil. Place the peppers in the pan and arrange the onion wedges close together in a line along one side of the pan to keep them intact. Scatter the garlic cloves on the bottom of the pan and distribute the thyme sprigs here and there. Drizzle the remaining 2 tablespoons olive oil over all the vegetables.

2. Cover the pan tightly with foil and bake on the bottom shelf of the oven for about 45 minutes, until the vegetables are tender. Set aside, covered, for 10 minutes.

3. Lift the foil and let the peppers cool enough to handle; they are easier to peel if still slightly hot. Working over a deep, wide dish to catch the juices, remove the stems, cores and as many seeds as possible from the peppers. (Don't worry if seeds fall into the dish with the pepper juices; they will be strained out.) Peel the peppers, tear them into ½-inch strips and place in a large bowl.

4. Gently remove the onion wedges from the pan and add them to the peppers. Strain the pepper juices into a small bowl. Squeeze the garlic pulp from the skins into the strained pepper juices and blend with a fork. Pour this dressing over the peppers and onion wedges and mix well. Season with salt and black pepper. Cover and refrigerate for up to 5 days if desired. To serve, scoop the peperonata onto plates with a slotted spoon and sprinkle generously with the basil.

—Marcia Kiesel

ROASTED VEGETABLE AND HOMINY CHILI

Here, hominy functions as an unusual alternative to beans.

♥ Look for a fruity, round California Merlot, such as 1990 St. Francis Reserve Estate or 1990 Shafer. A spicy beer, such as Anchor Steam or Samuel Adams, would work well, too.

8 Servings

5 medium pasilla, or negro, chiles
2 medium guajillo chiles
1 large chipotle chile
3 small zucchini, cut into ¾-inch dice
3 small yellow squash, cut into ¾-inch dice
4 baby eggplants, cut into ¾-inch dice
1 large red bell pepper, cut into ¾-inch dice
1 large yellow bell pepper, cut into ¾-inch dice
½ pound okra, cut into ¾-inch lengths
1 large Portobello mushroom, stem discarded and cap cut into ¾-inch dice, or ½ pound white mushrooms, stems discarded and caps quartered
¼ cup olive oil
Salt and freshly ground black pepper
2 tablespoons vegetable oil
1 medium onion, finely chopped
3 garlic cloves, minced
2 tablespoons ground cumin
1 28-ounce can tomato puree
1 6-ounce can tomato paste
1 tablespoon sugar
2 16-ounce cans yellow or white hominy, drained and rinsed
⅔ cup finely chopped fresh coriander leaves (cilantro)
Texmati rice or whole wheat pasta and sour cream, for serving

1. In a medium bowl, soak the pasilla, guajillo and chipotle chiles in 4 cups of hot water until softened, about 20 minutes. Pour off the soaking liquid, reserving 2 cups. Stem and seed the chiles and transfer them to a food processor or blender with the reserved soaking liquid. Puree until smooth. Pass the puree through a fine strainer into a small bowl.

2. Preheat the oven to 450°. On a large rimmed baking sheet, toss the zucchini, yellow squash, eggplants, bell peppers, okra and mushrooms with the olive oil. Spread the vegetables in a single layer and season with salt and pepper. Roast for about 20 minutes, stirring the vegetables occasionally, until lightly browned.

3. Heat the vegetable oil in a large enameled cast-iron casserole. Add the onion and garlic and cook over moderate heat, stirring occasionally, until translucent, about 3 minutes. Add the cumin and cook, stirring, until fragrant, about 1 minute. Stir in the pureed chiles, tomato puree, tomato paste, sugar and 1½ cups of water. Bring to a boil over moderately high heat. Lower the heat, cover partially and simmer, stirring occasionally, until thickened, about 1 hour. Fold in the roasted vegetables and hominy. (The chili can be made up to 1 day ahead; cover and refrigerate. Rewarm slowly over moderate heat.)

4. Stir half of the coriander into the chili and season with salt. Sprinkle with the remaining coriander and serve with Texmati rice and sour cream.

—Grace Parisi

GARDEN SQUASH AND PEA MEDLEY

This light and simple dish illustrates just how delicious freshly shucked peas are. However, you can substitute frozen peas if you wish. Serve the medley as a vegetarian meal with buttered noodles. ➤

177

Stir in ½ cup of the broth and boil until the pan is nearly dry, about 5 minutes.

2. Add the squash and the remaining ½ cup vegetable broth. Season with salt and pepper and cook over moderate heat, stirring occasionally, until the squash is crisp-tender, about 3 minutes. Stir in the peas and 1 tablespoon each of the basil and parsley and cook over moderate heat until the peas are tender, about 3 minutes. Remove from the heat.

3. Stir in the butter and the remaining 1 tablespoon each of basil and parsley. Serve at once.

—Deborah Madison

■

ZUCCHINI AND CARROTS PARMESAN

In this low-fat side dish, shredded zucchini and carrots are simmered in reduced chicken stock and sprinkled with a tiny bit of Parmesan cheese.

Garden Squash and Pea Medley

4 Servings
- 1 tablespoon extra-virgin olive oil
- 1 small onion, finely chopped
- 1 medium garlic clove, minced
- 1 cup homemade or canned vegetable broth
- 1 pound baby pattypan squash, cut into bite-size wedges, or small zucchini or yellow summer squash, sliced crosswise ¼ inch thick
  Salt and freshly ground pepper
- 1 cup shelled peas (from 1 pound fresh peas in the pod)
- 2 tablespoons thinly slivered fresh basil
- 2 tablespoons chopped fresh flat-leaf parsley
- 1 tablespoon unsalted butter

1. In a medium nonreactive skillet, combine the oil, onion and garlic and cook over moderately high heat, stirring often, until slightly softened, about 3 minutes.

4 Servings
- ½ cup Chicken Stock (p. 36), or canned low-sodium broth
- 1 pound medium zucchini, shredded
- 2 medium carrots, shredded
  Salt and freshly ground pepper
- 1 tablespoon freshly grated Parmesan cheese

In a medium skillet, boil the Chicken Stock over moderately high heat until reduced by half, about 2 minutes. Add the shredded zucchini and carrots and season with salt and pepper. Cook, stirring frequently, until the vegetables are just tender, about 4 minutes. Season with more salt and pepper, transfer to a serving dish and sprinkle the grated Parmesan on the top.

—Michele Scicolone

■

ZUCCHINI PARMESAN

No-fuss vegetables. Just layer the zucchini and onion slices and bake.

4 Servings

2 medium zucchini, sliced crosswise ¼ inch thick
1 medium onion, thinly sliced
2 tablespoons olive oil
 Salt and freshly ground pepper
3 tablespoons freshly grated Parmesan cheese

Preheat the oven to 375°. Layer the vegetable slices in a 9-by-13-inch glass or ceramic baking dish. Pour in 2 tablespoons or so of water to cover the bottom of the dish. Drizzle the oil over the vegetables and season lightly with salt and pepper. Sprinkle the cheese on top. Bake on the top shelf of the oven for 25 to 30 minutes, until the zucchini is tender and the top is browned. Serve hot or at room temperature.

—Marcia Kiesel

■

CORN, SQUASH AND GREEN CHILE STEW

Soft polenta or a fragrant rice, such as jasmine or basmati, is a nice companion to this dish.

4 Servings

4 medium ears fresh corn, shucked
2 tablespoons unsalted butter
1 tablespoon olive oil
1 large onion, finely chopped
1½ pounds small zucchini, cut into ¾-inch dice, or baby zucchini, sliced crosswise ¾ inch thick
6 ounces green chiles, such as Anaheim, New Mexico or Big Jim, cut into ½-inch dice
1 tablespoon coarsely chopped fresh marjoram or ½ teaspoon dried
 Salt
2½ ounces Monterey Jack cheese, cut into ¼-inch dice
 Freshly ground black pepper
¼ cup coarsely chopped fresh flat-leaf parsley

1. Using a thin sharp knife, slice the corn kernels from each cob into a glass measure until you have 2 cups.

2. In a large nonreactive skillet, melt the butter in the olive oil over moderate heat. Add the onion and cook, stirring occasionally, until it starts to color, about 10 minutes. Stir in the zucchini, chiles, marjoram and ½ cup of water. Season with ½ teaspoon of salt, cover and cook until the zucchini and chiles are nearly tender, about 8 minutes. Add the corn and cook, stirring occasionally, until crisp-tender, about 3 minutes. Remove from the heat.

3. Stir the Monterey Jack cheese into the stew and season well with salt and lots of black pepper. Sprinkle the parsley on top and serve.

—Deborah Madison

■

WINTER SQUASH WITH CROUTON STUFFING

When you have lots of people waiting for the carver to get at the bird, it is often faster and easier to serve the stuffing baked in a winter squash. This recipe works nicely with squash of any size; adjust the cooking time for the squash accordingly. To serve larger varieties, simply cut right through the squash and stuffing, making melon-shaped pieces. ➤

12 Servings

12 **small winter squash, such as**
buttercup, kabocha or acorn
(about ¾ pound each)
1 **stick (8 tablespoons) unsalted**
butter, plus 6 tablespoons melted
butter
Salt
Vegetable oil
1 **pound sliced firm-textured white**
bread, crusts removed, cut into
½-inch dice
1 **large Spanish onion, diced**
8 **medium celery ribs, diced**
1 **tablespoon chopped fresh sage**
Freshly ground pepper
2 **large eggs, lightly beaten**

1. Preheat the oven to 400°. Cut off the top third of each squash to form a lid. Scrape out all the seeds and strings from each squash and set them on an oiled baking sheet. Spoon ½ tablespoon of the melted butter into the cavity of each squash and sprinkle with salt. Replace the lids and lightly oil the outsides of the squash. Roast in the oven for 30 to 40 minutes, until the flesh of the squash is just tender when pierced.

2. Make the crouton stuffing: Lower the oven temperature to 350°. Spread the bread cubes in 2 large baking pans and toast in the oven for about 20 minutes, tossing occasionally, until lightly browned.

3. Melt the stick of butter in a large skillet. Add the Spanish onion and cook over moderately low heat until tender, 8 to 10 minutes. Add the celery and cook for 2 to 3 minutes longer. Transfer the vegetables to a bowl; stir in the croutons and sage. Season with salt and pepper. Blend in the eggs.

4. Raise the oven temperature to 375°. Spoon the stuffing into the squash and bake for about 30 minutes, until the squash is tender and the stuffing is heated through and beginning to brown.

—Julia Child

FRIED GREEN TOMATOES

For this recipe, use any tomato variety in its green (unripe) state. If you use Evergreens, which are green when ripe, be sure to select very firm ones.

4 Servings

½ **pound smoked bacon, cut into**
6 thick slices
½ **cup cornmeal**
3 **tablespoons freshly grated**
Parmesan cheese
¾ **teaspoon salt**
½ **teaspoon freshly ground pepper**
3 **tablespoons vegetable oil**
4 **medium green tomatoes, cored**
and sliced crosswise ¼ inch
thick

1. In a large skillet, fry the smoked bacon over moderate heat until crisp, about 8 minutes. Drain the bacon on paper towels and then crumble. Reserve 2 tablespoons of the fat and discard the remainder.

2. In a wide shallow dish, mix together the cornmeal, Parmesan cheese, salt and pepper. In the skillet, heat 1 tablespoon of the reserved bacon fat with half of the vegetable oil over moderately high heat. Press half of the tomato slices into the cornmeal mixture to coat both sides well. When the fat is sizzling hot, add the tomatoes and cook until crisp and lightly browned on one side, about 1 minute. Flip and cook the other side until crisp, another minute or so. Drain on paper towels. Fry the remaining tomato slices in the remaining 1 tablespoon bacon fat and 1½ tablespoons vegetable oil.

3. Transfer the fried tomatoes to a large plate, sprinkle the crumbled bacon on top and serve immediately.

—Marcia Kiesel

VEGETARIAN KOFTA CURRY

This Indian dish consists of deep-fried vegetable fritters (koftas) in a curry gravy. A mixture of diced onion and tomato with chopped mint is a good accompaniment.

❦ The mélange of flavors in this recipe will find affinities in a simple, fruity Sauvignon Blanc from California, such as 1992 Corbett Canyon Vineyards or 1992 Geyser Peak.

4 to 6 Servings

1 large Spanish onion, coarsely chopped
3 garlic cloves, finely chopped
2 tablespoons finely chopped fresh ginger
3 tablespoons safflower or canola oil
2 white or green cardamom pods, crushed, or ¼ teaspoon ground cardamom
1 1½-inch cinnamon stick
2 large tomatoes, peeled and coarsely chopped
1 heaping teaspoon turmeric
1 teaspoon garam masala*
½ teaspoon ground cumin
½ teaspoon cayenne pepper
½ teaspoon ground coriander
¾ teaspoon salt
Koftas (recipe follows)

*Available at Indian markets

1. In a food processor, puree the onion, garlic and ginger until smooth, stopping to scrape the bowl.
2. Heat the oil in a large nonreactive saucepan. Add the onion puree, the cardamom and cinnamon stick and cook over high heat, stirring constantly, until most of the moisture has evaporated, about 5 minutes.

3. Add the tomatoes and cook, stirring, for 3 minutes. Add the turmeric, garam masala, cumin, cayenne and coriander and cook for 2 minutes. Pour in 2 cups of hot water, stir in the salt and simmer over low heat until the gravy thickens, about 25 minutes. (The recipe can be made to this point up to 2 days ahead; refrigerate. To reheat, bring to a simmer over moderate heat.)
4. To serve, pour the gravy into a deep platter or shallow serving bowl and arrange the Koftas on top.

Koftas
Makes About 30 Balls

2 green serrano chiles, seeded if desired, and minced
½ cup whole blanched almonds (2 ounces), finely chopped
¼ cup coarsely grated carrot
1 small zucchini, peeled and sliced crosswise ½ inch thick (1 cup)
¾ pound pumpkin or butternut squash—peeled, seeded and cut into ¾-inch chunks (2 cups) ➤

CURRY SPICE GUIDE

- **BLACK (or BROWN) MUSTARD SEEDS:** Mustard's heat is due to an enzyme contained in the dried seeds. The longer they cook, the less pungent they become.
- **LAOS POWDER:** This is the dried and ground version of galangal, an Asian relative of ginger, whose flavor it resembles. It's a popular Thai spice.
- **CARDAMOM PODS:** Cardamom, a fragrant member of the ginger family, has a spicy-sweet taste. Crush to expose the seeds inside and release the full flavor.
- **GROUND CORIANDER:** Mild, sweet and vaguely orange flavored, coriander—both the whole seed and the ground version—is a common curry spice, particularly in India.
- **TURMERIC:** Another ginger cousin, sharp-tasting turmeric is remarkable for its brilliant orange hue and the yellow color it imparts to food.
- **GARAM MASALA:** This Indian spice blend, literally "hot mixture," is usually made with ground pepper, cardamom, cinnamon, cloves and coriander.

3. Return the saucepan of water to a boil, add the pumpkin chunks and cook until just tender, about 5 minutes. Drain the pumpkin thoroughly, transfer to a square of cheesecloth and squeeze it gently in the same manner as the zucchini.

4. In a food processor, puree the zucchini, pumpkin and onion for 30 seconds. Scrape the puree into the mixture of chiles, almonds and carrot. Season with the salt and cumin, add ½ cup of the chickpea flour and mix thoroughly with a wooden spoon. Cover and refrigerate the kofta batter for at least 1 hour or overnight.

5. Sprinkle the remaining ¼ cup chickpea flour on a large platter. With lightly floured hands, form the kofta batter into 1-inch balls. Place the kofta balls on the platter and gently roll them to coat evenly with the chickpea flour.

6. In a wok, heat the oil until it reaches 350° on a deep-fat thermometer. In batches of 4, fry the koftas, stirring gently, until browned all over, 1 to 2 minutes. Using a slotted spoon, transfer the balls to paper towels to drain. (The koftas can be made up to 1 day ahead; cover and refrigerate. Rewarm on a baking sheet in a 400° oven for about 5 minutes, until hot.)

—Jennifer Brennan

**Vegetarian
Kofta Curry**

1 **large Spanish onion, peeled and finely chopped (1½ cups)**
1 **teaspoon salt**
½ **teaspoon ground cumin**
¾ **cup chickpea flour (besan)***
1 **cup vegetable oil, for deep-fat frying**

*Available at Indian markets

1. Place the chiles, almonds and carrot in a nonreactive bowl.

2. Place the zucchini slices in a small strainer or a sieve. Submerge the strainer in a small saucepan of boiling water and cook until the zucchini slices are just tender, 1 to 2 minutes. Remove the strainer, reserving the saucepan of water. Rinse the zucchini slices under cold running water. Transfer the zucchini slices to a square of cheesecloth, pull up the corners and gently but firmly squeeze out the excess liquid.

Chapter 9 ▪ STUFFINGS & POTATOES

185   Bread Stuffing with Escarole and Ham

185   Corn Bread and Chestnut Stuffing

186   Two-Bread Stuffing with Sausage

187   Rice Stuffing with Fresh and Dried Mushrooms

188   Barley Stuffing with Dried Fruit

190   Bulgur Stuffing with Pears and Pecans

190   Classic Mashed Potatoes

191   Mashed Potatoes with Garlic

191   Low-Fat Garlic Mashed Potatoes

191   Potato Puffs

192   Potato and Red Pepper Frittata

193   Scalloped Potatoes

193   Roasted Potato Wedges with Salsa de Cilantro à la Presilla

194   Potato-Tomato Gratin

195   Six-Vegetable Curry

Corn Bread and
Chestnut Stuffing

BREAD STUFFING WITH ESCAROLE AND HAM

This stuffing forms a tasty, crisp crust when baked in a buttered casserole.

Makes About 12 Cups

- 12 cups ½-inch cubes of firm-textured white bread (from a 1-pound loaf)
- 1 stick (8 tablespoons) unsalted butter
- 2 pounds escarole, cored and cut into 1-inch pieces
- 3 ounces thinly sliced country ham or prosciutto, finely chopped
- 1 medium onion, finely chopped
- 4 large scallions, finely chopped
- 1 large green bell pepper, finely chopped
- 2 large eggs, lightly beaten
- 1 cup Chicken Stock (p. 36) or canned low-sodium broth
- ¾ teaspoon salt
- ¾ teaspoon freshly ground black pepper

1. Spread the bread cubes on 2 large rimmed baking sheets and air-dry thoroughly for 1 or 2 days. Alternatively, toast in a 300° oven for about 30 minutes, stirring occasionally, until toasted and dried.

2. Melt 3 tablespoons of the butter in a large skillet. Add the escarole. Cook over high heat, stirring, until wilted, about 4 minutes. Transfer to a very large bowl.

3. Melt the remaining 5 tablespoons butter in the skillet. Add the ham and cook over low heat, stirring, for 2 minutes. Add the ham to the escarole. Add the onion, scallions and green pepper and cook, stirring occasionally, until softened, about 8 minutes. Add to the escarole and let cool.

4. Add the bread cubes, eggs, Chicken Stock, salt and pepper to the escarole and ham and mix well. Let cool before stuffing the turkey.

5. Preheat the oven to 350°. Place the leftover stuffing in a shallow buttered baking dish. Cover with foil. Bake about 30 minutes, or until heated through. Uncover and cook for about 5 minutes longer, until the top is crisp and lightly browned.

—Marcia Kiesel

■

CORN BREAD AND CHESTNUT STUFFING

Create a modern classic by combining two popular stuffing ingredients, corn bread and chestnuts.

Makes About 12 Cups

Corn Bread:
- 3 tablespoons vegetable oil
- 1½ cups yellow cornmeal
- 1 cup flour
- 2½ tablespoons sugar
- 2 teaspoons baking powder
- ½ teaspoon salt
- ⅓ cup sour cream
- 1 large egg
- 1 cup milk

Stuffing:
- 4 cups ⅓-inch cubes of firm-textured white bread (from about ½-pound loaf)
- 1½ pounds fresh chestnuts
- 4 ounces lean smoked bacon, cut into 1-by-¼-inch strips
- 1 stick (8 tablespoons) unsalted butter
- ½ cup lightly packed fresh sage leaves
- 1 large onion, finely chopped
- 2 medium celery ribs, peeled and finely chopped
- ¼ cup coarsely chopped flat-leaf parsley
- 2 large eggs, lightly beaten
  About 2 cups Chicken Stock (p. 36) or canned low-sodium broth
- 1½ teaspoons salt
- ¾ teaspoon freshly ground pepper ➤

when pierced with a knife, about 15 minutes. Remove from the heat. Remove 2 or 3 chestnuts at a time from the water and peel off the shells and skins. If the shells stick, reheat the chestnuts in the hot water. Repeat with the remaining chestnuts. Break the nuts into ½-inch chunks. (The recipe can be prepared to this point up to 1 day ahead. Set the bread aside at room temperature. Refrigerate the chestnuts.)

5. Heat a large skillet. Add the bacon and cook over low heat, stirring often, until lightly browned but not crisp, about 5 minutes. Transfer to a paper towel. Pour off all but 1 tablespoon of the fat and melt the butter in the skillet. Scatter the sage leaves in the skillet in an even layer and cook over moderate heat, stirring once, for 2 minutes; you should have a mixture of crisp and soft sage leaves. Transfer to a plate. Let cool, then finely chop the sage.

6. Add the onion and celery to the skillet. Cook over moderately low heat, stirring, until softened, 8 minutes. Transfer to a very large bowl and stir in the chestnuts, bacon, sage and parsley. Let cool.

7. Add the corn and white breads to the chestnut mixture. Stir in the eggs. Add enough Chicken Stock so the stuffing forms a ball when squeezed. Season with the salt and pepper. Let cool before stuffing the turkey.

8. Preheat the oven to 350°. Place the leftover stuffing in a shallow buttered baking dish. Cover with foil. Bake about 30 minutes, or until heated through. Uncover and cook for about 5 minutes longer, until the top is crisp and lightly browned.

—Marcia Kiesel

■

TWO-BREAD STUFFING WITH SAUSAGE

This substantial stuffing makes delicious pan-fried patties.

Two-Bread Stuffing with Sausage

1. Make the corn bread: Preheat the oven to 375°. Heat 1 tablespoon of the oil in a 9- or 10-inch cast-iron skillet in the oven. Sift the cornmeal, flour, sugar, baking powder and salt into a large bowl.

2. In a small bowl, beat the sour cream and egg until smooth. Stir in the milk and remaining 2 tablespoons oil. Fold into the dry ingredients just until combined. Spoon into the hot skillet. Bake for about 20 minutes, until the bread springs back when lightly pressed. Invert on a rack. Let cool.

3. Prepare the stuffing: Crumble the corn bread onto a large rimmed baking sheet and air-dry thoroughly for about 3 days. Spread the white bread cubes on a second baking sheet and air-dry thoroughly for 1 or 2 days. Alternatively, in a 300° oven, toast the white bread cubes for about 20 minutes and the corn bread for about 30 minutes, stirring occasionally, until toasted and dried.

4. Make a small incision across the top of each chestnut. Place the chestnuts in a medium saucepan and cover with water. Simmer over moderate heat until tender

Makes About 12 Cups

9 cups ½-inch cubes of firm-textured white bread (from a ¾-pound loaf)

7½ cups ½-inch cubes of whole grain or whole wheat bread (from a ¾-pound loaf)

3 tablespoons unsalted butter, plus more for frying the patties

1 turkey liver or 6 ounces chicken livers, trimmed and cut into ⅓-inch pieces

1½ pounds sweet Italian sausage, removed from its casings

1 large onion, coarsely chopped

2 large celery ribs, finely chopped

1 teaspoon minced fresh thyme or ½ teaspoon dried

1 teaspoon minced fresh rosemary or ½ teaspoon dried

1½ teaspoons salt

1½ teaspoons freshly ground pepper

2 large eggs, lightly beaten

1 cup Chicken Stock (p. 36) or canned low-sodium broth

1 cup cranberry juice

⅓ cup coarsely chopped flat-leaf parsley

1. Preheat the oven to 225°. Spread the white bread cubes on a large rimmed baking sheet. Spread the whole wheat bread cubes on a second baking sheet. Bake for about 30 minutes, stirring, until lightly toasted outside. Let cool. Alternatively, let the cubes air-dry overnight.

2. Meanwhile, in a large heavy skillet, melt 1 tablespoon of the butter. Add the liver and cook over moderately high heat, turning once, until the liver is well browned, about 2 minutes. Transfer to a very large bowl. Crumble the sausage meat into the skillet and cook, stirring, until nicely browned and crisp, about 10 minutes. Add to the liver.

3. Melt 2 more tablespoons of the butter in the skillet. Add the onion and celery and cook over moderately low heat, stirring, until the onion is softened, about 15 minutes. Stir in the herbs and cook for 1 minute. Add the onion mixture and bread to the browned meat. Season with the salt and pepper and toss. (The recipe can be prepared to this point up to 1 day ahead. Cover and refrigerate.)

4. Stir the eggs, Chicken Stock, cranberry juice and parsley into the stuffing. Let cool before stuffing the turkey.

5. Shape the leftover stuffing into ¾-inch-thick patties; use about ¾ cup stuffing per patty. Melt about 1 tablespoon butter in a large heavy skillet. Add 4 patties and fry over moderate heat until browned outside and cooked through, about 3 minutes per side. Repeat with more butter and the remaining patties.

—Tracey Seaman

■

RICE STUFFING WITH FRESH AND DRIED MUSHROOMS

Fresh and dried mushrooms give this rice stuffing an intensely earthy flavor.

Makes About 12 Cups

1 ounce dried porcini mushrooms

3 cups hot water
About 3⅓ cups Chicken Stock (p. 36) or canned low-sodium broth

1 cup wild rice (6 ounces), rinsed

2 imported bay leaves

2 cups converted white rice (14 ounces)
Salt

4 tablespoons unsalted butter plus 1 tablespoon, cut into small pieces

1 large onion, finely chopped

3 medium celery ribs, finely chopped

1 large garlic clove, minced

1¼ pounds fresh white mushrooms, coarsely chopped
Freshly ground pepper

4 ounces finely chopped prosciutto

1 cup coarsely chopped flat-leaf parsley ➤

• Stuff the turkey just before roasting. The stuffing should be at room temperature, not warm or hot.

• Stuffing should be loosely packed in the cavity and neck to allow room for it to expand and cook through. If packed too tightly, the stuffing will be dense.

• Roast the turkey until the center of the stuffing reaches 165° on an instant-read thermometer. Stuffings baked in a casserole or fried in patties should be cooked until a metal skewer inserted in the center is hot to the touch.

• Scoop the leftover stuffing from the turkey and refrigerate separately.

1. In a bowl, soak the dried porcini mushrooms in the 3 cups hot water for 30 minutes. Remove the mushrooms from the soaking liquid, rinse and coarsely chop them.

2. Pour the liquid through a cheesecloth-lined strainer into a large measuring cup. Add enough Chicken Stock to make 5 cups of liquid. Pour into a medium saucepan. Add the wild rice and bay leaves and bring to a boil over high heat. Cover and simmer over very low heat for 15 minutes. Stir in the converted rice and 2 teaspoons salt, cover and simmer for 30 minutes longer. Remove from the heat and let stand uncovered until the liquid is absorbed, about 10 minutes.

3. Melt 2 tablespoons of the butter in a large skillet. Add the onion, celery and garlic and cook over moderate heat, stirring, until the onions soften and just begin to brown, about 12 minutes. Transfer to a very large bowl.

4. Add 2 more tablespoons of the butter to the skillet. Add the fresh white mushrooms and cook over moderately high heat, stirring, until the liquid has evaporated, about 8 minutes. Stir in the porcini mushrooms and cook for 2 minutes. Add the white and porcini mushrooms and the wild and white rices to the onion mixture. Discard the bay leaves, season the stuffing with salt and pepper and toss. (The recipe can be prepared to this point up to 1 day ahead. Cover and refrigerate.)

5. Add the chopped prosciutto and flat-leaf parsley to the stuffing. Season with salt and pepper and toss. Let cool before stuffing the turkey.

6. Preheat the oven to 350°. Place the leftover stuffing in a shallow buttered baking dish and drizzle with ⅓ cup Chicken Stock. Dot with the remaining 1 tablespoon butter pieces, cover with foil and bake for about 30 minutes, or until heated through.

—Diana Sturgis

■

BARLEY STUFFING WITH DRIED FRUIT

Dried apricots and prunes lend sweetness to this chewy barley stuffing.

Makes About 12 Cups

1 **pound medium pearl barley (2¼ cups)**
5 **cups Chicken Stock (p. 36) or canned low-sodium broth**
4 **imported bay leaves**
3 **tablespoons unsalted butter plus 1 tablespoon, cut into small pieces**
1 **cup blanched whole almonds, coarsely chopped (5 ounces)**
½ **pound shallots, finely chopped**
1 **tart apple, cut into ½-inch dice**
½ **pound dried sour apricots, coarsely chopped (1½ cups)**
½ **pound pitted prunes, coarsely chopped (1¼ cups)**
½ **cup coarsely chopped flat-leaf parsley**
1 **tablespoon coarsely chopped fresh thyme or 1½ teaspoons dried**
1 **tablespoon salt**
1½ **teaspoons freshly ground pepper**

1. In a medium saucepan, cover the barley with cold water. Rub the barley between your hands until the water turns cloudy. Drain and repeat until the water is clear; drain.

2. Return the barley to the saucepan, add the Chicken Stock and bay leaves and bring to a boil over high heat. Reduce the heat to low and simmer for 30 minutes. Cover and cook undisturbed over very low heat until the barley is tender, about 30 minutes.

3. Melt 1 tablespoon of the butter in a large skillet. Add the almonds and cook over moderate heat, stirring, until golden, 2 to 3 minutes. Transfer to a plate. Add 2

Barley Stuffing
with Dried Fruit

more tablespoons of the butter to the skillet. Add the shallots and cook, stirring, until softened, about 5 minutes. Add the diced apple and stir for 1 minute.

4. Place the barley in a very large bowl, discarding the bay leaves. Add the almonds, apple mixture, apricots, prunes, parsley, thyme, salt and pepper and toss. Let cool before stuffing the turkey.

5. Preheat the oven to 350°. Place the leftover stuffing in a shallow buttered baking dish. Dot with the remaining 1 tablespoon butter pieces, cover with foil and bake for about 30 minutes, or until heated through.

—Diana Sturgis

■

BULGUR STUFFING WITH PEARS AND PECANS

An unusual blend of flavors and textures provides a surprising twist on a holiday favorite.

Makes About 12 Cups
½ cup dried currants
¼ cup brandy
1 cup pecan halves (about 4 ounces)
2½ cups bulgur (14 ounces)
1 quart Chicken Stock (p. 36) or
   canned low-sodium broth
5 tablespoons unsalted butter
3 medium onions, coarsely chopped
2 large celery ribs, thinly sliced
⅓ cup finely chopped fresh sage
2 medium Bosc pears—peeled,
   cored and cut into ⅓-inch dice
1 tablespoon salt
1¼ teaspoons freshly ground
   pepper

1. Preheat the oven to 400°. In a bowl, soak the currants in the brandy until plumped, about 30 minutes.

2. Spread the pecans on a baking sheet. Toast for 8 to 10 minutes, until fragrant. Coarsely chop the nuts.

3. In a medium saucepan, combine the bulgur, Chicken Stock and 1 cup of water and bring to a boil over moderate heat. Cover and simmer until tender, about 15 minutes.

4. Melt the butter in a medium skillet. Add the onions and celery and cook over moderately low heat, stirring occasionally, until softened, about 15 minutes. Raise the heat to moderately high, add the sage and cook, stirring, for 2 minutes. Transfer to a very large bowl. Add the bulgur, pecans and pears. Drain the currants and stir them into the stuffing. Season with the salt and pepper. Let cool completely before stuffing the turkey.

5. Preheat the oven to 350°. Place the leftover stuffing in a buttered baking dish. Cover with foil and bake for about 40 minutes, or until heated through.

—Tracey Seaman

■

CLASSIC MASHED POTATOES

Save the boiling water from the potatoes and use it for making soup.

12 Servings
10 large baking potatoes, peeled and
   quartered
   Salt
About 3 cups hot milk or heavy cream
About 1 stick (8 tablespoons) softened
   unsalted butter
   Freshly ground white pepper

1. Put the potatoes in a large saucepan and cover with lightly salted water. Bring to a boil over high heat. Cover loosely and boil just until the potatoes are tender when pierced with a knife. Drain the water from the pan.

2. To dry the potatoes, toss them over moderate heat until they begin to stick to the pan, 1 to 2 minutes.

3. While still warm, either pass the potatoes through a ricer and return them to the pan, or place in the large bowl of an electric mixer and puree. Beat in the hot milk in driblets alternating with bits of the butter, then season with salt and pepper.

—Julia Child

■

MASHED POTATOES WITH GARLIC

For a mild garlic flavor, the sliced cloves are added to the cooking water but then removed before mashing the potatoes.

4 Servings
- **2 pounds baking potatoes, peeled and cut into 1-inch chunks**
- **4 medium garlic cloves, sliced**
  Salt
- **¾ to 1 cup milk or heavy cream**
  Freshly ground pepper

1. In a large saucepan, combine the potatoes, garlic, 1 teaspoon salt and enough water to cover by 1 inch. Bring to a boil, reduce the heat to moderate and simmer briskly until tender, about 15 minutes. Drain and return to the saucepan or transfer to a large bowl; discard the garlic.

2. Using a potato masher or electric mixer, mash the potatoes. Slowly stir in the milk and beat until fluffy. Season well with salt and pepper.

—Deborah Madison

■

LOW-FAT GARLIC MASHED POTATOES

Cooked garlic adds a mellow, sweet flavor to these low-fat mashed potatoes.

4 Servings
- **1½ pounds medium red or all-purpose potatoes, peeled and cut into 1-inch pieces**
- **5 large garlic cloves, thickly sliced**
  Salt
- **½ cup low-fat (one percent) milk**
  Freshly ground pepper
- **1½ teaspoons extra-virgin olive oil**

1. In a medium saucepan, combine the potatoes, garlic and enough water to cover by 2 inches. Add ½ teaspoon of salt and bring to a boil over moderately high heat. Cover the pan and simmer over moderate heat until the potatoes are tender, 20 to 25 minutes.

2. Drain the potatoes and garlic well, and pass them through a ricer or mash them with a potato masher. Stir in the milk and season with salt and pepper. Drizzle the mashed potatoes with the olive oil and serve.

—Georgia Chan Downard

■

POTATO PUFFS

Just like Italian gnocchi dough, these puffs are made with mashed potatoes and flour. They are excellent either served with cocktails or for a Sunday supper with a green salad tossed with tomatoes and black olives.

Makes About 15 Puffs
- **1 pound all-purpose potatoes, peeled and quartered**
  Salt
- **½ cup all-purpose flour**
- **1 quart corn oil, for frying**

1. In a medium saucepan, cover the potatoes with water, add salt and bring to a boil over moderate heat. Cook until the potatoes are very tender, 20 to 30

Potato and Red Pepper Frittata

minutes. Drain well. Quickly pass the potatoes through a ricer or food mill while they are still hot.

2. In a large bowl, stir the flour into the potatoes until smooth. On a lightly floured surface, using a floured rolling pin, gently roll out the dough to a 12-inch round. Stamp out 2½-inch rounds with a floured glass or a biscuit cutter. Place the rounds on a clean kitchen towel. Reroll the scraps and stamp out more rounds.

3. In a large deep skillet, heat the oil to 325°. Add the potato rounds in 3 batches and fry until puffed and golden brown. Line a serving platter with a clean kitchen towel and transfer the puffs to the towel. Sprinkle with salt and serve right away.

—Lydie Marshall

■

POTATO AND RED PEPPER FRITTATA

Indulge in eggs, ham and fried potatoes without squandering a week's worth of fat calories. The frittata is made leaner by substituting egg whites for some of the whole eggs. It also uses well-trimmed prosciutto, rather than a fattier type of ham, and a minimum of oil.

♟ A Sauvignon Blanc from the West Coast, such as 1992 Chateau Ste. Michelle or 1991 Benziger, would work particularly well.

4 Servings
1 **pound medium red potatoes, peeled and thinly sliced**
2 **teaspoons olive oil**
1 **medium red onion, thinly sliced**
2 **large garlic cloves, thinly sliced**
1 **large red bell pepper, thinly sliced**
2 **large jalapeño chiles, seeded and minced**
1 **ounce trimmed prosciutto or country ham, finely chopped**
¼ **cup coarsely chopped fresh coriander (cilantro)**
  Salt and freshly ground black pepper
2 **large whole eggs**
4 **large egg whites**

1. Rinse the potato slices in a bowl of cold water; drain and rinse again. Pat the slices dry with a dish towel.

2. Heat the oil in a large, heavy, nonstick or well-seasoned skillet. Spread the potato slices in the skillet. Cook over moderate heat, shaking the pan occasionally, for 15 minutes. Turn with a metal spatula. Cook until just tender and some slices are golden, about 5 minutes. Add the onion and garlic, turn and cook for 5 minutes longer.

3. Preheat the broiler. Add the red pepper and jalapeños to the potatoes, turn and cook, stirring once, until the pepper is tender, about 10 minutes. Sprinkle the prosciutto and 3 tablespoons of coriander on top and season with salt and pepper.

4. In a medium bowl, whisk the eggs and egg whites. Season with salt and pepper. Pour over the potatoes and cook without stirring until the eggs are firm at the edges but slightly runny on top, 6 to 7 minutes.

5. Broil the frittata for about 2 minutes, until golden and set. Sprinkle with the remaining 1 tablespoon coriander, cut into quarters and serve.

—Diana Sturgis

SCALLOPED POTATOES

Traditional American scalloped potatoes are made with milk. This old French recipe calls for chicken stock instead.

8 Servings

- **3 pounds all-purpose potatoes, peeled and sliced ¹⁄₁₆ to ⅛ inch thick**
- **1¼ cups grated Gruyère cheese (4 ounces)**
- **3 tablespoons all-purpose flour**
  Salt and freshly ground pepper
- **2 tablespoons unsalted butter at room temperature, cut into small pieces**
- **4 cups Chicken Stock (p. 36) or canned low-sodium broth**

1. Preheat the oven to 375°. Generously butter a 9-by-13-inch (3-quart) baking dish. In a large bowl, toss the potatoes with ½ cup of the cheese and the flour.

2. Arrange the potatoes in three layers, seasoning with salt and pepper and sprinkling the remaining ¾ cup Gruyère and the butter bits between each layer and on top. Pour the Chicken Stock over the top. Bake for about 1½ hours, until the potatoes are tender and golden brown on top.

—Lydie Marshall

ROASTED POTATO WEDGES WITH SALSA DE CILANTRO A LA PRESILLA

The easiest potatoes are baked potatoes; just wash them and stick them in the oven. These are a little harder; you wash them, cut them in eight pieces and stick them in the oven. Dip them in the coriander and garlic mayonnaise that follows, developed by Cuban food historian Maricel Presilla.

12 or More Servings

- **12 large baking potatoes (about 8 pounds), preferably Idaho Russets, scrubbed and dried**
- **¼ cup plus 2 tablespoons extra-virgin olive oil**
  Coarse (kosher) salt
  Salsa de Cilantro à la Presilla (recipe follows)

1. Preheat the oven to 450°. Quarter the potatoes lengthwise, then cut each quarter into 2 long wedges. In a very large bowl, toss the potatoes with the oil and 2 teaspoons coarse salt.

2. Arrange half of the potato wedges in rows on 2 large nonstick baking sheets, laying them flat on 1 cut side. Roast for 15 minutes. Flip each wedge over to its other cut side and roast for 10 to 15 minutes longer, until golden brown and crisp on the outside and very tender inside.

3. Transfer the potato wedges to a warmed platter, sprinkle with coarse salt and serve at once with the Salsa de Cilantro à la Presilla. Repeat with the remaining potato wedges.

Salsa de Cilantro à la Presilla
Makes About 2 Cups

- **4 medium garlic cloves**
- **1 large egg**
- **2 large egg yolks**
  Coarse (kosher) salt
- **1¼ cups extra-virgin olive oil**
- **1 cup (packed) fresh coriander (cilantro) leaves**
- **2 medium jalapeño peppers, seeded and finely chopped**
- **2 tablespoons fresh lemon juice**
- **¼ teaspoon ground cumin**

1. Halve the garlic cloves lengthwise. Cut out and discard the green sprouting "germ" that runs through the center, if there is one, and cut the garlic into large pieces. Turn on a food processor fitted with a steel blade and drop the garlic

pieces down the feed tube. Continue processing until finely chopped. Add the egg, egg yolks and 1 teaspoon coarse salt and process just until blended. With the machine on, add the olive oil in a thin, steady stream to make a mayonnaise.

2. Add the coriander, jalapeños, lemon juice and ground cumin. Process until smooth and creamy. Cover and refrigerate for at least 6 hours to let the flavors ripen. (The salsa can be prepared up to 1 day ahead; cover and refrigerate.)

3. Let the sauce stand at room temperature for 20 minutes. Season with more salt, lemon juice and cumin and serve with the potato wedges.

—Leslie Newman

■

POTATO-TOMATO GRATIN

Just a little of the concentrated Tomato Butter (recipe follows) enhances the mashed potatoes but doesn't overwhelm them. Parmesan cheese makes the top crusty. Serve this side dish with any roasted poultry or meat.

4 to 6 Servings
- 1½ pounds Idaho potatoes, peeled and halved
- 3 tablespoons plus 1 teaspoon unsalted butter
- ½ cup milk
- 4 to 5 tablespoons Tomato Butter (recipe follows)
- 1 tablespoon minced fresh flat-leaf parsley
  Salt and freshly ground pepper
- 1½ tablespoons freshly grated Parmesan cheese

1. Preheat the oven to 500°. In a large saucepan, cover the potatoes with cold water and boil over moderately high heat until fork tender, about 25 minutes.

Drain the water from the pan and return the potatoes to high heat. Shake the pan for about a minute to dry the potatoes thoroughly.

2. Using a potato masher or ricer, mash the boiled potatoes. Mix in the 3 tablespoons of unsalted butter and then beat in the ½ cup of milk until it is incorporated. Stir in 4 tablespoons of the Tomato Butter and the flat-leaf parsley. Season with salt and pepper. Add the remaining 1 tablespoon of the Tomato Butter if desired.

3. Lightly butter a 9-by-13-inch gratin or shallow baking dish and spoon the mashed potatoes evenly into it, making decorative strokes on the surface with a spatula. Cut the remaining 1 teaspoon unsalted butter into very small pieces and scatter them across the top. Sprinkle the Parmesan cheese evenly over the potatoes. Bake on the top rack of the oven for about 10 minutes, until hot and crusty. Serve at once.

Tomato Butter
Makes About 1½ Cups
- 2 tablespoons olive oil
- 5 medium garlic cloves, thinly sliced
- 5 pounds red or yellow tomatoes, cored and quartered
  Salt (optional)

In a large heavy nonreactive casserole, warm the olive oil over low heat. Add the garlic and cook until softened, about 3 minutes. Increase the heat to moderately high, add the tomatoes and cook, stirring often, until most of the liquid has evaporated and the mixture reduces to a thick paste, about 1 hour. Using a rubber spatula, press the tomato paste through a coarse strainer to remove the seeds and skin. Season with salt if you like. (Refrigerate for up to 1 week or freeze for up to 1 month.)

—Marcia Kiesel

■

SIX-VEGETABLE CURRY

This delicious mélange of vegetables in a thick spicy sauce tastes even better when made a day ahead; however, the chickpea flour will cause it to thicken, so add up to one-half cup of water when reheating. Chopped hard-cooked eggs sprinkled with paprika and pineapple dusted with cinnamon are tasty condiments for this curry.

🍷 This relatively mild curry requires only a simple, off-dry, pleasant white to support its flavor, such as 1992 Antinori "Capsula Viola" Galestro from Italy or 1992 Rosemount Estate Traminer-Riesling from Australia.

4 to 6 Servings

- 1 large all-purpose potato, peeled and cut into ¾-inch cubes
- 1 large sweet potato, peeled and cut into ¾-inch cubes
- 2 medium turnips, peeled and cut into ¾-inch cubes
- 2 large zucchini, sliced crosswise 1-inch thick
- ½ of a large eggplant, cut into ¾-inch cubes (about 12 ounces)
- 12 string beans, cut into 2-inch lengths
- 3 tablespoons safflower or canola oil
- 2 large onions, finely chopped
- 1 teaspoon cumin seeds
- ½ cup chickpea flour (besan)*
- 1 teaspoon ground fenugreek
- 6 fresh green chiles, such as New Mexico, finely chopped (seeded and deribbed if you like less heat)
- 2 tablespoons minced fresh ginger
- 1 tablespoon ground coriander
- 1 teaspoon turmeric
- 1 teaspoon dark brown sugar
- 1 teaspoon salt
- 4 medium tomatoes, peeled and coarsely chopped   ➤

Top: Roasted Potato Wedges with Salsa de Cilantro à la Presilla (p. 193). *Bottom*: Six-Vegetable Curry

4 **bay leaves**
1 **tablespoon tamarind concentrate***
dissolved in 3 tablespoons hot water
or 1 tablespoon molasses dissolved
in 3 tablespoons fresh lemon juice
¼ **cup finely chopped fresh coriander**
(cilantro)

***Available at Asian markets**

TYPES OF POTATOES

There are hundreds of varieties of potatoes known to potato growers. They are not usually called by name but rather are classified according to starch content and cooking method: high-starch baking potatoes, medium-starch all-purpose potatoes for roasting and boiling, and low-starch boiling potatoes. Straightforward as this may seem, it becomes confusing in supermarkets when, for example, baking potatoes (a type) are called Russets (a variety) or Idaho (the state renowned for growing the Russet potato).

To easily differentiate among the types, the basic rule of thumb is as follows: **baking potatoes** are generally oval shaped with thick brownish skin, **all-purpose potatoes** tend to be round with thinner, lighter skin, and **boiling potatoes** are round and red skinned. Of course, there are varieties that do not conform to these descriptions. In the Western United States, for example, the long white potato (White Rose variety) is an all-purpose potato that is oval shaped with very light beige skin. In many markets, you can find a **yellow-fleshed potato**, generally called Yukon Gold, which was developed by the Canadians. This potato has become the darling of chefs because it has a wonderfully rich, buttery flavor and can be fried, sautéed, baked, boiled and mashed.

In general, choose baking potatoes for baking, frying and mashing. All-purpose are very good for roasting and for making scalloped potatoes. Boiling potatoes are for just that—boiling and steaming—and eating as they are or in potato salads.

When shopping, look for firm, unblemished potatoes with smooth skins. Avoid buying those with a greenish tinge as it's a sign of poor storage and indicates the presence of a toxic alkaloid called solanine. Store potatoes in a brown paper bag in a ventilated, cool, dark place. It's best not to refrigerate them because the starch turns to sugar; however, if you do need to store them in the fridge, take them out a day or two before you plan to cook them because the sugar will revert to starch. In winter, potatoes tend to sprout easily. They'll still taste fine—just remove the sprouts before cooking.
—Lydie Marshall

1. Place the potato, sweet potato, turnips, zucchini, eggplant and string beans in a large bowl of ice water.

2. Heat the oil in a large enameled cast-iron casserole. Add the onions and cumin seeds and cook over moderately low heat, stirring, until the onions soften, 7 to 8 minutes. Stir in the chickpea flour and fenugreek and cook, stirring, until the chickpea flour becomes a paste and browns slightly, 2 to 3 minutes.

3. Pour in 2 cups of warm water and bring to a boil over moderately high heat. Cook, stirring, until the gravy begins to thicken, about 1 minute. Add 2 more cups of water and bring to a boil, then reduce the heat to low and cook until the gravy reduces and thickens slightly, about 10 minutes. Stir in the chiles, ginger, ground coriander, turmeric, brown sugar and salt and cook for 5 minutes, stirring gently.

4. Drain the vegetables and add them to the gravy. Stir in the tomatoes and bay leaves, cover and cook until the vegetables are tender but not mushy, 20 to 30 minutes. (If making this dish ahead, undercook the vegetables slightly. Refrigerate the dish for up to 2 days. Bring to a simmer over moderate heat before proceeding.)

5. Stir in the tamarind mixture and the fresh coriander and cook uncovered for 5 minutes. Discard the bay leaves and serve.
—Jennifer Brennan

Chapter 10 ▪ PIZZAS, GALETTES & BREADS

199   Grilled Pizza Bianca with Portobellos, Eggplant and Three Cheeses

200   Spicy Grilled Pizza with White Corn and Two Cheeses

200   Herbed Grilled Pizza with Summer Tomato and White Bean Salad

201   Grilled Pizza with Tomato, Basil and Prosciutto

202   Peppery Grilled Pizza with Broccoli, Sausage and Pecorino

203   Pizza with Red Onion, Rosemary and Hot Pepper

204   Cornmeal Pizzas with Spinach, Red Onion and Asiago Cheese

205   Tomato and Caramelized Onion Galette

206   Mushroom and Celery Root Galette with Mushroom Sauce

209   Leek and Goat Cheese Galette

211   Winter Squash and Blue Cheese Galette

212   Leafy Green and Ricotta Galette

213   White and Whole Wheat Bread

213   Sesame and Flaxseed Bread

215   Black Pepper Sally Lunn Bread

216   Potato Flat Bread

217   Onion-Parmesan Flat Bread

217   Skillet Corn Bread

218   Blue Cornsticks

218   Blue Corn Muffins with Pine Nuts

219   Smoky Chipotle Corn Bread

219   Rosemary Corn Cakes

220   Cheddar Corn Biscuits

Clockwise from upper left: Peppery Grilled Pizza with Broccoli, Sausage and Pecorino (p. 202), Spicy Grilled Pizza with White Corn and Two Cheeses (p. 200), Herbed Grilled Pizza with Summer Tomato and White Bean Salad (p. 200) and Grilled Pizza with Tomato, Basil and Proscuitto (p. 201)

GRILLED PIZZA BIANCA WITH PORTOBELLOS, EGGPLANT AND THREE CHEESES

The toppings, the crust and finally the whole pie are cooked on the grill for a deliciously different pizza.

❦ The smoky, cheesy topping here needs a crisp white as a refreshing foil. A California Sauvignon Blanc, such as 1992 Joseph Phelps or 1992 Chateau Souverain, would be a good choice.

Makes 4 Main-Course Pizzas

1 tablespoon plus 1 teaspoon minced garlic
  Virgin olive oil
4 4-inch Portobello mushrooms, stems discarded
20 slices of eggplant, cut ⅛ inch thick (from one narrow medium eggplant)
2 cups (loosely packed) shredded Fontina cheese (about ½ pound)
¾ cup freshly grated Parmigiano-Reggiano cheese (about 2½ ounces)
½ cup crumbled Gorgonzola cheese (about 2 ounces)
  Pizza Dough (at right)
¼ cup chopped fresh flat-leaf parsley

1. Prepare a hardwood charcoal fire and set the grill rack 3 to 4 inches above the coals.

2. In a bowl, mix the garlic with ¼ cup of olive oil. Liberally brush the oil on the mushrooms and eggplant. In another bowl, toss together the Fontina, Parmigiano-Reggiano and Gorgonzola. Cover and refrigerate.

3. When white ash begins to appear on the coals, the fire is ready. Grill the mushroom caps until softened and cooked through, about 4 minutes per side. Grill the eggplant slices until tender, about 2 minutes per side. Slice the mushroom caps ⅛ inch thick and set aside with the eggplant.

4. Divide the Pizza Dough into 4 equal pieces. Keep 3 pieces covered. On a large, lightly oiled unrimmed baking sheet, spread and flatten the fourth piece of dough with your hands to form a 12-inch free-form round about 1/16 inch thick; do not make a lip.

5. Gently drape the dough on the hot grill. Within a minute, the dough will puff slightly, the underside will stiffen and grill marks will appear.

6. Using tongs, immediately flip the crust over onto a warmed baking sheet. Brush with olive oil. Scatter one-fourth of the mixed cheeses, parsley and grilled vegetables over the crust. Drizzle the pizza with 1 to 2 tablespoons of olive oil. ➤

PIZZA DOUGH

Makes Enough Dough for Four 12-Inch Pizzas

1 envelope (¼ ounce) active dry yeast
1 cup warm water (110° to 115°)
  Pinch of sugar
2¼ teaspoons coarse (kosher) salt
3 tablespoons rye flour
  Virgin olive oil
2½ to 3 cups unbleached all-purpose flour

1. Place the yeast in a bowl and stir in the water and sugar. Let stand until foamy, about 5 minutes.

2. Stir in the salt, rye flour and 1 tablespoon of oil. Gradually add 2 cups of the all-purpose flour, stirring with a wooden spoon until the dough is fairly stiff.

3. Turn the dough out onto a well-floured work surface. Knead until smooth and elastic, 5 to 6 minutes, gradually kneading in as much of the remaining all-purpose flour as necessary to keep the dough from sticking.

4. Transfer the dough to a lightly oiled bowl and brush the surface with olive oil. Cover the bowl with plastic wrap and let the dough rise in a warm, draft-free place until doubled in bulk, 1½ to 2 hours.

5. Punch down the dough and knead it lightly. Return to the bowl, cover and let rise again until doubled, about 45 minutes. Punch down the dough again. Now it is ready to use.

—Johanne Killeen and George Germon

7. Slide the pizza back toward the hot coals but not directly over them. Using tongs, rotate the pizza frequently so that different sections receive high heat; check the underside often to see that it's not charring. The pizza is done when the cheeses are melted and the vegetables are heated through, 3 to 4 minutes. Serve the pizza hot off the grill. Repeat from step 4 to make the remaining pizzas.

—Johanne Killeen
and George Germon

■

SPICY GRILLED PIZZA WITH WHITE CORN AND TWO CHEESES

Serve this pizza hot off the grill as soon as the two cheeses—Pecorino Romano and Fontina—have melted.

Makes 4 Main-Course Pizzas

3 **cups white corn kernels, cut from the cob (from 4 medium-large ears)**
2 **cups (loosely packed) shredded Fontina cheese (about ½ pound)**
½ **cup freshly grated Pecorino Romano cheese (about 1½ ounces)**
1 **teaspoon crushed red pepper**
  Pizza Dough (p. 199)
  Virgin olive oil
1½ **cups chopped canned tomatoes in heavy puree**
½ **cup chopped mixed fresh herbs, such as parsley, thyme and basil**

1. Prepare a hardwood charcoal fire and set the grill rack 3 to 4 inches above the coals.

2. Bring a saucepan of lightly salted water to a boil. Add the corn kernels and blanch until just tender, 2 to 3 minutes. Drain and pat dry.

3. In a bowl, toss the Fontina and Pecorino Romano cheeses with the crushed red pepper. Cover and refrigerate until ready to use.

4. Divide the Pizza Dough into 4 equal pieces. Keep 3 pieces covered. On a large, lightly oiled, unrimmed baking sheet, spread and flatten the fourth piece of dough with your hands to form a 12-inch free-form round about ¹⁄₁₆ inch thick; do not make a lip.

5. When white ash begins to appear on the coals, the fire is ready. Gently drape the dough on the hot grill. Within a minute, it will puff slightly, the underside will stiffen and grill marks will appear.

6. Using tongs, immediately flip the crust over onto a warmed baking sheet and brush with olive oil. Scatter one-fourth of the mixed cheeses over the crust. Spoon 6 tablespoons of the tomatoes in small dollops over the cheese. Scatter one-fourth of the corn and fresh herbs over the pizza and drizzle with 1 to 2 tablespoons of olive oil.

7. Slide the pizza back toward the hot coals but not directly over them. Using tongs, rotate the pizza frequently so that different sections receive high heat; check the underside often to make sure that it's not charring. The pizza is done when the cheeses are melted and the other toppings are heated through, 3 to 4 minutes. Repeat from step 4 to make the remaining pizzas.

—Johanne Killeen
and George Germon

■

HERBED GRILLED PIZZA WITH SUMMER TOMATO AND WHITE BEAN SALAD

This is actually a departure from any formal pizza tradition. It's the same crust, brushed with oil and fresh herbs and used as a base for a refreshing bean salad. If you're pressed for time, canned cannellini beans can be substituted for freshly cooked ones, but drain and rinse them before using.

Makes 6 Light Main-Course Pizzas

Salad:
- ½ **pound dried white navy or cannellini beans, picked over and rinsed**
- 1 **onion, quartered**
- 2 **garlic cloves**
- 6 **ripe medium tomatoes, cored and cut into 1-inch chunks**
- 1 **large cucumber—peeled, seeded and cut into ½-inch dice**
- ½ **cup finely chopped fresh flat-leaf parsley**
- 1 **small fresh hot chile, seeded and minced**
- 3 **tablespoons virgin olive oil**
  Juice of 1 lemon
  Coarse (kosher) salt

Herbed Pizza Crust:
- **Pizza Dough (p. 199)**
- **Virgin olive oil**
- **Coarse (kosher) salt**
- 8 **fresh basil leaves, sliced into chiffonade (see How to Cut Basil, at right)**
- ¼ **cup chopped fresh coriander**
- ¼ **cup chopped fresh flat-leaf parsley**

1. Make the salad: In a bowl, cover the beans with cold water and soak them overnight.

2. The next day, drain and rinse the beans. In a large saucepan, combine the beans with the onion and garlic. Add 2 quarts of cold water and bring to a boil over high heat. Reduce the heat and simmer the beans until tender, 45 minutes to 1½ hours depending on the freshness of the beans.

3. Drain the beans; discard the onion and garlic. Transfer the beans to a bowl and add the tomatoes, cucumber, parsley and chile. Toss with the oil and lemon juice and season with coarse salt. Set aside at room temperature for up to 3 hours.

4. Make the herbed pizza crust: Prepare a hardwood charcoal fire and set the grill rack 3 to 4 inches above the coals.

5. Divide the Pizza Dough into 6 equal pieces. Keep 5 covered. On a large, lightly oiled unrimmed baking sheet, spread and flatten the sixth piece of dough with your hands into a 6- to 7-inch free-form round about ¹⁄₁₆ inch thick; do not make a lip. (Repeat and flatten as many pieces of dough as will fit on the grill at one time.)

6. When white ash begins to appear on the coals, the fire is ready. Gently drape the dough on the hot grill. Within a minute it will puff slightly, the underside will stiffen and grill marks will appear.

7. Using tongs, immediately flip the crust over onto a warmed baking sheet. Brush with olive oil, sprinkle with salt and scatter one-sixth of the fresh herbs over the entire surface.

8. Slide the pizza back toward the hot coals but not directly over them. Using tongs, rotate the pizza frequently so that different sections receive high heat; check the underside often to see that it's not charring. The pizza is done when the olive oil is bubbling, about 2 minutes.

9. Repeat from step 5 to form and grill the remaining pizzas. Transfer to individual plates. Spoon the bean and tomato salad onto the pizzas and serve at once.

—Johanne Killeen
and George Germon

■

GRILLED PIZZA WITH TOMATO, BASIL AND PROSCIUTTO

Cut the basil into a chiffonade (see How to Cut Basil, at right) just before serving for maximum flavor. ➤

HOW TO CUT BASIL

Begin by stacking the leaves in neat piles. Starting at a long side, roll up a stack of leaves, then thinly slice the roll crosswise. You'll end up with lovely fragrant ribbons of basil.

—Johanne Killeen
and George Germon

❦ The lively flavors of this pizza would be enhanced by a glass of fruity, spicy young red wine. A California Zinfandel, such as 1991 Rabbit Ridge or 1991 Franciscan, would be ideal.

Makes 4 Main-Course Pizzas

- ½ **cup freshly grated Pecorino Romano cheese (about 1½ ounces)**
- 2 **cups (loosely packed) shredded Fontina cheese (about ½ pound)**
  Pizza Dough (p. 199)
  Virgin olive oil, for brushing and drizzling
- 2 **teaspoons minced garlic**
- 1½ **cups chopped canned tomatoes in heavy puree**
- 32 **fresh basil leaves, sliced into chiffonade (see How to Cut Basil, p. 201)**
- 24 **paper-thin slices prosciutto or Parma ham**

1. Prepare a hardwood charcoal fire and set the grill rack 3 to 4 inches above the coals.

2. In a bowl, toss the grated Pecorino Romano cheese with the shredded Fontina cheese. Cover the bowl and keep the cheeses refrigerated.

3. Divide the Pizza Dough into 4 equal pieces. Keep 3 pieces covered. On a large, lightly oiled unrimmed baking sheet, spread and flatten the fourth piece of dough with your hands to form a 12-inch free-form round about ¹⁄₁₆ inch thick; do not make a lip.

4. When white ash begins to appear on the coals, the fire is ready. Gently drape the dough on the hot grill. Within a minute, the dough will puff slightly, the underside of the dough will stiffen and grill marks will appear.

5. Using tongs, immediately flip the pizza crust over onto a warmed baking sheet and brush the crust with olive oil. Scatter one-fourth of the garlic and cheese over the crust. Spoon 6 tablespoons of the

tomatoes in small dollops over the cheese. Drizzle the pizza with 1 to 2 tablespoons olive oil.

6. Slide the pizza back toward the hot coals but not directly over them. Using tongs, rotate the pizza frequently so that different sections receive high heat; check the underside often to see that it's not charring. The pizza is done when the cheese is melted and the other toppings are heated through, 3 to 4 minutes. Scatter ¼ of the basil chiffonade over the pizza and cover the entire surface with 6 slices of the prosciutto. Serve hot off the grill. Repeat from step 3 to make the remaining pizzas.

—Johanne Killeen
and George Germon

■

PEPPERY GRILLED PIZZA WITH BROCCOLI, SAUSAGE AND PECORINO

For this spicy pizza, look for the very freshest Pecorino Romano cheese you can find.

❦ The freshly ground pepper and Italian sausage on this pizza can be set off by a light, fruity-sweet California white Zinfandel, such as 1993 Monteviña, or by a flavorful beer, such as Anchor Steam or Samuel Adams.

Makes 4 Main-Course Pizzas

- 2½ **cups freshly grated Pecorino Romano (about 7½ ounces)**
- 1 **cup chopped fresh flat-leaf parsley**
- 1½ **teaspoons freshly ground pepper**
  Virgin olive oil
- 4 **hot or sweet Italian sausages (2 to 3 ounces each), meat removed from the casings**

**4 cups chopped fresh broccoli florets
and tender stems
Pizza Dough (p. 199)**

1. Prepare a hardwood charcoal fire and set the grill rack 3 to 4 inches above the coals.

2. In a bowl, toss the Pecorino Romano cheese with the parsley and pepper. Cover and refrigerate.

3. In a large skillet, heat 3 tablespoons olive oil. Add the Italian sausage meat and cook over moderately high heat, stirring until the sausage is cooked through and just beginning to brown, about 5 minutes. Add the broccoli florets and stems and 2 cups of water. Cover the skillet and cook until the pieces of broccoli are just tender, about 2 minutes. Uncover the skillet and cook until the liquid in the pan reduces to 1 cup. Stir in ¼ cup olive oil and set aside.

4. Divide the Pizza Dough into 4 equal pieces. Keep 3 pieces covered. On a large, lightly oiled unrimmed baking sheet, spread and flatten the fourth piece of dough with your hands to form a 12-inch free-form round, about ¹⁄₁₆ inch thick; do not make a lip.

5. When white ash begins to appear on the coals, the fire is ready. Gently drape the dough on the grill. Within a minute, the dough will puff slightly, the underside of the dough will stiffen and grill marks will appear.

6. Using tongs, immediately flip the pizza crust over onto a warmed baking sheet and brush it with olive oil. Scatter one-fourth of the Pecorino Romano cheese evenly over the pizza crust. Top the cheese with one-fourth of the Italian sausage and broccoli and drizzle lightly with olive oil.

7. Slide the topped pizza back toward the hot coals but not directly over them. Using tongs, rotate the pizza frequently so that different sections of the pie receive high heat; check the underside of the crust often to make sure that it's not charring. The pizza is finished when the cheese is melted and the sausage and broccoli toppings are heated through, 3 to 4 minutes. Serve the pizza hot off the grill. Repeat from step 4 to make the remaining pizzas.

—Johanne Killeen
and George Germon

■

PIZZA WITH RED ONION, ROSEMARY AND HOT PEPPER

These thin, cheeseless pizzas pack a punch with the assertive flavor of rosemary and the heat of crushed red pepper.

Makes Four 8-Inch Pizzas
Topping:
  **4 small red onions, sliced crosswise
into very thin rings**
  ½ cup extra-virgin olive oil
  ¼ cup fresh rosemary leaves, chopped
  ½ teaspoon crushed red pepper
  ¼ teaspoon fine sea salt

Dough:
  2 cups unbleached all-purpose flour
  1 cup fine semolina flour*
1½ teaspoons fine sea salt
**About 1¼ cups lukewarm water
(110° to 115°)**

  ***Available at specialty food shops
and Italian markets**

1. Make the topping: In a medium bowl, combine the onions, oil, rosemary, crushed red pepper and sea salt. Stir to evenly distribute the herbs and spices. Set aside to marinate for at least 1 hour or overnight. (Marinating softens the flavor of the onions.)

2. Make the dough: In a large shallow

Pizza with Red Onion, Rosemary and Hot Pepper

Cornmeal Pizzas with Spinach, Red Onion and Asiago Cheese

bowl, combine the all-purpose and semolina flours and sea salt. Mix thoroughly. Slowly add the lukewarm water, stirring with a wooden spoon just until a soft dough forms; you may not need to add all the water.

3. With your hands, work the dough into a ball and transfer to a clean work surface. Knead gently for about 1 minute; the dough should be firm and pliable but not sticky. Divide the dough into 4 even balls, then flatten each ball into a thick 4-inch disk. (The dough can be prepared to this point up to 1 day ahead. Wrap the disks in plastic wrap and refrigerate.)

4. Preheat the oven to 475°. If using a baking stone, place it in the oven. On a generously floured work surface, roll each disk of dough into an 8-inch round about ⅟₁₆ inch thick. Spoon the onion topping onto the dough, spreading it evenly

with the back of the spoon. Place the pizzas on the baking stone or on baking sheets and bake for about 10 minutes, until the dough is crusty and browned and the onions are sizzling. Serve immediately.

—Patricia Wells

■

CORNMEAL PIZZAS WITH SPINACH, RED ONION AND ASIAGO CHEESE

The pizza dough can be made a day ahead and allowed to rise very slowly in the refrigerator.

🍷 These savory cornmeal pizzas require nothing more than a straightforward, medium-bodied dry red, such as 1988 Castello di Gabbiano Chianti Classico Riserva or 1988 Bodegas Montecillo Viña Cumbrero Rioja.

Makes 6 Individual Pizzas

Dough:
- 1 cup lukewarm water (105° to 115°)
- 2 teaspoons sugar
- 1 envelope (¼ ounce) active dry yeast
- 2½ cups all-purpose flour
- ¾ cup coarse yellow cornmeal, plus more for sprinkling
- 1 teaspoon salt
- ¼ cup olive oil

Topping:
- 4 pounds fresh spinach, stemmed and leaves washed
- 3 tablespoons olive oil
- 4 garlic cloves, minced
- 9 ounces aged Asiago cheese, coarsely grated
- 1 medium red onion, coarsely chopped
- 3 ounces oil-packed sun-dried tomatoes, drained and cut into ¼-inch dice
- Freshly ground pepper

1. Make the dough: Pour the warm water into a small bowl and stir in the sugar. Sprinkle the yeast on top and let it dissolve for 5 minutes.

2. In a food processor, combine the flour with ¾ cup cornmeal and the salt. Process for 5 seconds to sift the dry ingredients. With the machine on, add the yeast mixture through the feed tube. Add the oil in a steady stream and process until the dough comes together. Turn the dough out on a lightly floured surface and knead until smooth, 2 to 3 minutes. Shape into a ball and transfer to a lightly oiled bowl. Turn the dough to coat with the oil, then cover and set aside in a warm, draft-free area until doubled in size, about 1 hour.

3. Prepare the topping: In a large saucepan, place half of the spinach with the water that clings to it. Cover and cook over moderate heat just until wilted, about 5 minutes. Drain well and transfer to a bowl. Repeat with the remaining spinach.

4. Heat the olive oil in the pan. Add the garlic and spinach and cook over moderate heat, stirring, for 5 minutes. Return to the bowl and let cool.

5. Preheat the oven to 500°. Sprinkle 3 cookie sheets with cornmeal.

6. Punch down the dough and cut it into 6 even pieces. Roll out each piece to a 7-inch disk and set it on a prepared baking sheet.

7. Sprinkle the dough with about a third of the Asiago, leaving a 1-inch border around each pizza. Cover the cheese with the spinach, onion and sun-dried tomatoes. Top with the remaining Asiago. Season with pepper.

8. Bake the pizzas, in batches if necessary, for about 8 minutes until the topping is melted and the bottom is crisp.

—Ann Chantal Altman

■

TOMATO AND CARAMELIZED ONION GALETTE

Both the dough and filling can be made ahead of time; then the galette can be assembled and baked when needed. Individual galettes, which are less fragile than large ones, can be made a few hours in advance and reheated in a hot oven before serving.

🍷 A Chianti will underscore the sweetness of the dish and will stand up to the sharpness of the tomatoes. Look for 1990 Castello di Gabbiano or 1990 Badia a Coltibuono. ➤

4 to 6 Main-Dish Servings or
10 to 12 First-Course Servings

2½ pounds yellow onions, coarsely
    chopped
6 fresh thyme sprigs or 2 pinches of
    dried thyme
¼ cup fruity olive oil
    Salt and freshly ground pepper
1 tablespoon minced fresh rosemary
    or 1 teaspoon dried
    Yeast Dough or Pastry Dough
    (p. 208)
3 ounces Gorgonzola cheese
1 pound large cherry tomatoes or
    plum tomatoes, sliced crosswise
    ⅓ inch thick
1 large egg, beaten

1. In a large, heavy, nonreactive saucepan, cook the onions and thyme over moderate heat, stirring once or twice, until the onions start to turn golden, about 15 minutes.

2. Add 3 tablespoons of the oil, cover and cook over low heat, scraping the pan every 10 minutes, until the onions are browned, about 1 hour. Season with salt, pepper and 2 teaspoons of the fresh rosemary (or all the dried rosemary). Let cool.

3. Preheat the oven to 400°. On a lightly floured baking sheet without sides, roll out the galette dough into a 14-inch round. (Alternatively, divide the dough into 4 even pieces and roll into 8-inch rounds.) Spread the filling over the dough, leaving a 2-inch border. Crumble the cheese on top and overlap the tomatoes in a ring. Season with salt and pepper and drizzle on the remaining 1 tablespoon oil. Fold up and pleat the border of the dough. Brush the dough with the egg.

4. Bake the galette until the crust is golden, about 20 minutes for Yeast Dough and 35 minutes for Pastry Dough. Sprinkle the remaining 1 teaspoon fresh rosemary over the top and serve hot or warm.

—Deborah Madison

■

MUSHROOM AND CELERY ROOT GALETTE WITH MUSHROOM SAUCE

This galette requires a reduced vegetable stock as the base for the mushroom sauce. Start by preparing all the vegetables (step one below). Then proceed with the stock, which is made with the vegetable trimmings.

4 to 6 Main-Dish Servings or 10 to 12
First-Course Servings

1 small celery root (about ¾ pound)
2 medium leeks
1 pound white mushrooms
3 tablespoons olive oil
1 large onion, finely chopped
1 lemon, halved
½ teaspoon dried tarragon
    Salt and freshly ground pepper
2 medium garlic cloves, minced
¼ cup chopped fresh flat-leaf parsley,
    plus more for garnish
    Mushroom Sauce (recipe follows)
½ cup crème fraîche or sour cream
2 tablespoons freshly grated
    Parmesan or Asiago cheese
    Yeast Dough or Pastry Dough
    (p. 208)
1 large egg, beaten

1. Preheat the oven to 375°. Thoroughly scrub the celery root, trim off a thin piece from both ends and peel; set aside the trimmings. Thinly slice the celery root crosswise, then cut into ¼-inch dice. Transfer to a nonreactive bowl and cover with cold water to prevent discoloration. Trim the root end and the dark green portion of the leeks; set aside. Coarsely chop the remaining white and tender green portion of the leek and rinse well but don't dry. Trim off the mushroom stems and set

aside. Slice the mushroom caps crosswise ½ inch thick. (Use the celery root trimmings, leek trimmings and mushroom stems to make the Mushroom Sauce.)

2. In a large nonreactive skillet, heat 2 tablespoons of the oil over low heat. Using a slotted spoon, transfer the diced celery root to the skillet. Add the chopped leeks and onion. Squeeze half a lemon over the vegetables, add the tarragon and cook until the liquid is evaporated and the vegetables

are tender and just beginning to brown, about 12 minutes. Season with salt and pepper. Transfer to a nonreactive bowl.

3. In the same skillet, heat the remaining 1 tablespoon oil over high heat until it starts to shimmer. Stir in the mushrooms until coated with oil, then squeeze the remaining lemon half over them. Cook until the mushrooms begin to color, about 2 minutes. Add the garlic and cook for 1 minute. Season with the parsley and salt

Tomato and Carmelized Onion Galette

GALETTE DOUGHS

The pastry dough is flaky and delectable. The yeast dough, which is a joy to handle, uses far less fat. You must, however, roll the dough very thin so that the finished crust won't be bready.

Yeast Dough

The crème fraîche or butter used in this dough makes it more tender than a typical pizza-type yeast dough.

Makes Enough for
One 12-Inch Galette
or Four 6-Inch Galettes

⅓   cup lukewarm water
     (105° to 115°)
1   teaspoon active dry
     yeast
½   teaspoon sugar
1½   cups all-purpose flour
½   teaspoon salt
1   large egg, at room
     temperature
3   tablespoons crème fraîche
     or softened unsalted
     butter

1. In a bowl, stir together the water, yeast and sugar. Let stand in a warm place until bubbly, about 10 minutes.

2. In a bowl, toss the flour with the salt and make a well. Add the egg, crème fraîche and yeast mixture to the well. Using a wooden spoon, incorporate the flour into the liquid ingredients to form a soft dough. Turn out onto a floured surface and knead briefly until smooth.

3. Transfer the dough to a lightly buttered bowl, cover with plastic wrap and let rise until doubled in bulk, about 45 minutes. Punch the dough down and let it rest briefly before rolling out.

Pastry Dough

Treat this dough like any other pie dough: Don't overmix and don't worry about an uneven texture. If the weather is very dry, you may need more water to bring the dough together. This dough freezes well for up to two weeks; so why not double or triple the recipe.

Makes Enough for
One 12-Inch Galette
or Four 6-Inch Galettes

1½   cups all-purpose flour
½   teaspoon salt
½   teaspoon sugar
1   stick (8 tablespoons)
     plus 1 tablespoon cold
     unsalted butter
About ¼ cup ice water

1. In a bowl, toss the flour with the salt and sugar. Cut in the butter until the mixture resembles coarse meal. Using a fork, stir in the ice water by tablespoons, until the dough holds together when pressed. Sprinkle in more water by the teaspoon if needed.

2. Flatten the dough into a disk, wrap well and refrigerate the dough for 15 minutes before rolling it out.

—Deborah Madison

and pepper. Remove from the heat and stir in the celery root mixture. Fold in ½ cup of the Mushroom Sauce, the crème fraîche and the Parmesan.

4. On a lightly floured baking sheet without sides, roll out the dough into a 14-inch round. (Alternatively, divide the dough into 4 even pieces and roll into 8-inch rounds.) Spread the filling over the dough, leaving a 2-inch border. Fold up and pleat the border of the dough. Brush with the beaten egg. Bake the galette until golden, about 30 minutes for Yeast Dough and 40 minutes for Pastry Dough.

5. To serve, pour ¼ cup of the Mushroom Sauce over the top of the galette. Garnish with chopped parsley. Cut into wedges and spoon sauce over each one.

Mushroom Sauce
Makes About 1 Cup

1   tablespoon olive oil
1   large onion, coarsely chopped
     Mushroom stems from 1 pound
     mushrooms
1   carrot, coarsely chopped
1   bay leaf
½   teaspoon dried tarragon
     Pinch of thyme
1   tablespoon all-purpose flour
1   tablespoon mushroom soy sauce
1   tablespoon tomato paste
     The peel and trimmed ends from
     1 scrubbed celery root
     Leek greens and root ends from
     2 leeks, thoroughly rinsed and
     coarsely chopped
     Parsley stems from 1 bunch
     Salt
1   teaspoon tarragon vinegar
2   tablespoons unsalted butter
     Freshly ground pepper

1. Heat the oil in a medium nonreactive saucepan. Add the onion, mushroom stems, carrot, bay leaf, tarragon and thyme. Cook over high heat, stirring, until

beginning to brown, about 10 minutes.

2. Stir in the flour, the soy sauce and the tomato paste. Add the celery root trimmings, leek trimmings, parsley stems, ½ teaspoon salt and 2½ cups of water. Bring to a boil, then lower the heat to moderately low, cover and simmer for 35 minutes. Strain.

3. Return the stock to the saucepan and boil over high heat until reduced to 1 cup, about 10 minutes. Stir in the vinegar. (The sauce can be made to this point up to 4 hours ahead. Rewarm over low heat.) Whisk in the butter and season the sauce with salt and pepper.

—Deborah Madison

Mushroom and Celery Root Galette with Mushroom Sauce

■

LEEK AND GOAT CHEESE GALETTE

For this galette, you can use a mixture of leeks and onions with equally good results.

🍷 Pinot Noir, Gamay and Beaujolais are light reds whose fruitiness will attractively accent the goat cheese. Good choices

HOW TO SHAPE GALETTES

• First make the dough; then make the filling and allow it to cool to room temperature.

• **To make a large galette:** Use a lightly floured baking sheet without sides (or use the underside of a rimmed baking sheet). Place the dough on the baking sheet and roll into a round about 14 inches in diameter. You can either leave the edges rough and irregular or trim them. Spread the filling over the dough, leaving a 2-inch border. Slide your hand under the border in one spot and fold it in to cover the outer portion of the filling. Repeat this motion all the way around the galette. As you shape the border, you can make neat, sharply defined pleats or soft irregular folds. The yeast dough lends itself much more to rounded edges and careful shaping than the pie dough.

• **To make individual galettes:** Divide the dough into 4 equal pieces and shape them into disks. On a lightly floured surface, roll the disks into rounds about 8 inches in diameter. Spread the filling, as above, leaving a 2-inch border, and then gently pleat all the way around. Or roll the dough into a square and fold the edges over the filling like an envelope. Place the individual galettes on a baking sheet.

• Before baking the galettes, brush the dough with beaten egg or melted butter to give it sheen and a golden color.

—Deborah Madison

Winter Squash and Blue Cheese Galette

would be 1990 Pinnacles Pinot Noir and 1993 Beringer Gamay Beaujolais from California or 1991 Louis Jadot Beaujolais from France.

4 to 6 Main-Dish Servings or
10 to 12 First-Course Servings
6 large leeks, white and tender green parts, thinly sliced (6 heaping cups)
3 tablespoons unsalted butter
1 teaspoon chopped fresh thyme or ½ teaspoon dried
½ cup dry white wine
½ cup heavy cream
Salt and freshly ground pepper
1 large egg, beaten
3 tablespoons finely chopped fresh flat-leaf parsley or chervil
Yeast Dough or Pastry Dough (p. 208)
½ cup soft goat cheese, such as Montrachet

1. In a large nonreactive skillet, combine the leeks, butter, thyme and ½ cup of water and cook over low heat, stirring frequently, until the leeks are tender, about 15 minutes. Raise the heat to moderate, add the wine and cook until almost evaporated, about 5 minutes. Stir in the cream and cook until it is reduced slightly, about 3 minutes. Season with salt and plenty of pepper. Let cool for 10 minutes.

2. Reserve 1 tablespoon of the beaten egg. Stir the remaining beaten egg and 2 tablespoons parsley into the leek mixture.

3. Preheat the oven to 400°. On a lightly floured baking sheet without sides, roll out the dough into a 14-inch round. (Alternatively, divide the dough into 4 even pieces and roll into 8-inch rounds.) Spread the leek filling over the dough, leaving a 2-inch border. Crumble the goat cheese over the leeks. Fold up and pleat the border of dough. Brush the dough with the remaining 1 tablespoon beaten egg.

4. Bake the galette until the crust is golden, about 20 minutes for Yeast

Dough and 30 to 35 minutes for Pastry Dough. Set aside to cool for a few minutes. Scatter the remaining 1 tablespoon parsley over the galette and serve warm.
—Deborah Madison

■

WINTER SQUASH AND BLUE CHEESE GALETTE

You can make either a large round or individual galettes.

❦ The slightly sweet taste of the squash, accented here by the sharp blue cheese, will contrast with a crisp fruity white, such as a 1991 Markham Sauvignon Blanc or 1992 Ferrari-Carano Fumé Blanc, both from California.

4 to 6 Main-Dish Servings or
10 to 12 First-Course Servings
2½ pounds winter squash, such as butternut
Olive oil
Salt and freshly ground pepper
1 small head of garlic, cloves separated but not peeled
1 small onion, finely chopped
10 fresh sage leaves, coarsely chopped, or 1½ teaspoons dried
½ cup freshly grated Romano or Parmesan cheese (about 1½ ounces)
⅔ cup crumbled Roquefort or other blue cheese (3 ounces)
Yeast Dough or Pastry Dough (p. 208)
1 large egg, beaten

1. Preheat the oven to 375°. Using a large sharp knife, halve the squash; scrape out and discard the seeds and fibers. Lightly brush each cut side of the squash with olive oil; season with salt and pepper. Place the garlic cloves in the cavities and

211

turn the squash halves cut side down on a baking sheet. Bake for about 1 hour, or until tender when pierced with a knife. Remove the garlic and if the cloves aren't soft, return to the oven and bake a little longer. (The recipe can be made to this point up to 3 days ahead; wrap the squash and garlic separately and refrigerate.)

2. Scoop out the squash flesh into a large bowl and mash with a fork until fairly smooth. (If the mashed squash is very wet, place it in a colander and let drain for 2 hours.) Squeeze the garlic out of its skin and mash with a fork.

3. In a small skillet, warm 2 teaspoons of olive oil over low heat. Add the onion and sage and cook, stirring occasionally, until the onions are soft and beginning to color, 6 to 7 minutes. Add to the squash along with the garlic and Romano. Mix well, season with salt and pepper and fold in half of the Roquefort.

4. Preheat the oven to 400°. On a lightly floured baking sheet without sides, roll out the galette dough into a 14-inch round. (Alternatively, divide the dough into 4 even pieces and roll into 8-inch rounds.) Spread the squash filling over the dough, leaving a 2-inch border. Sprinkle the remaining Roquefort on top. Fold up and pleat the border of the dough. Brush the dough with the beaten egg.

5. Bake the galette until the crust is nicely browned, about 25 minutes for Yeast Dough and 40 minutes for Pastry Dough. Serve hot or warm.

—Deborah Madison

■

LEAFY GREEN AND RICOTTA GALETTE

If the leeks brown before they soften, add a few tablespoons of water and simmer until all the water evaporates.

4 to 6 Main-Dish Servings or
10 to 12 First-Course Servings

- 2 **pounds spinach, stems discarded (8 packed cups)**
- 1 **pound beet greens, mustard greens or Swiss chard, stems and large ribs discarded (4 packed cups)**
- ½ **pound sorrel or arugula (2 packed cups)**
- 2 **teaspoons butter or olive oil**
- 2 **medium leeks, white and tender green, or 1 medium onion, finely chopped**
- 1 **cup ricotta cheese**
- ⅓ **cup freshly grated Parmesan cheese (about 1½ ounces)**
  Salt and freshly ground pepper
- 2 **large eggs, 1 beaten**
  Yeast Dough or Pastry Dough (p. 208)

1. In a large steamer, bring 1 inch of water to a boil over high heat. Pack the spinach, beet greens and sorrel—in that order—in the steamer basket, cover and steam until wilted and tender, about 4 minutes. Transfer the steamer basket to the sink and let the greens cool slightly. Squeeze out as much liquid as possible, then transfer to a cutting board and chop fine. Return the chopped greens to the steamer basket in the sink to drain further while you proceed.

2. In a medium skillet, melt the butter over low heat. Add the leeks and cook, stirring occasionally, until soft and golden, 8 to 10 minutes.

3. In a large bowl, mix together the ricotta and Parmesan cheeses with a wooden spoon. Stir in the greens and leeks and season well with salt and pepper. Stir in the unbeaten egg until thoroughly blended.

4. Preheat the oven to 400°. On a lightly floured baking sheet without sides, roll out the galette dough into a 14-inch round. (Alternatively, divide the dough into 4 even pieces and roll into 8-inch

rounds.) Spread the filling over the dough, leaving a 2-inch border. Fold up and pleat the border of the dough. Brush the dough with the remaining beaten egg.

5. Bake the galette until the filling is hot and the crust is browned, about 25 minutes for Yeast Dough and 35 minutes for Pastry Dough. Set aside to cool for a few minutes before cutting into wedges and serving.

—Deborah Madison

■

WHITE AND WHOLE WHEAT BREAD

To give this light bread more whole wheat flavor, change the proportions and use two cups of all-purpose flour and one and one-half cups of whole wheat flour. This recipe has been adapted from *Fanny at Chez Panisse* (HarperCollins).

Makes One 9-Inch Loaf
- **1 envelope (¼ ounce) active dry yeast**
- **3 cups all-purpose flour, plus more for sprinkling**
- **½ cup whole wheat flour**
- **½ cup milk, at room temperature**
- **2 teaspoons salt**
- **2 tablespoons olive oil, plus more for brushing**

1. In a small bowl, dissolve the yeast in ¼ cup of warm water. Combine the flours in a large bowl. Make a well in the center. Pour the yeast mixture into the well and stir it into the flour with a wooden spoon.

2. Make another well in the center of the flour. Mix the milk with ½ cup warm water and stir in the salt. Pour this into the well along with the olive oil. Mix it into the flour with the wooden spoon and then with your hands until the dough begins to come together. Gather the dough into a shaggy ball.

3. Knead the dough on a lightly floured surface: Use the heel of your hand to push down on the dough, fold it in half, turn it around a bit and push it down again. Repeat this process until the dough is smooth and elastic, about 2 minutes.

4. Clean out the bowl and lightly oil the inside. Put the dough in the bowl and roll it around so that it is oiled all over. Cover the bowl with a damp towel and set aside in a warm place until the dough has doubled in size, about 1 hour.

5. Oil a 9-by-5-by-3-inch loaf pan. Transfer the dough to a lightly floured surface and knead it hard for 5 minutes. To shape the bread, press the dough out flat, then roll it into a tight, 9-inch long cylinder. Tuck the ends under to make them a bit square and transfer the loaf to the pan, seam side down. Lightly oil the top and sprinkle with a little flour (this is just for looks). Cover with the towel and let the dough rise for about 1 hour. Remove the towel near the end of the rising. Test the dough by pressing with your fingertip; if the dough doesn't spring back and the impression remains, it is ready.

6. Preheat the oven to 425°. Bake the loaf for 15 minutes, then turn the oven down to 400° and bake for 30 minutes longer. The loaf is done when it feels hard and sounds hollow when tapped; if it makes a soft and dull sound, bake for another 5 minutes or so. Turn the bread out onto a rack (so that it doesn't steam in the pan and thus soften the crust) and let cool. Eat soon or use for toast the following day.

—Alice Waters

■

SESAME AND FLAXSEED BREAD

This yeast bread uses only a small amount of leavening (so there's more wheat, less yeast, flavor) and takes on its substantial

White and Whole Wheat Bread (p. 213)
Roasted Red Peppers with Vinaigrette (p. 176)
Carrot and Parsley Salad (p. 51)

character from long rising in the refrigerator. The loaf is kneaded with a mixer—rather than by hand—resulting in a glutinous, high-rising, more polished loaf with even air holes.

Makes 1 Large Loaf

- 4 cups lukewarm water (105° to 115°)
- 1 teaspoon active dry yeast
- 1 teaspoon sugar
- 1½ tablespoons fine sea salt
- 9 cups bread flour
- ½ cup hulled sesame seeds
- ½ cup flaxseeds*

*Available at health food stores

1. In the bowl of a standing mixer, combine 1 cup of the lukewarm water with the yeast and the sugar. Let stand until foamy, about 5 minutes.

2. Stir in the salt and another cup of the lukewarm water and mix with the paddle at low speed for 1 minute. Mix in the remaining 2 cups water. Slowly add 4 cups of the flour and mix until incorporated, about 3 minutes. Add the sesame seeds and flaxseeds and mix for 30 seconds. Add the remaining 5 cups flour and mix for about 3 minutes. Mix for 1 minute longer, until the dough pulls away from the sides of the bowl in a cohesive sticky ball. Scrape the paddle.

3. Cover the bowl with plastic wrap. Refrigerate the dough until doubled in bulk, about 8 hours.

4. Transfer the dough to a lightly floured work surface and knead for 2 minutes. Return the dough to the bowl, cover and refrigerate until doubled again, at least 8 hours or overnight.

5. Punch the dough down. Place in a clean bowl, cover and set aside at room temperature in a draft-free spot until doubled, 3 to 4 hours.

6. Shape the dough into a large round loaf. Place it on a large, lightly floured unrimmed baking sheet. Cover with a towel and set aside in a draft-free spot until doubled, about 1¼ hours.

7. Preheat the oven to 500°. Heat a baking stone or baking tiles on the middle rack of the oven for 30 minutes. Using a razor blade, slash the top of the dough crisscross fashion several times. Slide the loaf off the baking sheet onto the baking stone with a quick jerk. (Alternatively, bake the loaf directly on the lightly floured baking sheet.) Using a plant mister filled with water, generously spray the oven roof and walls, then quickly shut the oven door. Spray the oven three more times during the first 10 minutes.

8. Lower the oven temperature to 400° and bake the bread for about 45 minutes longer, until the crust is nicely browned and the loaf sounds hollow when it is tapped on the bottom. Transfer the loaf to a rack to cool for at least 1 hour before slicing.

—Patricia Wells

■

BLACK PEPPER SALLY LUNN BREAD

Start the bread at least one day ahead to allow time for the dough to rest overnight in the refrigerator.

Makes One Tall 8-Inch Loaf

- 1 cup milk
- 1 tablespoon active dry yeast
- ¼ cup sugar
- 3¾ cups all-purpose flour
- 1 tablespoon freshly ground pepper
- 1½ teaspoons salt
- 1 stick (8 tablespoons) unsalted butter, melted and cooled slightly
- 4 large eggs, at room temperature, lightly beaten
- 1 large egg yolk, lightly beaten, for glazing ➤

1. In a small saucepan, heat the milk to lukewarm (110°). Remove from the heat and stir in the yeast and sugar. Let stand for 5 minutes, until foamy.

2. In a standing mixer fitted with a paddle, blend 3 cups of the flour with the pepper and salt. Add the yeast mixture, melted butter and eggs and beat on moderate speed until blended. Beat in the remaining ¾ cup flour on low speed, ¼ cup at a time; the dough will be very soft, like a thick cake batter.

3. Transfer the dough to a large buttered bowl, cover with a kitchen towel and let rise in a warm place until doubled in bulk, about 1 hour. Punch down the dough, cover with plastic wrap and refrigerate overnight.

4. Butter an 8-by-4-inch loaf pan. Shape the cold dough into a loaf and transfer to the prepared pan. Cover with a cloth and let rise in a warm place until doubled, about 2 hours.

5. Preheat the oven to 350°. Brush the top of the loaf with egg yolk. Bake for about 1 hour, until the bread is golden and pulls away from the sides of the pan. Turn out the loaf to be sure the bread sounds hollow when tapped on the bottom. Transfer the loaf to a rack and let it cool completely. (The bread can be wrapped in foil and kept overnight at room temperature.)

—Ben Barker

■

POTATO FLAT BREAD

This is a rich, simple bread that's great on its own or with salad or soup.

♥ The elemental flavors of this simple bread make one reach for a glass of simple, straightforward white wine, such as nonvintage Corvo Bianco or Gallo Sauvignon Blanc.

Makes One 9-by-13-Inch Loaf

- **1 large baking potato (½ pound), unpeeled**
- **Salt**
- **¼ cup milk**
- **2 teaspoons active dry yeast**
- **½ teaspoon sugar**
- **1½ cups all-purpose flour**
- **1 large egg**
- **2 tablespoons unsalted butter, at room temperature**
- **1 tablespoon olive oil**
- **Coarse (kosher) salt, for sprinkling**

1. In a medium saucepan, cover the potato with cold water, add salt and bring to a boil over high heat. Reduce the heat and simmer until the potato is tender, about 30 minutes. Reserve ¼ cup of the potato cooking water in a medium bowl. Drain the potato and peel. Quickly pass the potato through a ricer or a food mill into a large bowl if you are making the bread by hand. Alternatively, mash the potato in a large standing mixer with the flat paddle. Let cool.

2. Stir the milk, yeast and sugar into the potato water and let stand until foamy, about 5 minutes. Combine the flour and 1 teaspoon of salt.

3. Beat the yeast mixture into the cooled mashed potato along with the egg and butter. Gradually beat in the flour until smooth. (The mixture will be more like batter than dough.) Cover the bowl and let stand until the dough doubles in bulk, about 1 hour. Punch down the dough, cover and refrigerate overnight.

4. Oil a 9-by-13-inch rimmed baking sheet. Using your hands, spread the cold dough evenly over the sheet. Let stand until the dough has doubled, 30 to 45 minutes.

5. Preheat the oven to 375°. Drizzle the olive oil over the bread and sprinkle with coarse salt. Bake for about 25 minutes, or until golden. Cut into wedges and serve.

—Lydie Marshall

■

ONION-PARMESAN FLAT BREAD

Prepared bread dough, available in the refrigerator or freezer section of super-markets, makes this focaccia-like treat quick and easy to put together.

4 Servings

1 tablespoon olive oil
1 pound cold prepared bread dough
¼ cup finely chopped onion
2 tablespoons freshly grated Parmesan cheese
2 teaspoons finely chopped fresh rosemary
½ teaspoon coarse salt

1. Preheat the oven to 450°. Brush a baking sheet with ½ teaspoon of the olive oil. Stretch the dough out to a 9-by-12-inch rectangle and transfer to the prepared baking sheet. Brush the dough with the remaining 2½ teaspoons oil and scatter the onion, Parmesan, rosemary and coarse salt on top.

2. Bake until crisp and lightly browned, about 20 minutes; transfer to a rack to cool slightly. Cut into pieces and serve hot, warm or at room temperature.

—Diana Sturgis

SKILLET CORN BREAD

"If I could choose one thing to eat before I die, this is it," says Park Kerr, owner of the El Paso Chile Company in El Paso, Texas, and author of *The El Paso Chile Company's Texas Border Cookbook* (Morrow). His rich corn bread is laced with chiles, bacon and cheese. If you're in a hurry, canned chiles and roasted red peppers from a jar can be used in place of fresh.

Makes One 9-Inch Corn Bread

2 hot green chiles, preferably New Mexicos or jalapeños
1 small red bell pepper
6 slices of bacon
Vegetable oil
1 cup cornmeal
½ cup all-purpose flour
2 tablespoons sugar
2 tablespoons pure hot New Mexico chile powder*
½ teaspoon salt
½ teaspoon baking soda
½ teaspoon baking powder
1 cup buttermilk
2 large eggs, beaten
1 cup grated sharp Cheddar cheese (4 ounces)
3 tablespoons melted unsalted butter

*Available at Latin American markets and specialty food shops

1. Preheat the oven to 350°. Roast the chiles and bell pepper over a gas flame or under the broiler until charred all over. Place in a paper bag, seal and set aside to steam for 5 minutes. Open the bag and, working over it, remove all the blackened skins, as well as the stems, cores and seeds; rinse briefly, if necessary, to remove any black bits. Cut into small dice and drain very well on paper towels.

2. In a 9-inch cast-iron skillet, cook the bacon over moderate heat until crisp, about 5 minutes. Drain the bacon and crumble it. Discard the bacon fat and wipe the skillet clean. Coat the skillet with a thin film of vegetable oil.

3. In a large bowl, stir together the cornmeal, flour, sugar, chile powder, salt, baking soda and baking powder. Add the buttermilk, eggs, cheese, bacon, chiles, bell pepper and the melted butter. Stir well. Pour the batter into the skillet and bake for about 40 minutes, until firm. Serve warm.

—Park Kerr

Blue Cornsticks

3 jalapeño chiles, seeded and minced
2 garlic cloves, minced
3 tablespoons chopped fresh coriander (cilantro)
Oil or melted butter, for brushing

1. Preheat the oven to 400°. Place a cast-iron cornstick mold in the oven to heat.

2. In a large bowl, sift together the cornmeal, flour, sugar, salt and baking powder. In a medium bowl, lightly beat the eggs. Beat in the melted butter and shortening. Stir in the milk. Add to the dry ingredients along with the jalapeños, garlic and coriander. Stir just to blend; do not overmix.

3. Remove the mold from the oven and brush with oil. Spoon about 2 tablespoons of the batter into each mold. Bake in the middle of the oven for 20 to 25 minutes, until golden brown around the edges and on the bottom. Turn out onto a rack to cool. Repeat with the remaining batter.

—Stephan Pyles

■

BLUE CORNSTICKS

These garlicky cornsticks flavored with fresh coriander are best when they are baked in a heavy cast-iron cornstick mold. This recipe has been adapted from *The New Texas Cuisine* (Doubleday).

Makes About 1½ Dozen Cornsticks
1½ cups blue cornmeal
¾ cup all-purpose flour
2 tablespoons sugar
1½ teaspoons salt
1 teaspoon baking powder
3 large eggs
6 tablespoons unsalted butter, melted and cooled slightly
6 tablespoons shortening, melted and cooled slightly
1¼ cups milk, at room temperature

■

BLUE CORN MUFFINS WITH PINE NUTS

From Coyote Cafe in Santa Fe, these light, sweet muffins are chock-full of crunchy toasted pine nuts and chewy roasted corn kernels.

Makes 1 Dozen Muffins
Vegetable cooking spray
¾ cup pine nuts (about 4½ ounces)
⅔ cup fresh or thawed frozen corn kernels
1½ cups unbleached all-purpose flour
1½ cups blue cornmeal
⅓ cup sugar
1 tablespoon baking powder
¾ teaspoon salt
3 large eggs, separated
1½ cups milk
⅓ cup wildflower honey

1 stick (8 tablespoons) plus 2
  tablespoons unsalted butter, melted
2 tablespoons chopped fresh herbs,
  such as marjoram or rosemary
  (optional)

1. Preheat the oven to 375°. Generously coat a 12-cup muffin pan with vegetable cooking spray. Place the pine nuts on a baking sheet and toast in the oven until golden brown, about 4 minutes. Transfer to a plate to cool.

2. In a cast-iron skillet, cook the corn over low heat, stirring often, until browned and slightly dry, 6 to 8 minutes. Transfer to a plate to cool.

3. In a large bowl, mix together the flour, cornmeal, sugar, baking powder and salt. In a medium bowl, whisk the egg yolks with the milk, honey and melted butter. In another bowl, beat the egg whites until stiff but not dry.

4. Make a well in the middle of the dry ingredients. Pour in the milk mixture with the pine nuts and corn; stir just to combine. Fold in the egg whites and herbs. Spoon into the prepared pan and bake for 20 to 25 minutes, until a tester inserted in the center of a muffin comes out clean. Let cool slightly in the pan. Turn out onto a rack.

—Mark Miller

■

SMOKY CHIPOTLE CORN BREAD

The southwestern-style Mesa Grill in New York City serves this delectable corn bread. The recipe has been adapted from *Bobby Flay's Bold American Food* (Warner Books).

Makes One 9-Inch Corn Bread
1 cup coarse yellow cornmeal
1 cup all-purpose flour
2 tablespoons sugar
1½ teaspoons baking powder

1 teaspoon salt
1 large egg, lightly beaten
½ cup buttermilk
½ cup milk
6 tablespoons unsalted butter, melted
4 canned chipotle chiles in adobo*—
  drained well, stemmed and pureed
  or minced
  Shortening

*Available at Latin American markets and specialty food shops

1. Preheat the oven to 450°. Place a 9-inch cast-iron skillet in the oven.

2. In a large bowl, stir together the cornmeal, flour, sugar, baking powder and salt. Fold in the egg, buttermilk, milk, butter and chipotle puree.

3. Generously brush the hot skillet with shortening. Pour in the batter. Bake for 20 to 25 minutes, or until the bread is brown around the edges and firm. Serve warm.

—Bobby Flay

■

ROSEMARY CORN CAKES

If you like corn and rosemary, you'll love these sweet, tender cakes that are somewhere between a corn bread and a biscuit. The recipe comes from Sumi Chang, the breakfast chef at Campanile in Los Angeles.

Makes About 15 Cakes
1 stick plus 6 tablespoons unsalted
  butter, at room temperature
½ cup light brown sugar
1 tablespoon honey
1 large egg
1 large egg yolk
1¾ cups unbleached all-purpose flour
1 cup cornmeal
1 tablespoon plus 1 teaspoon baking
  powder ➤

¼ teaspoon salt

2 teaspoons finely chopped fresh rosemary plus tiny sprigs for decoration

½ cup heavy cream

1. Preheat the oven to 350°. In a large bowl, using a hand-held electric mixer, beat the butter with the brown sugar on medium speed until light and fluffy. Beat in the honey, egg and egg yolk. Scrape down the sides of the bowl with a rubber spatula and beat in the flour, cornmeal, baking powder, salt and finely chopped rosemary. Pour in the cream and blend well; the dough will be quite sticky.

2. On a generously floured work surface, with floured hands, pat the dough into an 8-by-12-inch rectangle about ½ inch thick. Using a 2½-inch-round biscuit cutter dipped in flour, cut out individual cakes. Gently pat the dough scraps together and cut out more cakes.

3. Place the cakes about 2 inches apart on an ungreased baking sheet and place a tiny rosemary sprig in one corner of each cake. Bake for 30 to 35 minutes, until the bottoms are golden brown. Let the cakes rest for a few minutes on the baking sheets; they are very tender and quite fragile. Using a spatula, carefully transfer the cakes to a rack to cool.

—Sumi Chang

■

CHEDDAR CORN BISCUITS

These light, corn-studded biscuits are from The Lark Creek Inn in Larkspur, California.

Makes About 3 Dozen Biscuits

2 cups all-purpose flour

1 cup cornmeal

3 tablespoons sugar

2 tablespoons baking powder

¾ teaspoon salt

¼ teaspoon freshly ground pepper

1 stick (8 tablespoons) cold unsalted butter, cut into small pieces

1 cup grated Cheddar cheese (4 ounces)

1 cup fresh or thawed frozen corn kernels

1½ cups heavy cream

1. Preheat the oven to 375°. In a large bowl, stir together the flour, cornmeal, sugar, baking powder, salt and pepper. Using a pastry blender or 2 knives, cut in the butter until the mixture resembles coarse meal. Stir in the cheese and corn kernels. Pour in the cream and stir just until the dough begins to hold together.

2. On a well-floured surface, gently roll out the dough to a 9-by-10-inch rectangle about ¾ inch thick. Using a 1½-inch-round biscuit cutter, cut out as many biscuits as possible and place them 1 inch apart on ungreased baking sheets. Bake for 15 to 18 minutes, until lightly browned. Transfer to a rack. Reroll the scraps. Cut out and bake the remaining biscuits.

—Bradley Ogden

Chapter 11 ▪ PRESERVES & CONDIMENTS

223   Plum and Nectarine Jam

223   Cantaloupe and Black Pepper Jam

223   Peach and Lime Jam

225   Fig and Strawberry Jam

225   Strawberry and Sweet Plum Jam

226   White Peach Jam

226   Yellow Tomato, Lemon and Basil Jam

226   Green Cherry Tomato Pickles

227   Quick Pickled Cauliflower

227   Corn Dollar Pickles

228   Ginger-Spiced Pickled Peppers

228   Roasted Tomato Relish

229   Cucumber Raita

229   Tamarind Chutney

229   Horseradish with Beet

230   Cranberry Ketchup

230   Garlic Jam

Plum and Nectarine Jam

JAMS
IN A JIFFY

For all who love the taste of locally grown ripe fruit, summer is much too short. But having a few jars of easy-to-make jams tucked away in a cupboard will help us make it through the winter months. Each of the following seven recipes yields small, manageable batches (three to six half-pints) of intensely flavored jam.

Cantaloupe and Black Pepper Jam

Plum and Nectarine Jam
Makes 5 Half-Pints

2 pounds ripe red plums, such as Santa Rosa, pitted and cut into ½-inch pieces

2 pounds ripe nectarines or peaches— peeled, pitted and thinly sliced

2½ cups sugar

¼ cup fresh lemon juice

1. In a large, heavy, nonreactive skillet, combine the plums, nectarines, sugar and lemon juice. Using a potato masher, mash the mixture well. Let stand for 2 hours, stirring occasionally with a wooden spoon.

2. Bring the fruit mixture to a boil over moderately high heat, stirring often. Lower the heat to moderate and boil the jam, stirring often to prevent scorching, until thickened, 30 to 40 minutes. About halfway through the cooking time, using a large metal spoon, skim off any white foam that has accumulated on the surface.

3. Ladle the hot jam through a wide-mouthed funnel into 5 sterilized half-pint jars and process (see Jam-Making Tips, p. 225, for complete instructions).

Cantaloupe and
Black Pepper Jam
Makes 3 to 4 Half-Pints

7 cups ½-inch cantaloupe chunks (from 2 ripe medium cantaloupes)

1 tart green apple—peeled, cored and coarsely grated

1½ cups sugar

⅓ cup fresh lime juice

½ teaspoon coarsely ground black pepper

1. In a large, heavy, nonreactive skillet, combine the cantaloupe, apple, sugar and lime juice. Using a potato masher, mash the mixture well. Let stand for at least 1 and up to 2 hours, stirring occasionally.

2. Bring the fruit mixture to a boil over moderately high heat, stirring often. Lower the heat to moderate and boil the jam, stirring often to prevent scorching, until thickened, 20 to 30 minutes. About halfway through the cooking time, using a large metal spoon, skim off any white foam that has accumulated on the surface. Remove the skillet from the heat and stir in the pepper.

3. Ladle the hot jam through a wide-mouthed funnel into 3 to 4 sterilized half-pint jars and process (see Jam-Making Tips, p. 225, for complete instructions).

Peach and Lime Jam
Makes 5 Half-Pints

4 to 5 limes

3 pounds ripe peaches—peeled, pitted and thinly sliced

3 cups sugar ➤

223

**Peach and
Lime Jam**

1. Remove ½-inch-wide strips of zest from half of 1 lime. In a small saucepan of boiling water, blanch the lime zest for 5 minutes to remove bitterness. Drain and pat dry. Cut the strips lengthwise into very fine shreds.

2. Peel 2 of the limes, removing all the bitter white pith. Cut in between the membranes to release the sections; set the sections aside. Squeeze the membranes over a small bowl to extract all the juice and then squeeze juice from the remaining limes to make a total of ¼ cup. Chop the sections into small pieces.

3. In a large, heavy, nonreactive skillet, combine the peaches, sugar and lime juice, chopped sections and zest. Using a potato masher, mash well. Let stand for at least 1 and up to 2 hours, stirring occasionally.

4. Bring the fruit mixture to a boil over moderately high heat, stirring often. Lower the heat to moderate and boil the

jam, stirring often to prevent scorching, until thickened, 20 to 30 minutes. About halfway through the cooking time, using a large metal spoon, skim off any white foam that has accumulated on the surface of the jam.

5. Ladle the hot jam through a wide-mouthed funnel into 5 sterilized half-pint jars and process (see Jam-Making Tips, below, for complete instructions).

Fig and Strawberry Jam
Makes 6 Half-Pints

1½ pounds small green figs, such
   as white Kadota, white Adriatic
   or white Calimyrna, stemmed
   and cut into small pieces
2 pints ripe strawberries, hulled
   and quartered
2½ cups sugar
¼ cup fresh lemon juice

1. In a large, heavy, nonreactive skillet, combine the small green figs, the hulled and quartered strawberries, the sugar and the fresh lemon juice. Using a potato masher, mash the mixture. Let it stand for at least 1 and up to 2 hours, stirring occasionally.

2. Bring the fruit mixture to a boil over moderately high heat, stirring often. Lower the heat to moderate and boil the jam, stirring often to prevent scorching, until thickened, 20 to 30 minutes. About halfway through the cooking time, using a large metal spoon, skim off any white foam that has accumulated on the surface of the jam.

3. Ladle the hot jam through a wide-mouthed funnel into 6 sterilized half-pint jars and process (see Jam-Making Tips, at right, for complete instructions).

Strawberry and Sweet Plum Jam
Makes 5 Half-Pints

1 pound ripe red plums—halved,
   pitted and cut into ½-inch pieces
2 pints ripe strawberries, hulled
   and quartered
2½ cups sugar
¼ cup fresh lime juice

1. In a large, heavy, nonreactive skillet, combine the plums, strawberries, sugar and lime juice. Using a potato masher, mash well. Let stand for at least 1 and up to 2 hours, stirring occasionally.

2. Bring the fruit mixture to a boil over moderately high heat, stirring often. Lower the heat to moderate and boil the jam, stirring often to prevent scorching, until thickened, 20 to 30 minutes. About halfway through the cooking time, using a large metal spoon, skim off any white foam that has accumulated on the surface of the jam.

3. Ladle the hot jam through a wide-mouthed funnel into 5 sterilized half-pint jars and process (see Jam-Making Tips, below, for complete instructions).

JAM-MAKING TIPS

• To sterilize the jars: Rinse the half-pint jars and their lids, place in an 8- to 10-quart saucepan, add water to cover and bring to a boil. Remove the pan from the heat and set aside until the jam is made. Using a jar lifter or tongs, remove the jars and lids from the water and drain briefly on paper towels before filling.
• While the jam is cooking, place a rack or towel in the bottom of an 8- to 10-quart saucepan. Fill the saucepan halfway with water and bring to a simmer. Bring a large kettle of water to a simmer.
• Ladle the hot jam through a widemouthed funnel into the sterilized jars to within ½ inch of the top. Wipe the jar rims with a clean towel rinsed in hot water. Cover with the lids and screw on firmly but not too tightly.
• Using a jar lifter or tongs, place the filled jars in the saucepan of simmering water; the jars should not touch each other. Add enough simmering water from the kettle to cover the tops of the jars by two inches. Cover the pan and simmer for 10 minutes. Using the jar lifter or tongs, transfer the jars to a towel and drain. As the jars cool and the seal tightens, you will hear them "ping." (You can skip the last step of simmering the jars of jam and simply refrigerate them instead.)

—Marie Simmons

White Peach Jam
Makes 4 Half-Pints

3 **pounds ripe white peaches— peeled, pitted and thinly sliced**
2½ **cups sugar**
¼ **cup fresh lemon juice**

1. In a large, heavy, nonreactive skillet, combine the peaches, sugar and lemon juice. Using a potato masher, mash the mixture well. Let stand for 2 hours, stirring occasionally.

2. Bring the fruit mixture to a boil over moderately high heat, stirring often. Lower the heat to moderate and boil the jam, stirring often to prevent scorching, until thickened, 20 to 30 minutes. About halfway through the cooking time, using a large metal spoon, skim off any white foam that has accumulated on the surface of the jam.

3. Ladle the hot jam through a wide-mouthed funnel into 4 sterilized half-pint jars and process (see Jam-Making Tips, p. 225, for complete instructions).

Yellow Tomato, Lemon and Basil Jam
Makes 4 Half-Pints

2 **lemons**
3 **pounds ripe yellow tomatoes— peeled if the skins are tough, cored and cut into ½-inch pieces**
3 **cups sugar**
1 **tablespoon (packed) finely chopped fresh basil**

1. Using a small sharp knife, peel the lemons, removing all the bitter white pith. Holding the lemons over a bowl, cut in between the membranes to release the sections. Discard the seeds and membranes.

2. In a large, heavy, nonreactive skillet, combine the lemon sections, the tomatoes, the sugar and the basil. Using a potato masher, mash the mixture well. Let stand for at least 1 and up to 2 hours, stirring occasionally.

3. Bring the fruit mixture to a boil over moderately high heat, stirring often. Lower the heat to moderate and boil the jam, stirring often to prevent scorching, until thickened, 30 to 40 minutes. About halfway through the cooking time, using a large metal spoon, skim off any white foam that has accumulated on the surface of the jam.

4. Ladle the hot jam through a wide-mouthed funnel into 4 sterilized half-pint jars and process (see Jam-Making Tips, p. 225, for complete instructions).

—Marie Simmons

■

GREEN CHERRY TOMATO PICKLES

These quick pickles are reminiscent of the half-sour garlic pickles sold in kosher delicatessens.

Makes 1 Quart

1 **pound green cherry tomatoes, cored, or small green tomatoes cut in half**
⅓ **cup cider vinegar**
1½ **tablespoons coarsely chopped garlic**
1 **teaspoon salt**
½ **teaspoon freshly cracked black pepper**

1. Pack the tomatoes into a 1-quart canning jar. Combine 1 cup of water and the rest of the ingredients in a medium nonreactive saucepan, cover and bring to a boil. Remove from the heat and let infuse for a few minutes.

2. Pour the mixture over the tomatoes and let cool to room temperature. Cover and refrigerate overnight. (The pickles will keep for up to 3 days. Remove them from the refrigerator at least 15 minutes before serving.)

—Marcia Kiesel

■

QUICK
PICKLED
CAULIFLOWER

Saffron threads, lemon zest and fennel seeds bring special flavor to crunchy cauliflower pickles.

Makes About 2 Quarts

½ cup dry white wine
¼ teaspoon saffron threads
¼ cup sugar
¼ cup white wine vinegar
2 strips of lemon zest
2 bay leaves
1 tablespoon tomato paste
1 teaspoon fennel seeds
1 teaspoon salt
1 teaspoon whole black peppercorns
1 cinnamon stick
1 large garlic clove, finely chopped
1 head of cauliflower, cored and trimmed into 1- to 2-inch florets
2 teaspoons dry mustard

1. In a large nonreactive saucepan, warm the wine over low heat. Sprinkle in the saffron threads, crushing them between your fingers. Turn off the heat and let steep for 5 minutes. Add 3 cups of water and the sugar, vinegar, lemon zest, bay leaves, tomato paste, fennel seeds, salt, black peppercorns, cinnamon and garlic. Stir well and bring to a simmer over moderate heat. Cover, reduce the heat to low and cook for 5 minutes.

2. Stir in the cauliflower. Raise the heat to high and boil for 2 minutes. Remove from the heat and stir in the mustard. Cover and let cool to room temperature. Pack into canning jars and refrigerate for at least 1 and for up to 5 days.

—Marcia Kiesel

■

CORN DOLLAR
PICKLES

Slice through fresh corn, cobs and all, for these unusual pickles.

6 Servings

4 thin, medium ears of fresh corn, shucked
1 teaspoon cumin seeds
1 medium onion, thinly sliced
3 garlic cloves, thinly sliced
1 tablespoon sugar
1 tablespoon white wine vinegar
¾ teaspoon salt

1. Fit a food processor with a ¼- or ½-inch slicing disk. Turn the processor on and push the ears of corn through the feeder to slice them into rounds.

2. In a small dry skillet, toast the cumin seeds over high heat until fragrant, about 30 seconds. Transfer the cumin seeds to a plate to cool, then pound the seeds to a coarse powder in a mortar or finely chop with a knife.

3. In a medium nonreactive saucepan, combine the sliced onion and garlic cloves, the sugar, white wine vinegar, salt and cumin seeds. Pour in 2 cups of water and bring to a boil over high heat. Boil for 3 minutes. Add the corn slices and reduce the heat to low. Cover the saucepan and simmer until the corn is tender, about 3 minutes for thin slices and 5 minutes for thicker ones. Remove the saucepan from the heat and let the corn cool to room temperature.

4. Stack the corn dollars in a 1-quart canning jar, fitting in the onion and garlic slices as you go. Pour the cooking liquid into the canning jar to cover the corn completely. Refrigerate for at least 1 and for up to 5 days.

—Marcia Kiesel

From left:
**Ginger-Spiced
Pickled Peppers,
Roasted Tomato
Relish and
Tamarind
Chutney**

■

GINGER-SPICED
PICKLED PEPPERS

Allow time to make these pickles ahead so that their flavor develops. Serve them at room temperature or heated.

Makes About 1 Quart
- **1 red bell pepper, quartered lengthwise and thinly sliced crosswise**
- **1 green bell pepper, quartered lengthwise and thinly sliced crosswise**
- **1 yellow bell pepper, quartered lengthwise and thinly sliced crosswise**
- **1 jalapeño—halved, seeded if desired and thinly sliced lengthwise**
- **1 2-inch piece of fresh ginger, peeled and cut into thin matchsticks**
- **1 cup rice vinegar**
- **2 tablespoons sugar**
- **1½ teaspoons salt**

1. In a wide, shallow, nonreactive dish, toss the red, green and yellow bell peppers with the jalapeño and ginger. In a bowl, combine the vinegar, sugar and salt with 1 cup of water, stirring to dissolve. Pour over the peppers. Cover and refrigerate overnight.

2. Pack the peppers in a 1-quart canning jar and pour the liquid over to cover. Any remaining liquid can be stored separately. Refrigerate for at least 1 day and up to 1 month.

—Marcia Kiesel

■

ROASTED
TOMATO RELISH

Try this relish with roasted or grilled pork or chicken, or with shellfish, either warm or cold.

Makes About 1 Cup
- **1 pound plum tomatoes (6 to 8)**
- **1 medium jalapeño or 2 small serranos, stemmed**
- **½ pound shallots, unpeeled and halved lengthwise**
- **6 garlic cloves, unpeeled and halved lengthwise**
- **2 tablespoons fish sauce**
- **1 tablespoon light brown sugar**
- **½ teaspoon salt**

1. Preheat the broiler. Place the tomatoes and jalapeño on a rack in a broiler pan to catch any juices. Broil the tomatoes for about 8 minutes, turning occasionally, until the skin is charred and split. Transfer with tongs to a medium

bowl. Add the tomato juices and let cool for about 10 minutes. Peel the tomatoes and jalapeño.

2. Broil the shallots and garlic cloves, skin side up, for about 5 minutes, until nicely charred. Peel.

3. In a food processor, puree the tomatoes and their juices with the jalapeño, shallots, garlic, fish sauce, brown sugar and salt until relatively smooth. Use, or refrigerate in an airtight container for up to 1 week.

—Marcia Kiesel

■

CUCUMBER RAITA

Buttermilk makes a smooth substitute for the yogurt more traditionally used in this Indian condiment.

4 Servings
- 1 cup nonfat buttermilk
- 2 tablespoons finely chopped onion
- 1½ tablespoons finely chopped fresh mint
- ⅛ teaspoon ground cumin
  Salt and freshly ground pepper
- 2 medium cucumbers—peeled, halved lengthwise, seeded and thinly sliced crosswise

1. In a medium bowl, combine the buttermilk, onion, mint, cumin and ½ teaspoon each of salt and pepper. Cover and refrigerate for 1 hour to allow the flavors to blend.

2. Spread the cucumber slices on a large plate and sprinkle with 1 teaspoon salt. Let stand for 45 minutes to drain.

3. Transfer the cucumber slices to paper towels and pat dry. Stir the slices into the buttermilk mixture, season with salt and pepper and serve.

—Andrea Chesman

■

TAMARIND CHUTNEY

Spread this pungent chutney on grilled poultry or on sandwiches of smoked turkey breast and arugula.

Makes 1 Cup
- ½ cup tamarind pulp
- 1 tablespoon ground cumin
- ¼ cup minced onion
- 2 tablespoons minced fresh ginger
- 2 tablespoons brown sugar
- ¼ teaspoon cayenne pepper
- ¼ teaspoon salt

1. In a small bowl, cover the tamarind with 1 cup of warm water. Set aside to soak for at least 45 minutes, periodically stirring and mashing with a fork to break it down.

2. Meanwhile, in a dry skillet, toast the cumin over moderate heat, stirring, until fragrant, about 2 minutes.

3. Using a rubber spatula or a large spoon, press the tamarind pulp through a fine-mesh strainer set over a large bowl. Scrape the outside of the strainer often to remove the thick pulp. Keep working the mixture until you have nearly 1 cup.

4. Stir in the toasted cumin, onion, ginger, brown sugar, cayenne and salt. Use, or refrigerate in an airtight container for up to 5 days.

—Nancie McDermott

■

HORSERADISH WITH BEET

Fresh horseradish varies from mild to very strong; add more beets or vinegar to suit your taste. The texture of this condiment is best when the horseradish and beet are grated by hand. ➤

TAMARIND

Essential in Indian and Southeast Asian cooking, the ripe fruit of the tamarind tree has a smoky sweet-and-sour flavor reminiscent of raisins and limes. Tamarind pulp is sold in dark, moist bricks, well wrapped in plastic or cellophane. Fresh ripe tamarind is also available in season in both Asian and Hispanic markets. Look for dull brown, brittle, crackling, messy pods with exposed dark flesh (avoid smooth, firm tamarind; it is young and sour beyond expression). Soak tamarind pulp or peeled ripe pods in water to cover for 30 minutes to an hour, mashing occasionally. Press the softened fruit through a fine sieve or strainer, scraping the bottom. Use the thick, rich puree in soups and curries, dressings for fruit or vegetable salads, or marinades and sauces.

—Nancie McDermott

Makes About 1⅓ Cups

½ **pound fresh horseradish root, peeled and finely grated**
1 **small beet, peeled and finely grated**
½ **cup distilled white vinegar**
1 **teaspoon sugar**
1 **teaspoon salt**

Combine the horseradish and beet in a large bowl. Stir in the vinegar, sugar and salt. (The horseradish can be refrigerated in a tightly sealed jar for up to 3 days.) Serve chilled or at room temperature.

—Susan Shapiro Jaslove

■

CRANBERRY KETCHUP

This condiment can enliven a cold turkey sandwich or add a new kick to a broiled hamburger.

Makes 1½ Pints

1 **12-ounce bag whole cranberries, picked over (3⅓ cups)**
2 **large onions, finely chopped (2½ cups)**
1 **cup white wine vinegar**
2 **medium garlic cloves, minced**
1 **tablespoon ground allspice**
1 **teaspoon salt**
⅔ **cup sugar**

1. In a medium nonreactive saucepan, combine ⅔ cup water with the cranberries, onions, vinegar, garlic, allspice and salt. Bring to a simmer over moderately low heat and cook, stirring occasionally, until thick and pulpy, about 20 minutes. Stir in the sugar, return to a simmer and cook, stirring frequently, for 15 minutes longer. Let cool for 30 minutes.

2. Transfer the mixture to a blender and puree, then strain into a glass measure. Pour the ketchup into glass bottles.

(The ketchup will keep refrigerated for up to 2 months.)

—Diana Sturgis

■

GARLIC JAM

Roasting garlic whole gives it a mellow and surprisingly sweet flavor. Choose firm, fresh heads of garlic with plump, tightly clustered cloves and dry, papery skin from a good produce market. Use this condiment with roasted meats or as a spread for toasted croûtes or cold meat sandwiches, or try a spoonful of the jam mixed into homemade salad dressings and sauces.

Makes 1⅓ Cups

4 **whole heads of garlic (about 14 ounces)**
1 **tablespoon extra-virgin olive oil**
1 **medium onion, unpeeled and halved lengthwise**
Salt (optional)

1. Preheat the oven to 350°. Using a large sharp knife, cut off ½ inch from the top of each head of garlic to expose some of the flesh.

2. Drizzle 1 teaspoon of the oil over the bottom of a gratin or glass pie dish. Place the garlic and the onion halves cut sides down in the dish, cover tightly with foil and bake for 45 minutes, until very soft to the touch. Uncover and let cool for 20 minutes.

3. Peel the onion halves and finely chop them. Place in a medium bowl. Squeeze the garlic pulp from the skins into the bowl; discard the skins. Using a fork, stir in the remaining 2 teaspoons oil and mash with the onion and garlic until thoroughly incorporated. Season with salt if desired. (The garlic jam will keep refrigerated in a glass jar for up to 2 weeks.)

—Diana Sturgis

Chapter 12 ▪ DESSERTS

233   Chocolate Zabaglione Cream Trifle

233   Fondue au Chocolat

234   White Chocolate Ice Cream in Pecan Lace Cookie Cups

236   Mocha Mousse

236   Frozen Caffè Latte

239   Bittersweet Chocolate Pudding

239   Butterscotch Pudding

240   Basque-Flavored Pudding with Almond Praline

241   Cinnamon-Rice Crème Brûlée

243   Maple Indian Pudding

243   Arline Rodman's Minnesota Cheesecake

244   Ricotta Fritters

Chocolate
Zabaglione Cream
Trifle

CHOCOLATE ZABAGLIONE CREAM TRIFLE

A light zabaglione cream is layered with espresso-infused chocolate cake and covered with chocolate shavings in this elegant Italianate trifle, served at Stars in San Francisco.

10 Servings

Chocolate Cake:
- 1 cup all-purpose flour
- ¼ cup unsweetened cocoa powder
- 2½ teaspoons baking powder
- Pinch of salt
- 5 large eggs, at room temperature, separated
- 1¼ cups granulated sugar
- ⅓ cup boiling water
- 1 teaspoon pure vanilla extract
- Confectioners' sugar
- 1½ cups brewed espresso or very strong coffee

Zabaglione Cream:
- 8 large egg yolks
- ½ cup granulated sugar
- ½ cup Marsala
- ¼ cup sherry
- Pinch of salt
- 1½ cups cold heavy cream
- 6 ounces semisweet chocolate

1. Prepare the cake: Preheat the oven to 350°. Line a 10½-by-15½-by-¾-inch jelly-roll pan with parchment or wax paper.

2. In a medium bowl, sift the flour twice with the cocoa, baking powder and salt. In a large bowl, beat the egg yolks and granulated sugar at high speed until thick and pale, about 5 minutes. Gradually beat in the boiling water and vanilla at medium speed. Raise the speed to high and continue beating until the mixture is thick enough to hold a ribbon on the surface when the beaters are lifted, about 5 minutes. Fold in the dry ingredients.

3. In another medium bowl, beat the egg whites until soft peaks form. Fold half of the whites into the batter, then fold in the remaining whites.

4. Spread the batter evenly in the prepared pan. Bake for about 15 minutes, or until the top springs back when pressed lightly in the center. Invert the cake onto a clean kitchen towel sprinkled with confectioners' sugar and peel off the paper. Let cool completely.

5. Prepare the zabaglione cream: In a large bowl, whisk the egg yolks with the sugar, Marsala, sherry and salt. Set the bowl over a large saucepan filled with ¾ inch of simmering water. Beat the mixture at medium speed until it triples in volume and reaches 165°. Set the bowl in a larger bowl of ice water and continue beating until the zabaglione has cooled.

6. In another large bowl, beat the cream until soft peaks form. Fold the zabaglione into the whipped cream. Cover and refrigerate until chilled.

7. Pour 1¼ cups of the zabaglione into a 2½-quart glass bowl or trifle dish. Using a long serrated knife, cut the cake in half horizontally. Cut and fit cake pieces on top of the cream in a single layer, using one-third of the cake. Brush the cake generously with ½ cup of the espresso. Continue layering with the remaining ingredients so that you have 3 layers of cake and 4 layers of cream.

8. Using a vegetable peeler, shave the semisweet chocolate over the trifle. Cover with plastic wrap and refrigerate for at least 8 hours or up to 2 days.

—Emily Luchetti

■

FONDUE AU CHOCOLAT

At Le Cirque in New York City, this incredibly simple, sumptuous dessert is served with thin crisp cookies. ➤

4 to 6 Servings

- **1 cup heavy cream**
- **7 ounces imported bittersweet chocolate, such as Valrhona Manjari, finely chopped**
- **2 tablespoons green Chartreuse Seasonal fruits, such as pineapple, bananas, pears, kiwis, papayas and starfruits, cut into bite-size chunks or slices Unsweetened whipped cream**

1. In a small saucepan, bring the cream to a boil over moderate heat. Place the chocolate in a medium bowl and pour in the hot cream. Stir until smooth. Stir in the Chartreuse.

2. Divide the chocolate between two 1-cup ramekins. Set them on 2 large plates lined with doilies. Arrange the fruit around them. Garnish the fondue with a small dollop of whipped cream. Serve immediately.

—Jacques Torres

■

WHITE CHOCOLATE ICE CREAM IN PECAN LACE COOKIE CUPS

White chocolate lovers beware: This rich, sweet, silky smooth ice cream from The Trellis in Williamsburg, Virginia, is addictive. Tangy blood oranges make a striking substitute for the navels used here.

8 Servings

White Chocolate Ice Cream:
- **¾ pound white chocolate, coarsely chopped**
- **3¼ cups milk**
- **¾ cup granulated sugar**
- **3 large eggs**

Pecan Lace Cookies:
- **⅔ cup (packed) light brown sugar**
- **½ cup light corn syrup**

- **1 stick (8 tablespoons) unsalted butter**
- **1 cup pecans, finely chopped (about 4 ounces)**
- **⅔ cup cake flour**

- **4 medium navel oranges, washed**
- **4 ounces semisweet chocolate, finely chopped Fresh mint sprigs, for garnish**

1. Make the ice cream: In a medium bowl, combine the white chocolate with ¼ cup of the milk and cover tightly with plastic wrap. Set the bowl over a saucepan filled with ¾ inch of simmering water until the chocolate melts, about 10 minutes. Remove the bowl from the heat and stir until smooth.

2. In a medium nonreactive saucepan, bring the remaining 3 cups milk and ¼ cup of the sugar to a boil over moderately high heat, whisking occasionally.

3. In a large bowl, beat the eggs with the remaining ½ cup sugar at high speed until thick, about 3 minutes. Gradually whisk in the boiling milk. Return the custard to the saucepan. Cook over moderate heat, stirring constantly, until it reaches 185°, about 3 minutes. Strain into a bowl set in a larger bowl of ice water. Whisk in the melted white chocolate. Let stand, whisking occasionally, until chilled, about 45 minutes.

4. Freeze the custard in an ice cream maker according to the manufacturer's instructions. Scrape the ice cream into a chilled container and freeze until firm, about 4 hours.

5. Make the cookie cups: Preheat the oven to 325°. In a medium saucepan, bring the brown sugar, corn syrup and butter to a boil over moderate heat. Remove from the heat and stir in the pecans and flour.

6. Bake 2 cookies at a time: To make each cookie, drop 2 tablespoons of the batter onto a nonstick cookie sheet, allowing room for it to spread to 5 inches. Bake in the middle of the oven for about 12

Fondue au Chocolat

minutes, until golden brown. Let cool for 30 seconds. Carefully remove the cookies with a wide metal spatula and invert each one on a 19-ounce can. (If the cookies harden, rewarm them in the oven for 30 seconds.) Working quickly, loosely mold the cookies around the cans. Repeat until you have 8 cookie cups.

7. Make the cigar cookies: Drop teaspoons of the remaining batter about 3 inches apart on the cookie sheet. Bake for about 8 minutes, or until golden brown. Let cool 15 seconds. One by one, scrape up the cookies and roll them around a chopstick. Repeat until you have 8 cigars.

8. Using a zester, strip the zest from 2 of the oranges; alternatively, use a vegetable peeler to remove the zest in long strips, then cut the strips into thin matchsticks. Using a sharp knife, peel the 4 oranges, removing all the bitter white pith. Slice the oranges crosswise ⅜ inch thick.

9. To assemble, place each cookie cup on a dessert plate and arrange 4 or 5 overlapping orange slices alongside. Spoon 3 scoops of ice cream into each cookie cup and sprinkle the orange zest and chopped semisweet chocolate on top. Garnish with a cigar cookie and mint sprig.

—Marcel Desaulniers

■

MOCHA MOUSSE

This rich-tasting mousse gets its deep chocolate flavor from unsweetened cocoa—and has less than a gram of fat per serving.

8 Servings
- ¼ cup plus 1 tablespoon unsweetened cocoa powder
- 1 tablespoon instant espresso
- 1 envelope unflavored gelatin
- ½ cup plus 2 tablespoons sugar
- 1 cup low-fat (one percent) milk
- 2 large egg yolks
- ½ cup fromage blanc* or nonfat ricotta cheese
- 1 teaspoon pure vanilla extract
- 1 tablespoon light corn syrup
- 4 large egg whites
- ¼ teaspoon cream of tartar

*Available at specialty food stores

1. Sift the cocoa, espresso, gelatin and 2 tablespoons of the sugar into a small heavy saucepan. Whisk in the milk and egg yolks until smooth. Cook over moderate heat, stirring, until the mixture reaches 160° on a candy thermometer and starts to thicken, about 6 minutes. Strain the chocolate base into a medium bowl set over a larger bowl of ice water. Whisk until cool, then whisk in the fromage blanc and vanilla. Remove from the ice water bath and let stand, stirring occasionally.

2. Rinse out the saucepan. Add the remaining ½ cup sugar, the corn syrup and ¼ cup water. Cook over high heat until the syrup reaches 241°. Remove from the heat.

3. In a large bowl, beat the egg whites with the cream of tartar until soft peaks form. Bring the syrup back to a boil, then gradually beat the hot mixture into the egg whites. Continue beating until the meringue is glossy and cool, about 5 minutes.

4. Whisk the chocolate base until smooth. Stir in one-third of the meringue until combined, then gently fold in the remaining meringue. Spoon the mousse into parfait glasses and refrigerate for at least 1 or for up to 4 hours before serving.

—Ann Chantal Altman

■

FROZEN CAFFE LATTE

Caffè latte granita is a wonderful dessert and coffee combination. Or imitate the Sicilians and have it with breakfast instead of hot espresso. ➤

White Chocolate
Ice Cream in Pecan
Lace Cookie Cups

Top left: **Basque-Flavored Pudding with Almond Praline (p. 240)**

Top right: **Bittersweet Chocolate Pudding**

Bottom: **Butterscotch Pudding**

8 Servings

½ **cup sugar**
3 **cups freshly brewed espresso or strong coffee**
1 **cup whole milk**

1. Chill a 13-by-9-inch baking dish, preferably metal, in the freezer. In a medium bowl, stir the sugar into the coffee until dissolved; let cool completely. Stir in the milk.

2. Pour the coffee mixture into the chilled baking dish. Freeze until ice crystals form around the edges, about 30 minutes. Stir well to incorporate the ice. Continue freezing, stirring every 30 minutes (see How to Stir Granitas, p. 290), until all the liquid freezes completely, about 3 hours. Spoon the granita into bowls and serve.

—Michele Scicolone

■

BITTERSWEET CHOCOLATE PUDDING

To make this soft, rich pudding, use the best-quality chocolate you can find.

6 Servings

1 **cup whole milk**
½ **cup heavy cream, preferably not ultrapasteurized**
4 **ounces imported bittersweet chocolate, such as Callebaut, coarsely chopped**
1 **teaspoon pure vanilla extract**
½ **teaspoon instant espresso granules**
4 **large egg yolks**
¼ **cup sugar**
 Softly whipped cream, for topping

1. In a medium saucepan, warm the milk and cream over moderately high heat until steaming, about 2 minutes. Remove from the heat and stir in the chocolate, vanilla extract and instant espresso granules until smooth.

2. In the top of a double boiler, whisk the egg yolks and the sugar until combined. Gently whisk in the chocolate mixture without creating a foam. Cook the pudding over boiling water, stirring and scraping the bottom and sides of the pan constantly with a wooden spoon, until the pudding thickens slightly and reaches a temperature of 165° to 170°, 8 to 12 minutes. Do not overcook.

3. Strain the pudding into a medium heatproof bowl and stir constantly with a wooden spoon for 2 minutes to prevent a skin from forming. Transfer to 4- to 6-ounce ramekins (the larger ramekins will be about half full) and let cool to room temperature. Cover and refrigerate overnight or for up to 2 days. Serve chilled, topped with a generous dollop of whipped cream.

—Shelley Boris

■

BUTTERSCOTCH PUDDING

This recipe makes a rich, creamy and not-too-sweet pudding with a wallop of butterscotch flavor.

4 Servings

6 **large egg yolks**
1 **cup heavy cream, preferably not ultrapasteurized**
⅓ **cup (packed) dark brown sugar**
3 **tablespoons unsalted butter, cut into tablespoons**
¼ **cup whole milk**
½ **teaspoon pure vanilla extract**

1. In the top of a double boiler, lightly whisk the egg yolks. In a small saucepan, warm the cream over moderate heat until steaming; keep hot. ➤

2. In a heavy medium skillet, cook the brown sugar and butter over moderately high heat, stirring with a wooden spoon, until melted and bubbling, about 2 minutes. Remove from the heat and stir in the hot cream until blended. Let cool for 2 minutes, then stir in the milk.

3. Gently whisk the butterscotch mixture into the egg yolks. Stir in the vanilla. Set the pan over simmering water and cook over moderate heat, stirring, until the pudding thickens slightly and reaches 165° to 170°, about 6 minutes. Do not overcook.

4. Strain into a heatproof bowl and stir for 2 minutes to prevent a skin from forming. Transfer to 4-ounce ramekins and let cool to room temperature. Cover and refrigerate for at least 2 hours or up to 2 days.

—Shelley Boris

■

BASQUE-FLAVORED PUDDING WITH ALMOND PRALINE

Toasted almond praline provides a crunchy foil to this silky pudding made with an infusion of orange flower water and spirits. Both almonds and orange-flower water are typical Basque ingredients. There is enough topping for two batches of pudding.

4 Servings

Praline:
⅓ cup blanched sliced or slivered almonds (1 ounce)
¼ cup sugar

Pudding:
1 teaspoon orange flower water*
1 teaspoon anise-flavored liqueur
½ teaspoon dark rum
½ teaspoon Armagnac or Cognac

1½ cups heavy cream, preferably not ultrapasteurized
2 vanilla beans, split
2 2-by-¼-inch strips of lemon zest
6 large egg yolks
¼ cup sugar

***Available at specialty food shops**

1. Make the praline: In a dry skillet, toast the almonds over moderate heat, stirring, until fragrant, 4 to 5 minutes. Transfer to a plate to let cool.

2. Lightly grease a small baking sheet. Place the sugar in a small nonreactive skillet. Slowly and evenly drizzle ¼ cup of water over all the sugar. Cook over moderately high heat until the caramel turns a medium amber color, about 6 minutes; swirl the pan when the caramel begins to brown but do not stir. Remove the pan from the heat and stir in the almonds. Immediately pour the caramel onto the prepared pan; let it cool until firm, about 30 minutes.

3. Crack the brittle into 1-inch pieces and place in a food processor. Pulse until it resembles coarse salt; do not over-process. (The praline can be made up to 1 month ahead. Store in an airtight container in a cool, dry place.)

4. Make the pudding: In a small bowl, combine the orange flower water, anise liqueur, rum and Armagnac.

5. In a nonreactive saucepan, scald the cream with the vanilla beans and lemon zest over moderate heat.

6. In the top of a double boiler, whisk the egg yolks with the sugar. Slowly whisk in the hot cream. Place the pan over simmering water and cook over moderate heat, stirring constantly, until the mixture reaches 165° to 170°. Immediately pass the custard through a fine strainer into a glass measure.

7. Pour the custard into 4-ounce ramekins or custard cups. Cover with plastic wrap and refrigerate until chilled,

at least 6 hours or up to 2 days. To serve, sprinkle each custard with 1 tablespoon of the praline.

—Shelley Boris

■

CINNAMON-RICE CREME BRULEE

The easiest way to caramelize crème brûlée is to use a household propane torch (Julia Child swears by hers), which is available at hardware stores. But a hot broiler will also work well.

8 Servings
¼ **cup long-grain white rice**
1½ **cups milk**
¾ **cup plus 3 tablespoons sugar**
   Pinch of salt
½ **teaspoon plus ⅛ teaspoon cinnamon**
6 **large egg yolks**
3 **cups heavy cream**
1 **vanilla bean, split**

1. In a small heavy saucepan, using a wooden spoon, stir together the rice, milk, ¼ cup of the sugar and the salt. Bring to a gentle simmer over low heat, stirring occasionally, and cook until the rice is very tender and most of the liquid has been absorbed, about 30 minutes. Stir in ⅛ teaspoon of the cinnamon. Let cool. (The rice mixture can be made 1 day ahead; cover and refrigerate.)

2. Preheat the oven to 300°. Place eight 6-ounce ramekins or custard cups (see Crème Brûlée Tip, p. 243) in a large baking pan. Spoon the rice mixture evenly into the ramekins, smoothing the surface with the back of the spoon.

3. In a large bowl, whisk the egg yolks with ½ cup of the remaining sugar until thick and pale.

4. In a large saucepan, bring the heavy cream and vanilla bean to a boil. Gradually add the hot cream to the egg

Cinnamon-Rice Crème Brûlée

yolk mixture, whisking constantly to avoid curdling, until thoroughly combined. Strain through a fine sieve into a bowl. Rinse and reserve the vanilla bean for another use. Stir in the remaining ½ teaspoon cinnamon.

5. Pour the custard into the ramekins, filling them almost to the top. Set the baking pan in the lower part of the oven and pour enough hot water into the pan to reach halfway up the sides of the ramekins. Bake for about 50 minutes, or until the custard is just set. The center should wiggle very slightly but will firm

up as the custard cools. Let cool in the water bath for about 10 minutes, then remove the ramekins and let the custard cool to room temperature. Refrigerate the custard until well chilled, at least 3 hours or overnight.

6. Preheat the broiler. Sprinkle the remaining 3 tablespoons sugar evenly over the custards, making sure to cover the edges. With a damp cloth, wipe the rims of the ramekins. Set the ramekins on a baking sheet and broil as close to the heat as possible for about 1 minute, turning as necessary, until the sugar is evenly

Maple Indian Pudding

caramelized. Let sit for 1 to 2 minutes to set the caramel, then serve immediately or within 1 hour.

—Judith Sutton

■

MAPLE INDIAN PUDDING

Indian pudding is a classic New England dessert. The flavor, color and texture of this maple-syrup-sweetened version are lighter and more delicate than those of the traditional dessert made with molasses.

6 to 8 Servings
- 1 cup stone-ground yellow cornmeal
- 1 quart whole milk
- ½ cup maple sugar granules or light brown sugar
- 1 cup heavy cream, preferably not ultrapasteurized
- ½ cup pure maple syrup
- ⅛ teaspoon freshly grated nutmeg

1. Preheat the oven to 275°. Lightly butter a 1½-quart soufflé dish. In a heavy medium saucepan, whisk the cornmeal into the milk over moderately high heat until thickened slightly, about 5 minutes.

2. Remove from the heat and stir in the maple sugar granules. Stir in the cream, syrup and nutmeg. Pour into the prepared dish. Bake in the middle of the oven for about 4 hours, until bubbling and brown on top. Let rest 30 minutes before serving.

—Shelley Boris

■

ARLINE RODMAN'S MINNESOTA CHEESECAKE

First made by a novice baker in Virginia, Minnesota, this cheesecake is combined backwards. The cream cheese is beaten into the eggs instead of the eggs into the cream cheese. This method makes a lumpy filling. So to smooth it out, the mixture is beaten for half an hour. A mistake turned to triumph, because the cheesecake is exceptional.

10 to 12 Servings
Crust:
- 24 2½-inch-square plain graham crackers, roughly broken
- ⅓ cup sugar
- 4 tablespoons unsalted butter, cut into bits and softened
- ⅛ teaspoon cinnamon

Filling:
- 4 large eggs, at room temperature
- 1 cup sugar
- 1½ pounds cream cheese, at room temperature
- 2 tablespoons fresh lemon juice
- 1 teaspoon pure vanilla extract
  Pinch of coarse (kosher) salt

Topping:
- 1 cup sour cream
- 2 tablespoons sugar
- ½ teaspoon pure vanilla extract

1. Make the crust: In a food processor, process the graham crackers until they form fine crumbs. Add the sugar, butter and cinnamon and process just until well combined. Transfer the crumb mixture to an 8½- or 9-inch springform pan. Pat and press the mixture evenly over the bottom and about halfway up the sides of the pan. Refrigerate until firm.

2. Make the filling: Preheat the oven to 375°. In a heavy-duty mixer, beat the eggs lightly. Add the remaining filling ingredients, 1 at a time in the order given, beating briefly after each addition. When all the ingredients have been added, beat the filling at moderately low speed for 30 minutes, scraping down the sides of the bowl occasionally. Pour the filling into

Arlene Rodman's Minnesota Cheesecake

RICOTTA FRITTERS

These fritters are best while still hot, but they are very good lukewarm or even at room temperature.

4 Servings
½ **pound fresh ricotta cheese**
2 **eggs**
⅓ **cup flour**
1½ **tablespoons unsalted butter, at room temperature**
   Finely grated zest of 1 lemon
   Salt
   Vegetable oil
   Warmed honey, for drizzling

1. Put the ricotta in a bowl and crumble it using two forks held in one hand. Mix in the eggs. Work in the flour a little at a time. Add the butter, lemon zest and a tiny pinch of salt and beat until evenly combined. Set the batter aside and allow it to rest for at least 2 hours, but no more than 3½ hours.

2. Pour ½ inch of oil into a large frying pan and turn the heat to moderately high; the oil is ready when a driblet of batter dropped in floats instantly to the surface. Add tablespoons of the batter to the hot oil, pushing the batter off the spoon with the rounded corner of a spatula. Do not crowd the pan.

3. Fry the fritters until golden brown on one side, then turn them. If they are not puffing slightly into little balls, the heat is too high, so turn it down a little. When the fritters are brown on both sides, transfer them to a cooling rack with a slotted spoon to drain. Repeat with the remaining fritter batter.

4. Place the fritters on a serving platter and drizzle them liberally with the warm honey.

—Marcella Hazan

the crust and smooth the surface gently with a spatula.

3. Bake the cheesecake in the middle of the oven for about 50 minutes, until the top is golden brown and a toothpick inserted in the center comes out clean or with just a trace of moist batter clinging to it. Transfer the pan to a cooling rack and immediately raise the oven temperature to 475°. Let the cake stand for 10 minutes.

4. Make the topping: In a small bowl, combine the sour cream, sugar and vanilla. Spread the topping evenly over the surface of the cheesecake. Return to the oven and bake for 5 minutes. Remove and let cool completely on the rack, then cover the springform pan and refrigerate overnight. (The cheesecake can be refrigerated for up to 2 days.) Remove the sides of the pan and transfer the cake to a large serving plate. Serve cold, or let stand at room temperature for up to 1 hour before serving.

—Leslie Newman

Chapter 13 ▪ CAKES & COOKIES

247 Coffee-Almond Layer Cake with Raspberries

248 Orange Layer Cake with Orange Buttercream Frosting

250 Chocolate Hazelnut Cake

251 Simone Beck's Chocolate Cake

252 Roulé Confiture with Raspberry Coulis and Summer Berries

253 Bûche de Noël

255 Gingerbread-Pear Cake

256 Blueberry-Banana Crumb Cake

257 Hazelnut Pound Cake

258 Pumpkin Coffee Cake

259 Banana Madeleines

259 Maple Spice Cookies

260 Cocolocos

261 Chocolate-Walnut Brownie Drops

262 PB and Js

262 Pistachio Crumbles

263 Ginger-Ginger Shortbread Cookies

263 Lemon Poppy Stars

264 Fig Moons

265 Mochaccino Spirals

266 Chocolate Raspberry Squares

Coffee-Almond Layer Cake with Raspberries

COFFEE-ALMOND LAYER CAKE WITH RASPBERRIES

A perfect pedestal for delectable raspberries, this light cake is made with egg whites and yogurt cheese rather than yolks and butter.

10 Servings

Almond Cake:
    Vegetable cooking spray
¾ cup whole unblanched almonds (about 3 ounces)
¾ cup plus 2 tablespoons granulated sugar
2 tablespoons cornstarch
6 large egg whites
½ teaspoon cream of tartar

Coffee Buttercream:
½ cup granulated sugar
1 teaspoon light corn syrup
2 large egg whites
    Pinch of cream of tartar
1 teaspoon unflavored gelatin
1 tablespoon plus 1 teaspoon instant espresso, dissolved in 2 tablespoons boiling water
½ teaspoon pure vanilla extract
½ cup Yogurt Cheese (recipe follows)
1 pint fresh raspberries
2 tablespoons confectioners' sugar

1. Make the almond cake: Preheat the oven to 350°. Lightly coat a 10-by-15-inch jelly-roll pan with vegetable cooking spray. Line the pan with parchment or wax paper and lightly spray the paper.

2. Spread the almonds on a small baking sheet and toast for 8 to 10 minutes, or until fragrant. Let cool completely, then transfer to a food processor. Add ¾ cup of the granulated sugar and the cornstarch and process until the nuts are finely ground.

3. In a large bowl, beat the egg whites with the cream of tartar at medium speed until soft peaks form. Gradually beat in the remaining 2 tablespoons granulated sugar until glossy, about 1 minute. Using a rubber spatula, gently fold in the almond mixture. Spread the batter evenly in the prepared pan and bake for 30 to 35 minutes, or until the cake is lightly browned and springs back slightly when touched. Cool on a rack for 2 minutes.

4. Invert the almond cake onto a work surface and carefully peel off the paper; if it sticks, lightly brush the paper with a moistened pastry brush and wait 1 minute, then try again. Trim ½ inch from each edge of the cake, then cut crosswise into four 3½-by-9-inch rectangles.

5. Make the coffee buttercream: In a small saucepan, combine the granulated sugar, corn syrup and ¼ cup water and boil over high heat until the syrup reaches 241° on a candy thermometer, 4 to 5 minutes. Remove from the heat.

6. In a large bowl, beat the egg whites with the cream of tartar until soft peaks form. In a small bowl, sprinkle the unflavored gelatin over the dissolved instant espresso. Let stand for 1 minute. Set the bowl over a small pan of simmering water and stir to melt the gelatin. Remove from the heat and beat the gelatin mixture into the egg whites.

7. Bring the sugar syrup back to a boil. Gradually beat the hot syrup into the egg whites and continue beating until the meringue is glossy and cool, about 5 minutes. Stir the vanilla into the Yogurt Cheese, then fold the mixture into the coffee buttercream.

8. Place a cake layer on a rectangular platter and spread with a quarter of the coffee buttercream. Arrange ¾ cup of the raspberries on top. Cover with a second cake layer and lightly press down. Repeat with the remaining coffee buttercream, raspberries and cake layers, ending with a layer of buttercream; arrange the remaining raspberries around the base of the cake. (The cake can be refrigerated for up to 8 hours. Let stand at room temperature

for 10 minutes before serving.) Sprinkle the top with confectioners' sugar just before serving.

Yogurt Cheese
Makes ½ Cup
1 cup plain whole-milk yogurt

Set a strainer over a medium bowl and line it with a double layer of cheesecloth. Spoon the yogurt into the strainer. Cover and let drain in the refrigerator overnight. The drained yogurt, or yogurt cheese, can be refrigerated in a covered container for up to 4 days.

—Ann Chantal Altman

■

ORANGE LAYER CAKE WITH ORANGE BUTTERCREAM FROSTING

If you don't have time to make this multilayered cake all at once, make the orange buttercream and the cake layers in advance separately. The buttercream in this recipe is made with egg whites and has a lighter taste and texture than the classic French buttercream made with egg yolks. Candied orange slices are an appealing sweet-tart accompaniment to the cake. Any leftover slices and syrup can be refrigerated and served later over ice cream. If you don't have time to make the candied orange slices, just serve the cake with vanilla ice cream.

♥ This elegant cake, with its citrus accents, is a natural for fine sparkling wine. The sweetness of the cake, however, means that fruity California bottlings, such as 1988 Piper-Sonoma Brut, or slightly dry Champagnes, such as nonvintage Moët et Chandon "White Star," will match better than dry bubblies.

12 to 14 Servings
Candied orange slices:
  3 large navel oranges
  3 cups sugar

Buttercream:
  1 cup plus 2 tablespoons sugar
  4 large egg whites, at room temperature
  ¼ teaspoon cream of tartar
  3 sticks (¾ pound) unsalted butter, softened
  3 tablespoons orange liqueur

Cake:
  3 cups all-purpose flour
  1 tablespoon baking powder
  ¾ teaspoon salt
  1½ sticks (12 tablespoons) unsalted butter, at room temperature
  2 cups sugar
  4 large eggs, at room temperature
  2 teaspoons pure orange extract
  1 tablespoon plus 1 teaspoon minced orange zest
1½ cups milk

1. Make the candied orange slices: Using a very sharp knife, slice the oranges crosswise ⅛ inch thick (you should have 36 to 40 slices).

2. In a wide, 6-quart nonreactive saucepan, bring the sugar and 3 cups of water to a simmer, stirring until the sugar dissolves. Simmer for 5 minutes. Add the orange slices and simmer gently over low heat, occasionally spooning some of the syrup over the slices, until the orange peel is very tender and the white pith is almost translucent, about 2 hours; do not overcook the oranges or the centers will fall apart. Using tongs, carefully transfer the orange slices to baking sheets lined with wax or parchment paper to drain and cool. Reserve the orange syrup. (The orange slices and syrup can be prepared up to 3 days ahead; cover and refrigerate them separately.)

3. Make the buttercream: In a small heavy saucepan, bring 1 cup of the sugar and ⅓ cup of water to a boil over moderate heat, stirring until the sugar dissolves, about 3 minutes. Using a pastry brush dipped in cold water, wash down the sides of the pan to remove any sugar crystals. Then boil the sugar syrup, without stirring, until it reaches 238° on a candy thermometer, about 10 minutes.

4. Meanwhile, in a large bowl, using an electric mixer, beat the egg whites at low speed until foamy. Add the cream of tartar and beat until the whites hold soft peaks. Gradually add the remaining 2 tablespoons sugar. Increase the speed to high and beat until the whites are glossy and hold stiff peaks but are not dry.

5. Reduce the speed to medium low and beat in the hot sugar syrup in a thin steady stream; be careful to avoid splatters. Beat until the whites are thick and completely cool to the touch, 8 to 10 minutes.

6. Increase the speed to medium and add the butter, 1 tablespoon at a time; beat until the buttercream is smooth, thick and spreadable, about 5 minutes. If the mixture looks curdled at any time, increase the speed to high and beat until completely smooth, then reduce the speed to medium and beat in the remaining butter. (The buttercream can be covered and kept at room temperature for up to 4 hours or refrigerated for up to 5 days. Before using, bring the buttercream to room temperature and then beat with an electric mixer until smooth.) Just before using, beat in the orange liqueur.

7. Make the cake: Preheat the oven to 350°. Butter and flour two 9-by-1½-inch round cake pans. In a medium bowl, whisk the flour with the baking powder and salt.

8. In a large bowl, using an electric mixer, beat the butter and sugar at medium speed until light and fluffy, 8 to 10 minutes. Beat in the eggs 1 at a time, stopping to scrape the bowl with a rubber

spatula after each addition. Beat in the orange extract and orange zest. Beat in the dry ingredients at low speed alternately with the milk in 3 batches. Scrape the bowl frequently.

9. Pour the batter into the prepared pans and smooth the tops. (The pans will be almost three-quarters full.) Bake in the lower part of the oven for 35 to 40 minutes, or until a cake tester inserted in the center comes out clean.

10. Transfer the pans to a rack to cool for 10 minutes. Run a thin sharp knife around the edge of the pans and invert the cakes onto the rack. Turn the cakes right side up and let cool completely. (The cooled cakes can be wrapped well and kept at room temperature for up to 2 days.)

11. Using a serrated knife, trim the top of each cooled cake to make it level. Halve each cake horizontally. Place 1 top layer on a serving platter. Using a metal icing spatula, spread a scant ½ cup of the buttercream over the cake. Cover with a bottom layer and another scant ½ cup of buttercream. Repeat the layering with the second bottom layer and top layer and a

Orange Layer Cake with Orange Buttercream Frosting

Simone Beck's Chocolate Cake

scant ½ cup buttercream between them. Frost the top and sides of the cake with the rest of the buttercream. Let sit at room temperature for 1 to 2 hours before serving. (The cake can be covered and refrigerated for up to 3 days; return to room temperature before serving.)

12. Slice the cake and place 2 or 3 of the candied orange slices, along with a spoonful of the reserved orange syrup, next to each serving.

—Judith Sutton

■

CHOCOLATE HAZELNUT CAKE

The seductive flavor of hazelnut-and-chocolate *gianduja* makes this a popular dessert at Carlos' in Highland Park, Illinois. See Gianduja, at right, for a mail-order source.

12 Servings

Gianduja Cake:
- ⅔ cup shelled hazelnuts (3 ounces)
- 4½ ounces gianduja, coarsely chopped (see Gianduja, at right)
- 4 ounces bittersweet chocolate, coarsely chopped
- ½ cup plus 2 tablespoons sugar
- 1 stick (8 tablespoons) unsalted butter, softened
- 6 large eggs, separated
- ¼ cup unsweetened cocoa powder
- 3 tablespoons all-purpose flour

Gianduja Mousse:
- 1½ cups cold heavy cream
- 5 ounces gianduja, finely chopped
- 3½ ounces bittersweet chocolate, finely chopped

1. Make the *gianduja* cake: Preheat the oven to 375°. Lightly butter and flour a 10-by-2½-inch springform pan.

2. Toast the hazelnuts on a small rimmed baking sheet for about 8 minutes, or until fragrant. Transfer the hot hazelnuts to a kitchen towel and rub them together to loosen the skins. Finely chop one-third of the nuts; set the whole and chopped nuts aside separately to cool. Leave the oven on.

3. In a medium bowl, combine the chopped *gianduja* and bittersweet chocolate. Set the bowl over a saucepan filled with ¾ inch of simmering water and stir occasionally until melted. Remove from the heat.

4. In a food processor, pulse the whole hazelnuts with ½ cup of the sugar until finely ground. Stir the nuts into the melted chocolate.

5. In a large bowl, beat the butter until fluffy. Beat in the cooled chocolate mixture at medium speed, then beat in the egg yolks. Sift in the cocoa and flour and fold to combine.

6. In another large bowl, beat the egg whites with the remaining 2 tablespoons sugar until stiff peaks form. Fold a third of the whites into the chocolate batter, then fold in the remaining whites. Scrape the batter into the prepared pan and bake for about 35 minutes, or until puffed and set. Transfer the cake to a wire rack, remove the sides and let cool completely.

7. Make the *gianduja* mousse: In a small saucepan, bring ½ cup of the heavy cream to a boil over moderate heat. In a medium bowl, combine the chopped *gianduja* and bittersweet chocolate. Pour the hot cream over the chocolate and stir occasionally until smooth. Let cool completely.

8. In a medium bowl, whip the remaining 1 cup heavy cream until firm. Fold the whipped cream into the chocolate until no streaks remain.

9. Cut the cake in half horizontally with a serrated knife. Place the bottom layer on a serving plate, cut side up, and spread with 1 cup of the mousse. Cover with the second cake layer, cut side down. Frost the top and sides of the cake with the remaining mousse. Sprinkle the hazelnuts in a ring around the top. Serve the cake at room temperature or slightly chilled.

—Celeste Zeccola

■

SIMONE BECK'S CHOCOLATE CAKE

This cake has been adapted from *Simca's Cuisine* (Knopf) so that it can be served during Passover.

8 to 10 Servings

Cake:
- **2 tablespoons slivered blanched almonds**
- **¾ cup sugar**
- **6 ounces German sweet chocolate, coarsely chopped**
- **1½ sticks (12 tablespoons) unsalted butter or margarine**
- **4 large eggs, separated, at room temperature**
- **¼ cup cake flour or matzo cake meal Pinch of salt**

Glaze:
- **About ¼ cup slivered blanched almonds (about 1 ounce)**
- **3½ ounces German sweet chocolate, coarsely chopped**
- **2 tablespoons strong brewed coffee**
- **3 tablespoons cold unsalted butter or margarine, cut into bits**

1. Make the chocolate cake: Preheat the oven to 375°. Lightly butter an 8-by-2-inch round or springform pan. Line the pan with parchment or wax paper and butter the paper. Flour the pan, tapping out the excess.

2. In a food processor, pulse the almonds with 1 tablespoon of the sugar until very finely ground. Set aside. ➤

GIANDUJA

Gianduja, a milk chocolate and sweetened ground hazelnut paste, is available at specialty food stores. It can also be mail-ordered from Balducci's in New York City (800-225-3822).

RASPBERRY COULIS

When the season for fresh berries is past, I use unsweetened I.Q.F. (Individually Quick Frozen) raspberries in my coulis; since they are picked and frozen at the peak of ripeness, they're just as good as fresh berries when pureed. I do not, however, recommend serving thawed frozen berries because they tend to become mushy and bleed.

—Jacques Pépin

3. In a medium bowl set over a saucepan of simmering water, melt the chocolate and butter. Remove the bowl from the heat and let cool slightly.

4. In another medium bowl, beat the egg yolks with the remaining 11 tablespoons sugar at high speed until thick and pale. Stir in the warm chocolate until smooth. Fold in the cake flour and ground almonds.

5. In another large bowl, beat the egg whites with the salt until stiff peaks form. Stir one quarter of the beaten egg whites into the chocolate mixture, then fold in the remaining beaten egg whites just until combined. Scrape the batter into the prepared pan; tap the pan to spread the batter evenly.

6. Bake for about 30 minutes, or until moist crumbs cling to a toothpick inserted in the center and the cake springs back slightly when pressed. Transfer the cake to a rack and let cool in the pan for 1 hour. Loosen the cake from the sides of the pan, invert onto a rack and let cool completely. Remove the parchment paper. (The cake can be refrigerated, covered, for up to 1 day.)

7. Make the glaze: Preheat the oven to 350°. Toast the slivered blanched almonds on a baking sheet for about 7 minutes, until golden.

8. Meanwhile, in a small saucepan, melt the chocolate in the coffee over low heat, stirring, just until smooth, about 3 minutes. Remove the pan from the heat and stir in the butter.

9. Invert the cake onto a serving plate. Place 2-inch-wide strips of wax paper under the edges of the cake to keep the platter clean. Using a metal spatula, spread the chocolate glaze evenly over the top and sides of the cake. Discard the paper strips. Arrange the toasted nuts in a ring around the top of the cake and refrigerate for at least 30 minutes to set the glaze.

—Susan Shapiro Jaslove

■

ROULE CONFITURE WITH RASPBERRY COULIS AND SUMMER BERRIES

When berries are out of seaon, try winter fruit, such as pears.

8 to 10 Servings

The Roulé:
- 1 teaspoon unsalted butter
- 6 large eggs, separated
- ½ cup sugar
- 1 teaspoon pure vanilla extract
- ½ cup all-purpose flour
- 1½ tablespoons kirschwasser
- ½ cup seedless raspberry preserves

The Coulis:
- 1 pound fresh raspberries
- 1 cup seedless raspberry preserves

- 12 large fresh strawberries, sliced
- 2½ cups mixed fresh berries, such as blackberries, raspberries and red currants
- ½ cup small fresh mint leaves
- 1 cup chilled sour cream

1. Make the *roulé*: Preheat the oven to 350°. Butter a 15½-by-10½-inch jelly-roll pan. Spread the 1 teaspoon butter on a 14-by-18-inch sheet of parchment paper; cut a 2-inch long diagonal slit in each corner. Press the paper into the pan buttered side up, overlapping the cut corners.

2. In a large bowl, using an electric mixer, beat the egg yolks, sugar and vanilla on high speed for 2 minutes. Whisk in the flour until incorporated.

3. In another large bowl, using clean beaters, beat the egg whites on high speed until stiff peaks form. Whisk ¼ of the beaten whites into the egg yolk mixture, then gently fold in the remaining whites with a large rubber spatula. Transfer the

batter to the prepared pan and spread it evenly into the corners. Bake in the middle of the oven for about 10 minutes, until evenly golden. Let the cake cool on a rack for 30 minutes.

4. Hold the parchment paper at each end and lift the cake out onto a work surface. Sprinkle the cake evenly with the kirschwasser and spread the ½ cup preserves in a thin layer over the entire surface. Beginning at one of the short ends, grasp the parchment paper with both hands and push and roll the cake into a neat, tight scroll, peeling off the paper as you go. When the cake is compactly rolled, rewrap it in the parchment and refrigerate for at least 1 hour to firm it up.

5. Prepare the *coulis*: In a food processor, puree the raspberries with the 1 cup preserves. Press the puree through a fine sieve to remove the seeds. (The recipe can be prepared to this point up to 3 days ahead. Cover and refrigerate the *coulis*.)

6. To assemble, spoon a few tablespoons of *coulis* onto dinner plates and tilt to coat evenly. Using a sharp knife, cut the *roulé* in ¾- to 1-inch-thick slices and place one in the center of each plate. Scatter the fresh berries around the *roulé*. Arrange a few mint leaves between the berries and dot each plate with a few teaspoon-size dollops of sour cream. Serve immediately.

—Jacques Pépin

∎

BUCHE DE NOEL

The best, easiest and most attractive way to brown the meringue frosting on this Christmasy *bûche* is with a blowtorch. If you don't have one, assemble the cake on a heatproof platter and brown the meringue under a preheated broiler. If your oven is too small, simply make two separate cakes.

Makes One 20-Inch Cake

- ¼ **cup sugar**
- 2 **tablespoons dark rum**
- 2 **Genoise Sponge Sheets (recipe follows)**
  Chocolate Ganache (recipe follows)
  Italian Meringue and Meringue Mushrooms (recipe follows)

1. In a small bowl, dissolve the sugar in ½ cup of hot water and let cool. Stir in the dark rum.

2. Sprinkle the rum syrup over the Genoise Sponge Sheets. Spread the Chocolate Ganache evenly over the cakes. Beginning at the short ends, roll each cake into a cylinder. (At this point, the cakes can be well wrapped and frozen for up to 3 weeks. Defrost them completely before proceeding.)

3. Cut a 2-inch diagonal slice from the end of one cake and set aside; this will be the "knot." Place the cakes end to end on a long serving platter. Scoop the Italian Meringue into a large pastry bag fitted with a large star tip. Pipe the meringue onto the cake in lengthwise stripes to cover all but the ends. Place the reserved wedge of cake, cut side down, on top of the *bûche*. Pipe meringue around the sides of the "knot" and then on top. Similarly, pipe a swirl of meringue on both ends of the *bûche* to cover the cake completely.

4. Brown the meringue lightly all over with a blowtorch or under a hot broiler, watching carefully. Garnish the *bûche* and the serving platter with the Meringue Mushrooms.

Genoise Sponge Sheets
Makes Two 10½-by-15½-Inch Sheets

- 8 **large eggs, at room temperature**
- 1⅓ **cups granulated sugar**
- 1 **tablespoon plus 1 teaspoon pure vanilla extract**
  Finely grated zest of 1 small lemon ➤

1⅓ cups all-purpose flour
⅔ cup bleached cake flour
6 tablespoons melted unsalted butter, cooled
Confectioners' sugar

1. Butter two 10½-by-15½-inch jelly-roll pans. Cut two 12-by-17½-inch lengths of parchment paper to line the pans. With scissors, make a 2-inch diagonal slit in each corner; fit the paper into the pan, overlapping it neatly at the corners. Butter and flour the paper.

2. Preheat the oven to 375°. Break the eggs into a 3-quart stainless steel bowl and add the granulated sugar, vanilla and lemon zest. Set the bowl over a saucepan of almost simmering water. Using an electric mixer, beat at high speed for a few seconds to break up the eggs. Continue beating at moderately high speed until the eggs are warm to the touch. Remove the bowl from the saucepan and beat until the eggs are pale yellow and thick (when the beaters are lifted, the mixture should leave a fat, slowly dissolving ribbon on the surface).

3. In a medium bowl, mix the all-purpose flour with the cake flour. Sift ⅓ of the flour onto the eggs. Rapidly fold it in with a large rubber spatula until almost incorporated. Repeat with ⅓ of the remaining flour and fold in 2 tablespoons of the melted butter; then add half of the rest of the flour and 2 more tablespoons of butter; finally, fold in the last of the flour and butter.

4. Immediately turn the batter into the 2 prepared pans; spread it evenly with a large spatula. Bake the cakes on the upper and lower racks of the oven for about 8 minutes, until the cakes are barely starting to color and are lightly springy to the touch. (Do not overcook or the cakes will break when rolled.) Remove the cakes from the oven and quickly sift a thin layer of confectioners' sugar over them.

5. Spread a sheet of wax paper or parchment paper over each cake and top with a dampened towel. Invert the cakes onto baking sheets or a work surface; leave the pans in place and let cool for 10 minutes.

6. Lift off the pans. Peel the parchment off the cakes and discard. Trim any browned edges from the cakes and let them cool completely.

Chocolate Ganache
Makes About 2½ Cups
1½ cups heavy cream, chilled
6 ounces semisweet chocolate, finely chopped
2 tablespoons unsalted butter, cut into thin slices
2 teaspoons pure vanilla extract

1. In a small saucepan, bring ¼ cup of the cream just to a simmer over moderate heat. Remove from the heat. Add the chocolate, butter and vanilla and stir until the chocolate is melted. Let cool to room temperature.

2. In a medium bowl, beat the remaining chilled 1¼ cups heavy cream until thickened but a little too loose to hold soft peaks. Stir in the chocolate mixture with a large rubber spatula until just blended; it will be slightly thicker than whipped cream and will thicken a little more as it sits. (The ganache can be refrigerated, covered, for up to 2 days; stir until spreadable before using.)

Italian Meringue and Meringue Mushrooms
1 cup egg whites (7 to 8 large eggs), at room temperature
2 cups granulated sugar
1 3-ounce bar of imported bittersweet chocolate, melted, for the meringue mushrooms

1. In a large standing mixer, beat the egg whites to soft peaks on medium high speed. Beat in 3 tablespoons of the sugar

and beat to stiff shining peaks. Turn the mixer down to medium-low while you make the sugar syrup.

2. In a small saucepan, bring the remaining sugar and ⅔ cup of water to a simmer, swirling the pan frequently until the sugar has dissolved completely and the liquid is perfectly clear. Then cover the pan tightly and boil over moderately high heat to the soft-ball stage (240° on a candy thermometer), about 6 minutes.

3. Turn the mixer to medium-high and slowly pour in the boiling sugar syrup. Continue beating until the meringue is cool and stands in stiff shining peaks, 5 minutes or longer.

4. Make the meringue mushrooms: Preheat the oven to 200°. Butter and lightly flour a baking sheet. Scoop ¼ of the Italian meringue into a pastry bag fitted with a ¼-inch round tip. Pipe twenty ¼-inch domes onto the baking sheet to form the mushroom caps. Then pipe out twenty ¾- to 1-inch tall cones for the stems. Return any unused meringue to the mixer bowl.

5. Bake the caps and stems for about 1 hour, or until they are dry enough to lift off the pan; they should be a light cream color. Let cool.

6. Brush the underside of each mushroom cap with the melted chocolate; push in the pointy ends of the stems before the chocolate sets.

—Julia Child

■

GINGERBREAD-PEAR CAKE

In this recipe the texture and concentrated flavor of dried pears is preferable to those of fresh. Made with both ground and fresh ginger, this cake packs a gingery wallop. The coffee glaze is optional but is very easy to make, and it goes nicely with the pears and spices.

Gingerbread-Pear Cake

16 Servings

- 2 sticks (½ pound) unsalted butter, softened
- 1 cup granulated sugar
- ⅔ cup (packed) light brown sugar
- ½ cup unsulphured molasses
- 3 large eggs, at room temperature
- 2 large egg yolks, at room temperature
- 2 teaspoons pure vanilla extract
- 1½ tablespoons minced fresh ginger
- 3 cups unbleached all-purpose flour
- 1½ teaspoons baking soda
- 1½ teaspoons ground ginger
- 1 teaspoon ground cardamom
- ½ teaspoon salt
- 1 cup sour cream
- ¼ cup milk
- ½ pound dried pears (see Dried Pears, at left), cut into ½-inch pieces (about 1½ cups)
- 2 teaspoons freeze-dried instant coffee granules
- 1½ tablespoons boiling water
- ⅔ cup confectioners' sugar   ➤

1. Preheat the oven to 325°. Lightly butter and flour a 10-inch Bundt pan, preferably nonstick.

2. In a large bowl, using an electric mixer, beat the butter at high speed until creamy. Gradually beat in the granulated and brown sugars, then beat in the molasses. Beat in the eggs and egg yolks one at a time. Beat in the vanilla and fresh ginger just until blended. The mixture will appear slightly curdled.

3. In a medium bowl, sift the flour, baking soda, ground ginger, cardamom and salt. In a small bowl, mix the sour cream and milk. Alternately beat the dry ingredients and the sour cream mixture into the butter mixture in 5 additions, beginning and ending with the dry ingredients. Using a large rubber spatula, fold in the pears.

4. Scrape the batter into the prepared pan and smooth the surface. Bake for 65 to 70 minutes, until a cake tester inserted in the center of the cake comes out clean. Set the pan on a rack to cool for 5 minutes, then invert the cake onto the rack, remove the pan and let the cake cool completely. Transfer to a serving platter.

5. In a small bowl, stir the instant coffee granules into the boiling water until dissolved and then let cool. Whisk in the confectioners' sugar until smooth. Spoon the glaze evenly over the cake, letting it trickle down into the crevices. (The cake can be stored at room temperature, covered, for up to 2 days.)

—Ken Haedrich

■

BLUEBERRY-BANANA CRUMB CAKE

This cake is so great that no one is likely to care if the frozen blueberries aren't quite on a par with fresh. Serve with lemon yogurt for breakfast or vanilla ice cream for dessert. Wrap any leftovers in foil and freeze for up to one week; reheat the wrapped cake in a 400° oven for 10 to 15 minutes.

12 Servings

Crumb Topping:
- ¾ cup unbleached all-purpose flour
- ⅓ cup (packed) light brown sugar
- ½ teaspoon cinnamon
- ⅛ teaspoon salt
- 4 tablespoons unsalted butter, melted and cooled

Cake:
- 2 tablespoons fresh lemon juice
- 2 teaspoons cornstarch
- 2½ cups frozen blueberries (about 12 ounces)
- ¼ cup honey
- 1½ cups unbleached all-purpose flour, plus more for sprinkling
- ½ cup whole wheat flour
- ⅓ cup sugar
- 2 teaspoons baking powder
- ½ teaspoon salt
- 6 tablespoons cold unsalted butter, cut into ½-inch pieces
- 1 large, very ripe banana (about 7 ounces)
- 1 large egg
- ½ cup milk
- ½ teaspoon pure vanilla extract

1. Make the crumb topping: In a medium bowl, combine the flour, brown sugar, cinnamon and salt. Using a fork, stir in the melted butter. Then rub the mixture between your fingertips until crumbly; do not overmix.

2. Make the cake: In a small nonreactive bowl, stir the lemon juice and cornstarch until smooth. In a medium nonreactive saucepan, combine the blueberries with the honey and ⅓ cup of water and bring to a boil over moderate heat. Stir in

the cornstarch mixture and boil, stirring, for 1 minute. Scrape the blueberry mixture into a glass bowl and let cool.

3. Preheat the oven to 350°. Butter a 7½-by-11¾-by-2-inch glass or enameled baking dish.

4. In a large bowl, sift the unbleached and whole wheat flours with the sugar, baking powder and salt. Using your fingertips, a pastry blender or 2 knives, cut in the butter until the mixture resembles fine crumbs.

5. In a food processor, puree the banana with the egg. Add the milk and vanilla and process until blended. Make a well in the center of the flour mixture. Add the banana puree and stir with a wooden spoon just until blended and the dough comes together.

6. Scrape the dough into the prepared baking dish. Sprinkle the dough lightly with flour, and, with floured hands, press it evenly into the dish. Using a fork, prick the dough in about a dozen places. Pour the blueberry topping over the dough, smoothing the surface with a spoon. Sprinkle the crumb topping evenly over the berries.

7. Bake in the middle of the oven for 20 minutes. Transfer to the upper rack of the oven and bake for 15 minutes longer, or until the topping is golden brown. Transfer the cake to a rack to cool for about 10 minutes.

—Ken Haedrich

■

HAZELNUT POUND CAKE

This buttery pound cake calls for whole-wheat pastry flour, which contributes the nuttiness of whole wheat but keeps the texture of the cake tender. This pound cake is great all by itself for breakfast or topped with a scoop of coffee ice

cream for dessert. Let the cake cool completely before serving to allow the flavors to mellow.

12 to 16 Servings
1¾ cups hazelnuts (about 7 ounces)
2 sticks (½ pound) plus 1 tablespoon unsalted butter, softened
1 cup sugar
⅓ cup plus 3 tablespoons pure maple syrup, at room temperature
4 large eggs, at room temperature
1½ teaspoons pure vanilla extract
1 cup unbleached all-purpose flour
1 cup whole wheat pastry flour*
2½ teaspoons baking powder
½ teaspoon salt
⅓ cup buttermilk or plain yogurt

*Available at health food stores

1. Preheat the oven to 350°. Butter a 10-by-2½-inch springform pan. Spread the hazelnuts on a large baking sheet and toast in the oven for about 10 minutes, until the skins are blistered. Wrap the nuts in a towel and rub them vigorously to remove most of the skins. Let cool completely. Finely chop ¼ cup of the nuts. Place the remaining nuts in a food processor and pulse until finely ground.

2. In a large bowl, using an electric mixer, beat the 2 sticks of butter at high speed until creamy. Gradually beat in the sugar and ⅓ cup of the maple syrup until fluffy. Beat in the eggs one at a time, then beat in the vanilla. The mixture will appear slightly curdled.

3. In a medium bowl, sift the unbleached and whole wheat flours, baking powder and salt. Gently stir half of the flour mixture into the batter. Stir in the buttermilk, then stir in the remaining dry ingredients. Using a rubber spatula, fold in the ground nuts.

4. Scrape the batter into the prepared pan and smooth the surface. Bake in the middle of the oven for about 1 hour, until

If you make
Pumpkin Coffee
Cake, at right, with
fresh pumpkin
instead of canned,
the result will be
slightly less sweet.
Follow this method:
Break off the stem
of a small sugar
pumpkin (about 3
pounds) and bake at
375° until soft to the
touch, about 2
hours. Let cool, peel
and halve the
pumpkin, then
scoop out and
discard the seeds.
Puree the pumpkin
flesh in a food
processor or blender
or mash it with a
potato masher. Pass
the puree through a
fine sieve and
measure out 1 cup.
Freeze the
remainder for
another use.

—Ken Haedrich

a cake tester inserted in the center of the cake comes out clean. Transfer to a rack to cool completely. Remove the sides of the springform pan.

5. In a small saucepan, combine the remaining 3 tablespoons maple syrup and 1 tablespoon butter and bring to a boil over moderately high heat. Remove from the heat and swirl the pan to mix. Spoon the glaze evenly over the cooled cake and sprinkle the chopped hazelnuts on top. (The cake can be stored at room temperature, tightly covered, for up to 3 days.)

—Ken Haedrich

■

PUMPKIN COFFEE CAKE

This tender coffee cake is made with yeast and has a breadlike texture. The pumpkin and egg yolks give the cake a brilliant orange hue. The cake freezes well. Wrap any leftovers in foil and freeze for up to three days; reheat the wrapped cake in a 400° oven for 10 to 15 minutes.

12 to 15 Servings

- 1 **envelope (¼ ounce) active dry yeast**
- ¼ **cup lukewarm water (105° to 115°)**
- ½ **cup plus 1 tablespoon milk**
- ⅓ **cup honey**
- 1 **cup unsweetened canned pumpkin puree (see Fresh Pumpkin, at left)**
- 2 **large egg yolks**

About 3¼ cups unbleached all-purpose flour plus more for kneading
- ⅓ **cup yellow cornmeal, preferably stone ground**
- 1 **stick plus 2 tablespoons unsalted butter, melted and cooled**
- 1 **teaspoon salt**
- ¾ **cup (packed) light brown sugar**
- ½ **cup finely chopped walnuts (about 2 ounces)**
- 1 **teaspoon cinnamon**

1. In a small bowl, sprinkle the yeast over the water. Stir with a fork and set aside until foamy, about 5 minutes.

2. In a small nonreactive saucepan, warm the ½ cup milk with the honey over moderately low heat just until the honey dissolves. Transfer to a large nonreactive bowl and stir in the pumpkin puree, egg yolks and the yeast mixture. Using a wooden spoon, beat in 1½ cups of the flour and the cornmeal. Beat vigorously for 1 minute, then cover the sponge with plastic wrap and set aside in a warm place for 15 minutes.

3. Stir in 4 tablespoons of the melted butter and the salt. Stir in 1½ cups more flour, about ½ cup at a time, until a soft dough forms; stir in up to ¼ cup more flour if necessary.

4. Turn the dough out on a well-floured surface and knead for about 7 minutes, kneading in additional flour as necessary to prevent the dough from sticking. Place the dough in a large, lightly oiled bowl, turning the dough to coat it. Cover the bowl with plastic wrap and set aside in a warm place until the dough has doubled in bulk, about 1 hour. Butter a 13-by-9-by-2-inch glass baking dish.

5. Tap the dough to deflate it slightly. Turn it into the prepared dish and sprinkle lightly with flour. Using floured hands, press the dough evenly into the dish. Oil a sheet of plastic wrap and place it oiled side down over the dough. Let rest for 15 minutes.

6. Preheat the oven to 350°. In small bowl, combine the brown sugar, walnuts and cinnamon. Lightly brush the dough with the remaining 1 tablespoon milk. Sprinkle the brown sugar mixture evenly over the surface. Using a floured fingertip, poke 12 deep, evenly spaced holes in the dough (4 lengthwise rows of 3 holes each). Spoon the remaining 6 tablespoons melted butter over the dough, letting it run into the holes. Let the dough rest for 15 minutes.

7. Bake the cake for 35 minutes, until the top is lightly crusty. Transfer to a rack to cool for about 10 minutes before cutting into squares.

—Ken Haedrich

■

BANANA MADELEINES

For a dessert with a combination of flavors and textures, serve these cookies with Mocha Mousse (p. 236). Be sure to use overripe bananas for a pronounced banana flavor. Nonstick mini-muffin pans can be substituted for the madeleine pans.

Makes 2 Dozen Madeleines
Vegetable-oil cooking spray
⅓ cup pecan halves (1 ounce)
¾ cup cake flour
1 teaspoon baking powder
½ teaspoon salt
1 cup confectioners' sugar
2 overripe medium bananas
4 large egg whites
1 tablespoon unsalted butter, melted
1 teaspoon pure vanilla extract

1. Preheat the oven to 375°. Lightly coat two 12-mold madeleine pans with vegetable-oil cooking spray and flour them.

2. Place the pecans in a pie plate and toast until fragrant, about 8 minutes. Let cool, then finely chop.

3. In a medium bowl, sift the cake flour with the baking powder, salt and all but 2 tablespoons of the confectioners' sugar.

4. Puree the bananas in a food processor. Add the egg whites, melted butter and vanilla and process until blended. Add the dry ingredients and pulse just until combined. Scrape the batter into a large bowl and gently fold in the pecans.

5. Divide the mixture among the 24 madeleine molds and bake for about 12 minutes, or until puffed and browned.

Unmold onto a rack and let cool. Dust with the remaining 2 tablespoons confectioners' sugar and serve.

—Ann Chantal Altman

■

MAPLE SPICE COOKIES

For a change of pace, substitute chocolate chips for raisins in these cakey cookies.

Makes About 3 Dozen Cookies
2 cups all-purpose flour
1¼ teaspoons ginger
½ teaspoon cinnamon
½ teaspoon allspice
¼ teaspoon baking soda
¼ teaspoon salt
2 sticks (½ pound) unsalted butter, softened
½ cup (packed) dark brown sugar
¼ cup granulated sugar
¼ cup pure maple syrup
¼ cup unsulphured molasses
1 large egg
½ cup raisins
1½ cups coarsely chopped pecans (about 6 ounces)

1. Preheat the oven to 375°. In a medium bowl, sift the flour with the ginger, cinnamon, allspice, baking soda and salt.

2. In a large bowl, using an electric mixer, cream the butter with the brown sugar and granulated sugar until fluffy. Beat in the maple syrup, molasses and egg. Using a wooden spoon, stir in the dry ingredients. Stir in the raisins and pecans.

3. Spoon rounded tablespoons of the dough 2 inches apart on a large cookie sheet. Bake for about 12 minutes, until the cookies are set and browned at the edges. Transfer to a rack to cool completely. (The cookies can be stored for up to 1 week in an airtight container.)

—Tracey Seaman

Chocolate
Walnut
Brownie
Drops and
Fig Moons
(p. 264)

■

COCOLOCOS

These satisfying cookies get their crunch from pecans and their chewy texture from coconut and oats. Use the best chocolate you can buy to make the chunks.

Makes About 3 Dozen Cookies

2 sticks (½ pound) unsalted butter, softened
⅔ cup (packed) light brown sugar
⅔ cup granulated sugar
1 large egg
1 teaspoon pure vanilla extract
1¾ cups all-purpose flour
½ teaspoon baking soda
¼ teaspoon salt
½ pound semisweet or bittersweet chocolate, cut into ½-inch pieces
1½ cups old-fashioned rolled oats
1 cup sweetened grated coconut (about 3 ounces)
½ cup coarsely chopped pecans (about 2 ounces)

1. Preheat the oven to 375°. In a large bowl, using an electric mixer, cream the butter with the brown sugar and granulated sugar until fluffy. Beat in the egg and vanilla. Using a wooden spoon, stir in the flour, baking soda and salt. Stir in the chocolate, oats, coconut and pecans.

2. Spoon rounded tablespoons of the dough about 2 inches apart on a large cookie sheet. Bake for about 12 minutes, until golden. Transfer to a rack to cool completely. (The cookies can be stored for up to 1 week in an airtight container.)

—Tracey Seaman

■

CHOCOLATE-WALNUT BROWNIE DROPS

Stir all the ingredients together, drop the dough on cookie sheets and bake. That's all there is to these brownie-like cookies.

Makes About 2½ Dozen Cookies

- **4 ounces unsweetened chocolate**
- **1 stick (8 tablespoons) unsalted butter**
- **1½ cups sugar**
- **2 large eggs**
- **1 cup all-purpose flour**
- **½ cup unsweetened cocoa powder**
- **½ teaspoon baking soda**
- **¼ cup milk**
- **1 teaspoon pure vanilla extract**
- **1½ cups coarsely chopped walnuts (about 6 ounces)**

1. Preheat the oven to 375°. In a large saucepan, melt the chocolate and butter over low heat, stirring occasionally, until

Lemon Poppy Stars (p. 263) and PB and Js (p. 262)

261

smooth. Remove from the heat. Whisk in the sugar and then the eggs. Using a wooden spoon, stir in the flour, cocoa and baking soda. Add the milk and vanilla and stir until smooth. Stir in the walnuts.

2. Drop rounded tablespoons of the dough about 2 inches apart on a large cookie sheet. Bake for about 12 minutes, until the cookies are set. Let cool on the baking sheet for 2 minutes, then transfer to a rack to cool completely. (The cookies can be stored for up to 1 week in an airtight container.)

—Tracey Seaman

■

PB AND JS

Peanut butter and jelly sandwiches inspired these large thumbprint cookies. Chop the peanuts in a food processor or by hand.

Makes 2½ Dozen Cookies
1 stick (8 tablespoons) unsalted butter, softened
½ cup sugar
¼ cup creamy peanut butter
1 large egg yolk
1 teaspoon pure vanilla extract
1½ cups all-purpose flour
¼ teaspoon salt
Scant ½ cup unsalted roasted peanuts (about 2½ ounces), very finely chopped
About ⅔ cup good-quality strawberry or apricot jam

1. Preheat the oven to 375°. In a medium bowl, using an electric mixer, cream the butter and sugar until fluffy. Beat in the peanut butter, egg yolk and vanilla. Using a wooden spoon, stir in the flour and salt.

2. Form the dough into 1-inch balls. Roll the balls in the chopped peanuts and place them about 2 inches apart on a

large cookie sheet. Bake the cookies for 5 minutes. Using your thumb or a small melon baller, make a deep indentation in the center of each cookie so that it will flatten slightly. Spoon about 1 teaspoon of jam into each cookie; do not overfill. Bake for about 15 minutes longer, until the cookies are golden and cracked. Transfer to a rack to cool completely. (The cookies can be stored for up to 3 days in an airtight container.)

—Tracey Seaman

■

PISTACHIO CRUMBLES

The flavor of pistachios permeates these rich cookies. Surprisingly enough, the almond extract just makes the pistachio taste stronger.

Makes About 2 Dozen Cookies
2 cups shelled pistachio nuts (about 11 ounces)
2 sticks (½ pound) unsalted butter, at room temperature
¼ cup plus 2 tablespoons confectioners' sugar
½ teaspoon salt
2 cups sifted all-purpose flour
1 teaspoon pure vanilla extract
½ teaspoon pure almond extract
½ cup granulated sugar, for rolling

1. Preheat the oven to 300°. Spread the pistachios out on a baking sheet and roast in the oven for about 6 minutes, until fragrant. Let the nuts cool to room temperature. In a food processor, finely grind the pistachios.

2. In a large bowl, using an electric mixer, beat the butter with the confectioners' sugar and salt at high speed until light and fluffy. At low speed, blend in the flour until incorporated. Add the vanilla and

almond extracts and 1 tablespoon of water, then mix in the ground pistachios. Form the dough into a ball.

3. Roll tablespoons of the dough into balls. Roll the balls in the granulated sugar until completely coated. Arrange the balls about 2 inches apart on 2 lightly greased or nonstick baking sheets. Dip the buttered bottom of a small glass in the granulated sugar and press down lightly to flatten the cookies somewhat; dip the glass in sugar between cookies as necessary.

4. Bake the cookies on the top and middle shelves of the oven for 20 minutes, then switch the sheets and bake for about 20 minutes longer, or until the cookies are lightly browned. Let cool on the baking sheets for 5 minutes, then transfer the cookies to a rack to cool completely. (The cookies can be stored in an airtight tin for up to 1 week.)

—Bob Chambers

■

GINGER-GINGER SHORTBREAD COOKIES

Use cookie cutters to cut these delicate but rich morsels into stars, hearts and other fanciful shapes. Buy good-quality crystallized ginger in bulk at specialty markets; it is much less expensive and tends to be fresher than the variety found in small jars at supermarkets.

Makes About 7 Dozen
Small Cookies
2 cups all-purpose flour
¾ teaspoon ground ginger
¼ teaspoon salt
2 sticks (½ pound) unsalted butter, softened
⅔ cup confectioners' sugar
½ cup minced crystallized ginger (about 3 ounces)

1. In a medium bowl, whisk the flour with the ground ginger and salt.

2. In a large bowl, using an electric mixer, cream the butter and sugar until light and fluffy. Using a wooden spoon, gradually beat in the dry ingredients until they are incorporated. (The dough will be somewhat crumbly at this point.) Stir in the crystallized ginger until it is well distributed.

3. Gather the dough into a ball. Cut into quarters and pat into disks. Wrap each disk in wax paper and refrigerate until firm, about 1 hour.

4. Preheat the oven to 325°. On a lightly floured surface, roll out 1 disk of dough about ¼ inch thick. Using a 1½-inch cookie cutter, cut out as many cookies as possible. Place the cookies about 1 inch apart on ungreased cookie sheets. Repeat with the remaining disks of dough. Combine the scraps of dough from each disk, roll out once and cut out more cookies.

5. Bake the cookies on the upper and lower racks of the oven for 12 to 15 minutes, switching the pans after 6 minutes, just until the cookies are lightly golden on the bottom. Let the cookies cool on the sheets until firm, then transfer to racks to cool completely. (The cookies can be made up to 2 weeks ahead and stored in airtight tins.)

—Judith Sutton

■

LEMON POPPY STARS

This rich, delicate cream-cheese dough softens quickly; so roll out small amounts at a time.

Makes About 4½ Dozen Cookies
2 cups all-purpose flour
¼ teaspoon baking soda
¼ teaspoon salt ➤

2 tablespoons poppy seeds plus
  more for sprinkling
1½ sticks (12 tablespoons) unsalted
  butter, softened
4 ounces cream cheese, softened
¾ cup sugar plus more for
  sprinkling
1 large egg, at room temperature
1 tablespoon finely grated lemon
  zest
1 teaspoon pure vanilla extract
1 large egg white, lightly beaten

1. In a medium bowl, sift the flour with the baking soda and salt. Stir in the 2 tablespoons of poppy seeds.

2. In a large bowl, using an electric mixer, cream the butter and the cream cheese with the ¾ cup of sugar until fluffy. Beat in the egg, lemon zest and vanilla. Using a wooden spoon, stir in the dry ingredients.

3. Divide the dough in half. Pat each half into a disk and wrap in wax paper. Refrigerate until firm, at least 2 hours or overnight.

4. Preheat the oven to 350°. Cut each disk of dough into quarters. Set 1 quarter on a well-floured work surface; cover and refrigerate the remaining dough. Roll out the dough to about ⅛ inch thick. Cut with a 3-inch star-shaped cookie cutter. Transfer the poppy stars to a large cookie sheet, spacing them about ½ inch apart. Repeat with another piece of dough until the cookie sheet is filled. Knead any scraps together and refrigerate until chilled.

5. Brush each cookie with the beaten egg white and sprinkle lightly with poppy seeds and sugar. Bake the cookies for about 12 minutes, until golden. Transfer the cookies to a rack to cool completely. Continue making cookies with the remaining dough and scraps. (The cookies can be stored for up to 1 week in an airtight container.)

—Tracey Seaman

■

FIG MOONS

These are like the fig cookies of your childhood—only better.

Makes 2 Dozen Cookies
Dough:
1½ cups all-purpose flour
½ teaspoon baking powder
½ teaspoon baking soda
¼ teaspoon cinnamon
¼ teaspoon salt
4 tablespoons unsalted butter,
  softened
¼ cup vegetable shortening
⅓ cup (packed) light brown sugar
1 large egg
½ teaspoon finely grated lemon zest

Filling:
8 medium dried figs (about 6 ounces),
  stemmed and quartered
½ cup pitted dates (3 ounces)
2 teaspoons Cognac or water

1. Make the dough: In a medium bowl, stir the flour with the baking powder, baking soda, cinnamon and salt.

2. In a large bowl, using an electric mixer, cream the butter and shortening with the brown sugar until fluffy. Beat in the egg and zest. Using a wooden spoon, stir in the dry ingredients. Shape into a disk, wrap in wax paper and refrigerate until firm, at least 3 hours or overnight.

3. Make the filling: In a small nonreactive saucepan, combine the figs, dates and ⅓ cup of water. Bring to a simmer over moderate heat and cook until the figs are tender, about 12 minutes. Transfer the fruit and its cooking liquid to a food processor, add the Cognac and puree until smooth. Let cool completely.

4. Preheat the oven to 375°. Cut the dough into quarters. On a lightly floured work surface, roll out 1 piece of the dough

⅛ inch thick. Cut with a 3-inch fluted round cookie cutter. Arrange the rounds about 1 inch apart on a large cookie sheet. Continue rolling and cutting the dough until the cookie sheet is full. Knead the scraps together and refrigerate until chilled.

5. Spoon 1 teaspoon of the fig filling into the center of each round. Fold the dough over the filling to form a half-moon and press the edges with the tines of a fork to seal. Using a small sharp knife, cut 2 vents in the top of each cookie. Bake for about 12 minutes, until golden and set. Transfer to a rack to cool completely. Continue making cookies with the remaining dough, scraps and filling. (The cookies can be stored for up to 3 days in an airtight container.)

—Tracey Seaman

■

MOCHACCINO SPIRALS

These melt-in-your-mouth butter cookies have a cinnamony mocha swirl.

Makes About 2½ Dozen Cookies
1 **ounce unsweetened chocolate**
2 **cups all-purpose flour**
½ **teaspoon baking powder**
½ **teaspoon salt**
2 **sticks (½ pound) unsalted butter, softened**
1 **cup sugar**
1 **large egg yolk**
2 **tablespoons heavy cream**
1 **teaspoon pure vanilla extract**
1 **teaspoon instant espresso powder**
   Pinch of cinnamon

1. Melt the chocolate in a small bowl set over a small saucepan filled with ¾ inch of simmering water. Remove from the heat.

2. In a medium bowl, whisk the all-purpose flour with the baking powder and salt. In a large bowl, using an electric mixer, cream the butter and sugar until fluffy. Add the egg yolk and beat for 1 minute. Using a wooden spoon, stir in the heavy cream and vanilla extract. Stir in the dry ingredients.

3. Divide the dough in half. Pat half the dough out to a 5-inch square and wrap in wax paper. Add the melted chocolate, espresso powder and cinnamon to the remaining dough and stir until blended. Pat the mocha dough out to a 5-inch square and wrap in wax paper. Refrigerate the dough until firm, at least 3 hours or overnight.

4. Place the mocha dough on a large, lightly floured piece of wax paper and sprinkle lightly with flour. Hit the dough a few times with a rolling pin to soften and flatten it, then roll it out to an 8-by-12-inch rectangle. Slide the dough on the wax paper onto a cookie sheet and refrigerate for 5 minutes. Repeat the process with the plain dough.

5. Invert the plain dough onto a large clean piece of wax paper and peel off the top layer of paper. Invert the mocha dough on top of the plain dough so that the edges are aligned. Peel off the top layer of paper. With floured hands, pat the dough so that the layers adhere. Working from a longer side, roll the dough into a cylinder. If the dough becomes too soft, refrigerate briefly, then continue rolling. Wrap the cylinder in wax paper and re-frigerate until firm, at least 3 hours or overnight.

6. Preheat the oven to 375°. Unwrap the cookie dough. Cut enough thin slices (⅛ to ¼ inch thick) to fill a large cookie sheet, spacing the slices about 1 inch apart; refrigerate the remaining dough. Bake for about 10 minutes, until the cookies are set and the edges are golden. Transfer to a rack to cool completely. Slice and bake the remaining dough. (The cookies can be stored for up to 1 week in an airtight container.)

—Tracey Seaman

**Chocolate
Raspberry
Squares**

■

CHOCOLATE RASPBERRY SQUARES

A cross between brownies and cake, these chocolate squares are delicious even when adorned with only a dusting of confectioners' sugar. But topped with a rich raspberry-flavored ganache, they're irresistible. Use the best-quality chocolate you can find.

Makes 48 Squares

7 ounces bittersweet chocolate, finely chopped (1¼ cups)
¼ cup plus 2 tablespoons heavy cream
2 sticks (½ pound) plus 2 teaspoons unsalted butter, softened
1 teaspoon pure vanilla extract
1 tablespoon raspberry-flavored liqueur
1 cup all-purpose flour
¼ teaspoon salt
1¼ cups sugar
3 large eggs
½ cup seedless raspberry jam

1. Place ¾ cup of the chocolate in a medium bowl. In a small saucepan, combine the cream and 2 teaspoons of the butter and bring to a boil. Pour the cream over the chocolate. Let sit for 30 seconds, then whisk until completely smooth. Whisk in ½ teaspoon of the vanilla and the liqueur. Let cool, then refrigerate just until chilled to a spreadable consistency, 30 minutes to 1 hour. (The frosting can be made up to 5 days ahead; cover and refrigerate. Bring to room temperature before using.)

2. Preheat the oven to 350°. Lightly grease a 9-by-13-inch baking pan. Place the remaining ½ cup chocolate in a double boiler over simmering water. Stir occasionally until the chocolate melts. Remove from the heat.

3. In a medium bowl, whisk the flour and salt. In a large bowl, using an electric mixer, cream the remaining 2 sticks butter with the sugar until light and fluffy. Beat in the eggs 1 at a time, beating well after each addition. Beat in ¼ cup of the raspberry jam until well blended. (The batter may look slightly curdled at this point.) Beat in the melted chocolate and the remaining ½ teaspoon vanilla. On low speed, beat in the dry ingredients in 2 batches. Scrape the batter into the prepared pan and smooth the surface.

4. Bake in the middle of the oven for 20 to 25 minutes, until a cake tester inserted in the center comes out clean and moist. Transfer the pan to a rack and let cool completely.

5. Using a large metal spreading spatula, spread the frosting evenly over the top of the chocolate raspberry cake; refrigerate for 1 hour.

6. Spoon the remaining ¼ cup raspberry jam into a sturdy plastic bag. Snip off a generous ⅛ inch from one corner and squeeze decorative stripes on top of the cake. Cut into 1½-inch squares. Serve chilled or at room temperature. (The squares can be refrigerated, covered, for up to 3 days.)

—Judith Sutton

Chapter 14 ▪ PIES & TARTS

269   Double-Crusted Apple-Cranberry Pie

269   Apple Polenta Tart

270   Apple Tartlets with Browned Butter Filling

272   Apple-Cranberry Crumb Tart

273   Cranberry Caramel Tartlets

275   Pear-Ginger Custard Tart

275   Acorn Squash and Pear Pie

277   Spicy Pumpkin Pie

277   Sweet Mashed Potato Tart

278   Italian Almond Tart

280   Brown Butter Pecan Tart with Bourbon-Vanilla Ice Cream

282   German Chocolate Tartlets

283   Chocolate–Macadamia Nut Tart

Double-Crusted Apple-Cranberry Pie

DOUBLE-CRUSTED APPLE-CRANBERRY PIE

Any one of a variety of apples will work well in this pie from The Apple Tree in Gays Mill, Wisconsin. Try Spartan, Cortland, Empire, Greening, Granny Smith or Orange Winter.

Makes One 9-Inch Pie
Double-Crust Pastry (at right)
1½ **pounds tart apples**
 1 **cup fresh cranberries, rinsed and picked over**
 ¾ **cup sugar**
 2 **tablespoons all-purpose flour**
 2 **teaspoons finely grated orange zest**
 ¼ **teaspoon cinnamon**
 ⅛ **teaspoon salt**
 2 **tablespoons unsalted butter, cut into small pieces**

1. On a lightly floured surface, roll half of the Double-Crust Pastry into an 11-inch round about ⅛ inch thick. Transfer to a 9-inch pie pan and fit against the bottom and sides without stretching. Using a small sharp knife, trim the dough flush with the rim. Refrigerate for 30 minutes.

2. Using a small sharp knife, peel, quarter and core the apples. Slice them lengthwise ¼ inch thick. Toss in a medium bowl with the cranberries, sugar, flour, orange zest, cinnamon and salt; mix well. Pour into the pie shell. Dot with the butter.

3. Preheat the oven to 400°. Lightly moisten the edge of the pie shell with cold water. Roll out the remaining pastry into a 12-inch round. Drape it over the pie. Trim the overhanging dough to ½ inch. Tuck the excess under the rim of the bottom pie shell and press to seal; crimp decoratively. Cut 3 or 4 steam vents in the top.

4. Cover the rim with foil to prevent overbrowning. Bake the pie for 30 minutes, or until the apples feel tender when a cake tester is inserted into the center of the pie. Transfer to a rack to cool.

DOUBLE-CRUST PASTRY
Makes One Double-Crust 9-Inch Pie

2¼ **cups all-purpose flour**
 ½ **teaspoon salt**
 1 **stick (8 tablespoons) cold unsalted butter, cut into ½-inch pieces**
 3 **tablespoons cold vegetable shortening or lard**
4 to 5 **tablespoons ice water**

1. In a food processor, combine the flour and salt and pulse a few times to mix. Add the butter and shortening and process until the mixture is rough textured, with particles the size of peas.

2. Add 3 tablespoons of the ice water, 1 tablespoon at a time, pulsing briefly after each addition. Add another tablespoon of the water and pulse just until the dough begins to hold together. Add 1 more tablespoon of water if necessary.

3. Transfer the dough to a lightly floured surface. Gather it into a ball, handling it as little as possible. Divide the dough in half. Pat the 2 pieces into disks, wrap in wax paper and refrigerate for at least 20 minutes or overnight before rolling out.

■

APPLE POLENTA TART

This rustic-looking tart from the Downtown Bakery & Creamery in Healdsburg, California, has a not-too-sweet filling. The top crust may crack slightly as it cools.

Makes One 9-Inch Tart
Pastry:
 9 **tablespoons plus 2 teaspoons unsalted butter, at room temperature**
 ¾ **cup sugar**
 3 **large egg yolks**
1½ **cups all-purpose flour**
 ½ **cup polenta or yellow cornmeal**
 ¾ **teaspoon salt**

Filling:
 2 **pounds flavorful apples, such as McIntosh or Empire**
 1 **tablespoon sugar**
 1 **teaspoon all-purpose flour**
 3 **tablespoons polenta or cornmeal** ➤

Glaze:

1 **egg yolk mixed with 1 tablespoon heavy cream**
2 **teaspoons coarse sugar crystals or turbinado (partially refined) sugar**

1. Make the pastry: In a large bowl, using an electric mixer, beat the butter and sugar until light and creamy. Beat in the egg yolks until pale, about 1 minute. Sift together the flour, polenta and salt. Stir the dry ingredients into the butter-egg mixture. Form the dough into 2 balls, one slightly larger than the other. Flatten each of the balls into a ½-inch-thick disk; wrap the disks in wax paper and refrigerate for 30 minutes.

2. On a lightly floured surface, roll the larger pastry disk into an 11-inch fluted round. Transfer the dough to a 9-inch fluted tart pan with a removable bottom. Fit the dough evenly into the pan without stretching and run the rolling pin over the rim to trim away the extra dough. Prick the shell all over with a fork and refrigerate for 1 hour.

3. Preheat the oven to 375°. Bake the tart shell for about 15 minutes, until golden. Let cool slightly.

4. Make the filling: Using a small sharp knife, peel, quarter and core the apples. Slice them lengthwise ¼ inch thick. Toss the apples with the sugar and flour. Sprinkle the polenta over the bottom of the cooled shell. Spoon the apple filling into the shell.

5. On a lightly floured surface, roll the other pastry disk into a 10-inch round and lay it over the filling. Press the edges all around to seal and brush the dough with the egg glaze. Using a small sharp knife, cut a small hole in the center to vent steam. Sprinkle the coarse sugar over the top.

6. Lower the oven temperature to 350°. Bake the tart for about 1 hour, until the crust is golden brown all over. Transfer to a rack to cool.

■

APPLE TARTLETS WITH BROWNED BUTTER FILLING

These delicate individual tarts are as delicious as they are beautiful. The secret is a filling made with *beurre noisette*, browned butter, which is cooked until it acquires a nutty flavor.

8 Servings

1 **large egg**
⅓ **cup plus 4 teaspoons sugar**
3½ **tablespoons all-purpose flour**
4 **tablespoons unsalted butter**
½ **of a vanilla bean, split**
½ **pound frozen puff pastry, thawed but cold (see Puff Pastry, at left)**
6 **small Granny Smith or Golden Delicious apples**
1 **lemon, halved**
¼ **cup apricot preserves**
Chopped toasted pecans or walnuts, for garnish
Crème fraîche or vanilla ice cream, for serving

1. In a small bowl, whisk the egg with ⅓ cup of the sugar until well blended. Whisk in the flour until thoroughly incorporated.

2. In a small heavy saucepan, combine the butter and vanilla bean. Cook over high heat until the butter is golden brown and has a nutty aroma, about 10 minutes. Remove the vanilla bean, rinse and save for another use. Gradually whisk the browned butter into the egg-flour mixture. Let cool to room temperature, then cover and refrigerate for at least 1 hour, until chilled. (The browned butter filling can be prepared up to 3 days ahead.)

3. Halve the puff pastry. On a lightly floured surface, roll out one-half of the pastry into a 12-inch square. Using a sharp knife and a pot lid or a small plate

as a guide, cut out four 5½-inch rounds of dough. Arrange the dough rounds about 1 inch apart on a large, ungreased baking sheet; cover with plastic wrap and refrigerate. Repeat with the remaining pastry on another baking sheet, for a total of 8 rounds. Refrigerate the pastry for at least 30 minutes or overnight.

4. Preheat the oven to 400°. Using a small sharp knife, slice about ½ inch off the top and bottom of each of the apples. Peel, halve and core the apples. Rub the apple halves with the lemon halves to prevent discoloring. Place 1 apple half, cut side down, on a work surface and slice it crosswise about 1/16 inch thick; do not

Apple Tartlet with Browned Butter Filling

271

**Apple-Cranberry
Crumb Tart**

stirring, until smooth, 1 to 2 minutes. Brush the warm apricot glaze evenly over the apples. (The tartlets can be prepared up to 6 hours in advance and set aside, uncovered, at room temperature. Reheat them in a 375° oven for about 5 minutes before serving.)

7. Place the apple tartlets on individual dessert plates. Sprinkle chopped toasted nuts over them and place a dollop of crème fraîche or a small scoop of ice cream next to each serving.

—Judith Sutton

■

APPLE-CRANBERRY CRUMB TART

The soft pastry dough for this tart, from Bonnie's Patisserie in Southfield, Michigan, is not rolled out but simply pressed into the pan.

Makes One 11-Inch Tart

Dough:
- 1 stick (8 tablespoons) unsalted butter, at room temperature
- ¼ cup plus 1 tablespoon granulated sugar
- 1 egg yolk
- 1⅔ cups cake flour, sifted

Filling:
- 1½ pounds tart apples, such as Greening or Granny Smith
- 1 cup fresh cranberries, rinsed and picked over
- 2 tablespoons plus 2 teaspoons all-purpose flour
- ⅔ cup granulated sugar
- ½ teaspoon cinnamon

Topping:
- 1 cup rolled oats
- ¾ cup all-purpose flour
- ⅔ cup (packed) light brown sugar
- 6 tablespoons unsalted butter, melted

separate the slices. Repeat with the remaining apple halves. Squeeze lemon juice over them.

5. Place 1 tablespoon of the browned butter filling in the center of each puff pastry round. Cut across the tips of the apple slices to even the ends. Set aside 8 apple slices. Using about ¾ of a whole apple for 1 pastry round, arrange the apple slices in a tight overlapping circle, placing their trimmed ends flush with the edge of the dough. Repeat with the remaining pastry rounds and apples. Then cut the 8 reserved apple slices into short wedges and arrange in the center of each tartlet to form rosettes. Sprinkle ½ teaspoon sugar evenly over each tartlet. Bake for 18 to 20 minutes, or until the apples are tender and lightly browned on the edges. Transfer the baking sheets to racks to cool.

6. In a small nonreactive saucepan, combine the apricot preserves and 2 tablespoons of water. Melt over low heat,

1. Make the dough: In a large bowl, using an electric mixer, cream the butter and sugar on medium speed until light and fluffy. Beat in the egg yolk until incorporated. On low speed, mix in the flour until the dough just comes together. Turn out on a lightly floured surface and knead 3 or 4 times to form a smooth ball. Pat into a 6-inch disk. Press evenly into the bottom and up the sides of an 11-by-1-inch fluted tart pan with a removable bottom. Prick all over with a fork. Refrigerate for 1 hour.

2. Preheat the oven to 375°. Place the tart shell on a baking sheet. Bake 10 to 15 minutes, until just starting to color. Set aside.

3. Make the filling: Peel, quarter and core the apples; slice lengthwise ¼ inch thick. In a bowl, toss the apples and cranberries with the flour. Stir in the sugar and cinnamon. Mound the filling in the shell.

4. Make the topping: In a medium bowl, combine the oats, flour and brown sugar. Pour in the butter and crumble the mixture with your fingers. Pile it on the fruit to cover completely.

5. Bake the tart for about 40 minutes, or until the topping is golden, the filling is bubbling and the apples are tender when pierced. (Cover loosely with foil if the top gets too brown too soon.) Transfer to a rack to cool.

■

CRANBERRY CARAMEL TARTLETS

The pastry dough for these tartlets, from The City Bakery in New York City, was designed to be flaky and tender even after being kneaded well.

Makes Eight 4-Inch Tartlets

Pastry:
- 1 stick (8 tablespoons) plus 5 tablespoons cold unsalted butter, cut into ½-inch slices and slightly softened

- ⅓ cup confectioners' sugar
- 1 large egg yolk
- ¾ cup unbleached all-purpose flour, sifted
- ¾ cup bread flour, sifted

Filling:
- ¾ cup plus 2 tablespoons heavy cream
- ¾ cup granulated sugar
- 4 cups fresh cranberries, picked over
- 1 cup sliced almonds

Cranberry Caramel Tartlets

1. Make the pastry dough: In a medium bowl, using an electric mixer, beat the butter with the confectioners' sugar on medium speed for 2 minutes. Beat in the egg yolk, scraping the bowl with a rubber spatula. Using a wooden spoon, stir in half of the all-purpose flour and the bread flour until combined. Mix in the remaining all-purpose flour and bread flour to

**Pear-Ginger
Custard Tart**

try dough into 1 of the flan rings. Using your thumbs, gently but firmly press the dough into the ring, taking care to form a close fit around the base. Using a small sharp knife, trim the dough flush with the rim of the ring. Prick the dough all over with a fork. Repeat with the remaining pastry dough. Freeze the rings on the baking sheet until the pastry is firm, about 15 minutes.

4. Meanwhile, preheat the oven to 375°. Bake the tartlet shells on the baking sheet for about 12 minutes, until golden. (If the dough puffs up, tap it with a spoon; do not prick it.) Remove the tartlet shells and let cool on the baking sheet. Leave the oven on.

5. Make the filling: In a small saucepan, bring the heavy cream to a simmer over low heat. In a heavy medium saucepan, cook the granulated sugar over moderately high heat, stirring constantly with a wooden spoon, until melted, about 5 minutes. Swirling the pan occasionally, cook until the sugar is a rich golden brown, about 2 minutes. Immediately whisk the hot cream into the caramel, taking care to avoid splatters; do not let the mixture boil over. Cook, whisking constantly, until smooth. Strain the caramel into a medium bowl. Add the fresh cranberries and the sliced almonds and stir to coat completely.

6. Place the baking sheets with the tartlet shells on top of another baking sheet (to prevent the bottoms of the tartlets from burning). Mound the filling into the tartlet shells and bake them for 25 to 35 minutes, or until the cranberries have burst and the edges of the pastry have browned.

7. Remove the flan rings from the tartlets with tongs; if they stick, run a small sharp knife around the tartlet rims and then lift off the rings. Using a metal spatula, carefully transfer the tartlets to a rack to cool slightly. Serve warm or at room temperature.

form a soft, sticky dough. Scrape the dough onto a piece of wax paper and form it into a flat disk. Wrap and refrigerate the dough until firm, at least 2 hours or overnight.

2. On a lightly floured surface, cut the cold dough into 1-inch pieces. Using the heel of your hand, knead the pieces together until the dough is smooth but still cool, using a pastry scraper or metal spatula to free the dough from the work surface. Roll the dough into a 12-inch-long log and cut into 8 equal pieces. Transfer to a plate, cover with plastic wrap and refrigerate until cold, about 20 minutes.

3. Line a large baking sheet with parchment paper. Place eight 4-inch flan rings or 4½-inch fluted tartlet pans with removable bottoms on the baking sheet. Remove 1 piece of dough from the refrigerator and, on a lightly floured surface, roll it into a 5½-inch round. Ease the pas-

PEAR-GINGER CUSTARD TART

A tender cookie-like crust, soft pears and bits of chewy crystallized ginger give a wealth of textures and flavors to this tart from Fran Gage Patisserie Française in San Francisco.

Makes Two 9-Inch Tarts

Pastry:
- 1 stick (8 tablespoons) plus 2 tablespoons unsalted butter, slightly softened
- 1¼ cups plus ⅓ cup pastry flour
- ¾ cup confectioners' sugar
- ¼ cup blanched almonds (1¼ ounces), finely ground
- 1 large egg
- ¾ teaspoon pure vanilla extract
- ¼ teaspoon salt

Filling:
- 4 pears, preferably Bartlett or Comice
- 1 cup heavy cream
- 4 large eggs
- ½ cup granulated sugar
- 3 tablespoons blanched almonds, finely ground
- ¼ cup crystallized ginger, finely chopped (about 2 ounces)

1. Make the pastry: In an electric mixer, beat the butter at moderate speed until softened. Add the ⅓ cup flour, the confectioners' sugar, ground almonds, egg, vanilla and salt. Beat until well blended, scraping down the sides of the bowl once or twice. Add the remaining 1¼ cups flour and beat on low speed just until incorporated; do not overmix.

2. Halve the dough; flatten into 2 disks, wrap in wax paper and refrigerate for at least 1 hour or overnight.

3. Line 2 baking sheets without sides with parchment paper; dust very lightly with flour. Place 1 pastry disk on a prepared baking sheet; the dough will be sticky. Working quickly and using as little extra flour as possible, roll it out to an 11-inch round about ⅛ inch thick. Repeat with the other pastry disk. Refrigerate the pastry rounds on the baking sheets until firm, about 1 hour.

4. Flip 1 round of dough into a 9-inch fluted tart pan with a removable bottom. Peel off the parchment paper. Fit the dough into the pan, gently pressing the dough into the bottom and against the sides. Prick the tart shell all over with a fork. Repeat with the other round of dough. Freeze the tart shells for at least 30 minutes or up to 1 week.

5. Preheat the oven to 375°. Bake the tart shells for 10 minutes, then set aside to cool. Leave the oven on.

6. Make the filling: Using a small sharp knife, peel, quarter and core the pears. Slice them lengthwise ¼ inch thick. In a medium bowl, whisk the cream with the eggs, the granulated sugar and the ground almonds. For each of the tarts, arrange the pear slices in concentric circles, sprinkle the ginger over the pears and carefully pour the custard filling over the fruit.

7. Bake the tarts for 25 to 35 minutes, or until the custard is firm and the crusts are browned. Transfer the tarts to a rack and let cool to room temperature before serving.

ACORN SQUASH AND PEAR PIE

You will need a deep-dish (about two inches) pie pan for this recipe, from the Firehook Bakery & Coffee House in Alexandria, Virginia. This is one of the few pies that are better served cold than warm. ➤

Acorn Squash and Pear Pie

Makes One 10½-Inch Pie

Dough:

- 2 cups pastry flour (or ¾ cup unbleached all-purpose flour mixed with 1¼ cups cake flour)
- 1½ sticks (12 tablespoons) unsalted butter
- 1 large egg
- 1 tablespoon confectioners' sugar

Filling:

- 2 acorn squash (3 pounds)
- 1¼ cups light brown sugar
- 4 tablespoons unsalted butter
- 1 teaspoon ground ginger
- ⅛ teaspoon salt
- 3 large eggs
- 1½ pounds Bosc pears
- 1½ tablespoons granulated sugar
- 2 teaspoons cinnamon

1. Make the dough: In a food processor, combine 1 cup of the flour, the butter, egg and sugar. Pulse 10 to 15 times, or until the mixture is a fairly smooth paste. Add the remaining 1 cup flour and pulse until the dough comes together. Do not overwork. Form the dough into a ball, flatten into a disk, wrap in wax paper and refrigerate for at least 2 hours or overnight.

2. On a lightly floured sheet of parchment paper, roll the dough into a 13-inch round, about ⅛ inch thick. Transfer the dough to a 10½-inch deep-dish pie plate and fit it against the bottom and sides without stretching. Trim the overhanging dough to ½ inch, fold it under and crimp decoratively. Using a fork, prick the bottom and sides of the pie shell all over. Freeze the pie shell until firm, 10 to 15 minutes.

3. Preheat the oven to 400°. Bake the shell for 10 minutes, or until the edges begin to turn golden. Transfer to a rack to cool to room temperature. Leave the oven on.

4. Make the filling: Halve each squash lengthwise and, using a spoon, scoop out and discard the seeds. Place the squash halves, cut sides up, in a large baking dish. Pour ½ inch of water into the dish. Place 2 tablespoons of the brown sugar and 1 tablespoon of the butter in each squash cavity. Cover the dish with foil and bake the squash for 45 minutes, or until soft when pricked with a fork.

5. Using a spoon, scoop the squash flesh into a food processor, along with any cooking juices. Puree until smooth. Add the remaining ¾ cup brown sugar and the ginger and salt. Pulse several times to mix. Remove the food processor cover and let the puree cool for about 10 minutes. Add the eggs 1 at a time, pulsing until incorporated between each addition.

6. Using a small sharp knife, peel, quarter and core the pears. Slice them lengthwise ⅛ inch thick. Arrange the pear slices in the cooled pie shell. Mix the

276

granulated sugar and cinnamon and sprinkle on top of the pears. Pour the squash filling over the pears and smooth the surface with a spatula.

7. Bake the pie in the lower part of the oven for 15 minutes. Lower the temperature to 350° and bake for 40 to 50 minutes longer, or until the crust is golden brown and the filling is just set. (The center of the filling will continue to cook after the pie is removed from the oven). Transfer to a rack to cool completely, then refrigerate briefly before serving.

■

SPICY PUMPKIN PIE

You can buy pumpkin-pie spice at the supermarket, or you can make your own blend of ground cinnamon, ginger, nutmeg, allspice and cloves. Some nine-inch pie pans are deeper than others. For this recipe, from The French Loaf in Columbus, Ohio, look for pans that are about one and three-fourths inches deep.

Makes Two 9-Inch Pies
1 **29-ounce can of solid-pack pumpkin**
2 **cups (firmly packed) light brown sugar**
3 **tablespoons pumpkin pie spice**
1 **teaspoon salt**
5 **large eggs, lightly beaten**
2 **12-ounce cans of evaporated milk**
  Double-Crust Pastry (p. 269)

1. In a large bowl, whisk the pumpkin with the brown sugar, pumpkin pie spice and salt. Whisk in the eggs. Slowly whisk in the evaporated milk until completely blended. Refrigerate while you prepare the pie shells.

2. On a lightly floured surface, roll one half of the Double-Crust Pastry into an 11-inch round. Transfer the round to a 9-inch pie pan and fit it against the bottom

and sides without stretching. Trim the overhanging dough to ½ inch, fold it under and crimp decoratively. Prick the dough all over with a fork. Repeat with the other half of the pastry. Freeze the shells for at least 30 minutes.

3. Preheat the oven to 375°. Bake the shells for 10 minutes, or until they are just beginning to brown slightly. Let cool to room temperature.

4. Pour the filling into the cooled shells and bake for about 45 minutes, until the pies move slightly in one mass (no liquid center) when lightly jiggled. Transfer to a rack to cool.

■

SWEET MASHED POTATO TART

Make this sweetened mashed potato tart flavored with vanilla, lemon and Cognac in late winter, after apple and pear season and before the onset of spring. It is a surprising combination, but it works. The amount of water needed for the crust will be determined by the weather; less water is needed on humid days.

Makes One 11-Inch Tart
½ **pound yellow potatoes (Yukon Gold or Yellow Finn), peeled and cut into 1-inch cubes**
  Salt
½ **cup sugar**
1 **large egg, separated**
2 **tablespoons semolina or fine cornmeal**
1 **tablespoon Cognac**
1 **teaspoon pure vanilla extract**
1 **teaspoon finely grated lemon zest**
  Pastry Crust (recipe follows)
1 **cup sour cream mixed with 2 tablespoons sugar, for serving (optional)** ➤

1. In a medium saucepan, cover the potatoes with cold water, add salt and bring to a boil over moderately high heat. Simmer until the potatoes are very tender, 15 to 20 minutes.

2. Drain the cooked potatoes and quickly mash them in a ricer or a food mill before they cool.

3. Preheat the oven to 400°. In a large bowl, combine the potatoes with the sugar, egg yolk, semolina, Cognac, vanilla and lemon zest. Whisk until very smooth. Beat the egg white until firm and fold it into the mashed potatoes. Spread the mixture in the baked Pastry Crust.

4. Bake the tart in the middle of the oven for 30 minutes, or until golden. Serve warm as is or with the sweetened sour cream.

Pastry Crust
Makes One Thin 11-Inch
Tart Shell

1 **stick (8 tablespoons) unsalted butter**
1 **cup all-purpose flour**
   Pinch of salt

1. Cut the butter into teaspoons and freeze for 30 minutes. In a food processor, combine the flour, salt and butter. Process for 10 seconds. Add 2 to 3 tablespoons of cold water and process for another 10 seconds. Turn the dough out on a work surface. Working with small amounts at a time and using the heel of your hand, smear the dough against the work surface to fully blend the butter and the flour.

2. Gather the dough into a ball and flatten it into a disk. Wrap in wax paper and refrigerate for 15 minutes to firm up the butter.

3. Flour a work surface and rolling pin. Roll out the dough to a 13-inch round. Transfer the dough to an 11-inch tart pan with a removable bottom, fitting it in evenly without stretching. Trim the over-

hang. Prick the shell all over with a fork and refrigerate for 2 hours or freeze until ready to bake.

4. Preheat the oven to 400°. Line the tart shell with foil and fill it with pie weights or dried beans. Bake the shell in the middle of the oven for 15 minutes. Remove the weights and foil. Bake for about 10 minutes longer, until golden and the bottom is dried out. Let cool slightly before filling.

—Lydie Marshall

■

ITALIAN ALMOND TART

Regional variations of this tart are found all over Italy, but the addition of bits of chocolate makes this one unusual. The silken mascarpone and the bittersweet chocolate sauce perfectly complement the tart's not-too-sweet, macaroon-like filling.

8 Servings

2 **cups all-purpose flour**
1¼ **cups granulated sugar**
¼ **teaspoon salt**
1 **stick (8 tablespoons) plus 2 tablespoons unsalted butter, cut into small pieces and chilled**
4 to 5 **tablespoons ice water**
4 **large egg whites**
2 **cups blanched whole almonds, finely ground (11 ounces)**
3 **ounces semisweet chocolate, finely chopped (generous ½ cup)**
1 **large egg yolk beaten with 2 tablespoons water, for glazing**
8 **ounces mascarpone cheese**
2 **tablespoons confectioners' sugar Bittersweet Chocolate Sauce (recipe follows)**

1. In a medium bowl, stir together the flour, ½ cup of the granulated sugar and the salt. Using your fingertips, a pastry blender or 2 knives, cut the butter into the

flour until it resembles coarse meal. Drizzle 4 tablespoons of the ice water all over the top and, using a fork, stir until the dough just holds together when pinched, adding up to 1 tablespoon more ice water if necessary. Divide the dough in half. Shape each half into a disk, wrap well and refrigerate for 30 minutes. (The dough can be made up to 1 day ahead.)

2. On a lightly floured surface, roll out 1 disk of dough into a 12-inch round. Fold the dough in quarters and place in a 9-inch fluted tart pan with a removable bottom. Unfold the dough and press it gently into the pan without stretching. Trim the overhang to ½ inch and fold it in, pressing it against the sides to form a lip ¼ inch above the pan rim. Using a

Italian Almond Tart

fork, prick the bottom of the tart shell at 1-inch intervals. Refrigerate the tart shell for 30 minutes to firm up.

3. On a lightly floured surface, roll out the remaining disk of dough into an 11-inch round. Transfer the round to a baking sheet and refrigerate until ready to use.

4. Preheat the oven to 375°. Line the tart shell with aluminum foil and fill it with pie weights or dried beans. Bake the shell for 15 minutes. Remove the foil and weights and bake for about 5 minutes longer, just until the dough has lost its raw look. Let cool slightly. Leave the oven on.

5. In a large bowl, using an electric mixer, beat the egg whites at medium speed until they hold soft peaks. Gradually beat in the remaining ¾ cup granulated sugar. Increase the speed to high and beat until the whites are stiff and glossy. Using a large rubber spatula, gently but thoroughly fold in the ground almonds and then the chopped chocolate. Scrape the filling evenly into the partially baked tart shell and smooth the surface.

6. Remove the rolled-out dough from the refrigerator and, with a sharp knife, cut it into ten ¾-inch-wide strips. Evenly lay 5 parallel strips across the tart; lay the remaining strips diagonally across them to form a diamond lattice. Trim the ends of the strips flush with the tart shell and press them into the filling. Brush the pastry with the egg glaze.

7. Bake the tart for 30 minutes, or until the filling is puffed and golden and the pastry is light golden brown. Transfer to a rack and let cool to room temperature. (The tart can be made up to 1 day ahead; do not refrigerate.)

8. Place the mascarpone in a medium bowl. Using a wooden spoon, beat in the confectioners' sugar. Refrigerate until serving time.

9. To serve, using a fork, spoon or plastic squeeze bottle, decoratively drizzle 1 tablespoon of the Bittersweet Chocolate Sauce over 8 large dessert plates. Set a slice of the tart on each of the plates and place a dollop of the sweetened mascarpone next to it.

Bittersweet Chocolate Sauce
Makes About ½ Cup
- 1½ ounces bittersweet chocolate, finely chopped (generous ¼ cup)
- ⅓ cup heavy cream
- 2 tablespoons sugar
- ⅛ teaspoon pure vanilla extract

In a small heavy saucepan, combine the chocolate, the heavy cream and the sugar. Cook over low heat, stirring with a wooden spoon, until the chocolate is completely melted and the sugar is dissolved, 2 to 3 minutes. Transfer to a small bowl and stir in the vanilla. Let the sauce cool to room temperature. (The sauce can be made up to 4 days ahead; cover and refrigerate. Reheat in a double boiler before using.)

—Judith Sutton

BROWN BUTTER PECAN TART WITH BOURBON-VANILLA ICE CREAM

Rich pecan pie is better than ever with toasted pecans, brown butter and a touch of bourbon.

8 to 10 Servings
Pastry:
- 1¼ cups plus 2 tablespoons all-purpose flour
- 1 tablespoon plus 1 teaspoon sugar
  Pinch of salt
- 1 stick (8 tablespoons) cold unsalted butter, cut into small pieces
- 1 large egg yolk
- 1 tablespoon milk

Filling:

2½ **cups coarsely chopped pecans (9½ ounces)**

4 **tablespoons unsalted butter**

½ **cup light brown sugar**

¼ **cup granulated sugar**

1¼ **cups light corn syrup**

¼ **cup bourbon**

1 **teaspoon pure vanilla extract**

2 **large whole eggs**

3 **large egg yolks**

1 **large egg white, lightly beaten**

¾ **cup pecan halves (3 ounces)**
Bourbon-Vanilla Ice Cream (recipe follows)

1. Make the pastry: In a food processor, pulse the flour, sugar and salt to blend. Add the butter and pulse until the mixture resembles coarse meal. In a small bowl, combine the egg yolk and milk. Add to the processor and pulse just until the dough comes together. Pat the dough into a disk, wrap in plastic and refrigerate until firm, at least 1 hour or overnight. Let the dough soften slightly before rolling out.

2. Prepare the filling: Preheat the oven to 350°. Spread the chopped pecans on a baking sheet and toast for about 7 minutes, until fragrant. Leave the oven on.

3. In a small skillet, cook the butter over moderate heat until lightly browned, about 3 minutes. Transfer to a medium bowl. Whisk in the brown and granulated sugars, corn syrup, bourbon and vanilla. Whisk in the whole eggs and egg yolks.

4. On a lightly floured surface, roll out the dough to a 13-inch round. Gently transfer the dough to an 11-by-1-inch tart pan with a removable bottom, pressing it evenly into the pan without stretching. Trim any overlap. With a fork, prick the bottom of the tart shell and freeze until firm, about 5 minutes.

5. Line the pastry with foil and fill with pie weights, rice or dried beans. Bake for about 20 minutes, until set. Remove the foil and weights and bake for about 15 minutes, until golden. Immediately brush the pastry with the beaten egg white and put the pan on a baking sheet. Leave the oven on.

6. Spread the toasted pecan pieces in the tart shell. Arrange the pecan halves in a neat ring around the outer edge. Gently pour the filling over the nuts so that they are evenly covered.

7. Bake the tart for about 45 minutes, until the filling is set. Transfer the tart to a rack and let cool completely. Remove the sides of the pan, put the tart on a large plate and serve it with a scoop of Bourbon-Vanilla Ice Cream.

Bourbon-Vanilla Ice Cream
Makes 2 Quarts

3¾ **cups half-and-half**

3 **cups heavy cream**

1½ **large vanilla beans, split**

14 **large egg yolks**

1½ **cups sugar**

Pinch of salt

½ **cup bourbon**

1. In a large nonreactive saucepan, combine the half-and-half and heavy cream. Scrape the seeds from the vanilla beans into the cream and add the beans. Cook over moderate heat just until the cream comes to a boil.

2. Meanwhile, in a large bowl, whisk the egg yolks with the sugar and salt. Gradually whisk in the hot cream, then return the mixture to the saucepan. Cook over moderate heat, stirring constantly, until the custard reaches a temperature of 165° on a candy thermometer and coats the back of a spoon. Strain the custard into a large bowl and refrigerate until cold, about 2 hours.

3. Stir the bourbon into the cold custard. Pour half the custard into an ice cream maker. Freeze the custard according to the manufacturer's instructions. Transfer the frozen custard to a chilled

German Chocolate Tartlet

container and freeze for at least 3 hours or up to 3 days. Repeat with the remaining custard.

—Ben Barker

■

GERMAN CHOCOLATE TARTLETS

At Tapawingo in Ellsworth, Michigan, guests delight in this rendition of German chocolate cake. These fudgy tartlets can be served with a large spoonful of lightly sweetened whipped cream or vanilla ice cream.

Makes 6 Tartlets

Pastry:
1½ **cups plus 1 tablespoon all-purpose flour**
⅓ **cup sugar**

Pinch of salt
1½ sticks (12 tablespoons) cold unsalted butter, cut into small pieces
1 large egg yolk

Coconut and Chocolate Fillings:
¾ cup pecans (about 3 ounces)
¾ cup plus 3 tablespoons sugar
Pinch of cream of tartar
¾ cup unsweetened coconut milk*
1 cup plus 2 tablespoons unsweetened shredded coconut** (3 ounces)
6 ounces milk chocolate, coarsely chopped
2 ounces bittersweet chocolate, coarsely chopped
4 tablespoons unsalted butter
3 large egg yolks
½ of a large egg white
1 teaspoon pure vanilla extract

*Available at Asian markets
**Available at health food stores

1. Make the pastry: In a food processor, combine the flour, sugar and salt and pulse briefly to sift. Add the butter and pulse just until the mixture resembles coarse meal. Add the egg yolk and 1 tablespoon of water and process until the dough forms a ball. Shape the dough into a 5-by-2-inch log. Wrap the log in plastic or wax paper and refrigerate until firm, at least 1 hour.

2. Place six 4½-inch fluted metal tartlet pans on a baking sheet. Cut the chilled dough into 6 equal pieces. Set 1 piece of dough on a floured work surface; cover and refrigerate the remaining dough. Roll out the piece of dough to a 5-inch circle and press it into one of the tartlet pans. Prick the bottom with a fork. Repeat with the remaining pieces of dough and freeze the tartlet shells on the baking sheet until firm, about 15 minutes.

3. Preheat the oven to 325°. Bake the tartlet shells for 15 to 18 minutes, until golden. Remove the shells from the pans and let cool on a wire rack. Raise the oven temperature to 350°.

4. Make the coconut filling: In a small skillet, toast the pecans over moderate heat, shaking the pan occasionally, until fragrant, about 5 minutes. Finely chop the pecans and set aside.

5. In a medium saucepan, combine ¾ cup of the sugar with 2 tablespoons of water and the cream of tartar. Bring to a boil over moderately high heat and cook, brushing down the sides of the pan with a moistened pastry brush, until the caramel is a rich golden brown, about 5 minutes. Remove the saucepan from the heat and carefully pour in the coconut milk. Stir over moderately high heat until the caramel is completely dissolved, about 3 minutes. Remove the saucepan from the heat and stir in the shredded coconut and chopped pecans.

6. Make the chocolate filling: Place the milk chocolate, the bittersweet chocolate and the butter in a medium bowl. Set the bowl over a saucepan filled with ¾ inch of simmering water and stir until melted. Remove the chocolate mixture from the heat and beat in the egg yolks, egg white, the remaining 3 tablespoons sugar and the vanilla.

7. Spread 2 tablespoons of the coconut filling into each of the tartlet shells. Spoon the chocolate filling on top of the coconut filling. Bake the tartlets on the baking sheet for about 20 minutes, or just until set. Transfer the tartlets to a rack and let cool slightly.

8. To serve, top each of the warm tartlets with about 1 tablespoon of the reserved coconut filling, spreading it with the back of a fork. (The tartlets can be prepared up to 1 day ahead. Cover and refrigerate.) Serve the tartlets warm or at room temperature.

—Carl Duchaj

■

CHOCOLATE–MACADAMIA NUT TART

This tart from Patisserie Cafe Didier in Washington, D.C., is so chocolatey-rich that one tart will satisfy ten people nicely.

Makes One 8-Inch Tart

Dough:
- 1 stick (8 tablespoons) unsalted butter
- ¼ cup sugar
- ½ of a beaten large egg
- 1 cup plus 3 tablespoons cake flour
- ¼ cup plus 3 tablespoons unsweetened cocoa

Caramel:
- ½ cup heavy cream
- ½ cup plus 1½ tablespoons sugar
- 2 tablespoons unsalted butter

Chocolate cream:
- 3 ounces semisweet chocolate, broken into pieces
- ¾ teaspoon coffee liqueur
- ½ cup heavy cream

- 1 cup macadamia nuts (4 ounces)

1. Make the dough: In a large bowl, using an electric mixer, cream the butter and sugar until pale, about 3 minutes. Beat in the egg. In a separate bowl, stir together the flour and cocoa. Using a wooden spoon, stir the dry ingredients into the butter-sugar mixture and gather the dough into a ball. Flatten the dough into a disk, wrap in wax paper and refrigerate for at least 2 hours.

2. Preheat the oven to 325°. On a lightly floured surface, roll the chilled dough into a 10-inch round, slightly less than ¼ inch thick. Transfer the dough to an 8-

**Chocolate–
Macadamia
Nut Tart**

inch tart pan, gently pressing the dough evenly into the pan. Prick all over with a fork and freeze for 10 minutes.

3. Bake the tart shell for 12 minutes. Transfer to a rack to cool.

4. Make the caramel: In a small saucepan, bring the heavy cream to a simmer over low heat. Set a heavy medium saucepan over high heat and gradually add the sugar in small amounts, stirring constantly until it melts and turns golden brown. Remove the saucepan from the heat and slowly stir in the hot cream. Stir in the butter and let cool.

5. Make the chocolate cream: In a medium heatproof bowl, combine the chocolate and coffee liqueur. In a small saucepan, bring the heavy cream to a boil and pour it over the chocolate. Using a wooden spoon, stir until the chocolate is melted and completely smooth.

6. Reserve 13 whole macadamia nuts; finely chop and crush the rest. Pour the cooled caramel into the cooled tart shell and spread evenly with a metal spatula. Sprinkle the crushed macadamia nuts over the caramel. Pour the chocolate cream on top and spread evenly. Arrange 10 whole macadamia nuts around the edge of the tart to mark 10 slices; place the remaining 3 nuts in the center. Refrigerate the tart for 1 hour, or until firm.

Chapter 15 ▪ FRUIT DESSERTS

287   Green Apple Sorbet with Calvados

287   Bananas in Orange-Caramel Sauce

288   Chocolate-Banana Ice Cream Sandwiches

289   Banana Soufflés with Amaretti

290   Mixed Berry Shortcake

290   Blueberry Granita

292   Honeydew Granita

292   Melon with Mint-Lime Syrup and Jalapeño

292   Brandied Kumquats

293   Lemon Pudding Parfait

294   Lemon Pots de Crème

294   Creamy Lemon Ice

294   Lime Granita

295   Nectarine and Dried Cherry Clafoutis

296   Nectarine Crumble

296   Peachy Orange Shake

296   Peach and Red Wine Granita

297   Sourdough Bread Pudding with Caramelized Pears

298   Steamed Pears with Red Wine and Raspberries

298   Pear and Honey Napoleons with Hazelnuts

301   Caramelized Pineapple with Grilled Bananas and Tahitian Vanilla Sauce

303   Plum Cobbler

304   Rhubarb Compote with Strawberries

304   Strawberries Melba

306   Strawberry Semifreddo

307   Strawberry Meringues

308   Strawberries in Champagne Jelly

308   Strawberry Shortcake

**Green Apple Sorbet
with Calvados**

GREEN APPLE SORBET WITH CALVADOS

Champagne is a perfect stand-in for the apple brandy called for in this recipe, if you prefer.

8 Servings
2¼ pounds Granny Smith apples
¼ cup fresh lemon juice
1 cup plus 2 tablespoons sugar
Calvados
Fresh mint sprigs (optional)

1. Peel and core the Granny Smith apples, then cut them into ¼-inch dice. Place the diced apples in a bowl and toss with the lemon juice.

2. In a medium nonreactive saucepan, combine the sugar with 1⅓ cups of water. Bring the mixture to a boil over high heat, stirring occasionally. Add the diced apples and cook for 1½ minutes. Remove from the heat.

3. Transfer the apples and liquid to a blender and puree until completely smooth, scraping down the sides as necessary. Pour the puree into a 9-by-13-by-2-inch glass baking pan and freeze until thoroughly chilled.

4. Transfer the chilled apple puree to an ice cream maker and freeze according to the manufacturer's instructions. Alternatively, freeze the apple puree until it becomes icy around the edges, then stir well and refreeze. Repeat this procedure every 30 minutes for 4 to 5 hours, until the apple puree evenly frozen; when it is ready, you should not have any icy lumps. (The apple sorbet can be prepared up to 2 days ahead and frozen, tightly covered. Let the sorbet soften slightly before serving.)

5. To serve, scoop the apple sorbet into glass bowls, pour a splash of Calvados on top and garnish with a mint sprig.
—Bob Chambers

CARAMEL SAUCE TIPS

• Caramel sauce is ideal for dressing up fruit and is easily made without butter or cream, as in the version below flavored with orange juice. You can vary the flavor by using other fruit juices, such as pineapple or apple, or red wine. Or try stirring in a little rum or liqueur.
• The trickiest part of making caramel, which is done by melting sugar, is knowing when to stop the cooking. If you stop when the color is still light, the sauce will lack flavor; if you wait until the color is too dark, the sauce will taste burned. Look for a rich, golden-brown color; then remove the pan from the heat immediately and make the sauce.
—Michele Scicolone

BANANAS IN ORANGE-CARAMEL SAUCE

Banana slices in an orange-caramel sauce garnished with yogurt are a luscious and surprisingly low-fat finish.

4 Servings
½ cup sugar
½ cup fresh orange juice
2 teaspoons thinly sliced orange zest
4 ripe medium bananas, thinly sliced
1 cup plain low-fat yogurt

1. Make the caramel sauce: In a heavy, medium, nonreactive saucepan, combine the sugar and 3 tablespoons of water. Cook over moderate heat, stirring, until the sugar is dissolved. Bring to a boil and cook without stirring until the sugar becomes a rich golden brown caramel, about 5 minutes. Remove the pan from the heat. Add the orange juice, pouring it down the side of the pan so that the caramel does not boil over. Stir in the orange zest and cook the caramel over low heat, stirring, until smooth and melted, about 2 minutes. Let cool, then cover and refrigerate.

Chocolate-
Banana
Ice Cream
Sandwich

2. Just before serving, gently combine the banana slices and chilled caramel sauce in a medium bowl. Spoon the bananas into bowls and top each serving with ¼ cup of yogurt.

—Michele Scicolone

■

CHOCOLATE-BANANA ICE CREAM SANDWICHES

New York City's Mesa Grill offers this triple chocolate treat—chocolate and banana ice cream and chocolate–pumpkin seed cookies served with chocolate and Tia Maria sauce.

8 Servings

Banana Ice Cream:
- 1½ cups milk
- 1½ cups cream
- 1¾ cups sugar
- 9 large egg yolks
- 2 large ripe bananas
- 4 ounces semisweet chocolate, coarsely chopped

Chocolate Cookies:
- ¾ cup raw pumpkin seeds (about 3 ounces)*
- 3 ounces semisweet chocolate, coarsely chopped
- 1¾ cups all-purpose flour
- 1 teaspoon baking powder
- ¼ teaspoon salt
- 1 stick plus 2 tablespoons unsalted butter, at room temperature
- ¾ cup sugar
- 1 egg
- ¾ cup semisweet chocolate chips

Tia Maria Sauce:
- ½ cup heavy cream
- 2 ounces bittersweet chocolate, finely chopped
- ¼ cup Tia Maria or other coffee-flavored liqueur

*Available at health food stores

1. Make the ice cream: In a heavy medium saucepan, bring the milk, cream and ½ cup of the sugar just to a boil over moderate heat.

2. In a large bowl, whisk the egg yolks with 1 cup of the sugar. Gradually whisk in the hot milk. Return the mixture to the saucepan and cook over moderate heat, stirring constantly, until the custard reaches 175°. Strain into a bowl and let cool, then cover and refrigerate until chilled.

3. Mash the bananas to a puree with the remaining ¼ cup sugar. Stir the puree into the chilled custard. Transfer the custard to an ice cream maker and freeze according to the manufacturer's instructions.

4. Meanwhile, melt the chopped semisweet chocolate in a small bowl set over a small saucepan filled with ¾ inch of

simmering water. Remove the bowl from the heat and let cool slightly; reserve the saucepan on the heat.

5. Transfer the ice cream to a chilled bowl. Drizzle in the melted chocolate, folding constantly with a spatula. Cover and freeze for at least 3 hours and up to 3 days.

6. Make the cookies: Preheat the oven to 350°. Toast the pumpkin seeds on a cookie sheet until they pop for 1 full minute, about 5 minutes. Melt the semisweet chocolate in a small bowl set over the pan of simmering water. Set the bowl aside.

7. In a medium bowl, whisk the flour with the baking powder and salt. In a large bowl, beat the butter and sugar until creamy. Beat in the egg and melted chocolate. Add the dry ingredients in 3 additions, mixing just until combined. Stir in the pumpkin seeds and chocolate chips.

8. Shape the dough into 1-inch balls and arrange 2½ inches apart on a large non-stick cookie sheet. Flatten the cookies so they are ⅓ inch thick. Bake 10 minutes, or until firm. Transfer to a rack to cool.

9. Make the sauce: In a small saucepan, bring the cream just to a boil over moderate heat. Place the chocolate in a small bowl. Pour half of the hot cream over the chocolate and stir until smooth. Stir in the remaining cream and the Tia Maria.

10. To serve: Place 1 cookie on each large dessert plate, flat side up. Spoon 3 small scoops of ice cream onto each cookie. Pour 2 tablespoons of the Tia Maria sauce over the ice cream and top with another cookie. Pass the remaining sauce.
—Wayne Brachman

■

BANANA SOUFFLES WITH AMARETTI

The amaretti soaking liquid can be served as a sauce to accompany these fruity low-fat soufflés.

4 Servings
¼ teaspoon vegetable oil
3 tablespoons sugar plus more for sprinkling the ramekins
¼ cup brewed espresso or very strong coffee
1 tablespoon Marsala
4 amaretti cookies
3 ripe bananas (about 1 pound)
½ teaspoon fresh lemon juice
2 large egg whites
Pinch of salt

1. Preheat the oven to 400°. Coat four 1-cup ramekins with the vegetable oil, spreading it evenly with a paper towel. Sprinkle the ramekins with sugar; discard any excess.

2. In a small shallow soup plate, combine the espresso and Marsala. Add the amaretti cookies, flat side down, and let stand until the bottoms soften, about 20 minutes.

3. In a medium bowl, mash the bananas to a coarse puree with 2 tablespoons of the sugar. Stir in the lemon juice. In a medium bowl, beat the egg whites with the salt until soft peaks form. Add the remaining 1 tablespoon sugar and continue beating until glossy. Fold the egg whites into the banana puree until just combined.

4. Scrape the mixture into the prepared ramekins. Run your thumb around the inside edge of each ramekin to ensure even rising.

5. Bake the soufflés in the middle of the oven for 5 minutes. Remove the amaretti cookies from the soaking liquid and gently place 1 on each soufflé, soaked side down. Continue baking the soufflés for about 4 minutes longer, until they are puffed and barely set. Transfer the soufflés to individual plates. If you like, break open each soufflé alongside the cookie and spoon a little of the soaking liquid inside. Serve at once.
—Marcia Kiesel

FIVE TIPS FOR HIGH-RISING SOUFFLES

• Make sure your egg whites are firm but not overbeaten or dry.

• Fold the egg whites into the soufflé base until just combined; don't overmix or the whites will deflate.

• After you've filled the ramekins, run your thumb around the inside edge. This prevents the soufflés from sticking to the sides and helps them rise taller and straighter.

• Steady, uninterrupted heat is necessary for the soufflés to rise properly. Open the oven door during baking only when specified in the recipe.

• Don't overcook the soufflés. They should be a bit runny in the center.

Stir the granita
every 30 minutes
during freezing to
incorporate the ice
crystals that have
formed on the
bottom and sides
of the pan into the
mixture; if it is not
stirred regularly, it
will freeze solid. A
fork is the best
utensil to use for
stirring because the
tips of the tines can
be used to break up
larger ice crystals.
—Michele Scicolone

MIXED BERRY SHORTCAKE

Any combination of summer berries can
be used in this satisfying dessert. If you
omit the frozen yogurt, you will save 50
calories a serving.

4 Servings

3 **cups mixed summer berries,
such as raspberries, blueberries
and halved strawberries**
¼ **cup plus 1 teaspoon sugar**
1 **tablespoon orange liqueur**
½ **teaspoon finely grated orange zest**
1 **cup all-purpose flour**
1½ **teaspoons baking powder**
¼ **teaspoon baking soda
Pinch of salt**
2 **tablespoons cold vegetable
shortening**
½ **cup low-fat buttermilk**
1 **large egg white, lightly beaten
with 1 teaspoon water**
1 **cup nonfat frozen vanilla yogurt
(optional), for serving**

1. In a medium bowl, combine the
berries, 2 tablespoons of the sugar, the
orange liqueur and orange zest. Stir gently
to coat the berries, then cover and refrigerate for 2 hours.

2. Preheat the oven to 425°. Lightly
coat a cookie sheet with vegetable-oil
cooking spray.

3. In a large bowl, toss the flour with 2
tablespoons of the sugar, the baking powder, baking soda and salt. Using a pastry
blender or 2 knives, cut in the shortening
until it resembles coarse meal. Pour over
the buttermilk and stir with a fork to form
a soft dough.

4. Transfer the dough to the prepared
cookie sheet and pat it into a 6-inch disk,
about ½ inch thick. Lightly brush with the
egg white wash and sprinkle with the

remaining 1 teaspoon sugar. Using a
sharp knife, cut the dough into quarters.
Bake the wedges for about 15 minutes,
until golden and cooked through.
Transfer to a wire rack and let cool until
warm, about 5 minutes.

5. Split each shortcake wedge in half
horizontally and set a bottom half on
each plate. Spoon the berry mixture over
the shortcake and cover with the tops.
Garnish each serving with ¼ cup of
frozen yogurt.

—Georgia Chan Downard

BLUEBERRY GRANITA

Lemon juice intensifies the flavor of this
purple-hued ice.

6 Servings

½ **cup sugar**
1 **pint blueberries, rinsed and
stemmed**
1 **tablespoon fresh lemon juice**

1. Chill a 13-by-9-inch baking dish,
preferably metal, in the freezer. In a small
saucepan, combine the sugar with 1 cup of
water. Bring to a simmer over moderate
heat and cook, swirling occasionally, until
the sugar dissolves, about 5 minutes. Let
cool completely.

2. In a food processor or blender, combine the blueberries and sugar syrup.
Process until smooth. Strain the mixture
through a fine sieve set over a medium
bowl, pressing down on the solids. Stir in
the lemon juice.

3. Pour the blueberry mixture into the
chilled baking dish. Freeze the mixture
until ice crystals form around the edges,
about 30 minutes. Stir the mixture well to
incorporate the ice. Continue freezing,
stirring every 30 minutes (see How to Stir
Granitas, at left), until all of the liquid

Clockwise from top: Frozen Caffè Latte (p. 236), Honeydew Granita (p. 292)
and Peach and Red Wine Granita (p. 296)

Many store-bought fruit juices make great granitas. Keep a batch of sugar syrup in a covered container in the refrigerator ready to add to the fruit juice. Using the following recipe as a guideline, add sugar syrup to taste and balance it with an extra squeeze or two of fresh lemon juice, depending on the sweetness of the fruit juice:

Boil ½ cup sugar with 1 cup water until the sugar dissolves. Let cool, then stir into 3 cups bottled fruit juice; add about 2 teaspoons of fresh lemon juice. Pour into a chilled 13-by-9-inch baking dish and freeze, stirring every 30 minutes, until all the liquid freezes completely. This will serve 8.

—Michele Scicolone

freezes completely, about 2 hours. Spoon the granita into bowls and serve.

—Michele Scicolone

■

HONEYDEW GRANITA

This delicious icy treat is full of intense melon flavor.

6 Servings
- ½ **cup sugar**
- 1 **very ripe honeydew melon (about 4 pounds), peeled and cut into 1-inch chunks**
- 3 **tablespoons fresh lemon juice**

1. Chill a 13-by-9-inch baking dish, preferably metal, in the freezer. In a small saucepan, combine the sugar with 1 cup of water. Bring to a simmer over moderate heat and cook, swirling occasionally, until the sugar dissolves, about 5 minutes. Let cool completely. In a food processor or blender, working in 2 batches, combine the melon with the sugar syrup and lemon juice. Process until smooth.

2. Pour the melon mixture into the chilled baking dish. Freeze until ice crystals form around the edges, about 30 minutes. Stir well to incorporate the ice. Continue freezing, stirring every 30 minutes (see How to Stir Granitas, p. 290), until all the liquid freezes completely, about 3 hours. Spoon into bowls and serve.

—Michele Scicolone

■

MELON WITH MINT-LIME SYRUP AND JALAPENO

Cantaloupe and honeydew in a lime-and-mint-infused syrup are sprinkled with minced jalapeño for an unexpected kick.

4 Servings
- ½ **cup sugar**
- 2 **tablespoons fresh lime juice**
- ¼ **cup coarsely chopped fresh mint**
- 1 **small ripe honeydew (about 2 pounds), peeled and cut into 1-inch cubes**
- 1 **ripe medium cantaloupe (about 1½ pounds), peeled and cut into 1-inch cubes**
- 2 **teaspoons minced jalapeño chile**

1. In a small nonreactive saucepan, bring the sugar and ½ cup of water to a boil over moderately high heat. Lower the heat and simmer until the sugar is dissolved, about 3 minutes. Let cool completely. Stir in the lime juice and mint. Cover and refrigerate until chilled, at least 1 hour.

2. In a large bowl, combine the honeydew and cantaloupe cubes. Add the chilled syrup and jalapeño and toss gently to combine. Spoon the melon and syrup into 4 glass coupes and serve.

—Janet Hazen

■

BRANDIED KUMQUATS

Wonderful to have on hand, these will keep in the refrigerator for two months. When ready to serve, chop the kumquats and ladle, along with some of their syrup, over ice cream.

Makes About 3½ Cups
- 1 **pound kumquats, stems removed Boiling water**
- 1 **cup sugar**
- ½ **cup brandy**

1. In a bowl, cover the kumquats with boiling water; drain. Place the kumquats and 1½ cups of cold water in a medium nonreactive saucepan. Bring to a boil,

cover and simmer over low heat, stirring once, for 8 minutes. Using a slotted spoon, transfer the fruit to a bowl.

2. Add the sugar to the boiling liquid, stir to dissolve and boil over moderately high heat, skimming off the foam occasionally, until reduced to ¾ cup, about 10 minutes. Remove from the heat. Return the kumquats to the syrup and let cool to room temperature. Stir in the brandy.

—Diana Sturgis

■

LEMON PUDDING PARFAIT

The lemon pudding in this recipe is actually tart lemon curd lightened with cream. It is layered with fresh berries and whipped cream in a parfait glass. When available, blueberries make a nice alternative to raspberries.

6 Servings

- **4 large egg yolks**
- **2 large eggs**
- **⅔ cup fresh lemon juice (from 3 to 4 lemons)**
- **½ cup sugar**
- **4 tablespoons unsalted butter, cut into tablespoons**
  Finely grated zest of 1 lemon
- **½ pint heavy cream, preferably not ultrapasteurized, chilled**
- **1 pint fresh raspberries**

1. In the top of a double boiler, gently whisk the egg yolks, whole eggs, lemon juice, sugar, butter and lemon zest. Cook over boiling water, stirring constantly and scraping the bottom of the pan to prevent the eggs from overcooking, until the mixture thickens and reaches 165° to 170°, about 15 minutes. Immediately strain the curd through a sieve into a medium heatproof bowl, cover with

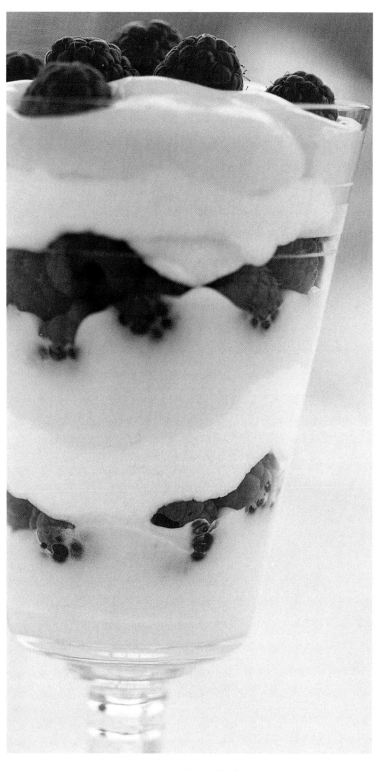

Lemon Pudding Parfait

plastic wrap and refrigerate until chilled, about 4 hours. (The curd can be made up to 1 week ahead.)

2. To assemble the parfaits, whip the heavy cream until it forms soft peaks. Stir half of the whipped cream into the lemon base. In 6 parfait glasses or wineglasses, alternate layers of lemon cream, raspberries and plain whipped cream, ending with the lemon cream. Sprinkle a few raspberries on top. Serve at once or refrigerate for up to 2 hours.

—Shelley Boris

■

LEMON POTS DE CREME

Smooth and light, with a gentle pucker, these individual golden lemon creams make a delightful dessert. They're delicious with crisp biscotti or a comforting madeleine.

4 Servings
½ **cup sugar**
½ **cup fresh lemon juice**
6 **large egg yolks**
1½ **cups heavy cream**

1. Preheat the oven to 325°. In a small bowl, stir the sugar with the lemon juice until thoroughly dissolved.

2. In a large bowl, gently whisk the egg yolks with the heavy cream. Whisk in the lemon juice mixture. Strain through a fine sieve or through several layers of cheesecloth set over a bowl. Let stand for 3 minutes and skim off any foam that rises to the surface.

3. Place four 1-cup custard cups or ramekins in a baking dish. Fill each cup about two-thirds full with the warm lemon cream. Place the baking dish in the oven. Pour enough hot tap water into the dish to reach halfway up the sides of the cups. Loosely cover the whole dish with

foil and bake for about 50 minutes, until the custards are just set around the edges but slightly loose in the center.

4. Carefully transfer the custard cups from the baking dish to a rack and let cool to room temperature. Cover loosely and refrigerate the custards for at least 3 hours or overnight. Serve chilled.

—Patricia Wells

■

CREAMY LEMON ICE

This refreshing ice is a cooling note at the end of a meal.

4 Servings
¾ **cup sugar**
½ **cup fresh lemon juice**
1½ **tablespoons finely grated lemon zest, preferably from organic lemons**
½ **cup heavy cream or crème fraîche**

1. In a small nonreactive saucepan, combine 1 cup of water with the sugar, lemon juice and lemon zest and bring to a boil over moderately high heat. Boil for 2 minutes, then strain the syrup into a medium bowl and let cool to room temperature.

2. Stir in the heavy cream. Transfer the mixture to an ice cream maker and process according to the manufacturer's instructions.

—Patricia Wells

■

LIME GRANITA

Made with fresh lime juice and flecks of grated peel, this frozen dessert is especially invigorating when topped with a splash of grappa, vodka or tequila.

8 Servings

¾ **cup sugar**
½ **cup fresh lime juice**
1 **teaspoon finely grated lime zest**

1. Chill a 13-by-9-inch baking dish, preferably metal, in the freezer. In a medium saucepan, combine the sugar with 3 cups of water. Bring to a simmer over moderate heat and cook, swirling occasionally, until the sugar dissolves, about 3 minutes. Let cool completely, then stir in the lime juice and zest.

2. Pour the lime mixture into the chilled baking dish. Freeze until ice crystals form around the edges, about 30 minutes. Stir well to incorporate the ice. Continue freezing, stirring every 30 minutes (see How to Stir Granitas, p. 290), until all the liquid freezes completely, about 2 hours. Spoon the granita into bowls and serve.

—Michele Scicolone

■

NECTARINE AND DRIED CHERRY CLAFOUTIS

Traditional French clafoutis, composed of fruit baked in an eggy batter, requires little adjusting to lower its fat content. Here, egg whites replace some of the whole eggs, and low-fat milk and yogurt are used instead of whole milk.

8 Servings

1 **tablespoon plus 1 teaspoon unsalted butter**
½ **cup plus 1 tablespoon granulated sugar**
½ **cup dried sour cherries***
¼ **cup plus 2 tablespoons all-purpose flour**
⅓ **cup whole blanched almonds (1 ounce)**
¼ **teaspoon salt**
1 **large egg**

3 **large egg whites**
¾ **cup low-fat (one percent) milk**
½ **cup plain whole-milk yogurt**
1 **teaspoon pure vanilla extract**
1½ **pounds firm ripe nectarines— halved, pitted and cut into ½-inch-thick wedges**
¼ **cup (packed) light brown sugar**
¼ **teaspoon cinnamon**
2 **teaspoons confectioners' sugar**

*Available at specialty food stores

1. Lightly grease a 10-inch glass or ceramic pie pan with 1 teaspoon of the butter and coat with 1 tablespoon of the granulated sugar. In a small bowl, soak the dried sour cherries in ½ cup of very hot water for 20 minutes. Drain well and set aside.

2. Preheat the oven to 400°. In a food processor, process the flour and almonds until the nuts are finely ground. Transfer to a medium bowl and stir in the salt. In another bowl, whisk the whole egg and egg whites until frothy. Stir in the milk, yogurt, the remaining ½ cup granulated sugar and the vanilla. Make a well in the almond flour and gradually whisk in the yogurt mixture until smooth. Let the batter rest for 10 minutes.

3. Meanwhile, melt the remaining 1 tablespoon butter in a large nonstick skillet. Add the nectarine wedges and cook over moderately high heat, stirring, for 2 minutes. Stir in the drained dried cherries and cook over moderate heat until the nectarine juices are exuded, about 2 minutes. Stir in the light brown sugar and the cinnamon. Cook, stirring occasionally, until the juices thicken and coat the fruit, 2 to 3 minutes.

4. Pour half of the batter into the prepared baking dish. Spoon the fruit over the batter in an even layer and cover with the remaining batter. Bake for about 45 minutes, or until the batter puffs up over the fruit and a small knife inserted in the

**Peachy Orange
Shake**

center comes out clean. Let cool for 20 minutes. Sift the confectioners' sugar on top of the clafoutis and serve warm.

—Ann Chantal Altman

■

NECTARINE CRUMBLE

This low-fat version uses less butter in the topping than most crisps or crumbles and is accompanied with thickened honey yogurt instead of whipped or ice cream.

8 Servings

- 1 **cup plain low-fat yogurt**
- 3 **pounds nectarines, pitted and cut into ½-inch-thick slices**
- 2 **tablespoons kirsch or plum or peach brandy**
- ¼ **cup plus 1 tablespoon mild-flavored honey, such as clover**
- 1 **cup old-fashioned rolled oats**
- ½ **cup all-purpose flour**
- ⅓ **cup (packed) dark brown sugar**
- ¼ **teaspoon freshly grated nutmeg**
- ¼ **teaspoon salt**
- 4 **tablespoons cold unsalted butter, cut into small bits**

1. Place the plain low-fat yogurt in a fine strainer set over a medium bowl. Allow the yogurt drain overnight in the refrigerator.

2. Preheat the oven to 375°. In a large bowl, toss the nectarines, kirsch and ¼ cup of the honey together. Spoon the mixture into a shallow 2-quart nonreactive baking dish.

3. In a medium bowl, combine the rolled oats, flour, dark brown sugar, nutmeg and salt. Work in the butter until the mixture resembles coarse crumbs. (The recipe can be prepared to this point up to 3 hours ahead. Set the fruit aside, covered, at room temperature and refrigerate the topping.)

4. Sprinkle the topping evenly over the nectarines. Bake for about 45 minutes, until lightly browned and bubbly. Let cool for at least 15 minutes.

5. In a small bowl, mix the thickened yogurt with the remaining 1 tablespoon honey. Serve with the warm crumble.

—Martha Rose Shulman

■

PEACHY ORANGE SHAKE

Peaches are pureed with buttermilk to make a refreshing no-fat dessert that celebrates summer fruit.

4 Servings

- 6 **ripe medium peaches, peeled and thickly sliced, plus 4 thin peach slices, for garnish**
- 8 **medium ice cubes**
- 2 **cups nonfat buttermilk**
- ¾ **cup fresh orange juice**
- ¼ **cup superfine sugar**
- ½ **teaspoon pure vanilla extract**
- 4 **thin orange slices, for garnish**
- 4 **fresh mint sprigs, for garnish**

In a blender, combine the thick peach slices with the ice cubes, buttermilk, orange juice, sugar and vanilla. Process until smooth. Pour the shake into 4 tall, chilled glasses and garnish each serving with a thin slice of peach and orange and a mint sprig.

—Andrea Chesman

■

PEACH AND RED WINE GRANITA

The classic Italian summer dessert of peaches in red wine inspires a zesty granita made with both these ingredients.

6 Servings

1½ **pounds large fresh peaches, peeled and thickly sliced**

¾ **cup sugar**

⅓ **cup dry red wine**

1 **tablespoon fresh lemon juice**

1. Chill a 13-by-9-inch baking dish, preferably metal, in the freezer. In a medium saucepan, combine the peaches with the sugar and 2 cups of water. Bring to a simmer over moderate heat. Lower the heat and cook, stirring occasionally, until the peaches are very tender when pierced with a fork, about 5 minutes. Let cool completely.

2. In a blender or food processor, working in 2 batches, combine the peaches and their cooking liquid with the wine and lemon juice. Process until smooth.

3. Pour the peach mixture into the chilled baking dish. Freeze until ice crystals form around the edges, about 40 minutes. Stir well to incorporate the ice. Continue freezing, stirring every 30 minutes (see How to Stir Granitas, p. 290), until all the liquid freezes completely, about 3 hours. Spoon the granita into bowls and serve.

—Michele Scicolone

■

SOURDOUGH BREAD PUDDING WITH CARAMELIZED PEARS

This pudding consists of chewy custard-soaked sourdough bread with a layer of juicy caramelized pears. It can either be served directly from the soufflé dish or unmolded onto a plate.

6 Servings

3 **large ripe Bartlett or Anjou pears**
Half of 1 lemon

3 **large eggs**

3 **large egg yolks**

1 **cup sugar**

2½ **cups whole milk**

1 **teaspoon pure vanilla extract**

¼ **teaspoon cinnamon**

¼ **teaspoon freshly grated nutmeg**

8 **slices dense sourdough bread (approximately 3 inches square by ¾ inch thick)**

3 **tablespoons unsalted butter, cut into tablespoons**

1 **vanilla bean, split**
Boiling water

1. Using a small sharp knife, peel, halve and core the pears. Slice them lengthwise ⅓ inch thick. Place in a medium bowl and squeeze the lemon half over the pear slices to prevent discoloration.

2. In a bowl, whisk the eggs with the egg yolks and ½ cup of the sugar.

3. In a small saucepan, warm the milk over moderately high heat until steaming. Whisk it into the egg mixture. Whisk in the vanilla extract, cinnamon and nutmeg. Add the bread and let soak, turning occasionally, until saturated, about 1 hour.

4. Preheat the oven to 350°. Lightly butter a 1½-quart soufflé dish.

5. Scatter the butter in a medium skillet. Sprinkle evenly with the remaining ½ cup sugar. Crisscross the split vanilla bean over the sugar and distribute the pears evenly on top. Cook over moderately high heat until the liquid is bubbling, syrupy and brown, about 20 minutes. (To avoid uneven browning, swirl the pan but do not stir. Watch closely; after the first 10 minutes it can burn.)

6. Neatly arrange the pears in the prepared soufflé dish, overlapping them slightly. Scrape the caramel on top. Remove the vanilla bean. Cover the pears with the soaked bread and pour any remaining custard on top.

7. Set the dish in a larger baking pan and place in the middle of the oven. Add enough boiling water to reach halfway up

Sourdough Bread Pudding with Carmelized Pears

the sides of the soufflé dish. Bake the pudding for about 1 hour, until golden and a knife inserted in the center comes out clean. Remove from the water bath and set aside to cool for 20 minutes.

8. To serve, run a thin knife around the inside of the soufflé dish. Invert onto a plate to unmold the pudding. Slice with a sharp knife and spoon into bowls. Alternatively, spoon the pudding from the soufflé dish into bowls; make sure you scoop up the pears and syrup from the bottom.

—Shelley Boris

■

STEAMED PEARS WITH RED WINE AND RASPBERRIES

These fragrant pears are first steamed until tender and then tossed in lightly sweetened red wine.

4 Servings

- **3 firm, ripe Anjou pears**
- **1 cup dry red wine**
- **3 tablespoons sugar**
- **½ pint fresh raspberries**

1. Peel, halve and core the pears. Put the pears in a steamer basket, cut sides down, and place over boiling water in a large saucepan. Cover and steam the pears over moderate heat until tender, about 5 minutes.

2. Meanwhile, combine the wine and sugar in a large serving bowl; stir to dissolve the sugar. Add the pears to the bowl along with the raspberries and let stand until cooled to room temperature. Serve as is or refrigerate and serve chilled.

—Stephanie Lyness

■

PEAR AND HONEY NAPOLEONS WITH HAZELNUTS

Sweet, tender fruit is frequently paired with a crunchy, buttery puff pastry, but how do you get that delightful contrast without all the fat? Wonton wrappers are one solution. Here, they are very lightly brushed with butter, then dipped in sugar, baked until crisp and layered with cooked fruit and a rich-tasting hazelnut-honey cream.

8 Servings

- **1 pint strawberries**
- **1 to 2 tablespoons pear brandy**
- **¾ cup sugar**
- **24 fresh wonton wrappers**
- **2 tablespoons unsalted butter, melted**
- **¼ cup hazelnuts (1 ounce)**
- **¼ cup fromage blanc* or Yogurt Cheese (p. 248)**
- **3 tablespoons mild honey**
- **2 teaspoons ground cinnamon** ➤

Steamed Pears with Red Wine and Raspberries

Pear and Honey Napoleon with Hazelnuts

8 medium Bartlett pears (about 3¼ pounds)
3 tablespoons fresh lemon juice
   Fresh mint sprigs, for garnish

*Available at specialty food stores

1. Preheat the oven to 375°. In a food processor, puree the strawberries with the pear brandy. Strain the strawberry sauce into a small bowl.

2. Line 2 large baking sheets with parchment paper. Place ½ cup of the sugar in a shallow bowl. For each wonton wrapper, lightly brush 1 side with a little of the melted butter and press the buttered side into the sugar. Repeat on the other side. Place the sugared wonton wrappers on the prepared baking sheets and bake, 1 sheet at a time, for 4 minutes. Turn the wrappers over and bake for 3 to 4 minutes longer, or until golden brown and caramelized. Transfer the wrappers to a rack to cool and bake the rest. (The recipe can be prepared to this point up to 1 day ahead. Cover and refrigerate the strawberry sauce. Store the wonton wrappers in an airtight container.)

3. Place the hazelnuts in a pie plate and toast in the oven for 8 to 10 minutes, or until fragrant. Wrap the nuts in a kitchen towel and let cool for 2 minutes. Rub them in the towel to remove the skins. Finely chop the hazelnuts and combine them with the *fromage blanc* and honey in a small bowl.

4. Lower the oven temperature to 350°. Line the baking sheets with fresh parchment paper. In a small bowl, combine the remaining ¼ cup of sugar and the ground cinnamon.

5. Peel, halve and core the pears. Transfer the pears to a large bowl and sprinkle them with the lemon juice. Place the pear halves on a work surface, cut side down, and thinly slice each of the halves crosswise.

6. Using a long flat spatula, transfer the pears to the baking sheets and press lightly on each half to fan out the slices slightly. Sprinkle with the cinnamon sugar. Bake the pears on the upper and lower racks of the oven for about 18 minutes, switching the pans halfway through cooking, until the fruit is soft and lightly colored. Let cool for 3 minutes. Separate the wider bottom halves of the pears from the narrower tops.

7. Lay a caramelized wonton wrapper on each dessert plate. Set a wide pear section on each wonton and top with a slightly rounded teaspoon of the hazelnut-honey cream. Cover with another wonton wrapper and place 2 narrow pear sections on top of each, overlapping the sections in opposite directions. Top with another rounded teaspoon of the hazelnut mixture. Finish with a third wonton wrapper, topped with the remaining broad pear section. Spoon 2 tablespoons of the strawberry sauce around each napoleon and garnish with mint sprigs.

—Ann Chantal Altman

CARAMELIZED PINEAPPLE WITH GRILLED BANANAS AND TAHITIAN VANILLA SAUCE

For this dessert, use firm, slightly under-ripe bananas that will hold their shape during cooking.

❦ The aromatic grapiness of Muscat de Beaumes-de-Venise from the Rhône Valley in France is a good match for the pointed flavors of vanilla, lemon and pineapple in this dessert. A 1990 Chapoutier or nonvintage Prosper Maufoux is an excellent choice.

8 Servings

- 1 **vanilla bean, split lengthwise**
- 1 **cup low-fat (one percent) milk**
- 1 **1-inch strip of lemon zest**
- 2 **large egg yolks**
  About ½ cup sugar
- ⅛ **teaspoon salt**
- 1 **medium pineapple (about 2¼ pounds)**
- 4 **slightly underripe medium bananas**
- 2 **tablespoons sugar-free pineapple jam or honey**
- 2 **tablespoons fresh lemon juice**
- 2 **tablespoons safflower oil**
  Fresh mint sprigs, for garnish

1. Scrape the seeds from the vanilla bean into a small heavy saucepan and add the bean. Add the milk and lemon zest and cook over moderate heat until small bubbles form around the edge of the pan. Cover, remove from the heat and let steep for 15 minutes.

2. Meanwhile, in a small bowl, beat the egg yolks and 3 tablespoons of the sugar until thick and pale, about 5 minutes. Reheat the milk to a simmer, then whisk the hot milk into the egg yolks. Return the mixture to the saucepan and cook over moderate heat, stirring constantly, until the custard just starts to thicken and reaches 160° on a candy thermometer, 3 to 4 minutes. Immediately strain the custard into a medium bowl and stir in the salt. (The sauce can be prepared up to 1 day ahead; cover and refrigerate.)

3. Trim off the top and bottom of the pineapple and slice off the skin. Using the tip of a vegetable peeler, remove the eyes. Cut the pineapple into eight ½-inch thick crosswise slices and cut out the core with a pineapple or apple corer or a sharp knife.

4. Heat a large nonstick skillet. Sprinkle 2 pineapple rings with 1 teaspoon of sugar each. Place the rings in the pan, sugared side down, and cook over high heat until the edges begin to caramelize, 2 to 3 minutes. Sprinkle each ring with 1 teaspoon sugar, turn them over and cook until the other side is caramelized, about 2 minutes. Transfer to a large plate. Repeat with the remaining pineapple rings and sugar. Spoon the caramelized juices from the skillet over the pineapple and set aside at room temperature for up to 2 hours.

5. Light a grill or heat a large heavy skillet. Cut the bananas in half lengthwise and then in half crosswise. In a small bowl, combine the jam and lemon juice. Brush the grill or skillet lightly with the oil (if using a skillet, you won't need as much oil). Add the bananas, cut side down (if grilling, arrange the bananas diagonally across the grill). Brush the banana tops lightly with the jam and grill or sauté until lightly browned, 2 to 3 minutes. Turn the banana quarters over and cook for 2 minutes longer.

6. To serve, arrange 2 banana quarters on each dessert plate and top with a caramelized pineapple ring, spooning any exuded juices over the pineapple. Spoon 1½ tablespoons of the custard sauce in a zigzag pattern over each serving and garnish the desserts with fresh mint sprigs.

—Ann Chantal Altman

Caramelized Pineapple with Grilled Bananas and Tahitian Vanilla Sauce (p. 301)

PLUM COBBLER

Fruit, with almost all its calories derived from carbohydrates, is a logical starting point for developing low-fat desserts. In this recipe, caramelized wedges of fruit are baked under a light biscuit topping.

♈ A slightly sweet sparkling wine would harmonize nicely with the sugariness of the cobbler, while its effervescence would provide a pleasing contrast. A demi-sec cuvée, such as the 1988 Schramsberg Crémant from California, is one possibility; another is a Moscato d'Asti from Italy, such as the nonvintage Bera.

8 Servings

- ¾ **cup all-purpose flour**
- ¾ **cup sugar**
- 1 **teaspoon baking powder**
  Pinch of salt
- ¼ **cup cold part-skim ricotta**
- 2 **tablespoons cold low-fat (one percent) milk**
- 3 **tablespoons cold unsalted butter, cut into small bits**
- 2 **drops pure almond extract**
- 1 **tablespoon corn syrup**
- 3 **pounds red plums—halved, pitted and cut into ¾-inch wedges**

1. In a food processor, combine the flour, ¼ cup of the sugar, the baking powder and salt. Process for 10 seconds. Add the ricotta, milk, 2 tablespoons of the butter and the almond extract and pulse until the dough just begins to come together in a ball. Pat the dough into a 5-inch disk, wrap well and refrigerate for at least 1 or for up to 24 hours.

2. In a heavy 10-inch ovenproof skillet, combine the remaining ½ cup sugar with the corn syrup and 2 tablespoons of water. Cook over high heat without stirring until

Plum Cobbler

a rich brown caramel forms, 6 to 8 minutes. Add the remaining 1 tablespoon butter and the plums and stir gently; the caramel may harden but will melt again. Cook, stirring occasionally, until the plums are coated with caramel and their juices are red and syrupy, about 8 minutes.

3. Pour the plums into a strainer set over a medium bowl. Let the plums cool for 10 minutes. Return the syrup to the skillet and cook over high heat until thickened, about 2 minutes.

4. Preheat the oven to 375°. On a lightly floured surface, roll out the chilled dough into a 10-inch round. Return the plums to the syrup in the skillet, spreading them out evenly. Lay the dough carefully on top of the plums, tucking in any edges. Cut 6 small slashes in the top of the dough to vent steam. Bake the cobbler for 30 to 35 minutes, or until the pastry is lightly browned. Let cool for 15 minutes before serving.

—Ann Chantal Altman

From left:
**Strawberry
Semifreddo
(p. 306)**

**Rhubarb
Compote with
Strawberries**

**Strawberry
Meringues
(p. 307)**

**Strawberries
Melba**

**Strawberries
in Champagne
Jelly (p. 308)**

■

RHUBARB COMPOTE WITH STRAWBERRIES

The berries, stirred into the warm poached rhubarb, soften slightly and flavor the tart fruit. A spoonful of vanilla yogurt adds a creamy flourish.

4 Servings

½ cup sugar
¾ pound fresh rhubarb, trimmed and cut into ¾-inch lengths
1 pint strawberries, hulled and thickly sliced
½ cup low-fat vanilla yogurt

1. In a medium saucepan, combine the sugar with 1½ cups of water. Bring to a boil over moderate heat, stirring occasionally, until the sugar is dissolved. Add the rhubarb and cook gently without stirring until just tender when pierced with a sharp knife, about 2 minutes. Don't overcook or the rhubarb will fall apart. Transfer the rhubarb and syrup to a medium bowl and let cool until warm.

2. Gently stir the sliced strawberries into the rhubarb compote. Cover and refrigerate until chilled, about 2 hours. Spoon into glass bowls and top each serving with 2 tablespoons of vanilla yogurt.

—Diana Sturgis

■

STRAWBERRIES MELBA

This twist on the classic peach melba is made with strawberry ice cream and sliced strawberries instead of vanilla ice cream and peaches. Serve with your favorite crisp cookies.

6 Servings

Strawberry ice cream:

¾ cup sugar

1 3-inch piece of vanilla bean, split

1½ cups heavy cream

3 large egg yolks

1½ pints strawberries—rinsed, dried and hulled

Pure vanilla extract (optional)

Raspberry sauce:

1 pint raspberries

¼ cup sugar

1 pint strawberries—rinsed, dried, hulled and thinly sliced lengthwise

About 1 tablespoon sugar

1. Make the strawberry ice cream: Place ¼ cup of the sugar in a heavy medium saucepan. Using the tip of a knife, scrape the seeds from the vanilla bean into the saucepan and add the bean. Using a wooden spoon, stir in the heavy cream and cook over moderate heat until the mixture begins to steam and bubbles appear around the edge of the pan.

2. In a medium bowl, lightly whisk the egg yolks. Whisk in the hot cream. Pour the mixture into the saucepan and cook over low heat, stirring with a wooden spoon, until the custard coats the spoon and reaches 170°, about 9 minutes. Do not overcook.

3. Strain the custard into a large bowl. Cover and refrigerate until cold, at least 2 hours. (Alternatively, set the bowl in a larger bowl of ice water and stir occasionally until chilled, about 30 minutes.)

4. Meanwhile, in a medium bowl, using a whisk or potato masher, coarsely crush the strawberries. Stir in the remaining ½ cup sugar. Set aside to macerate for 2 hours.

5. Mix the crushed strawberries into the chilled custard and flavor to taste with vanilla extract, if desired. Transfer the

strawberry custard to an ice cream maker and freeze according to the manufacturer's instructions.

6. Make the raspberry sauce: In a food processor, puree the raspberries. Strain over a bowl. Stir in the sugar until it dissolves, then stir in 2 tablespoons of water. (The sauce can be refrigerated overnight or frozen for up to 1 week.)

7. To serve, toss the sliced strawberries with the 1 tablespoon sugar; add more sugar if the berries are very tart. Scoop the ice cream into bowls, spoon the strawberries on top and drizzle the raspberry sauce over all.

—Lindsey Shere

■

STRAWBERRY SEMIFREDDO

This version of the classic Italian frozen dessert is made by layering vanilla sponge cake with homemade mascarpone and sugared strawberries. The mascarpone has a wonderful flavor and lovely soft texture; begin making it several days ahead. You can substitute about two and a half cups of store-bought mascarpone, if you prefer, with fine results.

8 to 10 Servings

- ½ cup unbleached all-purpose flour
- ⅓ cup cake flour
- ½ teaspoon nonaluminum baking powder (see Baking Powder, p. 308)
- ⅛ teaspoon salt
- 5 large eggs, at room temperature
- ¾ cup sugar
- 1 teaspoon pure vanilla extract
- 2 teaspoons milk, warmed
- 1 teaspoon kirsch, for brushing the cake
- 2 pints strawberries—rinsed, dried and hulled

- 2 tablespoons sugar
  Homemade Mascarpone (recipe follows)

1. Preheat the oven to 325°. Grease a 10-by-15-inch jelly-roll pan and line the pan with parchment or wax paper. Sift together the all-purpose flour, cake flour, baking powder and salt.

2. In a stainless steel bowl set over a pan of simmering water, whisk the eggs and sugar until warm, about 5 minutes; remove from the heat. Using a hand-held electric mixer, beat until the eggs are light and hold a ribbon on the surface for 3 seconds when the beaters are lifted, about 7 minutes.

3. Sprinkle in the vanilla and sift a third of the dry ingredients over the eggs. Using a whisk, fold them in until almost incorporated. Fold in the remaining dry ingredients in 2 batches, stopping just when all traces of flour disappear. Using a rubber spatula, quickly fold in the milk.

4. Pour the cake batter evenly into the prepared pan, tilting the pan to spread the batter. Gently smooth the surface with the spatula. Bake for about 25 minutes, or until golden brown and springy when pressed gently in the center. Let cool. (The cake can be made up to 2 days ahead. Cover the pan with foil and store at room temperature.)

5. In a small bowl, stir the kirsch with 6 tablespoons of water. Chop three-quarters of the hulled strawberries, place them in a bowl and stir in 1½ tablespoons of the sugar.

6. Spread a quarter of the Homemade Mascarpone over the bottom of an 8-inch round or square glass bowl or dish. Cut pieces of the sponge cake to cover the mascarpone (it isn't necessary to cover every bit). Brush the sponge cake with a third of the kirsch. Spread another quarter of the mascarpone on the cake. Spoon half the sugared strawberries evenly on top. Repeat the layering of cake, kirsch,

mascarpone and the remaining sugared berries. Add a layer of the remaining cake, brush with the remaining kirsch and spread the remaining mascarpone on top. Cover and refrigerate for 8 hours or overnight.

7. To serve, slice or halve the remaining strawberries, place in a small bowl and stir in the remaining ½ tablespoon sugar. Decorate the top of the semifreddo with the strawberries and scoop neatly onto plates.

Homemade Mascarpone
Makes 2½ Cups

- 2 cups heavy cream
- ⅛ teaspoon tartaric acid*
- 2 large eggs
- 2 tablespoons sugar

*Available at wine-making supply stores and some pharmacies

1. In a stainless steel bowl set over a saucepan of simmering water, stir the heavy cream until it reaches a temperature of 180°, about 15 minutes. Add the tartaric acid and stir for 30 seconds. Remove the bowl from the heat and stir the cream for 2 minutes. Transfer the cream to a nonreactive container and let cool, then cover and refrigerate for at least 2 and up to 4 days.

2. Whisk the eggs and the sugar in a stainless steel bowl set over simmering water until they reach a temperature of 150°, about 10 minutes. Place the bowl with the eggs and sugar in a larger bowl of ice water and chill for 20 minutes, stirring occasionally.

3. In a medium bowl, using a hand-held electric mixer, beat the chilled cream until it forms soft folds. Beat in the chilled egg mixture until it has the texture of very softly whipped cream. Refrigerate for 1 hour before using.

—Lindsey Shere

■

STRAWBERRY MERINGUES

Here is a dessert full of contrasts in tastes and textures: crunchy sweet meringues, billowy whipped cream and refreshing juicy berries. You will need a pastry bag to pipe out the meringue shells.

8 Servings

- 3 large egg whites, at room temperature
  Pinch of cream of tartar
  Pinch of salt
- 1 cup sugar
- ½ of a vanilla bean, split
- 2 pints strawberries
- 1½ cups heavy cream, chilled
- ¼ teaspoon pure vanilla extract
- 2 tablespoons coarsely crushed amaretti cookies

1. Preheat the oven to 200°. Butter and flour a large baking sheet and, using a glass or can as a template, mark eight 4-inch circles on the sheet.

2. Rinse a large bowl with hot water and dry it. Place the egg whites in the bowl and, using a hand-held electric mixer, beat until foamy. Add the cream of tartar and salt and beat until soft peaks form. Then beat in 9 tablespoons of the sugar, 1 tablespoon at a time, until the whites hold stiff peaks.

3. Using the tip of a knife, scrape the seeds from the vanilla bean into 3 tablespoons of the sugar and stir well. Fold the vanilla sugar into the egg whites with a rubber spatula until evenly incorporated.

4. Scoop the meringue into a pastry bag fitted with a ¼-inch fluted tip. Pipe the meringue in spirals to fill in the circles marked on the baking sheet; then build up the sides to give each meringue a rim about ½ inch high. Bake for about 1½ hours, until the meringues are crisp and

very lightly colored. (The meringues can be made up to 2 days ahead; store carefully in an airtight container.)

5. Rinse and dry the strawberries. Using a small sharp knife, hull the berries and thinly slice lengthwise. Place the berries in a bowl and toss them with 3 tablespoons of the sugar. Refrigerate until cold, 1 to 2 hours.

6. In a medium bowl, using the electric mixer, whip the chilled heavy cream with the remaining 1 tablespoon sugar and the vanilla extract until it forms soft peaks.

7. To serve, place the meringue shells on plates. Spoon the whipped cream into the shells. Spoon the strawberries and their juice over the whipped cream and sprinkle the amaretti crumbs over all. Serve at once.

—Lindsey Shere

■

STRAWBERRIES IN CHAMPAGNE JELLY

Making your own gelatin desserts will be a revelation if your only experience is with the hard-gelled artificially flavored commercial product. This recipe uses Champagne, but you might be inspired to make jellies with other wines or fresh fruit juices using the method described below. Serve this elegant, light dessert with crisp cookies of your choice.

6 Servings
1 envelope plus 1 teaspoon unflavored powdered gelatin (3½ teaspoons)
¾ cup plus 3 tablespoons sugar
1 bottle (750 ml) dry Champagne
1 pint strawberries

1. In a medium nonreactive saucepan, sprinkle the gelatin over 1 cup of water. Let soften until no dry spots are visible,

about 5 minutes. Place the saucepan over low heat and melt the gelatin, stirring with a wooden spoon just until no lumps remain; do not overcook. Remove from the heat and stir in ¾ cup plus 2 tablespoons of the sugar until thoroughly dissolved. Pour in the Champagne and stir briefly. Pour into a shallow bowl or a plastic container, cover and refrigerate until set, 6 hours or overnight.

2. Rinse the strawberries in a colander. Transfer to paper towels to drain; pat dry. Using a small sharp knife, hull the berries and thinly slice lengthwise.

3. To assemble, toss the sliced strawberries with the remaining 1 tablespoon sugar. Chop the gelatin with a knife or scramble in the bowl with a fork. Using about ½ cup gelatin per serving, layer one third in the bottom of a wineglass; add a layer of berries. Repeat the layering twice. Drizzle a little juice from the berries over the top. Serve cold. (You can refrigerate this dessert up to 4 hours ahead. Add the last layer of berries and the juice just before serving.)

—Lindsey Shere

■

STRAWBERRY SHORTCAKE

This shortcake is the real thing, made with biscuits, not cake.

4 Servings
1 pint strawberries—rinsed, hulled and thinly sliced lengthwise
2 tablespoons plus 3 teaspoons granulated sugar
1½ cups all-purpose flour
2¼ teaspoons nonaluminum baking powder (see Baking Powder, at left)
⅜ teaspoon salt
2 cups heavy cream, chilled
⅛ teaspoon pure vanilla extract
Confectioners' sugar, for dusting

1. In a medium bowl, toss the strawberries with 2 tablespoons of the granulated sugar. Refrigerate for 1 hour.

2. Preheat the oven to 400°. Lightly grease a large baking sheet. In a medium bowl, mix the flour, baking powder, salt and 2 teaspoons of the granulated sugar. Stir in 1 cup less 1 tablespoon of the heavy cream until just combined. Knead briefly.

3. Turn the dough out on a lightly floured surface and roll out to a scant ½-inch thickness. Using a biscuit cutter or a glass, cut out eight 2½-inch rounds. Place on the prepared baking sheet and bake them for 10 to 12 minutes, or until golden.

4. In a large bowl, using a hand-held electric mixer, whip the remaining 1 cup plus 1 tablespoon of heavy cream and 1 teaspoon of granulated sugar with the vanilla extract until the mixture holds a soft shape.

5. To serve, split the shortcakes horizontally and place 2 bottoms on each of 4 dessert plates. Spoon the strawberries and their juices on top of the biscuits. Dollop with whipped cream. Cover with the shortcake tops, set slightly askew. Lightly sift confectioners' sugar over the biscuit tops and serve.

—Lindsey Shere

Strawberry Shortcake

INDEX

Page numbers in **boldface** indicate photographs

A

Aioli, 85
ALMONDS
Almond-Date Haroset, 16
Basque-Flavored Pudding with
Almond Praline, **238**, 240
Coffee-Almond Layer Cake with
Raspberries, **246**, 247
Estouffade of Beef with Apricots,
Almonds and Raisins, **112**, 113
Italian Almond Tart, 278, **279**
ANCHOVIES
Celery Salad with Anchovy
Dressing, 50
Green Olive and Anchovy Puree,
10, 12
Pasta Puttanesca, 139
APPETIZERS, 11-24
APPLES
Apple-Cranberry Crumb Tart, 272,
272
Apple Haroset, 16
Apple Polenta Tart, 269
Apple Tartlets with Browned Butter
Filling, 270, **271**
Double-Crusted Apple-Cranberry
Pie, **268**, 269
Green Apple Sorbet with Calvados,
286, 287
Stir-Fried Collards with Apple and
Balsamic Vinegar, 173
ARTICHOKES
Artichoke Hearts with Tomatoes
and Balsamic Vinegar, 159
Baby Artichoke, Spinach and Fava
Bean Ragout, 164, **165**
Marinated Baby Artichokes in
Oil, 21
ASPARAGUS
Gratinéed Asparagus with
Parmesan and Fried Eggs, 160

B

BACON
Choucroute Garnie, 124, **125**
Potato Salad with Green Beans,
Bacon and Cremini Mushrooms, 51
BANANAS
Banana Madeleines, 259

Banana Raita, 129, **130**
Banana Soufflés with Amaretti, 289
Bananas in Orange-Caramel Sauce,
287
Blueberry-Banana Crumb Cake, 256
Caramelized Pineapple with Grilled
Bananas and Tahitian Vanilla
Sauce, 301, **302**
Chocolate Banana Ice Cream
Sandwiches, 288, **288**
BASIL
Capellini with Fresh Tomatoes,
Basil and Garlic Croutons, **134**, 135
Chilled Tomato Soup with Garlic
Oil, Basil and Mint, 27
Grilled Pizza with Tomato, Basil
and Prosciutto, 198, **201**
Soup of Broken Pasta and Beans
with Fresh Basil, 41
BEANS AND PEAS, DRIED
Chickpea and Celery Salad, 50
Curried Mussel Soup with Red
Lentils and Yogurt, 33
New Year's Peas and Greens, 166,
166
Smoky Beef and Red Bean Chili, 115
Turkey and Pinto Bean Chili, 96
See also Black Beans; White Beans
BEANS, GREEN
Blue Lake Beans with Red Wine–
Sweet Onion Pickle, 161, **162**
Green Beans with Tomato and
Fresh Coriander, 161
Potato Salad with Green Beans,
Bacon and Cremini
Mushrooms, 51
Spicy Tuna and Green Bean Salad
with Tomatoes, 79, **80**
See also Fava Beans
BEEF
Estouffade of Beef with Apricots,
Almonds and Raisins, **112**, 113
Middle Eastern Meatballs with
Swiss Chard, **116**, 117
Mom's Brisket with Dried Fruits,
110, **111**
New York Bowl of Red, 114
Penne with Ragù of Ground Pork
and Beef, 147
Smoky Beef and Red Bean Chili, 115
Wine-Merchant Steak, 109, **109**
BERRIES
Blackberry Dressing, 104

Mixed Berry Shortcake, 290
Roulé Confiture with Raspberry
Coulis and Summer Berries, 252
See also Blueberries; Cranberries;
Raspberries; Strawberries
BLACK BEANS
Black Bean Dip with Garlic, **10**, 11
Black Bean Salad with Chipotle
Vinaigrette, 46, **48**
Pork and Black Bean Chili Verde,
123
BLUEBERRIES
Blueberry-Banana Crumb Cake, 256
Blueberry Granita, 290
BREAD
Black Pepper Sally Lunn Bread, 215
Onion-Parmesan Flat Bread, 217
Potato Flat Bread, 216
Sesame and Flaxseed Bread, 213
White and Whole Wheat Bread,
213, **214**
See also Breads, Toasted; Corn
Breads; Stuffing
BREADS, TOASTED
Duck Liver Crostini, 100, **102**
Mushroom Toasts, 103
Pita Crisps, 11
BROCCOLI
Broccoli-Sauced Cauliflower, 168
Grilled Broccoli-Stuffed Onions, 167
Peppery Grilled Pizza with Broccoli,
Sausage and Pecorino, **198**, 202
Skillet-Steamed Broccoli with
Lemon, 167
BULGUR
Bulgur Salad with Watercress and
Sunflower Seeds, 53
Bulgur Stuffing with Pears and
Pecans, 190

C

CABBAGE
Choucroute Garnie, 124
Mustard Slaw, 49, **49**
Stir-Fried Cabbage with Green and
Red Peppers, 169
CAKE FILLINGS AND FROSTINGS
Buttercream (Orange), 248
Chocolate Ganache, 254
Coffee Buttercream, 247
Gianduja Mousse, 250

Glaze (Chocolate), 251
Italian Meringue, 254
CAKES
Bûche de Noël, 253
Blueberry-Banana Crumb Cake, 256
Chocolate Cake, 233
Chocolate Hazelnut Cake, 250
Coffee-Almond Layer Cake with
   Raspberries, **246**, 247
Genoise Sponge Sheets, 253
Gingerbread-Pear Cake, 255, **255**
Hazelnut Pound Cake, 257
Orange Layer Cake with Orange
   Buttercream Frosting, 248, **249**
Pumpkin Coffee Cake, 258
Roulé Confiture with Raspberry
   Coulis and Summer Berries, 252
Simone Beck's Chocolate Cake,
   250, 251
See also Cake Fillings and Frostings
Capon, Roast, 93
Caponata, 15
CARROTS
Carrot and Parsley Salad, 51
Carrots with Cornichon Dressing,
   50, 51
Curried Chicken with Spinach and
   Carrots, 89
Zucchini and Carrots Parmesan, 178
CAULIFLOWER
Broccoli-Sauced Cauliflower, 168
Penne with Cauliflower, Onions and
   Olive Oil, 138, **138**
Quick Pickled Cauliflower, 227
CELERY
Celery Salad with Anchovy
   Dressing, 50
Chickpea and Celery Salad, 50
Marinated Fennel, Pearl Onions
   and Celery, 169
Mushroom and Celery Root
   Galette, 206, **209**
Shrimp Salad with Celery, Olives
   and Tomatoes, 58
CHEESE
Cornmeal Pizzas with Spinach, Red
   Onion and Asiago Cheese, 204, **204**
Cheddar Corn Biscuits, 220
Cheese Grits Soufflé over Turnip
   Greens, 155
Creamy Polenta with Butter and
   Cheese, 156
Farfalle with Spicy Sausage and
   Smoked Mozzarella, 149
Grilled Pizza Bianca with
   Portobellos, Eggplant and Three
   Cheeses, 199
Peppery Grilled Pizza with Broccoli,
   Sausage and Peccorino, **198**, 202
Spicy Grilled Pizza with White Corn
   and Two Cheeses, **198**, 200

Winter Squash and Blue Cheese
   Galette, **210**, 211
Yogurt Cheese, 248
See also Cream Cheese; Goat
   Cheese; Parmesan; Ricotta
Cheesecake, Arline Rodman's
   Minnesota, 243, **244**
CHESTNUTS
Corn Bread and Chestnut Stuffing,
   184, 185
Oven-Roasted Parsnips with Onions
   and Chestnuts, 175
CHICKEN
Chicken Broth with Fregula, 36, **37**
Chicken in Green Sauce, 85
Curried Chicken Moghlai, 90
Curried Chicken with Spinach and
   Carrots, 89
Garlicky Chicken, 84
Roast Chicken with Herbs, **82**, 83
Steamed Chicken with Chinese
   Mushrooms, 83
Stewed Chicken with Pastis, 86, **87**
Thai Chicken and Eggplant Curry,
   88
See also Liver; Stock
CHILE PEPPERS
Black Bean Salad with Chipotle
   Vinaigrette, 46, **48**
Chicken in Green Sauce, 85
Corn, Squash and Green Chile
   Stew, 179
Fiery Cream Cheese Dip, 12
Lump Crab Chiles Rellenos with
   Chimayo Cream Sauce, 62
Melon with Mint-Lime Syrup and
   Jalepeño, 292
Peperonata, 176
Pickled Pepper Relish, 53
Pico de Gallo, 30
Poppy Seed-Coated Lamb Loins
   with Curried Couscous and
   Tamarind Chipotle Sauce, 127
Smoky Chipotle Corn Bread, 219
See also Chili; Salsa
CHILI
Lamb and White Bean Chili, 132
New York Bowl of Red, 114
Pork and Black Bean Chili Verde,
   123
Roasted Vegetable and Hominy
   Chili, 177
Turkey and Pinto Bean Chili, 96
CHOCOLATE
Bittersweet Chocolate Pudding, **238**,
   239
Bittersweet Chocolate Sauce, 280
Chocolate-Banana Ice Cream
   Sandwiches, 288, **288**
Chocolate Cake, 233
Chocolate Cookies, 288

Chocolate Filling, 282
Chocolate Ganache, 254
Chocolate Hazelnut Cake, 250
Chocolate–Macadamia Nut Tart,
   283, **284**
Chocolate Raspberry Squares, 266,
   266
Chocolate-Walnut Brownie Drops,
   260, 261
Chocolate Zabaglione Cream Trifle,
   232, 233
Cocolocos, 260
Fondue au Chocolat, 233, **235**
German Chocolate Tartlets, 282,
   282
Mochaccino Spirals, 265
Simone Beck's Chocolate Cake,
   250, 251
White Chocolate Ice Cream in
   Pecan Lace Cookie Cups, 234, **237**
Chutney: *See* Preserves & Condiments
Cilantro: *See* Coriander, Fresh
COCONUT
Brazilian-Style Shrimp and Coconut
   Soup, 35, **35**
Coconut Filling (for pie), 282
Pea Soup with Coconut, 28, **29**
COD
Cod Steaks with Red Pepper Sauce,
   72, **73**
Poached Cod with Tomatoes and
   Fennel, 72
Salt Cod Ragout on Steamed
   Spinach, **74**, 75
COFFEE
Coffee-Almond Layer Cake with
   Raspberries, **246**, 247
Coffee Buttercream, 247
Frozen Caffè Latte, 236
Mocha Mousse, 236
Mochaccino Spirals, 265
COOKIES
Banana Madeleines, 259
Chocolate Cookies, 288
Chocolate Raspberry Squares, 266,
   266
Chocolate-Walnut Brownie Drops,
   260, 261
Cocolocos, 260
Fig Moons, **260**, 264
Ginger-Ginger Shortbread Cookies,
   263
Lemon Poppy Stars, **261**, 263
Maple Spice Cookies, 259
Mochaccino Spirals, 265
PB and Js, **261**, 262
Pecan Lace Cookies, 234, **237**
Pistachio Crumbles, 262
CORIANDER, Fresh, 46
Green Beans with Tomato and
   Fresh Coriander, 161

Poached Shrimp with Coriander and Rice, 59
Roasted Potato Wedges with Salsa de Cilantro à la Presilla, 193, **195**

CORN
Corn Chowder, 27
Corn and Crab Gazpacho, 32
Corn Dollar Pickles, 227
Corn, Squash and Green Chile Stew, 179
Spicy Grilled Pizza with White Corn and Two Cheeses, 200

CORN BREADS
Blue Corn Muffins with Pine Nuts, 218
Blue Cornsticks, 218, **218**
Cheddar Corn Biscuits, 220
Rosemary Corn Cakes, 219
Skillet Corn Bread, 217
Smoky Chipotle Corn Bread, 219

CRAB
Corn and Crab Gazpacho, 32
Lump Crab Chiles Rellenos with Chimayo Cream Sauce, 62
Soft-Shell Crabs with Ginger-Lime Sauce, 63

CRANBERRIES
Apple-Cranberry Crumb Tart, 272, **272**
Cranberry Caramel Tartlets, 273, **273**
Cranberry Ketchup, 230
Double-Crusted Apple-Cranberry Pie, **268**, 269

CREAM CHEESE
Arline Rodman's Minnesota Cheesecake, 243
Fiery Cream Cheese Dip, 12

CUCUMBER
Cucumber Raita, 229
Lemon, Cucumber and Pepper Salad, 54
Tomato, Cucumber and Red Onion Salad, 49

CURRY
Curried Chicken Moghlai, 90
Curried Chicken with Spinach and Carrots, 89
Curried Mulligatawny Soup, **38**, 39
Curried Mussel Soup with Red Lentils and Yogurt, 33
Hot Curried Nuts, 20
Lamb, Spinach and Potato Curry with Banana Raita, 129, **130**
Malaccan Devil's Curry, 122, 122
Malay Prawn Curry, 60, **61**
Poppy Seed-Coated Lamb Loins with Curried Couscous, 127
Thai Chicken and Eggplant Curry, 88
Vegetarian Kofta Curry, 181, **182**

D

Dashi, 34

DESSERTS
Arline Rodman's Minnesota Cheesecake, 243, **244**
Chocolate Zabaglione Cream Trifle, **232**, 233
Fondue au Chocolat, 233, **235**
Lemon Pots de Crème, 294
Ricotta Fritters, 244
See also Cakes; Cookies; Desserts, Frozen; Desserts, Fruit; Meringues; Mousses, Dessert; Puddings; Tarts

DESSERTS, FROZEN
Bourbon-Vanilla Ice Cream, 281
Chocolate-Banana Ice Cream Sandwiches, 288, **288**
Creamy Lemon Ice, 294
Frozen Caffè Latte, 236
Green Apple Sorbet with Calvados, **286**, 287
Strawberries Melba, 304, **305**
White Chocolate Ice Cream in Pecan Lace Cookie Cups, 234, **237**
See also Granitas

DESSERTS, FRUIT
Bananas in Orange-Caramel Sauce, 287
Brandied Kumquats, 292
Caramelized Pineapple with Grilled Bananas and Tahitian Vanilla Sauce, 301, **302**
Melon with Mint-Lime Syrup and Jalapeño, 292
Mixed Berry Shortcake, 290
Nectarine Crumble, 296
Peachy Orange Shake, 296
Pear and Honey Napoleons with Hazelnuts, 298, **300**
Plum Cobbler, 303, **303**
Rhubarb Compote with Strawberries, 304, **304**
Steamed Pears with Red Wine and Raspberries, 298, **299**
Strawberries in Champagne Jelly, 308
Strawberry Meringues, **304-5**, 307
Strawberry Shortcake, 308, **309**
See also Desserts, Frozen; Puddings

DIPS
Black Bean Dip with Garlic, **10**, 11
Caponata, 15
Fiery Cream Cheese Dip, 12
Green Olive and Anchovy Puree, **10**, 11
Spicy Peanut Dip, **14**, 15
See also Spreads

DOUGHS
Gallette Doughs, 208

Pizza Dough, 199, 205
See also Pastry

DUCK
Duck Liver Crostini, 100, **102**
Roast Duck with Balsamic Vinegar, Summer Greens and Duck Liver Crostini, 98, **102**
Steamed Duck Breasts, 98, **99**
Dumplings, Green, with Shrimp and Peanuts, **22**, 23

E

EGGPLANT
Caponata, 15
Grilled Pizza Bianca with Portobellos, Eggplant and Three Cheeses, 199
Thai Chicken and Eggplant Curry, 88, **88**

EGGS
Egg Pasta, 142
Gratinéed Asparagus with Parmesan and Fried Eggs, 160
Pear-Ginger Custard Tart, **274**, 275
Potato and Red Pepper Frittata, 192
See also Meringues; Souffle's

ESCAROLE
Bread Stuffing with Escarole and Ham, 185
Fresh Fava Beans with Escarole and Tomato, 162, **163**

F

FAVA BEANS
Baby Artichoke, Spinach and Fava Bean Ragout, 164, **165**
Fresh Fava Beans with Escarole and Tomato, 162, **163**
Spaghetti with Fava Beans, 139

FENNEL
Lobster Salad with Fennel and Orange, 57
Marinated Fennel, Pearl Onions and Celery, 169
Poached Cod with Tomatoes and Fennel, 72
Skewered Shrimp with Fennel and Orange, 60

FETTUCCINE
Fettuccine with Radicchio and Sun-Dried Tomatoes, 135
Fettuccine with Sausage and Green Onions, 147, **148**

FIGS
Fig Moons, **260**, 264
Fig and Strawberry Jam, 225

FISH, 67-80
  Baked Whole Fish Stuffed with Shellfish, 67
  Fish in a Foil Packet, 68
  Grilled Whole Bluefish Rubbed with Garlic and Rosemary, 78
  Seared Pompano with Grapefruit Essence and Spinach, 70
  See also specific types of fish; Shellfish; Squid
Fregula, 36
Fruits: *See* specific names
FRUITS, DRIED
  Barley Stuffing with Dried Fruit, 188, **189**
  Estouffade of Beef with Apricots, Almonds and Raisins, **112**, 113
  Mom's Brisket with Dried Fruits, 110
  Nectarine and Dried Cherry Clafoutis, 295

G

GALETTES
  Dough for, 208
  How to shape, 209
  Leafy Green and Ricotta Galette, 212
  Leek and Goat Cheese Galette, 209
  Mushroom and Celery Root Galette with Mushroom Sauce, 206, **209**
  Tomato and Caramelized Onion Galette, 205, **207**
  Winter Squash and Blue Cheese Galette, **210**, 211
GAME
  Normandy-Style Rock Cornish Game Hens, 92, **93**
  Squab on Mushroom Toasts with Mixed Greens and Blackberry Dressing, 103
  See also Quail
GARLIC
  Aioli, 85
  Black Bean Dip with Garlic, 11
  Capellini with Fresh Tomatoes, Basil and Garlic Croutons, **134**, 135
  Chilled Tomato Soup with Garlic Oil, Basil and Mint, 27
  Garlic Butter, 87
  Garlic Jam, 230
  Garlicky Chicken, 84
  Grilled Whole Bluefish Rubbed with Garlic and Rosemary, 78
  Low-Fat Garlic Mashed Potatoes, 191
  Mashed Potatoes with Garlic, 191
  Roast Leg of Lamb with Garlic, 126
GIANDUJA, 251
  Gianduja Cake, 250

Gianduja Mousse, 250
GINGER
  Ginger-Ginger Shortbread Cookies, 263
  Ginger-Spiced Pickled Peppers, 228, **228**
  Gingerbread-Pear Cake, 255, **255**
  Pear-Ginger Custard Tart, 274
GOAT CHEESE
  Goat Cheese and Thyme Spread, 12, 13
  Goat Cheese, Walnut and Sun-Dried Tomato Spread, 15
  Leek and Goat Cheese Galette, 209
  Salad of Bitter Greens with Fallen Goat Cheese Soufflés, **44**, 45
GRAINS
  Barley Stuffing with Dried Fruit, 188, **189**
  Creamy Polenta with Butter and Cheese, 156
  Curried Couscous, 127
  See also Bulgur; Grits; Rice
GRANITAS
  Blueberry Granita, 290
  Frozen Caffè Latte, 236, **291**
  Honeydew Granita, **291**, 292
  Lime Granita, 294
  Peach and Red Wine Granita, **291**, 296
Grapefruit Essence, Seared Pompano with, 70
GREENS, **172-3**
  Broccoli Rabe and Potato Hash with Smoked Trout, 70
  Cheese Grits Soufflé over Turnip Greens, 155
  Leafy Green and Ricotta Galette, 212
  Mixed Greens, 172
  New Year's Peas and Greens, 166, **166**
  Quick-fix cooking suggestions, 173, **172-3**
  Smoky Potato Soup with Kale, 30
  Stir-Fried Collards with Apple and Balsamic Vinegar, 173
  See also Spinach; Swiss Chard
GRITS
  Cheese Grits Soufflé over Turnip Greens, 155
  Crisp Peppered Quail with Country Ham and Spicy Crayfish Hominy, 100
  Roasted Vegetable and Hominy Chili, 177

H

HAM
  Bread Stuffing with Escarole and Ham, 185

Crisp Peppered Quail with Country Ham and Spicy Crayfish Hominy, 100
  Grilled Pizza with Tomato, Basil and Prosciutto, **198**, 201
HAROSET
  Almond-Date Haroset, 16
  Apple Haroset, 16
HAZELNUTS
  Chocolate Hazelnut Cake, 250
  Hazelnut Pound Cake, 257
  Pear and Honey Napoleons with Hazelnuts, 298, **300**
HERBS
  Grilled Salmon with Potato-Herb Dressing, 77
  Pappardelle with Pork, Porcini and Herbs, 151
  Roast Chicken with Herbs, 83
  See also Basil; Coriander, Fresh; Mint; Sage

J

JAMS
  Cantaloupe and Black Pepper Jam, 223, **223**
  Fig and Strawberry Jam, 225
  Peach and Lime Jam, 223, **224**
  Plum and Nectarine Jam, **222**, 223
  Strawberry and Sweet Plum Jam, 225
  Yellow Tomato, Lemon and Basil Jam, 226
  White Peach Jam, 226
Jimaca Salad, 62

L

LAMB
  "Guitar" Maccheroni with Lamb Ragù, 153
  Lamb, Spinach and Potato Curry with Banana Raita, 129, **130**
  Lamb and White Bean Chili, 131
  Middle Eastern Meatballs with Swiss Chard, 117
  Poppy Seed-Coated Lamb Loins with Curried Couscous and Tamarind Chipotle Sauce, 127
  Pot-Roasted Lamb with Juniper Berries, 129
  Roast Leg of Lamb with Garlic, 126
Lasagna, Swiss Chard, 174, **174**
Leek and Goat Cheese Galette, 209
LEMON
  Creamy Lemon Ice, 294
  Lemon, Cucumber and Pepper Salad, 54
  Lemon Poppy Stars, **261**, 263

Lemon Pots de Crème, 294
Lemon Pudding Parfait, 293, **293**
Perciatelli with Zucchini and
  Lemon, 137
Skillet-Steamed Broccoli with
  Lemon, 167
Yellow Tomato, Lemon and Basil
  Jam, 226
LIMES
  Lime Granita, 294
  Peach and Lime Jam, 223, **224**
LINGUINE
  Veal and Linguine alla Pizzaiola, 146
  Wild Mushroom Linguine, 136
LIQUEURS AND LIQUOR
  Bourbon-Vanilla Ice Cream, 281
  Brandied Kumquats, 292
  Green Apple Sorbet with Calvados,
    286, 287
  Tia Maria Sauce, 288
LIVER
  Chopped Liver, 19
  Duck Liver Crostini, 100, **102**
  Le Grand Colbert's Calf Liver with
    Sherry Vinegar and Pearl Onions,
    108
  Pâté de Campagne with Pecans and
    Mushrooms, 18
LOBSTER
  Lobster Salad with Fennel and
    Orange, **56**, 57
  Lobster and White Bean Soup, 40

M

MAPLE
  Maple Indian Pudding, **242**, 243
  Maple Spice Cookies, 259
Marinade, Garlic-Red Pepper, 97
Mascarpone, Homemade, 307
Mayonnaise, Lemon Sage, 69
Meat: *See* specific types
MELONS
  Cantaloupe and Black Pepper Jam,
    223, **223**
  Honeydew Granita, 292
  Melon with Mint-Lime Syrup and
    Jalapeño, 292
MERINGUES
  Italian Meringue and Meringue
    Mushrooms, 254
  Strawberry Meringues, **304-5**, 307
MINT
  Chilled Tomato Soup with Garlic
    Oil, Basil and Mint, 27
  Melon with Mint-Lime Syrup, 292
  White Bean Puree with Mint, **10**, 11
Miso Clam Soup with Julienned
  Vegetables and Shiitake
  Mushrooms, 34, **34**

MOUSSES, DESSERT
  Gianduja Mousse, 250
  Mocha Mousse, 236
MOUSSES, SAVORY
  Salmon Mousse with Dill and
    Capers, 17, **17**
  Tuna Mouse with Lemon and
    Oregano, 18
MUSHROOMS
  Grilled Pizza Bianca with
    Portobellos, Eggplant and Three
    Cheeses, 199
  Miso Clam Soup with Julienned
    Vegetables and Shiitake
    Mushrooms, 34
  Mushroom and Celery Root
    Galette, 206, **209**
  Mushroom Sauce, 209
  Mushroom Toasts, 103
  Orecchiette with Porcini and
    Pancetta, 150, **151**
  Pappardelle with Pork, Porcini and
    Herbs, 151
  Pâté de Campagne with Pecans and
    Mushrooms, 19
  Potato Salad with Green Beans,
    Bacon and Cremini Mushrooms, 51
  Rice Stuffing with Fresh and Dried
    Mushrooms, 187
  Steamed Chicken with Chinese
    Mushrooms, 83
  Wild Mushroom Linguine, 136
Mustard Slaw, 49, **49**

N

NECTARINES
  Nectarine Crumble, 296
  Nectarine and Dried Cherry
    Clafoutis, 295
  Plum and Nectarine Jam, **222**, 223
Noodles, Bean Thread, Spinach Soup
  with, 32
NUTS
  Blue Corn Muffins with Pine Nuts,
    218
  Chocolate–Macadamia Nut Tart,
    283, **284**
  Hot Curried Nuts, 20
  Pistachio Crumbles, 262
  See also specific types

O

OILS
  Garlic Oil, 27
  Marinated Baby Artichokes in
    Oil, 21
  Olio Santo, 77

Penne with Cauliflower, Onions and
  Olive Oil, 138, **138**
OLIVES
  Fettuccine with Sausage and Green
    Olives, 147, **148**
  Green Olive and Anchovy Puree,
    10, 12
  Shrimp Salad with Celery, Olives
    and Tomatoes, 58
  Spicy Squid Salad, 67
ONIONS
  Blue Lake Beans with Red Wine–
    Sweet Onion Pickle, 161, **162**
  Cornmeal Pizzas with Spinach, Red
    Onions and Asiago Cheese, 204, **204**
  Grilled-Broccoli-Stuffed Onions, 167
  Le Grand Colbert's Calf's Liver
    with Sherry Vinegar and Pearl
    Onions, 108
  Marinated Fennel, Pearl Onions
    and Celery, 169
  Onion-Parmesan Flat Bread, 217
  Oven-Roasted Parsnips with Onions
    and Chestnuts, 175
  Penne with Cauliflower, Onions and
    Olive Oil, 138, **138**
  Pizza with Red Onion, Rosemary
    and Hot Pepper, 203, **204**
  Tomato and Caramelized Onion
    Galette, 205, **207**
  Tomato, Cucumber and Red Onion
    Salad, 50
ORANGES
  Candied Oranges, 248
  Lobster Salad with Fennel and
    Orange, 57
  Orange Layer Cake with Orange
    Buttercream Frosting, 248, **249**
  Peachy Orange Shake, 296
  Skewered Shrimp with Fennel and
    Orange, 60

P

PANCETTA
  Grilled Brook Trout with Pancetta,
    69
  Orecchiette with Porcini and
    Pancetta, 150, **151**
PARMESAN
  Creamy Polenta with Butter and
    Cheese, 156
  Gratinéed Asparagus with
    Parmesan and Fried Eggs, 160
  Onion-Parmesan Flat Bread, 217
  Potato-Tomato Gratin, 194
  Spinach and Red Pepper Gratin,
    170, **171**
  Zucchini and Carrots Parmesan, 178
  Zucchini Parmesan, 129

Parsnips, Oven-Roasted, with Onions and Chestnuts, 175
PASTA
Capellini with Fresh Tomatoes, Basil and Garlic Croutons, 135
Egg Pasta, 142
Farfalle with Spicy Sausage and Smoked Mozzarella, 149, **149**
Fresh Pappardelle, 153
"Guitar" Maccheroni with Lamb Ragù, 153
Orecchiette with Porcini and Pancetta, 150, **151**
Pappardelle with Pork, Porcini and Herbs, 151
Pasta and Potatoes, **140**, 141
Pasta Puttanesca, 139
Perciatelli with Zucchini and Lemon, 137
Seafood Cannelloni, **144**, 145
Soup of Broken Pasta and Beans with Fresh Basil, 41
Swiss Chard Lasagna, 174, **174**
Tuscan Ricotta and Spinach Ravioli with Sage, 142, **143**
See also Fettuccine; Linguine; Penne; Spaghetti
PASTRY
Double-Crust Pastry, 269
Pastry Crust, 278
with Polenta, 269
Puff Pastry, 270
Pâté de Campagne with Pecans and Mushrooms, 18
PEACHES
Peach and Lime Jam, 223, **224**
Peachy Orange Shake, 296
White Peach Jam, 226
PEANUTS
Green Dumplings with Shrimp and Peanuts, **22**, 23
PB and Js, **261**, 262
Spicy Peanut Dip, **14**, 15
PEARS
Acorn Squash and Pear Pie, 275, **276**
Bulgur Stuffing with Pears and Pecans, 190
Gingerbread-Pear Cake, 255, **255**
Pear-Ginger Custard Tart, **274**, 275
Pear and Honey Napoleons with Hazelnuts, 298, **300**
Pear and Watercress Salad, 54
Sourdough Bread Pudding with Caramelized Pears, 297, **298**
Steamed Pears with Red Wine and Raspberries, 298, **299**
PEAS
Fried Rice with Peas and Sun-Dried Tomatoes, 154
Garden Squash and Pea Medley, 177, **178**

Pea Soup with Coconut, 28, **29**
Spring Pea Soup with Scallops and Sorrel, 27
See also Beans and Peas, Dried
PECANS
Brown Butter Pecan Tart with Bourbon-Vanilla Ice Cream, 280
Bulgur Stuffing with Pears and Pecans, 190
Pâté de Campagne with Pecans and Mushrooms, 19
PENNE
Penne with Cauliflower, Onions and Olive Oil, 138, **138**
Penne with Ragù of Ground Pork and Beef, 147
Peperonata, 176
PEPPERS, SWEET
Cod Steaks with Red Pepper Sauce, 72
Ginger-Spiced Pickled Peppers, 228, **228**
Lemon, Cucumber and Pepper Salad, 54
Peperonata, 176
Pickled Pepper Relish, 53
Potato and Red Papper Frittata, 192
Roasted Red Peppers with Vinaigrette, 176
Roasted Yellow Pepper Soup with Pico de Gallo, 30
Silky Peppers, **13**, 20
Spaghetti with Fresh Tuna and Roasted Red Peppers, 144
Spinach and Red Pepper Gratin, 170, **171**
Stir-Fried Cabbage with Green and Red Peppers, 169
See also Chile Peppers
PICKLES
Blue Lake Beans with Red Wine–Sweet Onion Pickle, 161, **162**
Corn Dollar Pickles, 227
Ginger-Spiced Pickled Peppers, 228, **228**
Green Cherry Tomato Pickles, 226
Pickled Pepper Relish, 52
Quick Pickled Cauliflower, 227
Pico de Gallo, 30
Pie crust: *See* Pastry
PIES
Acorn Squash and Pear Pie, 275, **276**
Double-Crusted Apple-Cranberry Pie, **268**, 269
See also Tarts
PIZZA
Cornmeal Pizzas with Spinach, Red Onion and Asiago Cheese, 204, **204**
Pizza with Red Onion, Rosemary and Hot Pepper, 203, **204**
See also Pizza, Grilled

Pizza Dough: *See* Dough
PIZZA, GRILLED
Grilled Pizza Bianca with Portobellos, Eggplant and Three Cheeses, 199
Grilled Pizza with Tomato, Basil and Prosciutto, **198**, 201
Herbed Grilled Pizza with Summer Tomato and White Bean Salad, **198**, 200
Peppery Grilled Pizza with Broccoli, Sausage and Pecorino, **198**, 202
Spicy Grilled Pizza with White Corn and Two Cheeses, **198**, 200
PLUMS
Abundance Plum Chutney, 120
Plum Cobbler, 303, **303**
Plum and Nectarine Jam, **222**, 223
Strawberry and Sweet Plum Jam, 225
POLENTA
Apple Polenta Tart, 269
Creamy Polenta with Butter and Cheese, 156
PORK
Choucroute Garnie, 124, **125**
Hickory-Smoked Pork Tenderloins, 117
North Carolina Chopped Barbecue, 120, **121**
Pappardelle with Pork, Porcini and Herbs, 151
Penne with Ragù of Ground Pork and Beef, 147
Pork and Black Bean Chili Verde, 123
Roast Double Loin of Pork with Port Wine Sauce, 118
See also Bacon; Ham; Pancetta; Sausage
POTATOES, 196
Broccoli Rabe and Potato Hash with Smoked Trout, 70
Classic Mashed Potatoes, 190
Grilled Salmon with Potato-Herb Dressing, 77
Low-Fat Garlic Mashed Potatoes, 191
Mashed Potatoes with Garlic, 191
Pasta and Potatoes, **140**, 141
Potato Flat Bread, 216
Potato Puffs, 191
Potato and Red Pepper Frittata, 192
Potato Salad with Green Beans, Bacon and Cremini Mushrooms, 51
Potato-Tomato Gratin, 194
Roasted Potato Wedges with Salsa de Cilantro à la Presilla, 193, **195**
Scalloped Potatoes, 193
Smoky Potato Soup with Kale, 30
Sweet Mashed Potato Tart, 277
POULTRY, 36-40, 83-104

Roast Capon, 93-94
See also Chicken; Duck; Game;
 Turkey
PRESERVES & CONDIMENTS
 Abundance Plum Chutney, 119
 Cranberry Ketchup, 230
 Garlic Jam, 230
 Horseradish with Beet, 229
 Roasted Tomato Relish, 228, **228**
 Tamarind Chutney, **228**, 229
 See also Jams; Pickles; Raita
PUDDINGS
 Basque-Flavored Pudding with
  Almond Praline, **238**, 240
 Bittersweet Chocolate Pudding,
  238, 239
 Butterscotch Pudding, **238**, 239
 Cinnamon-Rice Crème Brûlée,
  241, **241**
 Lemon Pudding Parfait, 293, **293**
 Maple Indian Pudding, **242**, 243
 Nectarine and Dried Cherry
  Clafoutis, 295
 Sourdough Bread Pudding with
  Caramelized Pears, 297, **298**
 Strawberry Semifreddo, **304**, 306
PUMPKIN
 Pumpkin Coffee Cake, 258
 Spicy Pumpkin Pie, 277

QUAIL
 Crisp Peppered Quail with Country
  Ham and Spicy Crayfish Hominy,
  100, **102**
 Grilled Quail with Cumin, 101
 Pan Roasted Quail, **102**, 103

RAITA
 Banana Raita, 129, **130**
 Cucumber Raita, 229
RASPBERRIES
 Chocolate Raspberry Squares, 266
 Coffee-Almond Layer Cake with
  Raspberries, **246**, 247
 Raspberry Coulis, 252
 Raspberry Sauce, 305
 Steamed Pears with Red Wine and
  Raspberries, 298, **299**
Ravioli. *See* Pasta
RICE
 Cinnamon-Rice Crème Brûlée,
  241, **241**
 Fried Rice with Peas and Sun-Dried
  Tomatoes, 154
 Shrimp with Coriander and Rice, 59

Rice Stuffing with Fresh and Dried
 Mushrooms, 187
Risotto with Zucchini Blossoms and
 Sage, 154
RICOTTA
 Leafy Green and Ricotta Galette, 212
 Ricotta Fritters, 244
 Tuscan Ricotta and Spinach Ravioli
  with Sage, 142, **143**
Rillettes, Astier's Salmon, 17
ROSEMARY
 Grilled Whole Bluefish Rubbed with
  Garlic and Rosemary, 78
 Rosemary Corn Cakes, 219
 Pizza with Red Onion, Rosemary
  and Hot Pepper, 203, **204**
Rutabaga Soup, Creamy, 31

SAGE
 Risotto with Zucchini Blossoms and
  Sage, 154
 Turkey Cutlets with Grainy Mustard
  and Sage, 94
 Tuscan Ricotta and Spinach Ravioli
  with Sage, 142
SALAD DRESSINGS
 Blackberry Dressing, 104
 Lemon Vinaigrette, 65
 See also Salads
SALAD GREENS
 Fettuccine with Radicchio and Sun-
  Dried Tomatoes, 135
 Grilled Salmon with Potato-Herb
  Dressing, 78
 Mixed Greens, 172
 Roast Duck with Balsamic Vinegar,
  Summer Greens and Duck Liver
  Crostini, 98, **102**
 Salad of Bitter Greens with Fallen
  Goat Cheese Soufflés, **44**, 45
 Squab on Mushroom Toasts with
  Mixed Greens and Blackberry
  Dressing, 103
 Tomato and Arugula Salad, 46, **47**
 See also Escarole; Spinach;
  Watercress
SALADS
 Black Bean Salad with Chipotle
  Vinaigrette, 46, **48**
 Bulgur Salad with Watercress and
  Sunflower Seeds, 53
 Carrot and Parsley Salad, 51
 Carrots with Cornichon Dressing, 51
 Celery Salad with Anchovy
  Dressing, 50
 Chickpea and Celery Salad, 50
 Grilled Squid Salad with Tomato
  and Mint Bruschetta, 65

Jicama Salad, 62
Lemon, Cucumber and Pepper
 Salad, 54
Mustard Slaw, 49, **49**
Pear and Watercress Salad, 54
Potato Salad with Green Beans,
 Bacon and Cremini Mushrooms, 51
Shrimp Salad with Celery, Olives
 and Tomatoes, 58
Spicy Squid Salad, **66**, 67
Spicy Tuna and Green Bean Salad
 with Tomatoes, 79
Spinach and Cherry Tomato Salad,
 46
Sweet Potato Salad, 52, 52
Tomato and Arugula Salad, 46, **47**
Tomato, Cucumber and Red Onion
 Salad, 49
Tomato and White Bean Salad,
 198, 200
See also Salad Greens
SALMON
 Astier's Salmon Rillettes, 17
 Grilled Salmon with Potato-Herb
  Dressing, 77
 Salmon Mousse with Dill and
  Capers, 17, **17**
 Steamed Salmon, 78, **79**
SALSA
 Salsa de Cilantro à la Presilla,
  193, **195**
 Salsa Verde, 77
SAUCES, DESSERT
 Bittersweet Chocolate Sauce, 280
 Low-Fat Caramel Sauce, 287
 Mint-Lime Syrup, 292
 Orange-Caramel Sauce, 287
 Raspberry Sauce, 305
 Tahitian Vanilla Sauce, 301
 Tia Maria Sauce, 288
SAUCES, SAVORY
 Aioli, 85
 Chimayo Cream Sauce, 63
 Dipping Sauce, 59
 Fresh Plum Sauce with Basil, 97
 Garlic Butter, 87
 Ginger-Lime Sauce, 64
 Grapefruit Essence, 72
 Grilled Tomato Sauce, 58
 Lemon-Sage Mayonnaise, 69
 Mopping and Mixing Sauces, 120
 Mushroom Sauce, 209
 Port Wine Sauce, 118
 Tamarind Sauce, 127
 See also Salsa
SAUSAGE
 Choucroute Garnic, 124, **125**
 Farfalle with Spicy Sausage and
  Smoked Mozzarella, 149
 Fettuccine with Sausage and Green
  Olives, 147, **148**

Peppery Grilled Pizza with Broccoli, Sausage and Pecorino, 198, 202

Two-Bread Stuffing with Sausage, 186, **186**

SCALLOPS

Grilled Scallop Skewers with Grilled Tomato Sauce, 57

Spring Pea Soup with Scallops and Sorrell, 27

Sesame and Flaxseed Bread, 213

SHELLFISH

Baked Whole Fish Stuffed with Shellfish, 67

Crisp Peppered Quail with Country Ham and Spicy Crayfish Hominy, 100

Curried Mussel Soup with Red Lentils and Yogurt, 33

Miso Clam Soup with Julienned Vegetables and Shiitake Mushrooms, 34

Seafood Cannelloni, **144**, 145

See also Crab; Lobster, Scallops; Shrimp

SHRIMP

Brazilian-Style Shrimp and Coconut Soup, 35, **35**

Green Dumplings with Shrimp and Peanuts, **22**, 23

Low-Country Pickled Shrimp, 24

Malay Prawn Curry, 60, **61**

Poached Shrimp with Coriander and Rice, 59

Shrimp Salad with Celery, Olives and Tomatoes, 58

Skewered Shrimp with Fennel and Orange, 60

SOUFFLES

Banana Soufflés with Amaretti, 289

Cheese Grits Soufflé over Turnip Greens, 155

Salad of Bitter Greens and Fallen Goat Cheese Soufflés, 45

SOUPS, CHILLED

Chilled Tomato Soup with Garlic Oil, Basil and Mint, **26**, 27

Corn and Crab Gazpacho, 32

Pea Soup with Coconut, 28, **29**

Roasted Yellow Pepper Soup with Pico de Gallo, 30

SOUPS, HOT

Brazilian-Style Shrimp and Coconut Soup, 35, **35**

Chicken Broth with Fregula, 36, **37**

Corn Chowder, 27

Creamy Rutabaga Soup, 31

Curried Mulligatawny Soup, **38**, 39

Curried Mussel Soup with Red Lentils and Yogurt, 33

Smoky Potato Soup with Kale, 30

Soup of Broken Pasta and Beans with Fresh Basil, 41

Spinach Soup with Bean Thread Noodles, 32

Spring Pea Soup with Scallops and Sorrel, 27

SPAGHETTI

Spaghetti with Fava Beans, 139

Spaghetti with Fresh Tuna and Roasted Red Peppers, 144

SPINACH

Baby Artichoke, Spinach and Fava Bean Ragout, 164, **165**

Cornmeal Pizzas with Spinach, Red Onion and Asiago Cheese, 204, **204**

Curried Chicken with Spinach and Carrots, 89

Salt Cod Ragout on Steamed Spinach, **74**, 75

Seared Pompano with Grapefruit Essence and Spinach, 70

Spinach and Cherry Tomato Salad, 46

Spinach and Red Pepper Gratin, 170, **171**

Spinach Soup with Bean Thread Noodles, 32

Spinach-Stuffed Veal Rolls in Tarragon Tomato Sauce, 107

Tuscan Ricotta and Spinach Ravioli with Sage, 142, **143**

SPREADS

Astier's Salmon Rillettes, 17

Chopped Liver, 19

Goat Cheese and Thyme Spread, 12, **13**

Goat Cheese, Walnut and Sun-Dried Tomato Spread, 15

Pâté de Campagne with Pecans and Mushrooms, 18

Salmon Mousse with Dill and Capers, 17, **17**

Tuna Mousse with Lemon and Oregano, 18

White Bean Puree with Mint, **10**, 11

See also Dips

Squab on Mushroom Toasts with Mixed Greens and Blackberry Dressing, 103

SQUASH

Acorn Squash and Pear Pie, 275, **276**

Garden Squash and Pea Medley, 177, **178**

Winter Squash and Blue Cheese Galette, **210**, 211

Winter Squash with Crouton Stuffing, 179

See also Zucchini

SQUID

Grilled Squid Salad with Tomato and Mint Bruschetta, 65

Spicy Squid Salad, **66**, 67

STEWS

Corn, Squash and Green Chile Stew, 179

Estouffade of Beef with Apricots, Almonds and Raisins, 113

Garlicky Chicken, 84

Mom's Brisket with Dried Fruits, 110

Pot-Roasted Lamb with Juniper Berries, 129

Salt Cod Ragout on Steamed Spinach, 75

Stewed Chicken with Pastis, 86

Veal Shanks with White Beans, 107

See also Chili

STIR-FRYING

Stir-Fried Cabbage with Green and Red Peppers, 169

Stir-Fried Collards with Apple and Balsamic Vinegar, 173

STOCK

Chicken Stock, 36

Lamb Stock, 128

Rich Chicken Stock, 40

Tomato-Crayfish Stock, 101

STRAWBERRIES

Fig and Strawberry Jam, 225

Rhubarb Compote with Strawberries, 304, **304**

Strawberries Melba, 304, **305**

Strawberry Meringues, **304-5**, 307

Strawberry and Sweet Plum Jam, 225

Strawberry Ice Cream, 305

Strawberry Semifreddo, **304**, 306

STUFFING

Barley Stuffing with Dried Fruit, 188, **189**

Bread Stuffing with Escarole and Ham, 185

Bulgur Stuffing with Pears and Pecans, 190

Corn Bread and Chestnut Stuffing, **184**, 185

Rice Stuffing with Fresh and Dried Mushrooms, 187

Two-Bread Stuffing with Sausage, 186, **186**

Winter Squash with Crouton Stuffing, 179

Sweet Potato Salad, 52

SWISS CHARD

Middle Eastern Meatballs with Swiss Chard, **116**, 117

Swiss Chard Lasagna, 174, **174**

SWORDFISH

Grilled Swordfish with Salsa Verde, 77

Grilled Swordfish, Sicilian Style, 76

T

TARTS
Apple-Cranberry Crumb Tart, 272, **272**
Apple Polenta Tart, 269
Apple Tartlets with Browned Butter Filling, 270, **271**
Brown Butter Pecan Tart with Bourbon-Vanilla Ice Cream, 280
Chocolate–Macadamia Nut Tart, 283
Cranberry-Caramel Tartlets, 273, **273**
German Chocolate Tartlets, 282, **282**
Italian Almond Tart, 278, **279**
Pear-Ginger Custard Tart, **274**, 275
Sweet Mashed Potato Tart, 277
TOMATOES
Artichoke Hearts with Tomatoes and Balsamic Vinegar, 159
Capellini with Fresh Tomatoes, Basil and Garlic Croutons, **134**, 135
Chilled Tomato Soup with Garlic Oil, Basil and Mint, **26**, 27
Fresh Fava Beans with Escarole and Tomato, 162, **163**
Fried Green Tomatoes, 180
Green Beans with Tomato and Fresh Coriander, 161
Green Cherry Tomato Pickles, 226
Grilled Pizza with Tomato, Basil and Prosciutto, **198**, 201
Grilled Tomato Sauce, 58
Herbed Grilled Pizza with Summer Tomato and White Bean Salad, **198**, 200
Oven-Roasted Tomatoes, 21
Poached Cod with Tomatoes and Fennel, 72
Potato-Tomato Gratin, 194
Roasted Tomato Relish, 228, **228**
Shrimp Salad with Celery, Olives and Tomatoes, 58
Spicy Tuna and Green Bean Salad with Tomatoes, 79, **80**
Spinach and Cherry Tomato Salad, 46
Spinach-Stuffed Veal Rolls in Tarragon Tomato Sauce, 107
Tomato and Arugula Salad, 46, **47**
Tomato Butter, 194
Tomato and Caramelized Onion Galette, 205, **207**
Tomato Crayfish Stock, 101
Tomato, Cucumber and Red Onion Salad, 49

Tomato and Mint Bruschetta, 65
Yellow Tomato, Lemon and Basil Jam, 226
See also Tomatoes, Sun-Dried
TOMATOES, SUN-DRIED
Fettuccine with Radicchio and Sun-Dried Tomatoes, 135
Fried Rice with Peas and Sun-Dried Tomatoes, 154
Goat Cheese, Walnut and Sun-Dried Tomato Spread, 15
TROUT
Broccoli Rabe and Potato Hash with Smoked Trout, 70
Grilled Brook Trout with Pancetta, 69
TUNA
Spaghetti with Fresh Tuna and Roasted Red Peppers, 144
Spicy Tuna and Green Bean Salad with Tomatoes, 79, **80**
Tuna Mousse with Lemon and Oregano, 18
Turkey Tonnato, 95, **95**
TURKEY
Turkey Burgers, 97
Turkey Cutlets with Grainy Mustard Sauce, 94-95
Turkey and Pinto Bean Chili, 96
Turkey Tonnato, 95, **95**

V

VEAL
Le Grand Colbert's Calf's Liver with Sherry Vinegar and Pearl Onions, 108
Spinach-Stuffed Veal Rolls in Tarragon Tomato Sauce, **106**, 107
Veal and Linguine alla Pizzaiola, 146
Veal Shanks with White Beans, 107
VEGETABLES, 157-182
Roasted Vegetable and Homini Chili, 177
Six-Vegetable Curry, 195, **195**
Spring Vegetable Medley, **158**, 159
Vegetarian Kofta Curry, 181, **182**
See also Greens; names of specific vegetables
VINEGAR, BALSAMIC
Artichoke Hearts with Tomatoes and Balsamic Vinegar, 159
Stir-Fried Collards with Apple and Balsamic Vinegar, 173
VINEGARS
Le Grand Colbert's Calf's Liver with Sherry Vinegar and Pearl Onions, 108
See also Vinegar, Balsamic

W

WALNUTS
Goat Cheese, Walnut and Sun-Dried Tomato Spread, 15
Chocolate-Walnut Brownie Drops, **260**, 261
WATERCRESS
Bulgur Salad with Watercress and Sunflower Seeds, 53
Pear and Watercress Salad, 54
WHITE BEANS
Carefree Boston Baked Beans, 167
Herbed Grilled Pizza with Summer Tomato and White Bean Salad, **198**, 200
Lamb and White Bean Chili, 131
Lobster and White Bean Soup, 40
Soup of Broken Pasta and Beans with Fresh Basil, 41
Veal Shanks with White Beans, 107
White Bean Puree with Mint, **10**, 11
WINE
Blue Lake Beans with Red Wine–Sweet Onion Pickle, 161, **162**
Peach and Red Wine Granita, **291**, 296
Roast Double Loin of Pork with Port Wine Sauce, 118
Steamed Pears with Red Wine and Raspberries, 298
Strawberries in Champagne Jelly, 308
Wine-Merchant Steak, 109, **109**

Y

YOGURT
Curried Mussel Soup with Red Lentils and Yogurt, 33
Yogurt Cheese, 248

Z

Zabaglione Cream, **232**, 233
ZUCCHINI
Corn, Squash and Green Chile Stew, 179
Perciatelli with Zucchini and Lemon, 137
Risotto with Zucchini Blossoms and Sage, 154
Zucchini and Carrots Parmesan, 178
Zucchini with Fresh Thyme, 23
Zucchini Parmesan, 179·

CONTRIBUTORS

Jody Adams is a partner and chef of the Rialto Restaurant and Bar at the Charles Hotel in Cambridge, Massachusetts.

Katherine Alford is a food writer, recipe developer and cooking teacher in New York City.

Ann Chantal Altman is the executive chef for Seagram's, a cooking teacher at Peter Kump's New York Cooking School and a food writer.

Ben Barker is the chef/owner of Magnolia Grill in Durham, North Carolina.

Jo Bettoja is a Rome-based food writer and the author of *Southern Italian Cooking, Family Recipes from the Kingdom of the Two Sicilies* (Bantam) and *Italian Cooking in the Grand Tradition* (Dial; available in paperback from Fireside), with Anna Maria Cornetto.

Shelley Boris is a caterer and food writer in Cold Spring, New York.

Wayne Brachman is the head pastry chef at both the Mesa Grill and Bolo in New York City. He is also the author of *Cakes and Cowpokes* (Morrow).

Jennifer Brennan is a Japan-based food writer and teacher and the author of several books, including *Curries and Bugles: A Memoir and a Cookbook of the British Raj* (HarperCollins).

Anna Teresa Callen is a food writer and the owner of Anna Teresa Callen's Italian Cooking School in New York City. She's also the author of the forthcoming *Food and Memories of Abruzzo* (Macmillan).

Bob Chambers is a New York–based chef, recipe developer and food stylist.

Sumi Chang is the breakfast chef at Campanile in Los Angeles and is currently at work on a book, *Breakfast at Campanile*.

Andrea Chesman is a food writer and the author of *Simply Healthful Skillet Suppers* and *Simply Healthful Pasta Salads* (both from Chapters Publishing) and a forthcoming collection of recipes for *Together Times: The Disney Book of Family Activities, Celebrations, and Fun* (Hyperion).

Julia Child is the country's foremost television cooking teacher and the doyenne of French cooking in America. She is working on the TV series and book, *In Julia's Kitchen with Master Chefs*, for PBS.

Anna Del Conte is the author of *Anna Del Conte's Italian Kitchen* (Simon & Schuster) and *Gastronomy of Italy* (Prentice Hall). She is contributing recipes to a forthcoming book on fungi.

Julia della Croce is a cooking teacher and the author of *The Vegetarian Table: Italy; Antipasti: The Little Dishes of Italy; The Pasta Book: Recipes in the Italian Tradition;* and *Pasta Classics: The Art of Italian Pasta Cooking* (all from Chronicle Books).

Erica De Mane is a chef and food writer, and the author of a forthcoming book on an improvisational approach to Italian cooking.

Lorenza de' Medici is a cooking teacher (The Villa Table, Siena, Italy) and the author of many cookbooks, including *The Villa Table* (Fawcett Columbine).

Marcel Desaulniers is executive chef/co-owner of The Trellis in Williamsburg, Virginia, and the author of *The Trellis Cookbook* (available in paperback from Simon & Schuster), *Death by Chocolate* (Rizzoli) and *The Burger Meisters* (Simon & Schuster). He is working on *Desserts to Die For* (Simon & Schuster), to be published in the fall of 1995.

Hubert Des Marais is the executive chef at the Four Seasons Ocean Grand in Palm Beach, Florida.

Georgia Chan Downard is a food consultant, teacher and stylist, and the author of *The Big Broccoli Book* (Random House).

Celestino Drago is the executive chef/owner of Drago in Santa Monica, California.

Carl Duchaj is the pastry chef at Tapawingo in Ellsworth, Michigan.

Mary Ann Esposito is a cookbook author and the host of PBS's *Ciao Italia* cooking series.

Mike Fennelly is the chef/owner of Mike's on the Avenue in New Orleans, Louisiana, and the author of *East Meets Southwest* (Chronicle Books of San Francisco).

Bobby Flay is the executive chef/proprietor of the Mesa Grill in New York City. He recently opened Bolo, another New York restaurant. His most recent cookbook, *Bobby Flay's Bold American Food* (Warner Books), includes recipes, tips and techniques from the Mesa Grill.

Jim Galileo, formerly the executive chef of Oceana in New York City, will open his own place in New Jersey in 1995.

Kevin Graham, formerly of the Windor Court Hotel in New Orleans, has opened his own restaurant, called Graham's, also in New Orleans. He is the author of *Kevin Graham's Book of Seafood and Shellfish* (Stewart, Tabori & Chang) and has two other books in the works.

Ken Haedrich is a cookbook author and consultant. His most recent book is *Country Breakfasts,* and he is currently working on *Simple Desserts* (both from Bantam).

Marcella Hazan is the owner of the cooking school Master Class in Classic Italian Cooking in Venice, Italy, and a renowned author, most recently of *Essentials of Classic Italian Cooking* (Knopf).

Janet Hazen is a food writer, cooking teacher and restaurant critic, and the author of a number of cookbooks, including *Pears: A Country Garden Cookbook* (Collins), *Hot, Hotter, Hottest* and *Janet's Juice Book* (both from Chronicle Books). She is working on a cookbook about vanilla and on a sequel to *Hot, Hotter, Hottest.*

Susan Shapiro Jaslove is a food writer and recipe developer. She is currently working on a cookbook about baking with children.

Park Kerr is the owner of the El Paso Chile Company in El Paso, Texas, and the author of *The El Paso Chile Company's Texas Border Cookbook* (Morrow).

Lynne Rossetto Kasper is a cooking teacher and lecturer and the author of *The Splendid Table* (Morrow).

Marcia Kiesel is the associate director of *Food & Wine* magazine's test kitchen and co-author of *Simple Art of Vietnamese Cooking* (Prentice Hall).

Johanne Killeen and **George Germon** are cookbook authors and the chefs/owners of Al Forno in Providence, Rhode Island. They are the authors of *Cucina Simpatica* (HarperCollins).

Jonathan Levine is the director of the New York State Chili Cook-Off and a member of the International Chili Society Advisory Board.

Eileen Yin-Fei Lo is a cooking teacher at the China Institute in New York City, and the author of five cookbooks, including *From the Earth: Chinese Vegetarian Cooking.*

Alexander Lobrano is a Paris-based food, travel and style writer.

Emily Luchetti is the executive pastry chef at Stars Restaurant and Stars Cafes and a co-owner of Star Bake in San Francisco. She is also the author of *Stars Desserts* (HarperCollins).

Pino Luongo is a restaurateur and the author of *Fish Talking* and *A Tuscan in the Kitchen* (both from Clarkson Potter).

Stephanie Lyness is a food writer, recipe developer and cooking teacher in New York City.

Deborah Madison is a cooking teacher and chef, and the author of *The Savory Way* and *The Greens Cookbook* (both from Bantam). *The Joy of Vegetarian Cooking* (Bantam) is forthcoming.

Lydie Marshall is a food writer and cooking teacher and the author of *A Passion for Potatoes* and an upcoming cookbook, *Chez Nous: Home Cooking from the South of France* (both from HarperCollins).

Nancie McDermott is a cooking teacher and the author of *Real Thai: The Best of Thailand's Regional Cooking* (Chronicle Books) and *The 5 in 10 Pasta and Noodle Cookbook* (Hearst Books).

Mark Miller is a chef and the owner of the Coyote Cafe in Santa Fe, New Mexico, the Coyote Cafe in Las Vegas, Nevada, and Red Sage in Washington, D.C. He is also the author of several cookbooks, including *The Great Chile Book* and *Coyote's Pantry* (both from Ten Speed Press).

Leslie Newman is the author of *Feasts* (HarperCollins) and is currently working on a cookbook called *The Family Table*.

Anna Amendolara Nurse is a cooking teacher (Anna Amendolara Nurse Cooking Classes, Brooklyn, and Peter Kump's New York Cooking School), a consultant and a contributor to many cookbooks.

Nancy Oakes is the chef/owner of Boulevard in San Francisco, California. She was included in the recently published *Cooking & Entertaining with America's Rising Star Chefs* (Santa Fe Publishing).

Bradley Ogden is executive chef/co-owner of The Lark Creek Inn in Larkspur, California. He is the author of *Bradley Ogden's Breakfast, Lunch & Dinner* (Random House).

Grace Parisi is a New York food writer and chef; she is currently working on an upcoming television cooking show.

Jacques Pépin is a cooking teacher and the author of numerous cookbooks, the most recent of which are *Today's Gourmet* and *Today's Gourmet II* (KQED, Inc.). Soon to be published is *Jacques Pépin's Light and Healthy Cooking* (Rodale Press).

James Peterson is a cooking teacher at Peter Kump's New York Cooking School and the author of *Splendid Soups* (Bantam). He is working on *The Complete Guide to Cooking Seafood* (Morrow).

Stephan Pyles is the chef/owner of Star Canyon in Dallas and the author of *The New Texas Cuisine* (Doubleday).

Anne Rosenzweig is the chef/owner of Arcadia in New York City.

Michele Scicolone is a food and travel writer and the author of *The Antipasto Table, La Dolce Vita* (both from Morrow) and a forthcoming book on Italian regional cooking.

Tracey Seaman is a recipe tester-developer for *Food & Wine* magazine.

Larkin Selman, formerly chef at Gautreau's in New Orleans, is interim chef at the Upperline Restaurant and will open his own restaurant, Legumes, also in New Orleans, early this year.

Lindsey Shere is a partner in the Downtown Bakery and Creamery in Healdsburg, California, a pastry chef and the author of *Chez Panisse Desserts* (Random House).

Martha Rose Shulman is the author of *Provençal Light* (Bantam Books).

Marie Simmons is a cooking teacher (The New School Culinary Center and New York University) and the author of several cookbooks, including *365 Ways to Cook Pasta* (HarperCollins) and *The Light Touch* (Chapters).

Ilana Sharlin Stone is the executive chef/owner of Rustica in Cape Town, South Africa, where she also teaches cooking.

Diana Sturgis is the test-kitchen director of *Food & Wine* magazine.

Judith Sutton is a food writer and freelance chef in New York City.

Jacques Torres is the pastry chef at Le Cirque in New York City. He teaches at several cooking schools, including The French Culinary Institute in New York City. Among his awards is James Beard Pastry Chef of the Year, 1994.

Candy Voytershark is a perennial gardener in Washington, Connecticut, who grows jalapeños.

Alice Waters is the owner of Chez Panisse in Berkeley, California, and the co-author of many cookbooks, including *Fanny at Chez Panisse* (HarperCollins) and *Chez Panisse Cooking* (Random House).

Patricia Wells is a journalist and the author of numerous food books, including *Patricia Wells' Trattoria* (Morrow) and an upcoming book tentatively titled *Patricia Wells Cooks at Home*.

Don Yamauchi is the executive chef at Carlos' in Highland Park, Illinois.

Celeste Zeccola is the pastry chef at Carlos' in Highland Park, Illinois.

PHOTO CREDITS

William Abranowicz: 198, 238, 242, 293, 298; Christopher Baker: 291; Mary Ellen Bartley: 192, 304; Antoine Bootz: 207, 209, 210, back cover; Fran Collin: 102 (top left), 102 (top right); Tom Eckerle: 73, 79, 99, 163, 299; John Reed Forsman: 52, 162; Dennis Galante: 48, 49, 82, 102 (bottom right), 121, 195 (top), 214, 244, 255; Gentl & Hyers: front cover, 109, 158, 165, 178; Susan Goldman: 184, 186, 189, 218; Robert Jacobs: 10, 14, 17, 246, 268, 272, 273, 274, 276, 284, 300, 302, 303; Rita Maas: 136, 296; David Phelps: 102 (bottom left); Maria Robledo: 47, 87, 95, 171; Victor Schrager: 61, 88, 122, 182, 195 (bottom); Ellen Silverman: 1, 4, 13, 22, 29, 38, 66, 74, 91, 106, 112, 144, 166, 172-3,174, 204, 222, 223, 224, 260, 261; Mark Thomas: 2, 26, 37, 44, 56, 80, 93, 111, 116, 125, 130, 138, 140, 143, 148, 228, 241, 249, 266, 271, 279, 286, 304 (left), 304-5, 305, 309; William Waldron: 250; Lisa Charles Watson: 34, 35, 134, 149, 151; Elizabeth Watt: 6, 232, 235, 237, 282, 288; Walter Wick: 50.